Criminal Law and Criminal Justice

Criminal Law and Criminal Justice: Morals and Policy goes beyond the traditional criminal law textbook, inviting students to question why we criminalise certain behaviour and whether the decisions made by the courts can be justified according to legal principle, morals, and policy.

Providing an overview not only of the legal doctrine of criminal law, but also of the underpinning theory behind the legal doctrine, the book encourages critical thinking around the context behind, and implementation of, legal decisions. It applies this to current issues, such as respect for personal autonomy, prevention of domestic abuse, and discouraging gang activity, while providing a clear overview of the law relating to *actus reus*, *mens rea*, property offences, homicide, non-fatal offences, sexual offences, accessorial liability, and defences. Using hypothetical scenarios, students will develop an understanding of why certain rules exist and then be able to critically analyse why certain behaviour is criminalised. An in-depth study of several key cases will show how the rules and theory play out in practice, and students will examine how morals and policy have influenced these decisions.

Featuring thinking points as well as further reading suggestions, this textbook is suitable for all students of criminal law, as well as for those studying jurisprudence.

Amy Elkington is a Senior Lecturer in Law, who manages the undergraduate and postgraduate Law programmes at the University of Chichester.

Criminal Law and Criminal Justice

Morals and Policy

Amy Elkington

Routledge
Taylor & Francis Group
LONDON AND NEW YORK

Designed cover image: DNY59 / Getty Images ®

First published 2025
by Routledge
4 Park Square, Milton Park, Abingdon, Oxon OX14 4RN

and by Routledge
605 Third Avenue, New York, NY 10158

Routledge is an imprint of the Taylor & Francis Group, an informa business

British Library Cataloguing-in-Publication Data
A catalogue record for this book is available from the British Library

Library of Congress Cataloging-in-Publication Data
Names: Elkington, Amy, author.
Title: Criminal law and criminal justice : morals and policy / Amy Elkington.
Description: Abingdon, Oxon [UK] ; New York, NY : Routledge, 2025. | Includes bibliographical references and index.
Identifiers: LCCN 2024061077 | ISBN 9781032527833 (hardback) | ISBN 9781032527826 (paperback) | ISBN 9781003408383 (ebook)
Subjects: LCSH: Criminal law—Philosophy. | Criminal law—Moral and ethical aspects. | Criminal justice, Administration of—Moral and ethical aspects. | Criminal intent—Moral and ethical aspects.
Classification: LCC K5018 .E45 2025 | DDC 345/.001—dc23/eng/20250111
LC record available at https://lccn.loc.gov/2024061077

ISBN: 978-1-032-52783-3 (hbk)
ISBN: 978-1-032-52782-6 (pbk)
ISBN: 978-1-003-40838-3 (ebk)

DOI: 10.4324/9781003408383

Typeset in Joanna
by Apex CoVantage, LLC

For my wonderful husband, Colin, who makes everything possible.

Contents

Table of Statutes

D

E

F

H

I

L

M

N

O

P

R

S

T

W

Overseas Countries

Table of International Instruments

Table of Statutory Instruments

Table of Cases

I

J

K

L

M

N

P

R

S

T

W

Y

Introduction

This book provides a novel insight into criminal law and the underpinning theory behind the legal doctrine. This goes beyond the traditional criminal law textbook, and considers why the law has developed in the way it has. Using hypothetical scenarios, you, the reader, are invited to question why we criminalise certain behaviour and why we find some behaviours more blameworthy than others. You will be asked to consider whether the decisions made by the courts can be justified according to established legal principles, morals values and policy considerations. To do this, the chapters of the book focus on a series of current issues in criminal law.

Chapters 1 and 2 provide the foundation for the book by examining what is meant by morals and policy in the context of criminal law. The concepts studied in these first two chapters are referred to throughout the remaining chapters. They provide reasoning for why the law has developed as it has, and are used to critique the law when it diverges from what would be expected. Chapter 1 considers two of the traditional schools of thought on the meaning of law: positivism and natural law. This is to demonstrate that there is no agreement about what is meant by law and what it ought to achieve. Furthermore, that how the law is viewed can impact how the law is developed and interpreted. The Hart–Devlin and Hart–Fuller debates are used to further illustrate this.

Chapter 2 further examines the underpinning principles of criminal law to elucidate what criminal law is and how it operates. This considers the different understandings of what is meant by justice, and the importance of fair labelling. The requirement of the coincidence and correspondence of *actus reus* and *mens rea* will also be considered, alongside the principles of voluntariness, the harm principles, and no punishment without just cause. These concepts illustrate how it can be identified, and limited, who is to blame.

Chapter 3 defines the concept of *actus reus*, with a focus on causation and unlawful act manslaughter. What amounts to a *novus actus interveniens* is considered in the context of taking drugs and euthanasia. The cases of *R v Blaue*,[1] *R v Kennedy*,[2] and *R v Wallace*[3] are examined to explore how the law has developed to ensure those who are responsible for certain consequences are held to blame. It will be seen that a victim has no obligation to accept life-saving treatment, as the law will hold to blame the person who initiated the need for treatment. Actions of doctors and police, aimed at assisting the victim, will not be held to break the chain of causation from the earlier actions of the defendant. Thus, fault will remain on the person who caused the original harm. In a move to uphold policy considerations, doctors should be free to treat patients, and police officers should be able to reasonably exercise their legal duty, without fear of condemnation. It will be examined how a victim's actions, if free, deliberate, and informed, can amount to a break in the chain of causation. It will be shown how morals and policy have influenced the discussion of when the victim's actions will fulfil these criteria.

1 [1975] 1 WLR 1411.
2 [2007] UKHL 38.
3 [2018] EWCA Crim 690.

DOI: 10.4324/9781003408383-1

Chapter 4 continues this examination of *actus reus* in relation to omissions and gross negligence manslaughter. Consideration is made of whether someone who fails to act is as blameworthy as someone who does, and in what situations the law can justly impose liability. This will consider the arguments for retaining the conventional view of omissions that is currently recognised in English law, compared with a social responsibility view that is adopted in other jurisdictions. Exploration of *R v Adomako*[4] and *R v Bowditch*[5] will examine the limits of when a duty to act will be imposed with comparison to civil law. Furthermore, it will be discussed whether the law is, or should, move towards having a "Good Samaritan" law that in line with moral values would impose a duty to act in easy rescue cases.

Chapter 5 introduces the concept of *mens rea* and considers how this legal construct is used to determine who can rightly be held to blame and to what extent they are blameworthy. The differing levels of *mens rea* of intention, recklessness, and negligence are defined. A focus on *R v Woollin*,[6] and the offence of murder, is used to discuss when intention can be inferred from foresight. Furthermore, what place morals and policy have in determining blameworthiness or whether the use of different levels of *mens rea*, such as intention and recklessness, make this a value neutral judgement.

Chapter 6 delves into the requirement of dishonesty in relation to property offences. This considers the question of whether a person should objectively be judged by what ordinary people would think is dishonest, or whether a subjective approach should be used. It considers when a person will be deemed honest under section 2 of the Theft Act 1968, before then considering how the common law definition of dishonesty as applied in theft and fraud cases has developed in *R v Ghosh*[7] and *Ivey v Genting Casinos (UK) Ltd t/a Crockfords*.[8] The common law's move away from a subjective assessment of dishonesty will be examined and the impact of this discussed, to show how the law requires that the standards of honest and reasonable people in society are upheld.

Chapter 7 considers how the courts have tried to address the balance of allowing people to choose what happens to their own bodies while ensuring that people, especially those who are vulnerable, do not cause harm to each other for no good reason. There is examination of how the defence of consent works in relation to different non-fatal offences in different situations, as well as considering implied and mistaken consent. An examination of *R v BM*[9] and *R v Brown*[10] considers the conflict between legal paternalism and personal autonomy. The judgments in these cases show how morals and policy have been used to draw the line of what harm a person can consent to and in what circumstances.

Chapter 8 continues to analyse the defence of consent, by examining *R v R* and how the law of consent in sexual offences has developed in line with society's moral values in relation to marital rape.[11] The statutory definition of consent provided in the Sexual Offences Act 2003 is then considered. The evidential and conclusive presumptions for when consent will not be present are examined, highlighting some of the issues that the law causes. The interaction between sexual offences and strict liability is also considered with examination of *R v G*.[12] Strict liability is normally reserved for crimes that are regulatory in nature, as further considered in Chapter 14, but the imposition of strict liability for those who engage in sexual conduct with children under the age of 13 shows strict liability being adopted for policy reasons to combat this serious crime.

---

4 [1995] 1 AC 171.
5 (Unreported) 26 January 2017 (Crown Ct (Maidstone)).
6 [1999] 1 AC 82.
7 [1982] QB 1053.
8 [2017] UKSC 67.
9 [2019] QB 1.
10 [1994] 1 AC 212.
11 [1992] 1 AC 599.
12 [2008] UKHL 37.

Chapter 9 examines the law of intoxication. In an area of law that is truly driven by morals and policy, it is considered how legal principle can be set aside so that people cannot rely on being drunk or drugged as an excuse for committing crime. While aiming to achieve justice, this leads to arbitrary rules. As set out in *DPP v Majewski*,[13] these rules distinguish between voluntary and involuntary intoxication, and basic and specific intent crimes. This leads to an uncertain and unsatisfactory approach, which will be shown, has not been adopted in other commonwealth jurisdictions.

Chapter 10 explores the moral concept of the sanctity of human life in the context of the defences of necessity and duress, and the cases of *R v Dudley and Stephens*[14] and *R v Howe*.[15] It will be seen how this moral concept has restricted the availability of these defences, despite the different theoretical underpinnings of necessity being regarded as a justificatory defence and duress as excusatory. The result is that the law expects a person to act as a hero, and choose to sacrifice themselves or their loved ones, when faced with the moral dilemma of who should live and who should die.

Chapter 11 considers how the law of accessorial liability was developed to reduce gang association and protect society from gang activity. The case of *R v Jogee*[16] is examined to show how the law that enabled a secondary party to be criminally liable without the perquisite *mens rea* was considered a wrong turn. The judgment in *R v Hasan*[17] is then explored, to show how the same policy concerns over gang activity were used to restrict the defence of duress for those who voluntarily associate to those who could subject them to compulsion. The result of the way the law has developed, for both secondary parties and those who act under duress, is law that discriminates against, and fails to protect, certain sections of society.

Chapters 12 and 13 consider the special, partial defences of loss of control and diminished responsibility. In the Chapter 12, focus is placed on the requirement of a qualifying trigger for the defence of loss of control to reduce murder to manslaughter. The dual policy aims of making sure the law is not discriminative towards men who kill out of jealousy and providing a defence to women who kill from fear of serious violence are examined. This includes a discussion of why women who kill their abusers cannot rely on the defence of self-defence, and how they might be afforded less protection than householders who kill intruders. Furthermore, an examination of *R v Clinton*[18] is used to support the conclusion that the law has had mixed success in achieving these policy aims. In Chapter 13, the meaning of domestic abuse is considered. The relationship between diminished responsibility and coercive and controlling behaviour following *R v Challen*[19] is also examined, to show how coercive control is an offence and not a defence. Together, these two chapters demonstrate that women who kill their abuser are unlikely to be afforded the defence of self-defence or loss of control by the jury, and instead will be labelled as having an abnormality of mental functioning under the defence of diminished responsibility in order to achieve a reduction in conviction from murder to manslaughter.

Chapter 14 provides a different outlook on criminal liability by examining when a corporation can be found blameworthy, and the moral and policy reasons of why it might be desirable to hold a corporation criminally responsible. It considers strict liability, and the common law devices used to assign fault to a corporation. This includes an examination of *Tesco Supermarkets Limited v Nattrass*,[20] and the resulting difficulties that arise from assigning liability to a corporation

13 [1977] AC 443.
14 (1884) 14 QBD 273.
15 [1987] AC 417.
16 [2016] UKSC 8.
17 [2005] UKHL 22.
18 [2012] EWCA Crim 2.
19 [2019] EWCA 916.
20 [1972] AC 153.

in a system of criminal law designed to hold individuals responsible. Recently introduced statutory crimes that impose corporate liability will also be considered, to conclude that an overarching schema has not been considered or enacted. The result is piecemeal law, with the uncertainties this causes.

The overall aim of this book is to highlight that criminal law is not black and white. It does not just consist of the words as written in Acts by Parliament or laid down in previous precedents by judges. Legal rules are applied and interpreted in various ways to achieve an outcome that could be considered morally correct, or to advance policy aims. As society changes and develops, legal rules continue to change too. While this results in a complex and uncertain system of rules, it is done under the guise of ensuring that substantive justice is achieved. What remains to be seen throughout the course of this book is whether this is actually achieved.

Chapter 1

The Nature of Criminal Law

Chapter Contents

DOI: 10.4324/9781003408383-2

1.1 Chapter Aims and Objectives

This chapter will consider the nature of criminal law by examining different understandings of the meaning of law, and where law derives its authority from. The relationship between law, morals, and policy, which is the basis for this book and referred to throughout, will also be outlined.

By the end of this chapter, you should be able to:

- Identify and contrast different approaches to determining the nature of criminal law.
- Discuss the meaning of morals within criminal law.
- Discuss the policy aims of criminal law.

1.2 The Nature of Law

For centuries, philosophers and academics have been trying to answer questions such as what is law, where is the authority to make law derived from, and why law is necessary. The enormity of these questions is beyond the scope of this book.[1] This section will, however, briefly summarise two of the classic schools of thought on the nature of law. These are natural law and positivism, which will be framed in the context of criminal law.

1.2.1 Natural Law

Natural law stems from the idea that underneath all that we do there is a body of rules based on a universal and immutable moral code of what is right and what is wrong. Natural law argues that laws are evaluated in terms of these higher values and if the law deviates, then they are unjust and not morally binding. Natural law can thus be viewed as distinct from man-made law. As such, in one of the leading Christian expositions of natural law by Aquinas,[2] law is categorised into four different types:

1. God's Eternal Law – Divine reason known only to God, which is unfathomable to human beings.
2. Divine Law – Law revealed in the scriptures.
3. Natural Law – Divine law discoverable by rational creatures.
4. Human Law – Created by people for the common good.

Thus, natural law is the means by which human beings participate in divine law to ensure that good is done and evil is avoided. The operation of natural law, and its distinction from human law, can be seen below.

> Divine law includes the Ten Commandments revealed to Moses by God, which included "Thou shalt not kill" and "Thou shalt not steal". Human beings discovering this divine law and abiding by it shows natural law in operation. This also coincides with the human made laws of murder and theft, which prohibits such behaviour. The Ten Commandments, however, include "Thou shall not commit adultery". This would be considered divine law and should be followed as a requirement of natural law, but is not part of English human law.

---

1 This section aims to introduce some of the key theories and theorists and not an in-depth analysis of the different schools of thought. For a detailed and accessible examination of legal jurisprudence, see Raymond Wacks, *Understanding Jurisprudence* (6th edition, Oxford University Press 2020).

2 St Thomas Aquinas, *Summa Theologiae* in *Selected Political Writings* trans JG Dawson, ed A Passerin D'Entreves (Basil Blackwell 1970).

Natural law has also been considered as a secular concept by Fuller, who considers that natural law derives from the law having an "inner morality".[3] Notwithstanding its evolving nature natural law was challenged in the eighteenth century, and seemingly relegated to history, by the advent of the more scientific Positivist school of legal thought.[4] Nonetheless, natural law saw a resurgence in the twentieth century following the atrocities of World War II and the development of human rights law. As such, a contemporary understanding of natural law with a focus on human rights is provided by Finnis.[5]

An example of natural law's application can be seen in criminal law through the Nuremberg Trials.

The Nuremberg Trials

The Nuremberg Trials were a series of 13 trials carried out in Nuremberg, Germany, between 1945 and 1949 for the purpose of bringing 185 people indicted as Nazi war criminals to justice. These trials were notable for being the first international criminal court to be set up between the four allied sovereign nations of France, Britain, the Soviet Union and the United States. These countries, with different legal traditions and practices, agreed to the London Charter of the International Military Tribunal (IMT) on 8 August 1945. This established the laws and procedures for the Nuremberg trials.

The basis of the trials was the implementation of repressive and violent policies introduced by Adolf Hitler, which persecuted German-Jewish people and other perceived enemies of the Nazi state. These policies resulted in the state-sponsored murder of 6 million European Jews (along with an estimated 4 million to 6 million non-Jews) by the end of World War II. While Hitler himself committed suicide before he could be brought to trial, the first Major War Criminal Trial included twenty-four Nazi Party officials and high-ranking military officers. These defendants were charged under the Charter with Crimes against Peace, War Crimes, and Crimes against Humanity. This led to one key issue with the Nuremberg trials. When the actions of the defendants were undertaken these offences were not in existence. Moreover, the defendants were following the stated law of Germany as it stood at the time. Despite this, all but three of the defendants were found guilty. Thus, while natural law theory was not directly referred to in reaching this outcome, it provides an important example that what actions are legitimate cannot always be determined by reference to the stated law.

This suggests that the only legitimate law is law that reflects what society finds acceptable. Thus, the (criminal) law should develop to reflect society's moral values. As Devlin states, "it is clear that the criminal law as we know it is based upon moral principle. In a number of crimes its function is simply to enforce a moral principle and nothing else".[6] Further below, and throughout this book, the proper role of morals in shaping criminal law will be discussed. Before this, however, the alternative positivist school of thought will be considered.

---

3 Lon L Fuller, *The Morality of Law* (revised edition, Yale University Press 1969).

4 See Chapter 2.4.2.

5 John Finnis, *Natural Law and Natural Rights* (2nd edition, Clarendon Press 2011).

6 Patrick Devlin, *The Enforcement of Morals* (Oxford University Press 1970) 7.

1.2.2 Positivism

Austin, one of the first legal positivists, sought to show that law is a scientific concept that is separate from personal values and individual manipulation. He stated that law differs from other rules because it is the command of the sovereign body and can be enforced by the state through punishment[7] This, however, fails to recognise that not all laws command us to do something. Bentham,[8] another legal positivist, held that law is all rules that are legitimately made by Parliament and objectively applied by judges. As such, like Austin, argued that the law does not rely on the interpretation or application of some higher or intrinsic value. Dworkin was a strong critic of positivism and argued, in Law's Empire, that law is integrated with morality.[9] Positivism, however, focuses on what the law is, rather than what law ought to be. That said, positivists do not necessarily reject the importance of the influence of morality on the law, but hold that what law is, can be determined without reference to morals.

Hart provided a more contemporary view of legal positivism by considering its practical application. Moving away from the largely coercive nature of law prescribed by Bentham and Austin, Hart instead viewed law as a social phenomenon that can be observed through social practices within a community. In other words, law only exists as society recognises and accepts that it exists. Thus, in *The Concept of Law* he argued that rules could be split into:

> Primary rules – rules to protect persons and property, which a fair and just society needs to survive. For example, criminal laws such as do not steal and do not kill.
>
> Secondary rules – rules needed by more complex societies, which can be categorised into: (i) Rules of change that set out the processes for changing primary or secondary rules, for example, Parliamentary law making. Rules of change also confer power on individuals to change their legal status. For example, by forming contracts, entering into a marriage, or becoming a homeowner. (ii) Rules of adjudication, which are the rules for conferring power to those who resolve disputes. This includes giving power to individuals, such as judges, to come to decisions on guilt and pass sentences. (iii) Rules of recognition, which determine criteria for ensuring the validity of all primary and secondary rules.[10]

Hart summarises the positivist position:

1. Laws are commands of humans.
2. There is no necessary connection between law and morals.[11]
3. The analysis of legal concepts is worth pursuing without sociological, and historical enquiries.
4. Correct decisions can be deduced from predetermined legal rules by logical means alone.
5. Moral judgments cannot be established as statements of fact.[12]

---

7 John Austin, *The Province of Jurisprudence Determined* (Harvard University Press 1832).

8 See writings including: Jeremy Bentham, *A Fragment on Government* (2nd edition, W. Pickering 1823); Jeremy Bentham, *An Introduction to the Principles of Morals and Legislation* (Clarendon Press 1789); Jeremy Bentham, *Of Laws in General* (ed HLA Hart, Athlone Press 1970).

9 Ronald Dworkin, *Law's Empire* (Harvard University Press 1986).

10 HLA Hart, *The Concept of Law* (Clarendon Press 1961).

11 See also Hans Kelson, *The General Theory of Law and State* (New York, 1945), 5, who states, "the concept of law has no moral connotation whatsoever". Additionally, Joseph Raz, *The Authority of Law: Essays on Law and Morality* (Oxford University Press 1979) 38, states "the identification of law involves no moral argument, it follows that conformity to moral values or ideals is in no way a condition for anything being a law or legally binding. Hence, the law's conformity to moral values and ideals is not necessary."

12 HLA Hart, *Definition & Theory in Jurisprudence: An Inaugural Lecture Delivered before the University of Oxford on 30 May* (Clarendon Press 1953).

In a distinction from legal formalism[13] or the declaratory theory of law,[14] which assumes there is always one correct answer to a legal problem which it is judge's role is to state, Hart acknowledges that judges have a role in making law by the choices they make and the discretion they exercise.[15] Bentham accepts this legislative function of judges but strongly objects to it because of the problem it creates with retrospective law making.[16] As discussed further in Chapter 2,[17] this retrospectivity and lack of certainty goes against the underpinning principles of criminal law, and means that people cannot adjust their behaviour in accordance to the law before being charged with a crime. Moreover, the positivist approach means that people will not necessarily avoid criminal liability by following their own, or what they believe is society's, moral compass.

1.2.2.1 The Hart–Devlin Debate

The conflict between the positivist school of thought and natural law informed by morals, can be seen in the renowned Hart–Devlin debate. This is just one example of the debates that exist between leading theorists, to determine what the true nature of law is. In this debate, the question was one of how far morals should influence the content of the law that is made. The debate between Professor Hart and Patrick Devlin was an attempt to contribute to the findings of the Wolfenden Committee. In 1957 the Wolfenden Committee Report, of the Committee on Homosexual Offences and Prostitution, recommended the decriminalisation of private homosexual activity between consenting adults over the age of 21.[18] At the time of publication there was not wholesale support for these recommendations. Discussing the report's findings, Hart agreed that homosexuality should be made legal to reflect individual freedom of choice and to respect privacy. Therefore, the law should not be based on popular morality in the absence of other harms.[19] Opposingly, Devlin, in delivering the Maccabaean Lecture in Jurisprudence at the British Academy in 1959, took a legal moralism approach to the role of law in society. He argued that the collective judgment of a society should guide enforcement of laws against both private and public behaviour that was deemed immoral. While he did not advocate that all immoral behaviour should be criminalised, Devlin stated that when behaviour reached the limits of "intolerance, indignation and disgust", legislation against it was necessary.[20]

Unlike the proposals recommended in the Wolfenden Report to restrict prostitution, which were enacted shortly after the report's publication,[21] it was another 10 years before homosexuality was legalised for those over 21 years of age.[22] During this time there was a clear division of support for the Wolfenden Report's recommendations relating to legalising homosexuality when the proposals were discussed in Parliament. Furthermore, there was a lack of clarity as to whether the role of the law was to enforce moral values.[23] Eventually, the Sexual Offences Act was passed in 1967. It cannot, however, be said that this shows that Hart's arguments triumphed over Devlin's. In the intervening years there had been a clear shift in moral views, or at least how openly these views

---

13 For more discussion, see Paul Troop, "Why Legal Formalism Is Not a Stupid Thing" [2018] Ratio Juris 428.

14 William Blackstone, *Commentaries on the Laws of England: A Facsimile of the First Edition of 1765–1769*, vol I (The University of Chicago Press 1979) 69.

15 HLA Hart, *The Concept of Law* (Clarendon Press 1961) 124–154.

16 Jeremy Bentham, *Truth versus Ashurst, Or, Law as It Is, Contrasted with What It Is Said to Be: Written in December 1792* (T. Moses 1823) 13.

17 See Chapter 2.3.3.

18 Home Office, *Wolfenden Committee Report of the Committee on Homosexual Offences and Prostitution* (HL 1957) 115–116.

19 HLA Hart, *Law, Liberty and Morality* (Oxford University Press 1963).

20 Patrick Devlin, *The Enforcement of Morals* (Oxford University Press 1970) 17.

21 Street Offences Act 1959.

22 Sexual Offences Act of 1967.

23 For example, see HL Deb 4 December 1957, vol 206, cols 753–832; HC Deb 26 November 1958, vol 596, cols 365–508.

were expressed, towards tolerating and accepting homosexuality. Thus, arguably the change in law represented what was by then the collective view of society.[24]

1.2.2.2 The Hart–Fuller Debate

Another famous example of the clash between positivism and natural law can be seen in the Hart–Fuller debate. Unlike the above debate, this did not concern what should be made into law, but the veracity of law already in force. Central to this argument was a case commonly referred to as the "Grudge Case".[25] The facts of the case were that in 1944, a woman in Germany, in a bid to rid herself of her husband, reported him to the authorities for derogatory remarks he had made about Hitler. At the time, it was illegal to make statements that were detrimental to the government of the Third Reich. As such, the husband was arrested and sentenced to death by a military tribunal. He was not executed but instead, after a time in prison, was sent to serve on the front line. Following the defeat of the Nazi regime, the wife was prosecuted and convicted in a West German court in 1949 under section 289 of the German Criminal Code of 1871. This section provided for the crime of depriving a person of his freedom. The wife pleaded that she had committed no crime as her husband's imprisonment had been in accordance with the law. Moreover, that at the time her conduct in reporting him was actively encouraged. In an appeal to a German court of last resort in criminal cases, the court held that she had been under no duty to report her husband. She had utilised the Nazi law out of free choice, which was contrary "to the sound conscience and sense of justice of all decent human beings".[26] In the "Separation of Law and Morals", reviewing this case, Hart comments: "This reasoning was followed in many cases which have been hailed as a triumph of the doctrines of natural law and as signalling the overthrow of positivism. The unqualified satisfaction with this result seems to me to be hysteria".[27] Hart considered that while allowing the woman to escape punishment was not a suitable option, the alternative lesser evil of introducing a retrospective statute to deem her actions illegal could have been implemented.[28] Fuller, however, responds with criticism of Hart's approach.[29] He exposes a key problem with Hart's positivist thinking: If the positivist approach is based on fidelity to the law as it stands at the time, rather than recourse to moral values, how can a later statute deem that the earlier law is void at the time it was in force?[30] While Fuller acknowledges that a retrospective statute would be strongly symbolic in signalling "a sharp break from the past",[31] he argues that due to the immoral nature of the Nazi informer laws they were never valid law:

> To me there is nothing shocking in saying that a dictatorship which clothes itself with a tinsel of legal form can so far depart from the morality of order, from the inner morality of law itself, that it ceases to be a legal system. When a system calling itself law is predicated upon a general disregard by judges of the terms of the laws they purport to enforce, when this system habitually cures its legal irregularities, even the grossest, by retroactive statutes, when it has only to resort to forays of terror in the streets, which no one dares challenge,

24 For example, the Homosexual Law Reform Society (HLRS) was formed in 1958 to campaign for the implementation of the reforms recommended by the Wolfenden Report. The HLRS lobbied Parliamentarians about the importance of legislative change in light of societal changes. The popularity of their appeal was seen in 1960 when an unprecedented crowd of over 1000 people attended a HLRS open meeting at Caxton Hall, London.

25 Judgment of 27 July 1949, Oberlandesgericht, Bamberg, 5 St Deutsch Juristen-Zeitung 207 (Germany 1950) [1951] Harv L Rev 1005.

26 Judgment of 27 July 1949, Oberlandesgericht, Bamberg, 5 St Deutsch Juristen-Zeitung 207 (Germany 1950) (1951) Harv L Rev 1005, 1006.

27 HLA Hart, "Positivism and the Separation of Law and Morals" [1958] Harv L Rev 593, 619.

28 HLA Hart, "Positivism and the Separation of Law and Morals" [1958] Harv L Rev 593, 619–621.

29 Lon L Fuller, "Positivism and Fidelity to Law: A Reply to Professor Hart" [1958] Harv L Rev 630.

30 Lon L Fuller, "Positivism and Fidelity to Law: A Reply to Professor Hart" [1958] Harv L Rev 630, 649.

31 Lon L Fuller, "Positivism and Fidelity to Law: A Reply to Professor Hart" [1958] Harv L Rev 630, 649.

> in order to escape even those scant restraints imposed by the pretence of legality – when all these things have become true of a dictatorship, it is not hard for me, at least, to deny to it the name of law.[32]

While these debates focus on specific issues within the law, this does not detract from the difficulty they illustrate in determining what our law should be and how its legitimacy should be viewed. Even within the recognised schools of thought of natural law and positivism there is much diversity as to what the nature of law is. As will be examined throughout this book, these questions of what the law is, and what it ought to be, are still evident in the law today.

1.3 The Role of Morals and Policy in Shaping Criminal Law

Morals and policy have an important role in determining how the law should be defined and interpreted. As will be explored during the chapters of this book, particular events, or the occurrence of unwanted behaviour, can trigger law to be made to penalise and deter such wrongdoing. As such, the law aims to reflect the standards of behaviour that society finds acceptable and operate in the public's best interests, while also maintaining certainty and respecting personal autonomy by being minimally intrusive.

Once law is created through legislation, or the establishment of judicial precedent, a standard is set to which citizens must abide. The number of cases reaching the courts, however, show that there is uncertainty as to how law will be interpreted. Even positivists acknowledge that judges can make law through their interpretation.[33] This leads to the question of how judges decide what is the correct position to take when faced with making a judgment, and what influences them to reach the conclusions that they do.

The difficulty of determining the correct role of morals and policy in shaping the criminal law can be seen by considering the majority and dissenting judgments in *Shaw v DPP*.[34]

Shaw v DPP

Shaw was convicted of, among other things, conspiracy to corrupt public morals after he published a directory advertising the names and addresses of prostitutes. He argued that no such offence existed and resultingly the matter was appealed to the House of Lords for their consideration. As part of the majority decision to dismiss Shaw's appeal, Viscount Simonds stated:

> In the sphere of criminal law I entertain no doubt that there remains in the courts of law a residual power to enforce the supreme and fundamental purpose of the law, to conserve not only the safety and order but also the moral welfare of the State, and that it is their duty to guard it against attacks . . .[35]

32 Lon L Fuller, "Positivism and Fidelity to Law: A Reply to Professor Hart" [1958] Harv L Rev 630, 660.

33 See Chapter 1.2.2.

34 *Shaw v DPP* [1962] AC 220.

35 *Shaw v DPP* [1962] AC 220, 267.

Thus, judging that the duty of the courts was to uphold the moral values of society. Lord Morris, in determining that the offence of conspiracy to corrupt public morals did exist, makes a similar point in stating: "There are certain manifestations of conduct which are an affront to and an attack upon recognised public standards of morals and decency, and which all well-disposed persons would stigmatise and condemn as deserving of punishment".[36] Lord Tucker, giving the leading judgment to dismiss Shaw's appeal on this indictment, argues that a conspiracy to corrupt morals is as blameworthy as a conspiracy to commit a wrongful act which is calculated to cause public injury.[37] Thus, corruption of morals can be equated to causing harm to another. Moreover, Lord Tucker states that in deciding what behaviour would be deemed immoral and attract criminal censure, it should be for the jury to decide as: "They alone can adequately reflect the changing public view on such matters through the centuries."[38] Therefore, a person's behaviour is judged by his peers to determine what is acceptable in society, and therefore what actions are blameworthy, and thus criminal.

Alternatively, Lord Reid dissenting, states: "Notoriously, there are wide differences of opinion today as to how far the law ought to punish immoral acts which are not done in the face of the public."[39] This suggest that private acts, done in the privacy of the home, should not warrant intrusion by the criminal law even if some would deem the acts immoral. Moreover, Lord Reid warns against the influence of public policy. In his judgment, referring to previous cases, he opines:

> I think that the following comments are as valid today as they were in 1824: "I am not much disposed to yield to arguments of public policy. I think the courts of Westminster Hall . . . have gone much further than they were warranted in going in questions of policy: they have taken on themselves, sometimes, to decide doubtful questions of policy; and they are always in danger of so doing because courts of law look only at the particular case, and have not the means of bringing before them all those considerations which ought to enter into the judgment of those who decide on questions of policy" (*per* Best C.J. in *Richardson v. Mellish*. "I . . . protest . . . against arguing too strongly upon public policy – it is a very unruly horse, and when once you get astride it you never know where it will carry you. It may lead you from the sound law. It is never argued at all but when other points fail" (*per* Burrough J.).[40]

Lord Reid iterates the importance of certainty in criminal law,[41] stating: "It has always been thought to be of primary importance that our law, and particularly our criminal law, should be certain: that a man should be able to know what conduct is and what is not criminal, particularly when heavy penalties are involved."[42] Resultingly, Lord Reid concludes that: "Where Parliament fears to tread it is not for the courts to rush in."[43] Therefore, he is of the opinion that for matters of morals and policy it should be left to Parliament to decide what the law should be.

36 *Shaw v DPP* [1962] AC 220, 292.
37 *Shaw v DPP* [1962] AC 220, 290.
38 *Shaw v DPP* [1962] AC 220, 289. See also Lord Morris at 292, who makes a similar point.
39 *Shaw v DPP* [1962] AC 220, 275.
40 *Shaw v DPP* [1962] AC 220, 276 (footnotes omitted).
41 See Chapter 2.3.3 for more discussion of the importance of certainty in criminal law.
42 *Shaw v DPP* [1962] AC 220, 281.
43 *Shaw v DPP* [1962] AC 220, 275.

Many well-known and authoritative academics have spent considerable time and effort examining the relationship between legal rules, morals and policy. Reference to some of the leading work can be seen in the further reading at the end of this chapter.[44] One such writer, Dworkin, identifies that law consists of not only rules, but also principles and policies that judges may consider in reaching decisions.[45] He defines principles as a standard to be observed, weighted against other principles, to achieve justice, fairness, or some other dimension of morality.[46] Conversely, policy is a goal to be achieved, weighted against other policies, for example, an improvement of an economic, political or social feature of society.[47] The adoption of principles when deciding cases, in addition to applying rules, leads Dworkin to conclude, in opposition to what positivists hold, that "no ultimate distinction can be made between legal and moral standards".[48] While Dworkin acknowledges that weighing up principles can fall within the remit of a judge's decision making, he argues that matters of policy should be left to the legislature. This avoids the uncertainty of making decisions based on achieving different policy aims in individual cases,[49] and the legislature is better suited to make law as they are elected, can be held accountable, and do not make law retrospectively.[50] Greenawalt, however, argues that judges do rely on policy to make decisions.[51] As will be shown throughout this book, it appears that judges are influenced by both morals and policies when exercising their judicial functions in determining what the law is, or even what the law should be. This is not to say that judges make law,[52] but that there are multiple considerations in determining what the law truly is. Thus, the premise of this book is that criminal law is shaped not only by the application of legal rules, but also by morals and policy.

1.3.1 Morals

As discussed above,[53] natural lawyers argue that law comes from a higher being or values, so it is in line with moral ideals. This can be seen in the common law of England and Wales, which has its roots in Christianity. Positivists, on the other hand, argue that law is what is authoritatively stated and can be formed without reference to morals.[54] Laws could be considered as stating and enforcing a minimum standard of behaviour to avoid punishment, whereas morals require a higher standard of how one ought to behave. Therefore, even if it is accepted that morals form part of the intrinsic nature of law it still needs to be determined when it is just to enforce these moral values. This section will consider the meaning of morals, and the difficulties in determining what they are. The aim is to outline this concept, which will run throughout this book when considering the way judges have addressed the different moral issues in the cases presented to them.

It is important to consider what moral values are. Morals can exist implicitly, and with no reference to religion. They are shown to exist when people's attitudes and behaviour conform to them, even when there is no legal penalty for not doing so. Notwithstanding this, moral values can exist even when they are often breached. For example, many would argue that it is morally

44 See Chapter 1.5.

45 Ronald Dworkin, *Taking Rights Seriously* (Gerald Duckworth & Co 1977) 38–39.

46 See Joseph Raz, "Legal Principles and the Limits of Law" (1972) 81 Yale LJ 823 for a contrary view. He argues that what Dworkin refers to as principles are actually laws.

47 Ronald Dworkin, *Taking Rights Seriously* (Gerald Duckworth & Co 1977) 22–23.

48 Ronald Dworkin, *Taking Rights Seriously* (Gerald Duckworth & Co 1977) 46.

49 Ronald Dworkin, *Taking Rights Seriously* (Gerald Duckworth & Co 1977) 88.

50 Ronald Dworkin, *Taking Rights Seriously* (Gerald Duckworth & Co 1977) 84–86.

51 Kent Greenawalt, "Policy, Rights, and Judicial Decision" (1976) 11 Ga L Rev 991.

52 For an alternative viewpoint, consider legal realism – for example, Karl Llewellyn, "Some Realism About Realism" (1931) 44 Harv L Rev 1222.

53 See Chapter 1.2.1.

54 See Chapter 1.2.

wrong to lie, but this does not prevent lying occurring on a frequent basis. Moreover, moral values can exist even though they may conflict with other moral values. For example, many would agree that it is wrong to steal, however, they may not condemn a shop assistant who takes perishing products at the end of the day without permission to give to another to prevent them from starving. There may be certain fundamental moral values that are shared by the majority of society, for example, that it is wrong to kill. Even such fundamental moral values are not, however, free from debate. There is still strong division among societal views about the morality of certain kinds of intentional killing. For example, the use of death penalty to punish certain crimes, or assisted dying for the terminally ill. As such, the same actions can provoke differing views on what is acceptable depending on the context. To further illustrate this point, sexual activity with a child under 16 is illegal, whether or not the child consents.[55] Society would likely condemn a 50-year-old man engaging in sexual activity with a 15-year-old child. Society might not feel this is as immoral, however, if the matter instead involves a kiss between two consenting 15-year-old children, which would still amount to a sexual offence.[56]

In a pluralist society it can be difficult to establish shared values. Fuller discusses how primitive societies may have shared moral values but how this becomes harder to achieve as societies become more complex. He observes that despite a reduction in shared values there are more criminal laws (mostly for regulatory matters) as societies develop. This may seem counterintuitive, as it would become harder to determine what the law should be if the population do not form a consensus on what is right and what is wrong. Alternatively, the requirement for more law may be because there is more conflict between citizens due to this lack of shared values.[57] Therefore, as we grow and advance as a society it becomes harder to reach an agreement about what the law should be.

An additional problem in establishing what moral values are is that morals are not a static concept. They evolve and change over time and place.[58] For example, historically, animal cruelty or pollution may not have been considered immoral, but now may generally be accepted as such. In most parts of the United Kingdom, it has become illegal to smack your child, when once such behaviour was seen by many as beneficial. Equally, historically, homosexuality may have been considered by some (or even the majority) to be deviant behaviour, but by many (at least in certain parts of the world) will no longer even be considered a moral issue.[59] In this way morals are unlike laws. Laws can be deliberately created, amended, or repealed, at will, with fairly prompt implementation. Morals, however, may take much longer to change and it is difficult to pinpoint exactly what they are at one specific point in time.

Even if it can be established what a society's shared moral values are, it still needs to be considered what the state's role is in upholding these moral values. Kant argued that it is not for the state to tell individuals how they ought to act as this would infringe personal autonomy. Instead, Kant believed that every human being is endowed with a conscience that makes him or her aware that moral law has authority over them to determine right from wrong.[60] While this may be true, the problem is that it is not easy to identify or define these moral laws. Thus, if there were no formal laws, and people were regulated by their own conscience, there would be no certainty of what behaviour was acceptable. The fabric of society is maintained by shared morality, and social

55 Sexual Offences Act 2003, section 9.

56 Sexual Offences Act 2003, section 13.

57 Richard C Fuller, "Morals and Policy in Criminal Law" (1942) J Crim L Criminol 624.

58 For an alternative view see Patrick Devlin, *The Enforcement of Morals* (Oxford University Press 1970) 18, who argues that our morals values do not change, but the limits of our tolerance does.

59 For a further discussion of this and how a change in law can change morals see, L Green, "Should Law Improve Morality" [2013] University of Oxford Legal Research Paper Series, Paper No. 73, 14–24.

60 Immanuel Kant, *The Metaphysical Elements of Justice: Part I of the Metaphysics of Morals* (Bobbs-Merrill, 1965).

cohesion would be undermined by what is deemed by others as immoral behaviour. Societies made up of individuals with differing values can lead to civil unrest, as seen throughout history across the world. This means, that with no consensus within communities, it is left to the state to determine what values should be protected by law and how. Devlin argues that this should be achieved through the idea of public morality, based on what a reasonable person would find injurious to society, while protecting as much as possible the private rights and freedoms of the individual within limits of tolerance.[61] This has the potential to discriminate against minority beliefs with the law reflecting populist views. Moreover, even if society does agree that certain behaviours are wrong, this still does not mean that such behaviour should be illegal. For example, many would agree that committing adultery is not morally praiseworthy, but would not necessarily think it should be contrary to criminal law. Furthermore, many established crimes seem not to involve questions of morality. Instead they are more regulatory in nature. For example, requiring a licence to drive a car or the requirement for businesses to follow weights and measures regulations. Thus, it could be concluded that many crimes have no moral underpinning, and so the question of how morality shapes the criminal law becomes irrelevant. But, even with regulatory crimes there are moral considerations, such as the unacceptable risk of potential danger to other drivers that driving without a licence may cause, or the unfair advantage gained in business by not following weights and measures requirements. Therefore, the consideration of morals is central to determining what the law is and what it ought to be.

1.3.2 Policy

When Parliament are deciding what the content of a law should be, or when judges are determining how the content should be interpreted, there are many differing considerations. For example, the law may aim to address a particular issue, prevent certain unwanted behaviour, or aim to protect certain individuals. These considerations, which consider what the purpose of the law is or what it was trying to achieve, can be described as the policy aims of the law. Policy goals will often achieve results that will be considered morally correct by the majority. It is not, however, always easy to establish what the policy aims of the law are, nor, as stated by Kenny, "is the policy always followed consistently or logically".[62] As will be shown throughout this book, this means that those judges who consider policy in their judicial decision making, will have to determine what the policy of the law is. As such, they may come to differing conclusions about what the law was trying to achieve and, as a result, how it should be interpreted.

As well as specific stated Government policies within criminal law, such as tackling hate crime or reducing knife violence, there are general policy aims that underpin what policy makers are trying to achieve through the imposition of criminal law. For example, as discussed in Chapter 2, Mill's harm principle provides one rationale for criminalising behaviour.[63] By ensuring that people do not cause harm to others, this achieves the policy aim of protecting the public and reducing the associated costs of crime detection, prosecution, and incarceration. This is in addition to reducing the related health care costs of treating those who are victims to crime.

Laws are also written to provide particular protection to those who are especially vulnerable. For example, section 5 of the Domestic Violence, Crimes and Victims Act 2004 allows any person in a household to be prosecuted for failing to intervene to protect a child victim from domestic crime.

---

61 Patrick Devlin, *The Enforcement of Morals* (Oxford University Press 1970) 16.

62 JW Cecil Turner, *Kenny's Outlines of Criminal Law* (18th edition, Cambridge University Press 2013) 4.

63 See Chapter 2.3.6.

In November 2006, Rebecca Lewis was one of the first people to be convicted of familial homicide, under section 5 of the Domestic Violence, Crimes and Victims Act 2004, for not preventing her partner from killing her 13-month-old son. Although largely absent when the 50 injuries were inflicted upon the baby that led to his death, she did not prevent them through her silence.

Criminal law aims to achieve certain policy aims through the imposition of punishment once wrongdoing has been established. One aim of punishment is denunciation. The infliction of punishment means the defendant is publicly denounced for his actions in the hope that this will prevent future offending.[64] Walker, however, argues that the theory of denunciation is flawed as many crimes go unpunished or unpublicised, and the crimes that are publicised are often because of the leniency of the sentence.[65] Therefore, if the sole purpose of punishment is to denounce, it could be argued that punishment is without just cause and no policy aims are achieved.

Punishment, however, also aims to achieve retribution. Corrective justice[66] is attained by the defendant receiving the punishment they deserve for their blameworthy conduct. This means it is important to determine who is to blame for a particular outcome and whether it is just to impose a punishment upon them. The punishment can be calculated objectively, considering what society would consider a just punishment in the circumstances. This "just deserts" methodology was championed by Kant who argued that each defendant must be treated individually and humanely, rather than a means of achieving utilitarian goals.[67] While the retributivist theory focuses on the offence the individual has committed, and the appropriate punishment for that person, retribution does also provide wider social control. As von Hirsch asserts, for example, giving proportionate punishments will lead to respect for the law, which in turn could result in the utilitarian aim of crime reduction.[68] Moreover, punishment can be seen as providing a deterrent not only to the individual who is punished, but to society as a whole. As Stephen states the "criminal law is . . . a system of compulsion on the widest scale".[69] In other words, the threat of what will happen if we break the law should compel society to abide by it. Thus, imposing punishment achieves a general policy aim of deterring crime and achieving a safer society.

Punishment can also act to protect society by incapacitating those who are likely to reoffend and are dangerous to society, for example, by putting them in prison. While this might control the individual for the period that they are incapacitated it could, however, be deemed ineffectual in the longer term. For example, as Gross identifies "the places to which those convicted are removed are themselves breeding places for crime".[70] The reality of this statement can be seen in high re-offending rates.

Therefore, when Parliament is determining actions that should be criminal, and judges are interpreting these laws, careful consideration must be taken of what policy aims are hoped to be achieved before conviction and punishment is imposed.

64 This highlights the importance of fair labelling, as discussed in Chapter 2.3.2.

65 Nigel Walker, *Why Punish?* (Oxford University Press 1991) 26.

66 See Chapter 2.3.1. for more discussion of justice.

67 Immanuel Kant, *Groundwork of the Metaphysics of Morals* (Harper Torchbooks 1964).

68 Andrew von Hirsch, "Proportionality in the Philosophy of Punishment" (1992) 16 Crime & Justice 55, 68–69.

69 James Fitzjames Stephen, *History of the Criminal Law of England*, vol II (Macmillan 1883) 97.

70 Hyman Gross, *A Theory of Criminal Justice* (Oxford University Press 1979) 386.

1.4 Conclusion

This chapter has demonstrated that there is not one agreed-upon definition of the nature of law. Some legal philosophers have argued that the law is what is written, while others argue that the law will not be valid unless it reflects the accepted values of society. It is also unclear whether the purpose of law is to set a minimum standard that is demonstrated by citizens, or set a higher moral standard to be achieved that reflects how society ought to be.

Criminal law is intrinsically linked with morals. By finding an individual to blame, labelling them as a criminal, and inflicting punishment on them, society is imposing moral censure upon that individual. Thus, questions of what behaviour is deemed right, and what is deemed wrong, become central to establishing criminal liability. In a pluralist society there may be no clear, or agreed upon, division of what is right and what is wrong. Moreover, the law aims to achieve certain policy goals. These are set by the legislature with the purpose of achieving a some common good. As such, they will often be in line with popularly held moral values. Judges, attempting to give effect to what the law was trying to achieve, will have to discover and uphold these policy aims.

As will be shown throughout this book, the law is not something that is easy to define. Judges when deciding cases have to interpret what a law means. This is not always a straightforward task. As such, they use morals and policies to shape the meaning of criminal law.

1.5 Further Reading

Devlin P, *The Enforcement of Morals* (Oxford University Press 1970)
Dworkin R, *Taking Rights Seriously* (Gerald Duckworth & Co 1977)
Greenawalt K, "Policy, Rights, and Judicial Decision" (1976) 11 Ga L Rev 991
Gross H, *A Theory of Criminal Justice* (Oxford University Press 1979)
Hart HLA, *Law, Liberty and Morality* (Stanford University Press 1963)
Kant I, *Foundations of the Metaphysics of Morals* (Scribner 1957)
Mills JS, *On Liberty* (Penguin Books 1974)
Raz J, "Legal Principles and the Limits of Law" (1972) 81 Yale LJ 823
Salmond J, *Jurisprudence: or the Theory of the Law* (Stevens & Haynes 1902)
Simmonds N, *Law as a Moral Idea* (Oxford University Press 2007)
Wacks R, *Understanding Jurisprudence* (6th edition, Oxford University Press 2020)

Chapter 2

Principles of Criminal Law

Chapter Contents

DOI: 10.4324/9781003408383-3

2.1 Chapter Aims and Objectives

Criminal law provides a means by which the state can denounce and punish an individual's actions for not conforming to the stated law. Such denouncement demonstrates public disapproval of what the person has done, and imposition of punishment can adversely affect the individual's freedom, future opportunities, relationships, and status.

Thus, with such extensive potential repercussions, careful consideration needs to be given of what restrictions and obligations the criminal law should impose on society. The way this law operates through how it is interpreted and applied in cases, also necessitates contemplation of the outcome this will cause and the wider implications that may result. A balance needs to be achieved between the state regulating people's unwanted behaviour, and ensuring personal liberty and autonomy.

This chapter will consider the underpinning principles of criminal law that try to achieve this balance. It will be considered why we need criminal law, what the purpose of criminal law is, and how imposing criminal liability can be justified.

By the end of this chapter, you should be able to:

- Define what criminal law is.
- Identify the principles underpinning criminal law.
- Examine examples of the principles underpinning criminal law in practice.

2.2 What Is Criminal Law?

Criminal law is a body of rules that regulates the relationship between the individual and the state. While when we think of criminal law it may bring to mind offences such as murder and theft, many criminal offences are far more regulatory in nature. These cover matters such as health and safety or road safety violations. As such, the nature of criminal offences can range vastly in seriousness, but the common thread is that violation of one of these rules leads to censure by the state and potential punishment or penalty.

This book does not purport to examine the many criminal offences that exist. Instead, in the subsequent chapters focus is placed on a selection of offences to examine how the principles set out below play out in practice.

2.3 Principles of Criminal Law

There are several key principles that underpin criminal law. These include:

- Justice.
- Fair labelling.
- Certainty within the law and avoidance of retrospective law making.
- Requirement and coincidence of *actus reus* and *mens rea*.
- Importance of voluntariness.
- The harm principle.
- No punishment without just cause.

Below, each of these principles is summarised with reference to some of the leading academic discourse in each area. These principles will be referred to in the subsequent chapters to provide rationalisation of why the criminal law has developed in the way it has.

2.3.1 Justice

Justice can be interpreted as meaning that there should be fairness within the law.[1] Simplistically, this would mean that there is one objective, impartial, standard of justice to which everyone agrees. However, this is not so. Individuals seem to be born with an innate sense of what they deem is fair, which can be seen as specific to each person's internal beliefs. Furthermore, throughout a person's life their view of what is fair is shaped by their experiences and knowledge, meaning that the concept is not static. Moreover, what is just is not necessarily linked with morals. For example, it can be deemed immoral to kill, but it may seem unjust to punish a person who has killed under duress in the same way as someone who has undertaken desired murder. Equally, not everyone holds the same belief as to what is fair or just, making it difficult to define what justice means.

Justice is not a new concept, nor is the debate as to what it means. For example, the ancient philosophers Aristotle and Plato took opposing views of the meaning of justice when considering what is meant by the good life. Plato promoted justice as harmony between different sectors and classes,[2] whereas Aristotle considered that proportionately equals should be treated equally and "unequals" unequally to achieve equality.[3]

Alternatively, utilitarians, such as Bentham,[4] hold that justice means achieving happiness for the greatest number of people. This takes a consequential view, by examining the impact of a person's actions, and places happiness above other (potentially conflicting) values. As examined in later chapters, this approach means that individual justice can be sacrificed for the greater good.

Justice can be categorised in different ways:

- **Substantive justice** – the content of enacted law, and the way it is interpreted by the judiciary, is fair. In the context of criminal law, this would include considering the restrictive or oppressive nature of the law balanced against the harm it was preventing.
- **Procedural justice** – the methods and procedures adopted by the criminal justice system are fair. For example, the criminal justice system is based on the premise that a person is innocent until proven guilty, and there are strict rules of evidence to ensure fair and impartial trials.
- **Distributive justice** – the burdens and benefits of society are allocated justly. This would include, for example, that those who need legal representation are provided with it by the state if they cannot afford it. Legal rules would not allow one person to gain an unfair advantage over others.
- **Corrective justice** – People pay fairly for the harms they have done to others. In a criminal case, this could mean, for example, a person being sent to prison for life for killing someone.

The focus of this book in subsequent chapters is substantive justice. It is considered whether this is achieved through the laws that are made, and the way in which they are applied in the courts.

1 John Rawls, *A Theory of Justice* (Belnap Press 1971).
2 Plato, *The Republic* (ed GRF Ferrari, trans Tom Griffith, Cambridge University Press 2000).
3 Aristotle, *Politics* (ed RF Stanley, trans Sir Ernest Barker, Oxford University Press 2009)
4 Jeremy Bentham, *An Introduction to the Principles of Morals and Legislation* (Batoche Books 1781).

2.3.2 Fair Labelling

Fair labelling is a principle introduced by Ashworth (who referred to it as "representative labelling"),[5] with the term "fair labelling" first coined by Williams.[6] It is based on the premise that labelling a person in a specific way for a crime has a symbolic function. It signals to society the degree of condemnation that should be shown towards the offender.[7] Therefore, fair labelling is concerned with making sure that the distinctions between different types of crimes, in terms of their seriousness, nature, and associated stigma, are known. Fair labelling communicates this to the offender, the victim, and the public. This in turn, enables people to form opinions and make decisions on the information received from the type of label imposed.[8] As such, while a criminal conviction signals state censure of the person's actions, the exact label can inform the responding level of stigma imposed by society. For example, society mostly likely would feel differently towards someone who has been labelled as a fly-tipper compared to someone who is a rapist. Names given to certain offences not only reflect society's disapproval of certain actions, but also "allow criminal law to shape social morality on certain matters".[9] Using labels as a means of reflecting or creating public stigma towards certain behaviours assumes, however, that society holds shared values about the degree of wrongfulness of particular crimes. Moreover, that the labels that have been attached to certain crimes fairly reflect an accepted level of wrongfulness. This is not only important in terms of the intrinsic value of truth and fairness to the defendant's reputation,[10] but also has practical implications for the defendant. For example, a criminal conviction can have a serious detrimental effect on an individual's chances of employment and future earning potential, and so it would be unfair to misrepresent the defendant's wrongdoing.[11]

The requirement to impose a fair label does, however, need to be balanced against the need to make sure the law does not become too convoluted. For example, section 8 of the Theft Act 1968 defines the crime of robbery. This requires that the defendant steals, and immediately before or at the time of doing so, and in order to do so, he uses force on any person or puts or seeks to put any person in fear of being then and there subjected to force. This shows that the force can either be used or threatened, and the victim can be put in fear of force being used or the defendant just has to seek to put the victim in fear of force being used. Moreover, the amount of force that needs to be used is not defined, and could vary from something relatively minor to something far more significant. The amount of ways this section can be interpreted and applied means that a person could be liable for robbery having undertaken very different actions. This keeps the law simple, as the different ways the offence can be undertaken are encompassed in one offence. The degree of force used or threatened can then be considered when sentencing. This, however, does not change the fact that the label remains the same when very different consequences may have been caused. This can be compared with the Offences against the Person Act 1861 which takes the opposite approach, and has many very specific offences. For example, section 22 defines the offence of using chloroform to commit any indictable offence, and section 28 defines causing bodily injury by gunpowder. Such an approach means that the label applied will truly reflect the crime that has been committed. Nonetheless, this has led to criticisms by the Law Commission about the unneeded degree of

---

5 Andrew Ashworth, "The Elasticity of Mens Rea" in Colin Tapper (ed) *Crime, Proof and Punishment: Essays in Memory of Sir Rupert Cross* (Butterworths 1981) 53.

6 Glanville Williams, "Convictions and Fair Labelling" (1983) 42 CLJ 85, 85.

7 Chambers and Fiona Leverick, "Fair Labelling in Criminal Law" (2008) 71 MLR 217, 226.

8 James Chambers and Fiona Leverick, "Fair Labelling in Criminal Law" (2008) 71 MLR 217, 238.

9 For a detailed discussion of the justifications of fair labelling see, Matthew Gibson, "Three Justifications of Fair Labelling" (2024) 140 LQR 431. See also, Victor Tadros, "Fair Labelling and Social Solidarity" in Zedner and Roberts (eds), *Principles and Values in Criminal Law and Criminal Justice: Essays in Honour of Andrew Ashworth* (Oxford University Press 2012).

10 James Chambers and Fiona Leverick, "Fair Labelling in Criminal Law" (2008) 71 MLR 217, 227.

11 James Chambers and Fiona Leverick, "Fair Labelling in Criminal Law" (2008) 71 MLR 217, 223. See also Z Hoskins, *Beyond Punishment: A Normative Account of the Collateral Legal Consequences of Conviction* (Oxford University Press 2019).

specificity and proposed reforms that would remove this complexity.[12] Therefore, the law has to be broad enough to cover a range of actions within one offence, but not so broad that the label then becomes unfair.

2.3.3 Certainty within the Law and the Avoidance of Retrospective Law Making

Lord Bingham, in his seminal work *The Rule of Law*,[13] defined the Rule of Law as "all persons and authorities within the state, whether public or private, should be bound by and entitled to the benefit of law publicly and prospectively promulgated and publicly administered in the courts".[14] He then further elaborated on this constitutional principle by identifying eight sub-rules to explain what is meant by this definition of the Rule of Law. The first of these sub-rules is that "the law must be accessible and so far as possible intelligible, clear and predictable".[15] In other words, the law must be certain. This is of obvious importance when discussing criminal law, as a person will tailor their behaviour according to what they believe the law to be. Furthermore, there is a clear injustice if a person believes they are doing everything in order to obey the law, only to then be taken to court to find that they have in fact breached a law that they could not have conceivably discovered. This importance of certainty in criminal law can be exemplified by the House of Lords waiting 20 years to first use the Practice Statement 1966 (which gave them the power to overrule their own previous decisions) in a criminal case.[16]

Moreover, to ensure predictability in the law it must be possible to determine the outcome of a case before it is heard. Prospectively promulgating the law ensures adequate notice of any changes that are due to be made, thus giving fair warning. This enables solicitors to advise their clients, and for individuals to change their behaviour or plan accordingly. Therefore, one of the principles of criminal law to ensure its certainty is that criminal law should not be made or enforced retrospectively.[17]

2.3.4 Requirement, Correspondence, and Coincidence of *Actus Reus* and *Mens Rea*

Criminal law generally requires that a person should only be held criminally responsible for the actions that they have committed, and moreover that they have committed these actions knowingly or purposively. As is examined below, the devices the criminal law uses to ensure that only those who have undertaken blameworthy conduct are *actus reus* and *mens rea*.

2.3.4.1 Requirement of *Actus Reus* and *Mens Rea*

One of the fundamental maxims of criminal law is *actus reus non facit reum nisi mens sit rea*, meaning that an act is not necessarily a guilty act unless the accused has the necessary accompanying guilty state of mind required for that offence. Resultingly, apart from crimes of strict liability (which tend to be regulatory in nature) the prosecution will need to prove that the defendant committed the required *actus reus* with the necessary *mens rea*.

---

12 Law Commission, *Reform of Offences against the Person* (Law Com No 361, 2015).

13 Tom Bingham, "The Rule of Law" (2007) 66(1) CLJ 67.

14 Tom Bingham, "The Rule of Law" (2007) 66(1) CLJ 67, 69.

15 Tom Bingham, "The Rule of Law" (2007) 66(1) CLJ 67, 69. See also J Raz, *The Authority of Law* (2nd edition, Oxford 1999) 214–216.

16 In *R v Shivpuri* [1986] UKHL 2 the House of Lords used the Practice Statements for the first time in a criminal case to overrule their previous decision in *Anderton v Ryan* [1985] AC 560, that a person could not be guilty for attempting the impossible under the Criminal Attempts Act 1981.

17 This also links to the ideal that there should be no punishment without law. See Chapter 2.3.7.

Actus reus can be described as the physical element of the crime. It includes conduct such as stabbing someone. *Actus reus* can also include the conditions that the conduct must take place under, and the consequence that the conduct must cause. For example, the crime of murder requires that it is a human being that is killed, and that this killing is under the King's Peace. These are both conditions that the offence must take place under. Furthermore, the required consequence is that the defendant's conduct must cause the victim's death. Crimes, such as murder, that require a particular consequence, are known as result crimes.

Mens rea is the mental element of a crime. If a person accidently trips and falls into another, he will not be guilty of battery as his actions were not done with a guilty mind. Therefore, as will be furthered discussed in Chapter 5, *mens rea* acts as a device to ensure only those who are blameworthy are held criminally to account. *Mens rea* covers a range of mental states, which vary according to the crime. The most serious of which tend to require the mental state of intention. Other mental states include being dishonest (normally associated with property offences) or being knowingly reckless, for example, as to causing harm to another or damaging property.

Therefore, a person who accidently trips and falls into another person, hurting them, will not be guilty of a crime as despite having the *actus reus* they have no *mens rea*. Equally, someone who thinks about committing a crime, but takes no action to realise it, will also not be guilty. A person's thoughts are not regulated. Moreover, a person who takes a risk by starting a bonfire near their neighbour's garden fence will not be as blameworthy as someone who sets out with the intention to set the fence on fire. Consequently, the requirements of *actus reus* and *mens rea* set limits on who can be found criminally liable, and also provide a means of distinguishing between the levels or seriousness of the offence committed.

2.3.4.2 Correspondence Theory

Ashworth identifies that a consequent underpinning theory of *actus reus* and *mens rea* is that the *actus reus* and *mens rea* of a crime should correspond.[18] Or, in other words, they should match. This ensures that not only is the defendant being tried for the crime that they caused, but that they can be considered blameworthy as they intended or foresaw that particular result. Some crimes, however, do not require that the *actus reus* and *mens rea* correspond. These crimes are said to create constructive liability, as criminal liability is constructed from what the defendant has done. For example, this can be seen in the offence of unlawful act manslaughter.

> Lord Hope in *Attorney General's Reference [No 3 of 1994]* defined unlawful act manslaughter, which can be summarised as when:
>
> > D commits an unlawful act, the act is intentionally performed, in circumstances rendering it dangerous, and it causes death.[19]
>
> As can be seen from the definition of unlawful act manslaughter, while the defendant must cause death, they only need to intend the lesser unlawful dangerous act that they have committed. Thus, liability is constructed from the crime they have committed, and they is held to blame for a result that he did not mean to occur.

18 Andrew Ashworth, "A Change of Normative Position: Determining the Contours of Culpability in Criminal Law" (2008) 11 New Crim LR 232.

19 [1998] AC 245, 270.

2.3.4.3 Coincidence Theory

In addition to the correspondence theory, it can also be considered that the *actus reus* and *mens rea* should occur at the same time. This, again, ensures that the defendant is being held accountable for the actions that he committed and that at the time he intended or foresaw the result. Once more, however, it can be seen that this is not always applied in practice.

> **Mela v The Queen**[20]
>
> The four defendants had taken the victim to a hut and struck him on the head in a plan to kill him. Believing that this had killed him, to dispose of the body they rolled him over a low cliff and left him outside. The medical evidence showed that the victim had died due to exposure from being left outside and not from the head injury. At trial the four defendants were convicted of murder. They appealed their convictions arguing that there was no coincidence of *actus reus* and *mens rea*.

Thinking points:

- At the moment in time when defendants struck the victim what was their *mens rea*? At this point had they completed the *actus reus* of causing the victim's death?
- When the victim died, what did the defendants believe (what was their *mens rea*)?
- How do you think the court resolved this?

The defendants argued that there was no coincidence of *actus reus* and *mens rea*. They did not cause the victim's death at the time they intended to, and then when the death was actually caused they only intended to dispose of the body, not kill. The Privy Council held that these were not two separate events but instead one continuous act. This meant that it could be said that there was coincidence of *actus reus* and *mens rea*.

2.3.5 Importance of Voluntariness

Voluntariness is an important principle that appears regularly in the discourse of criminal law. For example: the question of whether a defendant has become voluntarily or involuntarily intoxicated is central to the way the defence of intoxication operates; manslaughter can be categorised as voluntarily when the defendant has the *mens rea* for murder but has a special partial defence, or involuntarily when the defendant has killed without malice aforethought. Voluntariness is, therefore, essential for determining criminal liability as it provides a means to distinguish between those who should be held responsible for their actions and those who are not (as) blameworthy.

In criminal law the traditional view is that before someone is convicted of a crime, and consequently punished, it must be established that they acted voluntarily in infringing the law.[21] "Moralists and lawyers regard the individual's will as the autonomous prime cause of his behaviour."[22] As

20 [1954] 1 WLR 228.

21 HLA Hart, *Punishment and Responsibility: Essays in the Philosophy of Law* (2nd edition, Oxford University Press 2008); Jeremy Horder, *Ashworth's Principles of Criminal Law* (10th edition, Oxford University Press 2022) 76; AP Simester, "On the So-called Requirements for Voluntary Action" [1998] Buffalo Criminal Law Review 403, 404–407; James Fitzjames Stephen, History of the Criminal Law of England (Vol II Macmillan 1883) 97; JW Cecil Turner, *Kenny's Outlines of Criminal Law* (17th edition, Cambridge University Press 1953) 26–27, 90; Nigel Walker, *Why Punish?* (Oxford University Press 1991) 1–3.

22 Glanville Williams, "Finis for Novus Actus?" (1989) 48(3) CLOJ 391, 392.

Blackstone states, "punishments are only inflicted for the abuse of free-will"[23] and punishment is not appropriate where the defendant acts without freewill.[24] Therefore, the way a person chooses to exercise their free will in reference to established laws, or whether they have been free and informed in the choices made, determines whether they have acted voluntarily and should be subject to the criminal law and the associated penalties. As such, as will be further examined in Chapter 3, the principle of voluntariness is essential for determining, and limiting, who is rightly held to blame for their actions.

2.3.6 The Harm Principle

One rationale for criminalising behaviour is the Harm Principle. This principle was famously first articulated by John Stuart Mill in *On Liberty*.[25] It states in the absence of harm to another the state is not morally entitled to intervene and interference should be kept to the minimum necessary to maximise individual autonomy.[26] This theory does not necessarily mean that if there is harm to another that the state can automatically intervene. This was addressed by Feinberg in *Harm to Others*,[27] who offered a wider definition of the harm principle that enables criminalisation of actions to prevent or reduce harm to others. Whereas Mill focused on a negative obligation for the state to not intervene, Feinberg provided a positive obligation to protect.

Mill did not define harm but stated that acts that could be considered injurious to others and subject to punishment were an: "Encroachment on their rights; infliction on them of any loss or damage . . . falsehood or duplicity . . .; unfair or ungenerous use of advantages . . .; even selfish abstinence from defending them against injury . . ."[28] He separated these acts of harm from an individual's acts that caused no harm to others. He argued that while acts that caused no harm they might resort in moral censure from society, they should not be subject to state interference. Under Feinberg's harm principle, there should also not be criminalisation for non-harmful moral wrongs.[29] It must be shown that wrongful harm was directly or indirectly suffered, meaning that there was a set-back to one or more of a person's interests or their well-being.[30] Even where there is harm, in order to limit the application of state interference there must be a balancing of the harm caused and the implications of criminalisation. This includes considering how much interference there would be with personal autonomy, and the social value of allowing the harm.[31]

Legal moralists, such as Devlin, however, state that behaviour can be criminalised for being immoral even when it does not cause direct harm or offence.[32] For example, this could mean that abusive language used by an individual could be criminalised even if no one was offended. Moreover, consensual actions between individuals could be made illegal if they were deemed immoral. While the harm principle requires that harmful consensual conduct was conducted in public before it could be said to have caused an indirect set-back to society, moralists would not make the same distinction between acts conducted in public or private. According to moralists, not criminalising immoral behaviour, even if carried out in private, would in itself lead to the disinte-

---

23 W Blackstone, *Commentaries on the Laws of England: A Facsimile of the First Edition of 1765–1769*, vol IV (The University of Chicago Press 1979) 27.

24 Nigel Walker, *Why Punish?* (Oxford University Press 1991) 1–3; and James Fitzjames Stephen, *History of the Criminal Law of England*, vol II (Macmillan 1883).

25 John Stuart Mill, *On Liberty* (2nd edition, Parker and Son 1859)

26 John Stuart Mill, *On Liberty* (2nd edition, Parker and Son 1859) 101.

27 J Feinberg, *Harm to Others: The Moral Limits of the Criminal Law* (Oxford University Press 1987).

28 John Stuart Mill, *On Liberty* (2nd edition, Parker and Son 1859) 140.

29 J Feinberg, *Harm to Others* (Oxford University Press 1984) 36.

30 J Feinberg, *Harm to Others* (Oxford University Press 1984) 215–216.

31 J Feinberg, *Harm to Others* (Oxford University Press 1984) 221–225.

32 P Devlin, *The Enforcement of Morals* (Oxford University Press 1970) 14.

gration of society and thus (indirect) harm to the public.[33] Therefore, sometimes criminal sanctions can be imposed on what is deemed to be immoral conduct carried out in private even when the harm was desired by the victim.[34]

2.3.7 No Punishment without Just Cause

Punishment of an offender expresses the view that their behaviour was unacceptable and therefore they should be made to suffer in some manner.[35] Punishment, however, should not be imposed without just cause. Not only would this offend the ideals of corrective justice and infringe the liberty and reputation of the individual, the cost to society is vast.[36] Bentham argues that punishment is itself an evil and should only be used where it will avoid a greater evil.[37] Therefore, it must be fairly established beyond doubt that the defendant has committed a crime. Furthermore, before punishment is imposed it should be considered that if the punishment would have no impact on the defendant's behaviour (or society more generally) then punishment is inappropriate.

This requirement is more than just an underpinning principle of criminal law as it is a legal requirement through Article 7 of the European Convention on Human Rights (ECHR). The UK is a signatory to the Convention and has adopted its provisions into domestic law by means of the Human Rights Act 1998. Article 7 states:

> 1. No one shall be held guilty of any criminal offence on account of any act or omission which did not constitute a criminal offence under national or international law at the time when it was committed. Nor shall a heavier penalty be imposed than the one that was applicable at the time the criminal offence was committed.
> 2. This Article shall not prejudice the trial and punishment of any person for any act or omission which, at the time when it was committed, was criminal according to the general principles of law recognised by civilised nations.

The vague definition of legal concepts can lead to the claim that the law infringes Article 7.[38] Moreover, the retrospective nature of judicial law making can lead to arguments that when such judgments are made they are in conflict with this Article. This is demonstrated in Chapter 7, in the discussion of *SW v UK*,[39] in relation to marital rape. As will be shown, however, Article 7(2) allows for the application of what the law is generally believed to be, even if this is not what it is expressly stated as. Thus, while this principle, and law enacted in Article 7, provides protection for individuals, it is not guaranteed that a person will be found not guilty of a crime even when there was previously no written evidence of the crime's existence.

2.4 Conclusion

This chapter has identified several important principles that underpin criminal law. These principles, if observed, restrict the scope of the criminal law. They require that the law is applied in

---

33 P Devlin, *The Enforcement of Morals* (Oxford University Press 1970) 13.

34 For example, as seen in Chapter 7 in the discussion of *R v Brown* [1994] 1 AC 212.

35 Andrew von Hirsch, "Proportionality in the Philosophy of Punishment" (1992) 16 Crime & Justice 55, 66.

36 Data from the Ministry of Defence for 2022–2023 show that the annual overall resources expenditure for prisons was £4,007,980,534. See Ministry of Justice, "Costs per Place and Costs per Prisoner by Individual Prison", 21 March 2024, https://assets.publishing.service.gov.uk/media/65f4229810cd8e001136c655/costs-per-place-per-prisoner-2022-2023-summary.pdf, accessed 26 November 2024.

37 J Bentham, *An Introduction to the Principles of Morals and Legislation* (Batoche Books 1781) 134–135.

38 For example, see *Kokkinakis v Greece* (1994) 17 EHRR 397.

39 (1995) 21 EHRR 363.

a just, certain, and prospective manner. The requirements of *actus reus* and *mens rea*, coupled with voluntariness, mean that only those who have committed the offence with a blameworthy state of mind will be subject to the criminal law. Nonetheless, the examples examined above, and those that are considered throughout this book, demonstrate that strict legal principle is not always followed. As will be discussed, the justification for this is that the law has to also uphold moral values and achieve policy aims.

2.5 Further Reading

Bingham T, "The Rule of Law" (2007) 66(1) CLJ 67
Feinberg J, *Harm to Others* (Oxford University Press 1984)
Mill JS, *On Liberty* (Penguin Books 1974)
Rawls I, *A Theory of Justice* (Belnap Press 1971)
Walker N, *Why Punish?* (Oxford University Press 1991)
Williams G, "Convictions and Fair Labelling" (1983) 42 CLJ 85

Chapter 3

Voluntary Actions, Causation, and Causing Euthanasia

Chapter Contents

DOI: 10.4324/9781003408383-4

3.1 Chapter Aims and Objectives

This chapter will consider the concept of *actus reus*, by considering how the principles of causation have been developed, with the influence of morals and policy, to establish when someone can rightly be held legally responsible for the consequences of their actions. This will be achieved through the examination of three key cases: *R v Blaue*,[1] *R v Kennedy*,[2] and *R v Wallace*.[3]

By the end of this chapter, you should be able to:

- Outline the requirements of causation.
- Define unlawful act manslaughter.
- Identify the key issues in *R v Blaue*, *R v Kennedy (no 2)*, and *R v Wallace*.
- Discuss the influence of morals and policy in the development of causation.

The issues that will be addressed in this chapter can be exemplified by considering the following situations. Before starting the chapter, consider who, if anyone, is to blame and should be held criminally responsible for the resulting deaths:

- Abdul and Brad are arguing in a car. Abdul pulls out a knife, so Brad jumps out of the moving car to avoid being stabbed. As a result of jumping out of the car, he dies from his injuries.
- Carrie stabs Davinder. Davinder is taken to hospital but, due to his religious beliefs, refuses a blood transfusion, which is needed to save his life. As a result, he dies.
- Ethan supplies Frankie with drugs. Frankie takes these drugs, overdoses, and dies.
- Georgio supplies and injects Henry with drugs. Henry overdoses and dies.
- India wants her husband Jacob dead. She supplies him with a bottle of strong alcohol hoping that he will drink himself unconscious, to give her the opportunity to smother him. Jacob drinks the alcohol, becomes unconscious and India does nothing to help. Jacob dies from the alcohol before India can carry out the rest of her plan to smother him.
- Keith provides his friend Laura with drugs, which they take together by each injecting themselves. Laura starts to overdose and Keith puts her in the recovery position but then does nothing more to help her. As a result, Laura dies.
- Maurice throws acid over Nigella. This leaves her disfigured and with life-altering injuries. Nigella decides that she wants to die. Her friend, Omar, assists her to do this by providing a large amount of painkillers and helping Nigella to take them. As a result, Nigella dies.
- Penny throws acid over Quentin. This leaves him disfigured and with life-altering injuries. Quentin decides that he wants to die. His father, who is a Belgium national, takes Quentin to Belgium where euthanasia is legal. Quentin chooses to be euthanised and dies as a result of the doctor's legal life ending actions.

1 [1975] 1 WLR 1411.

2 [2007] UKHL 38

3 [2018] EWCA Crim 690.

3.2 The Need for Voluntary Action

As discussed in Chapter 2 it is a fundamental principle of criminal law that the defendant acted voluntarily when completing the *actus reus* of a crime.[4] Voluntariness has particular relevance when considering issues of causation, as Hart and Honore state:

> voluntary human action . . . has a special place in causal inquiries . . . because, when the question is how far back a cause shall be traced through a number of intervening causes, such a voluntary action is often regarded both as a limit and also as still the cause even though other later abnormal occurrences have provisionally been recognised as causes.[5]

Through the examination of the rules of causation, this chapter will consider voluntary actions, by the defendant and the victim, as both a cause and a limit of criminal liability.

3.3 Causation

Actus reus is the physical element of a crime. As discussed in Chapter 2.3.4 it can be derived from conduct, circumstances, or consequences. There may be lots of contributing causes to an outcome, but causation as a legal principle acts to determine who should be held responsible. This is a value judgment. As Simester states: "The unwelcome nature of criminal conviction . . . naturally creates pressure to accommodate moral considerations within the causation doctrine."[6] It considers who can justly be held legally accountable (and labelled) for the outcome.

Causation only relates to result crimes, when it is required to establish the defendant's practical contribution resulted in a certain outcome. This is necessary where the offence, such as murder or manslaughter, could occur by natural causes or accident, rather than the wrongful behaviour that is required for theft.[7] For example, if a person dishonestly takes an item from a shop, while there maybe multiple reasons for this, it is not difficult to determine where the legal responsibility for the theft should lie. In comparison, a person may punch another, causing the victim to fall and bang his head. The ambulance may be delayed, the doctor may treat the patient negligently, or the victim may have an underlying health condition that causes further complications. If the victim dies, the question of who has caused this death becomes more complex.

Causation is split into two branches, the first asking whether the defendant is the factual cause of the outcome and the second questioning whether the defendant is the legal cause. In other words, causation asks who is responsible (factual causation) and who ought to be responsible (legal causation). While the factual cause can often be straight forward to determine, by asking the question "but for the defendant's actions would that result have occurred?"[8] legal causation is more complex. This is because it becomes an enquiry of where the correct place is to draw the line between what the defendant ought and ought not be responsible for.

Causation adopts a number of principles to establish where the line should be drawn for what prohibited consequences can be attributed to the defendant's voluntary action. These include:

- The *de minimis* rule,[9] which requires that the defendant's actions are more than a minimal cause of the prohibited consequence.

---

4 See Chapter 2.3.5.

5 HLA Hart and A Honoré, *Causation in the Law* (2nd edition, Oxford University Press 1985) 2.

6 AP Simester, *Fundamentals of Criminal Law: Responsibility, Culpability and Wrongdoing* (Oxford University Press 2021) 95.

7 George P Fletcher, *Basic Concepts of Criminal Law* (Oxford University Press 1998) 62.

8 *R v White* [1910] 2 KB 124.

9 *R v Pagett* (1983) 76 Cr App R 279.

- *Novus Actus Interveniens*,[10] which considers if there has been a new intervening act, from the victim or a third party, between the defendant's voluntary actions and the prohibited consequence.
- The Thin skull rule,[11] which requires that a defendant takes their victim as they find them.

These principles of causation, and the influence of morals and policy in the development of the law, can be seen being played out in practice through an examination of *R v Blaue*.[12]

R v Blaue

In *Blaue*, the victim, Jacolyn Woodhead, refused to have sex with the defendant with the result that he stabbed her four times. She was taken to hospital, where, due to her religion, she refused a potentially life-saving blood transfusion and as a result died. The defendant was charged with murder. On trial he was found guilty of voluntary manslaughter, based on the defence of diminished responsibility, and sentenced to life imprisonment. The defendant appealed his conviction, arguing that the matter of causation had not been properly put to the jury. The Court of Appeal dismissed the defendant's appeal.

Thinking points:

- If the victim had accepted the blood transfusion, as medical treatment advised, she would not have died. The defendant would then have been charged with wounding contrary to section 18 of the Offences against the Person Act 1861, instead of murder reduced to manslaughter. Why might this be seen as important?

While section 18 has the same maximum sentence as manslaughter, being labelled as someone who has committed wounding is arguably different to being labelled a manslayer. The term manslayer denotes that the defendant has performed a role in the killing of another, and as such will be stigmatised by society according to their disdain of such a serious offence. Therefore, while the sentencing outcome of a conviction may have stayed the same regardless of whether section 18 or manslaughter was found, the issue of what outcome the defendant's voluntary actions caused is important when considering what label should be applied.[13]

- In considering the appeal Lawton LJ stated that the trial judge's direction to the jury reflected the common law legal principles: "He who inflicted an injury which resulted in death could not excuse himself by pleading that his victim could have avoided death by taking greater care of himself."[14] This common law rule dates back to the work of Sir Matthew Hale,[15] and reference was made to its application in *R v Holland*.[16] The defence argued that medical treatment had substantially changed since the nineteenth century and, thus, while at the time *Holland* was decided the medical treatment advised could have quite easily led to victim's death, this was not true in the current case. Does this mean that because medical treatment is now not as

10 *R v Jordan* (1956) 40 Cr App R 152.
11 *R v Blaue* [1975] 1 WLR 1411.
12 [1975] 1 WLR 1411.
13 See Chapter 2.3.2 for a further discussion of the importance of fair labelling.
14 *R v Blaue* [1975] 1 WLR 1411 at 1414.
15 MS Hale, *Historia Placitorum Coronae* 1736 (Classical English Law Texts 1971) 427–428.
16 (1841) 2 Mood & R 351.

dangerous as it was in the eighteenth century, that a victim should be placed under a duty to take care of themselves or accept the treatment offered?

Lawton LJ stated that it did not mean this, as: "The common law in Sir Matthew Hale's time probably was in line with contemporary concepts of ethics. A man who did a wrongful act was deemed morally responsible for the natural and probable consequences of that act."[17] The physical cause of Jacolyn Woodhead's death was the bleeding into the pleural cavity. Therefore, it can be said that it was not the victim's decision to refuse treatment, but the more than minimal voluntary actions of the defendant causing a stab wound to the victim's lung, that caused her death.

- While most would agree that more than 200 years after the writing of Hale the defendant should still be morally held to account for the natural and probable outcomes of his actions, this does not address whether he should be held equally accountable for any improbable consequences.

In this case, the victim's refusal to accept life-saving treatment was improbable, or in other words, unforeseeable. Thus, the defendant should not be held morally to blame for the death. The fact remains, however, that death is not an improbable or unforeseeable result of stabbing someone four times and seriously wounding them. Thus, the victim's failure to accept the treatment offered would not amount to a new intervening act that removed culpability from the defendant, as the defendant's voluntary actions were still the operating and substantial cause of the death.[18]

- The defence tried to argue that the decision to not have a blood transfusion was an unreasonable one, and thus, could amount to a break in the chain of causation.[19] Is it unreasonable to refuse medical treatment on the grounds of your religious beliefs?

The law holds that if the victim acts in a foreseeable but unreasonable or disproportionate way then the defendant could avoid liability. This is because the victim's voluntary actions amount to a new intervening act.[20] Therefore, considering the scenarios at the start of the chapter, for Abdul to avoid liability it would need to be established that Brad jumping from the car due to his fear was unreasonable, or daft, and as such amounted to a new intervening act. In *Blaue*, however, the victim's decision to refuse a blood transfusion was based on her faith as a Jehovah witness. Lawton LJ deemed that what religious belief it would be reasonable for her to hold could not be determined by the defendant,[21] and therefore while her actions might seem unreasonable for a person not of that faith (and juries might reach opposing verdicts according to their own values) it could not be deemed that the victim acted unreasonably in this situation. Thus, in the scenarios given at the start of the chapter Carrie can be found responsible for the death of Davinder.

- Was it acceptable for the court to take the victim's unforeseeable religious beliefs into consideration?

Lawton LJ stated that this was based on the policy of a defendant having to take their victim as they finds them, and that this covers wider attributes than just physical ones.[22] In other words, a person

---

17 *R v Blaue* [1975] 1 WLR 1411, 1414.
18 *R v Smith* [1959] 2 QB 35.
19 *R v Blaue* [1975] 1 WLR 1411, 1415.
20 *R v Williams* [1992] 1 WLR 380.
21 *R v Blaue* [1975] 1 WLR 1411, 1415.
22 *R v Blaue* [1975] 1 WLR 1411, 1415.

cannot be allowed to avoid blame and punishment for their voluntary actions due to the characteristics of the victim. This is because policy[23] dictates that it would not be deemed acceptable to allow a potentially dangerous individual (who stabs a woman who refuses to have sex with him) to avoid criminal liability due to the beliefs of the victim.

- One final thought: in civil law legal principle requires that a claimant must mitigate their loss. The Court of Appeal's decision in *Blaue* suggests that this legal principle does not apply in criminal cases. Why might this be?

In many types of civil case, such as negligence, the defendant has not acted deliberately. The courts are trying to reach a compromise in the situation and provide justice through fair loss allocation for the harm suffered. Criminal law, as discussed in Chapter 2.3.1, is also concerned with achieving justice. The Criminal Justice System achieves this through reflecting moral values and achieving policy aims. It determines who is blameworthy and when punishment is appropriate. As a result, is more adversarial in nature, with less room for compromise, than its civil counterpart. Therefore, there is no expectation to mitigate loss when making the binary decision of whether or not someone is blameworthy.

3.4 Causing Death through the Supply of Drugs

In December 2021 the Government released a policy paper entitled "From Harm to Hope: A 10-Year Drugs Plan to Cut Crime and Save Lives". This paper identifies that drugs have a ruinous effect on our society by driving half of all homicides with nearly 3,000 drug misuse related deaths in England and Wales in 2020. Additionally, that the cost of drugs to society is almost £20 billion a year. The policy aim of this paper was to reduce the supply and demand for drugs.[24]

With this policy aim in mind, one area where the courts have struggled is determining when the defendant's voluntary actions of supplying drugs can be said to have caused a victim's death. This becomes a particular issue when the victim has acted voluntarily to take the drugs, and thus arguably, the victim's voluntary action, if informed and free, should limit the defendant's blameworthiness. Such an outcome, however, directly conflicts with the policy aim to reduce the supply of drugs by not holding to account those who are supplying drugs that have "a ruinous effect on our society".

As discussed above,[25] the principles of causation are one way of ensuring only those who are blameworthy are held to blame. The problem, as illustrated by the cases below, is finding the correct balance between deterring the supply of drugs and only punishing those who are blameworthy. Thus, should a person who supplies drugs that leads to the death of the victim be only charged with supply of the drugs or should they face a charge of unlawful act manslaughter?

3.4.1 Unlawful Act Manslaughter

Lord Hope in *Attorney General's Reference (No 3 of 1994)* defined unlawful act manslaughter as requiring an unlawful act, intentionally performed, in circumstances rendering it objectively dangerous, which

23 See Chapter 2.5.2.

24 Home Office *et al.*, "From Harm to Hope: A 10-Year Drugs Plan to Cut Crime and Save Lives", 29 April 2022, www.gov.uk/government/publications/from-harm-to-hope-a-10-year-drugs-plan-to-cut-crime-and-save-lives/from-harm-to-hope-a-10-year-drugs-plan-to-cut-crime-and-save-lives, accessed 26 November 2024.

25 See Chapter 3.3.

causes death.[26] The unlawful act from which the conviction is based must be a crime, rather than a civil wrong.[27] The defendant must complete the *actus reus*[28] with the associated *mens rea* for that crime.[29] An omission will not suffice,[30] and crimes that can be completed negligently will generally not be sufficient.[31] The crime does not, however, have to be dangerous *per se*.[32] It is enough that the way the unlawful act is carried out makes it objectively dangerous.[33] The unlawful act does not need to be directed at the eventual victim,[34] or even at a person,[35] but it must be established that the unlawful act caused the death in fact and law.[36]

The constructive nature of this crime raises an issue regarding the legal principles of the correspondence theory.[37] The defendant having to cause death, but only have *mens rea* for the unlawful act committed (which might be quite minor) suggests a lack of correspondence, or an imbalance, between the *actus reus* and *mens rea*. This also creates an issue with the principle of fair labelling.[38] The defendant could be labelled as a manslayer for a death they did not foresee, following an act that they subjectively may not think was dangerous. The constructive nature of unlawful act manslaughter has caused particular problems in cases when the unlawful act has been the supply of drugs.

3.4.2 Supply and Administration of Drugs

In *R v Cato*[39] the defendant injected the victim with heroin. This caused the victim's respiratory system to stop functioning and as a result he died. It was established that the injection was the factual and legal cause of the death. The victim's consent to the injection was not a defence. The defendant was convicted of manslaughter based on the unlawful act of administering a noxious thing, heroin, contrary to section 23 of the Offences against the Person Act 1861.

But what if the defendant has only supplied the drugs, but not injected the victim; is the defendant still rightfully the cause of the death? In *R v Dalby*[40] the defendant lawfully obtained on prescription a class A controlled drug. He supplied some to the victim, who was a friend he was staying with. Each injected themselves intravenously before parting. Later, the victim injected himself intravenously twice more with the help of another person. He was found dead in the morning. The defendant pleaded guilty to supplying a class A controlled drug but denied manslaughter. He was convicted of manslaughter but appealed. The Court of Appeal allowed his appeal stating that for a conviction of unlawful and dangerous act manslaughter there must be a dangerous act directed at the victim, and that "the supply of drugs would itself have caused no harm unless the deceased had subsequently used the drugs in a form and quantity which was dangerous".[41] Thus, if the victim injected himself, it would appear that the defendant would not be held to blame for causing the victim's death despite supplying the drugs.

---

26 [1998] AC 245, 270.
27 *R v Franklin* (1883) 15 Cox CC 163.
28 *R v Arobieke* [1988] Crim LR 314.
29 *R v Lamb* [1967] 2 QB 981.
30 *R v Lowe* [1973] QB 703.
31 *Andrews v DPP* [1937] AC 576.
32 *R v Long, Bowers and Cole* [2020] EWCA Crim 1729.
33 *R v Church* [1966] 1 QB 59; *R v Newbury* [1977] AC 500; *R v Watson* [1989] I WLR 684; *R v JF* [2015] EWCA Crim 351.
34 *R v Mitchell* [1983] 2 WLR 938.
35 *R v Goodfellow* (1986) 83 Cr App R 23.
36 *R v Johnstone* [2007] EWCA Crim 3133; *R v Lewis* [2010] EWCA Crim 151.
37 See Chapter 2.3.4.2.
38 See Chapter 2.3.2.
39 [1976] 1 WLR 110.
40 [1982] 1 WLR 425.
41 [1982] 1 WLR 425, 429.

The matter was approached differently in the trial of *R v Dias*.[42] The victim had self-injected with heroin that had been supplied by the defendant. The judge directed the jury that the victim's self-injection amounted to an unlawful act, and they convicted the defendant of aiding and abetting an unlawful and dangerous act that led to the victim's death. The Court of Appeal rendered the conviction unsafe by virtue of the judge having wrongly directed the jury as the victim's self-injection did not amount to a crime, and a person cannot generally aid and abet something that is not a crime.[43]

Perhaps, unsatisfied with the lack of deterrent effect these rulings achieved, the matter then became clouded in *R v Rogers*.[44] The defendant pled guilty to administering a noxious substance under section 23 of the Offences against the Person Act 1861 and to manslaughter as a joint principal, after the judge had directed that no defence was available. The defendant had tied and held the tourniquet while the victim injected. The defendant appealed on the grounds that the judge had erred in his direction to the jury. The defendant claimed that tying a tourniquet was not a crime, and that you could not be a joint principal to something that was not an offence. The Court of Appeal, moving towards an approach similar to that seen in Scotland where no absolute distinction is drawn between a defendant who recklessly supplies drugs and a defendant who injects, dismissed the appeal. In reasoning that is arguably somewhat contradictory to the position taken two years earlier in *Dias*, the court stated that whether the victim's self-injection was an offence was immaterial. The court held that by applying and holding the tourniquet, the defendant was playing a part in the mechanics of the injection which caused death.[45]

Following this decision, Reed noted in 2005 that "a dissonance has arisen in this area because UK courts have been more concerned about moral fault attached to drug administration than with strict legal principles".[46] Therefore, perhaps it is not surprising that the matter then came before the House of Lords not long after in *R v Kennedy*.[47]

R v Kennedy

In *Kennedy* the defendant supplied his friend with a syringe of heroin. The victim injected himself with the drug and returned the syringe to the defendant, who then left the room. The victim later died from inhalation of his gastric contents while acutely intoxicated by opiates and alcohol. The defendant was convicted of unlawful act manslaughter and appealed. Following the same reasoning as in *Rogers* the Court of Appeal upheld the conviction, but the matter was referred to the House of Lords. The question of public importance for them to decide was: When is it appropriate to find someone guilty of manslaughter where that person has been involved in the supply of a class A controlled drug, which is then freely and voluntarily self-administered, and that administration causes the victim's death? The House of Lords allowed the appeal and held that in the case of a fully informed and responsible adult, the answer was "never".[48]

---

42 [2001] EWCA Crim 2986.

43 One exception is assisted suicide.

44 [2003] 1 WLR 1374.

45 *R v Rogers* [2003] 1 WLR 1374, 1377.

46 Alan Reed, "Causation and Assisting Drug-Abuse Injection" [2005] J Crim L 384.

47 *R v Kennedy* (No 2) [2008] 1 AC 269.

48 *R v Kennedy* (No 2) [2008] 1 AC 269, 279.

Thinking points:

- Unlawful act manslaughter requires death to be caused from an unlawful and objectively dangerous act. Why is this particularly problematic in drugs cases?

Supply of drugs is a crime under the Misuse of Drugs Act 1971. Nonetheless, as established in *Dalby*, supply of the drugs is not itself harmful and cannot cause death unless the drugs are taken. Therefore, as Lord Bingham states in *Kennedy* supply of drugs cannot be the unlawful act for the charge of unlawful act manslaughter.[49] Furthermore, as seen in *Dias*, self-injection of drugs is not a crime. Therefore, the unlawful act cannot stem from aiding and abetting the victim to take the drugs.

Maliciously administrating a noxious substance is a crime under section 23 of the Offences against the Persons Act 1861, but if the victim has self-injected then there is a question of whether the defendant has administered anything. Even if the term administered was interpreted widely to encompass supply of the drugs, which was one argument made by the Crown in *Kennedy*,[50] then there is still the issue of whether the victim's action amounted to a new intervening act. If it was, then this would break the chain of causation, and remove criminal liability from the defendant.

- In the judgment, Lord Bingham states: "The criminal law generally assumes the existence of free will." Does this mean that despite the harm the government states is caused by drugs, that a person should be able to overdose with no one being held to blame for supplying the means for them to do so?

The judgment in *Kennedy* holds that people are autonomous beings who are free to make their own decisions. Therefore, the court found that it was inappropriate to place blame for the victim's death with the defendant when the victim's decision to administer the drugs was free, deliberate, and informed. As the House of Lords said, "the deceased had a choice whether to inject himself or not. He chose to do so, knowing what he was doing. It was his act."[51] This then poses the question of when the victim's actions can be deemed truly free, deliberate, and informed. This was not an issue addressed directly in *Kennedy*, but Lord Bingham recognised that sometimes people may not be free to make their own decisions. He gives the examples of those who are young, those who for any reason are not fully responsible for their actions, and the vulnerable.[52] Despite this, the judgment ignores that drug addicts' may fall into the category of those who are vulnerable, and that their actions are not truly free if they are determined by their addiction. Such an approach seems to have been taken in *R v Rebelo*, when considering gross negligence manslaughter.[53] The jury convicted the defendant on retrial for gross negligence manslaughter, after he provided weight loss drugs to someone who was addicted to the drugs. The trial judge had directed the jury to consider whether the victim's actions were "fully free, voluntary and informed" considering her vulnerability caused by addition.[54] The Court of Appeal held there had not been a misdirection.[55]

---

49 *R v Kennedy (No 2)* [2008] 1 AC 269, 274.

50 *R v Kennedy (No 2)* [2008] 1 AC 269, 272.

51 *R v Kennedy (No 2)* [2008] 1 AC 269, 277.

52 *R v Kennedy (No 2)* [2008] 1 AC 269, 275.

53 [2021] EWCA Crim 306.

54 *R v Rebelo* [2021] EWCA Crim 306, [30].

55 *R v Rebelo* [2021] EWCA Crim 306, [32]–[39].

- Does the judgment in *Kennedy* support the Government's policy aim to reduce the supply and demand for drugs?

The judgment in *Kennedy* does not achieve the Government's policy aims of reducing the supply and demand for drugs. A person who supplies drugs can avoid liability for unlawful act manslaughter, for any resulting death, if the victim's actions are voluntary. Thus, there is a lack of deterrent effect. While the alternative of prosecuting for gross negligence manslaughter could provide a solution, if all the elements of that offence are met, Elliot and de Than argue that the issue could be resolved with the introduction of a new statutory offence for deaths caused by the supply of class A drugs.[56] This would satisfy the requirements of fair labelling while still conveying a message of moral condemnation.[57]

Alternatively, to achieve the policy aim of deterring the supply of drugs, when the victim's actions would break the chain of causation for unlawful act manslaughter could be narrowed. This is seen in *R v Field*.[58] The defendant has befriended an older man with the alleged intent of killing him and inheriting his estate. The Court of Appeal held that the victim, who was deceived as to the defendant's murderous desires when he supplied the victim with "deadly whisky",[59] would not be considered informed in his decision to drink it. Thus, the chain of causation would not be broken between the defendant's supply of a (legal) substance and the victim's death. As such, the defendant could be found guilty of murder. In reaching this decision the court claimed to follow the *ratio* from *Kennedy*, but distinguished *Field* on its facts.[60] As Rasiah argues:

> the Court of Appeal is willing to explore the range of the evaluative concept of voluntariness and whether an act is free, deliberate and informed, in order to limit the exculpatory effect of the *novus actus interviens* principle articulated by Lord Bingham in *Kennedy*.[61]

Therefore, the outcome is that actions that appear to be voluntary – such as the victim in *Field* choosing to drink whisky – are regarded as involuntary, but the actions of a drug addict injecting drugs are deemed to be voluntary. Perhaps policy can be used to explain what could otherwise appear as an anomalous outcome. As Azmeh states, the outcome in *R v Field* is a logical construal of the rule set out in *Kennedy* as "from a policy perspective . . . it is important that the law is workable when grounded in practicalities, rather than being an abstruse and rigid set of legal niceties that may lend itself to injustice".[62] Thus, flexibility in the application of the rule in *Kennedy* means that guilt can be achieved in cases, such as *Field*, when the defendant wants to harm another and their actions are infinitely blameworthy. This, however, leaves the law uncertain as to when the chain of causation will be left intact or when it will be broken. It will hinge on judging the voluntariness of the defendant's actions – a decision that may be swayed by morals and policy considerations.

In relation to the scenarios at the start of the chapter, it can be seen that Georgio, who supplies and injects Henry with drugs, will be the cause of the resulting death. Alternatively, Ethan who has supplied Frankie with drugs will not be considered the legal cause when Frankie voluntarily takes these drugs, overdoses and dies. On the other hand, India, who supplies her husband Jacob with a bottle of strong alcohol that Jacob drinks himself, could still be considered the cause due to her undisclosed desire that Jacob dies.

---

56 C Elliot and C de Than, "Prosecuting the Drug Dealer When a Drug User Dies: *R v Kennedy (No 2)*" (2006) 69(6) MLR 986, 991–992.

57 See Chapter 2 for further discussion of fair labelling and the deterrent value of the law.

58 *R v Field* [2021] EWCA Crim 380.

59 GR Sullivan and AP Simester, "Deadly Whisky" (2022) 138 LQR 11.

60 *R v Field* [2021] EWCA Crim 380.

61 Nathan Rasiah, "Homicide: Novus Actus Interveniens" (2021) 8(2) CLJ 213, 215.

62 Umar Azmeh, "Murder: R v Field" [2021] Crim LR 980, 984.

An alternative, and perhaps more satisfactory way to view the situation of India and Jacob, and by analogy *Field*, is through the lens of omissions.[63] While drug dealers, or in this situation suppliers of strong alcohol, have been held not to have a general duty of care to their customers,[64] a person can be held responsible for failing to act when they have voluntarily assumed a duty of care[65] or due to a relationship.[66] This means that if India failed to summon help when Jacob became unconscious, paired with her murderous intent, she could be found guilty of his murder.

As such, in the scenario at the start of the chapter Keith could be held responsible for the death of Laura. This is despite her injecting herself, as Keith has assumed a responsibility to her and then failed to call for help.[67] The principles of causation will not be applied to ask whether the supply of drugs caused Laura's death, but instead the question becomes whether Keith has breached his duty to act and this has caused the death.[68]

3.5 Causing Euthanasia

This chapter has so far considered some of the fundamental principles of causation, and seen how they operate in practice through case law. In *Blaue* the victim had refused to accept treatment, which ultimately led to their death, but what if the victim does a positive act that leads to their death? This final section will consider whether a person can be criminally responsible for causing another to commit suicide.

Traditionally, suicide was considered a sin, and until the Suicide Act 1961 was a criminal offence. It still is a crime in over 20 countries worldwide, many of which are former British Colonies applying the English common law. These countries include Malaysia, Kenya, Nigeria, and Bangladesh. Despite suicide no longer being illegal in the United Kingdom, it is illegal to assist someone in committing suicide. This creates an anomalous situation when you can be guilty, and sentenced to up to 14 years in prison, for assisting and encouraging something that is not a crime.

Assisted dying is the term used when a person helps someone else to die who is terminally ill. The medical form of this is known as euthanasia. A YouGov poll in 2024 showed a majority of UK citizens want to legalise euthanasia.[69] There have been several attempts to legalise assisted dying in the UK,[70] alongside court challenges to argue for the right to assisted suicide.[71] Regardless, as the law stands at the time of writing, helping someone to die through assisted suicide, assisted dying, or euthanasia, remains illegal.

It is easy to establish a causal relationship between a doctor's actions to euthanise and a patient's death. The situation is not, however, always so straightforward. For example, can it be said that an online bully that has led another person, whom they have never met, to commit suicide has caused their death? If a person chooses to kill himself in response to the defendant's actions, can this be said to be a new intervening act? In his discussion of causation Wilson argues:

> If a person chooses to kill themselves because of something somebody else does it is their choice not the other's. If the other has done something wrong then the appropriate response

---

63 See Chapter 4 for more discussion of omissions.

64 *R v Khan* [1998] 3 WLUK 350.

65 *R v Evans* [2009] 1 WLR 1999.

66 *R v Hood* [2003] EWCA Crim 2772; *R v Broadhurst* [2019] EWCA Crim 2026.

67 *R v Ruffell* [2003] EWCA Crim 122.

68 *R v Broughton* [2020] EWCA Crim 1093.

69 Matthew Smith, "Three Quarters Support Assisted Dying Law", 22 November 2024, https://yougov.co.uk/politics/articles/50989-three-quarters-support-assisted-dying-law, accessed 26 November 2024.

70 At the time of writing the most recent of these was the Terminally Ill Adults (End of Life) Bill 2024–2025.

71 For example, the law preventing assisted dying was challenged in the Supreme Court in *R (on the application of Nicklinson) v Ministry of Justice* [2014] UKSC 38.

> is to censure and punish for that wrong rather than use the victim's unusual reaction as an occasion to pile on added criticism and punishment . . .
>
> The purpose of a criminal conviction is not simply to pinpoint a convenient wrongdoer upon which to pin responsibility, but to declare a moral truth about the undesired event, namely that it was the wrongdoer's "doing" for which he is accountable.[72]

The question of whether you can be held responsible for causing someone to choose to die, was addressed in *R v Wallace*.[73]

R v Wallace

Wallace was charged with murder and applying corrosive substance with intent, after pouring acid over her ex-boyfriend while he slept. The acid caused life-threatening injuries and permanent disfigurement to the victim. After several months of suffering and limited recovery, the victim's father took him to Belgium where he voluntarily requested medical euthanasia and died because of this treatment. At the trial the offence of murder was withdrawn from the jury, and the prosecution appealed, arguing that the defendant had caused the death. The defence responded that the defendant's actions, or those of the doctors (which would be considered illegal in the UK), broke the chain of causation. The Court of Appeal agreed that the matter of whether the defendant's actions had caused the death should have been put to the jury and a retrial was ordered.

Thinking points:

- In reaching their decision the Court of Appeal said that policy and value judgments had made their assessment of causation particularly complex.[74] Should morals and policy have influenced this decision?

Simester and Sullivan agree that this case was morally charged and submit that this makes it understandable that the court would strive to hold the defendant legally responsible for the victim's death.[75] The Court of Appeal considered the Canadian case of *R v Maybin*,[76] which stated that focus should be maintained on whether the defendant should be held legally responsible or whether holding the accused responsible for the death would be punishing a moral innocent.[77] This suggests that the question of whether someone is the legal cause of death becomes a judgment of whether they are morally blameworthy or innocent. As with the discussion above,[78] regarding *R v Field*,[79] this means a level of uncertainty will be present in decision making. It cannot be determined exactly how morals will influence the outcome of any particular case.

---

72 William Wilson, *Central Issues in Criminal Theory* (Hart Publishing 2002) 177.
73 [2018] EWCA Crim 690.
74 [2018] EWCA Crim 690, [52].
75 AP Simester and GR Sullivan, "Causing Euthanasia" [2019] LQR 21, 25.
76 [2012] 2 SCC 24.
77 *R v Maybin* [2012] 2 SCC 24, [29].
78 See Chapter 3.4.2.
79 [2021] EWCA Crim 380.

- Accepted legal principle from *Kennedy* states that free, deliberate, and informed conduct on the part of the victim or a third party, which supervenes over the defendant's act, will start a new chain of causation.[80] Therefore, can voluntarily choosing euthanasia be considered a new intervening act?

The Court of Appeal distinguished *Wallace* from *Kennedy*, and stated that although the victim's actions were voluntary under the required meaning for euthanasia in Belgium, they were not truly free. This was because the acid attack had made the victim feel that they had no choice but to end their life. The victim was in indescribable pain with no hope for recovery. Therefore, as the victim's actions were not truly voluntary, they did not break the chain of causation.

Moreover, the doctor's actions were not deemed to have started a new chain of events. In *R v Smith*[81] it was established that when the original stab wound was still "operating", despite the subsequent incompetent medical treatment that most likely increased the risk of death, the defendant was still the cause of the death.[82] Furthermore, in *R v Cheshire*,[83] when the defendant's injuries had almost healed, the doctors' actions did not break the chain of causation as the defendant's actions of shooting the victim were held to have contributed significantly to the victim's death.[84] In *Wallace*, despite the time delay between the actions of throwing the acid and the victim's death, the original wounds were still operating and contributed significantly, if not solely, to the defendant's decision to request euthanasia. So, it seems logical that the doctor's actions would not amount to a new intervening act. This, however, raises three observations when applying the established rules of causation.

First, the actions of a third party reasonably exercising a legal duty will not break the chain of causation.[85] Unlike the doctors in *Smith* and *Cheshire* who had a duty to treat their patients, the doctor in *Wallace* was under no legal duty to carry out the euthanasia. Therefore, the doctor's actions could be considered free, deliberate, and informed, and thus under the principle from *Kennedy* could be deemed a new intervening act that broke the chain of causation. The court in *Wallace* held, however, that despite the medical cause of death being from the lethal administered injection the doctor's act did not supervene what the defendant did.Second, in *R v Jordan*,[86] doctors twice unintentionally administering a drug that the victim was allergic to was considered a new intervening act. This was due to the doctor's actions being deemed "palpably wrong".[87] In *Wallace* the lethal drugs were intentionally given. The Court of Appeal acknowledged that giving the victim a lethal injection in this country would have been unlawful, but stated that actions being unlawful were not determinative of a new intervening act.[88]

Third, the victim would have survived, albeit it is unclear for how long, were it not for the lethal injection. As seen above, in the discussion of *Blaue*, there is no requirement that the victim take greater care of themselves by accepting potentially lifesaving treatment. This same principle could be applied in *Wallace* to state that there is no requirement that the victim does not request life-ending treatment. The difference is, however, that *Blaue* was refusing treatment and *Wallace* was requesting it. The cases of *Adams*[89] and *Cox*[90] make it clear that doctors cannot give treatment

---

80 *R v Kennedy* [2007] UKHL 38, [14].
81 [1959] 2 QB 35.
82 *R v Smith* [1959] 2 QB 35, 42–43.
83 [1991] 1 WLR 844.
84 *R v Cheshire* [1991] 1 WLR 844, 852.
85 *R v Pagett* (1983) 76 Cr App R 279, 290.
86 (1956) 40 Cr App R 152.
87 *R v Jordan* (1956) 40 Cr App R 152, 158.
88 [2018] EWCA Crim 690, [77].
89 [1957] Crim LR 365.
90 (1992) 12 BMLR 38.

for the purpose of accelerating an inevitable death, unless the is an alternative justified therapeutic reason for the administration of the medicine. The Court of Appeal, however, in *Wallace* stated that the doctor's actions had to be considered against the law in Belgium, where they had acted lawfully.[91]

- In *Wallace*, at the end of the judgment, the Court of Appeal gave a model direction for juries. This stated: "Are you sure that at the time of the acid attack it was reasonably foreseeable that the *defendant* would commit *suicide* as a result of his injuries?"[92] (emphasis added). Why is the final part of this direction particularly problematic?

This part of the judgment seems to linguistically make two significant errors. Firstly, it refers to the "defendant" committing suicide, rather than the victim. Secondly, it uses the word "suicide" when the matter in question was euthanasia or assisted dying.

Beyond that, this model direction includes a question of foreseeability in the assessment of causation. As discussed above,[93] a victim's actions can break the chain of causation if they are considered unforeseeable, or daft. This has been seen in cases, such as the scenario at the start of the chapter involving Abdul and Brad, when the victim has injured themselves in response to some threat from the defendant.[94] There is no existing authority, however, that the victim's actions have to be reasonably foreseeable in response to a substantive and operative injury that that defendant has already caused.[95] As *Blaue* states, the defendant has to take their victim as they find them. This means that if the victim responds in an unexpected way due to their physical makeup or beliefs, the defendant cannot avoid liability. The requirement that the victim's actions are not daft does not apply when they are in response to an injury that has already been caused by the defendant.

Therefore, considering the final scenario at the beginning of the chapter, you were asked to consider the criminal liability of Penny, who had thrown acid over Quentin. According to the precedent set by *Wallace*, Penny could be convicted for causing Quentin's murder. The model direction from *Wallace*, however, would require a jury foreseeing that the victim would undergo euthanasia in a country where this is illegal. This perhaps explains why, on the retrial of *Wallace*, the jury found her not guilty.

3.6 Conclusion

This chapter has demonstrated how the rules of causation can enable the law to hold to account those who are morally to blame, while still respecting an individual's free will. First, in *Blaue* it was seen that the defendant who stabbed a woman because she would not have sex with him could not escape liability because the victim refused treatment due to her medical beliefs. The victim's choice did not break the chain of causation despite being unforeseeable. Next, it was considered that notwithstanding the policy of wanting to reduce drug offences, *Kennedy* establishes that a defendant will not be held responsible when they have just provided the opportunity of taking drugs. The victim's actions in taking the drugs are viewed as voluntary. This again respects personal autonomy, although perhaps provides insufficient protection for those who are vulnerable through addiction. Finally, *Wallace* examines whether you can cause someone to choose to die through euthanasia. It

91 [2018] EWCA Crim 690, [77].
92 [2018] EWCA Crim 690, [86].
93 See Chapter 3.3.
94 *R v Roberts* (1972) 56 Cr App R 95; *R v Williams* [1992] 1 WLR 380; *R v M* [1999] 11 WLUK 937.
95 *R v Dear* [1996] Crim LR 595.

was held that the victim's decision to choose euthanasia was capable of not being a voluntary act as the decision was not freely made. Thus, the law holds that it is theoretically possible for a person to cause another's unlawful death through their decision to undertake euthanasia. In the circumstances of *Wallace*, it would have been the morally palatable outcome to find that the defendant had caused the victim's death, nonetheless the jury on retrial did not agree.

The significance of causation as a device to limit, or extend, liability to those who are deemed blameworthy should not be underestimated. The pull of moral and policy considerations has been shown to have an extensive impact on how causation is applied in cases. The concept of voluntariness of the victim's actions, is used to determine when the defendant will be blameworthy. It could be argued that the ends justify the means, with the results of cases upholding an ideal of public morality. This, however has led to precedent which find that a drug addict's actions in taking drugs are voluntary, but a person who freely chooses to drink whisky or voluntarily undergoes euthanasia are involuntary. The flexibility afforded by these legal rules to achieve particular outcomes means that the law is left uncertain.

3.7 Further Reading

Elliot C and de Than C, "Prosecuting the Drug Dealer When a Drug User Dies: *R v Kennedy (No 2)*" (2006) 69(6) MLR 986
Reed A, "Causation and Assisting Drug-Abuse Injection" [2005] J Crim L 384
Rogers J, "Death, Drugs and Duties" [2009] Pitts LJ 6
Simester AP and Sullivan GR, "Causing Euthanasia" [2019] LQR 21
Stephen CG, "Causation, Drugs and Culpable Homicide in the High Court" [2009] SLT 27
Sullivan GR and Simester AP, "Deadly Whisky" [2022] LQR 11
Williams G, "Finis for Novus Actus?" (1989) 48(3) CLJ 391

Chapter 4

Omissions and a Good Samaritan Law

Chapter Contents

DOI: 10.4324/9781003408383-5

4.1 Chapter Aims and Objectives

This chapter will continue to study the concept of *actus reus*, by considering the law of omissions. It will examine the cases of *R v Adomako*[1] and *R v Bowditch*[2] to discuss whether the law needs reforming to introduce a Good Samaritan law.

By the end of this chapter, you should be able to:

- Outline the law relating to omissions.
- Define gross negligence manslaughter.
- Identify the key issues in *R v Adomako* and *R v Bowditch*.
- Discuss whether the law should be reformed to enforce a Good Samaritan law, to be more in line with moral values.

The issues examined in this chapter can be illustrated through the following scenarios. Before starting the chapter, consider who, from these situations, is most blameworthy.

- Abe gets into a fight with Ben. Abe intentionally stabs Ben, and Ben dies.
- Cerise sees a child drowning in a paddling pool but intentionally decides to do nothing to help. The child dies.
- Danielle intentionally fails to feed her child, with the result that her child dies.
- Edgar lives next door to Frankie. Edgar is aware that Frankie's child is seriously emaciated but does nothing. The child dies.
- Gertrude is an on-duty lifeguard. She sees a child drowning in the sea but does nothing to help, with the result that the child dies.
- Hermione goes out drinking with her friend Ian. They get very drunk and decide to go for a swim in the sea. Hermione loses sight of Ian. She knows he is not a strong swimmer, but she just leaves him and falls asleep on the beach. Ian gets into difficulties and drowns.

4.2 Omissions

An omission is a failure to act. As discussed in Chapter 2, to establish criminal liability there is normally the requirement of some prohibited conduct, which might have to occur in certain circumstances and result in an unlawful consequence.[3] As Wilson enunciates, wrongdoing that attracts punishment "is the requirement of some prohibited conduct on the part of the accused for which he bears moral responsibility".[4] But, as Wilson goes on to state, this moral responsibility does not necessarily depend on doing something we should not, as someone can be equally morally blameworthy for not doing what they should.[5] In reference to the scenarios at the start of the chapter, this would mean that Abe's action of stabbing Ben is morally as blameworthy as Cerise failing to help the drowning child. Alternatively, Williams argues that there can be a moral

1 [1995] 1 AC 171.
2 (Unreported) 26 January 2017 (Crown Ct (Maidstone)).
3 See Chapter 2.3.4.1.
4 William Wilson, *Central Issues in Criminal Theory* (Hart Publishing 2002) 86.
5 William Wilson, *Central Issues in Criminal Theory* (Hart Publishing 2002) 86.

distinction between an act an omission, as our attitudes to each differ.[6] Arguably we have a different psychological approach to acts than we do to omissions, meaning that individuals find it much harder to decide to actively commit a crime than to fail to do something.[7] This would mean that Cerise is not as blameworthy as Abe.

4.3 Crimes that Can Be Committed through Omission

Not all crimes can be committed by omission.[8] For example, as discussed in Chapter 3, the courts have decided that an omission is insufficient for the crime of unlawful act manslaughter.[9] The fact that not all crimes can be committed by a failure to act caused complexity in *Fagan v Commissioner of the Police of the Metropolis*.[10] The courts interpreted the defendant's failure to remove his car, which he had accidently driven onto a police officer's foot, as a continuing act rather than an omission. This ensured there was coincidence of the *actus reus* and *mens rea*.[11]

The courts have, however, deemed that crimes including murder,[12] gross negligence manslaughter,[13] and arson[14] can be committed through omission. Williams argues that judges should not be deciding which crimes should be capable of completion through an omission, especially in relation to statutory offences when judges are making this decision based on their interpretation of the words of the act. As will be discussed below, some statutes make it clear that failure to act will amount to a crime.[15] Williams argues, however, that there are acts which are not so clear. He gives the example that the courts have held that you can "obstruct" a constable (now called obstructing a police officer) through a failure to act, whereas "obstructing" a highway requires a positive act. Williams argues that this has nothing to do with the linguistic meaning of "obstruct", but instead is a policy decision made to support the police.[16] This means that it will not always be certain as to which crimes can be completed by omission. Moreover, as with *Fagan*, even if it is decided that an omission is insufficient for that particular crime, the facts of the case can be interpreted to mean that the defendant's failure is part of a larger continuing act.

One crime that the courts have deemed can be committed through omission is the common law offence of gross negligence manslaughter, as will be examined below.

4.3.1 Gross Negligence Manslaughter

The definition of gross negligence manslaughter was clarified by the House of Lords in *R v Adomako*.[17]

---

6 Glanville Williams, "Criminal Omissions – The Conventional View" [1991] LQR 86. See also Michael S Moore, *Act and Crime: The Philosophy of Action and its Implications in Criminal Law* (Clarendon Press 1993) 350; and A. Honore, "Are Omissions Less Culpable?" in Peter Cane and Jane Stapleton (eds) *Essays for Patrick Atiyah* (Oxford University Press 1991).

7 Glanville Williams, "Criminal Omissions – The Conventional View" [1991] LQR 86, 88.

8 For example, see *R v Ahmad* (1986) 84 Cr App R 64 where a positive act was required to fulfil the statutory definition of the crime.

9 See Chapter 3.4.1.

10 [1969] 1 QB 439.

11 See Chapter 2.3.4.3 for more discussion on the coincidence of *actus reus* and *mens rea*.

12 *R v Gibbins and Proctor* (1919) 13 Cr App R 134.

13 *R v Pittwood* (1902) 19 TLR 37; *R v Stone and Dobinson* [1977] QB 354; *R v Adomako* [1995] 1 AC 171.

14 *R v Miller* [1983] 2 AC 161.

15 See Chapter 4.4.1.

16 Glanville Williams, "Criminal Omissions – The Conventional View" [1991] LQR 86, 94.

17 [1995] 1 AC 171.

R v Adomako

An anaesthetist failed to notice for over four minutes that a patient undergoing eye surgery was not receiving oxygen, with the result that the patient died. The tube supplying the oxygen had become disconnected during the surgery, which an expert at trial claimed should have been noticed within 15 seconds. Adomako did not deny that he had been negligent, but claimed that this was not to the extent to make him criminally liable. Nonetheless, the jury found him guilty of gross negligence manslaughter. The defendant appealed arguing that the law of involuntary manslaughter lacked certainty, and that the required standard of *mens rea* should be recklessness.

Lord Mackay stated that for a conviction of gross negligence manslaughter:

> [T]he ordinary principles of the law of negligence apply to ascertain whether or not the defendant has been in breach of a duty of care towards the victim who has died. If such breach of duty is established the next question is whether that breach of duty caused the death of the victim. If so, the jury must go on to consider whether that breach of duty should be characterised as gross negligence and therefore as a crime. This will depend on the seriousness of the breach of duty committed by the defendant in all the circumstances in which the defendant was placed when it occurred. The jury will have to consider whether the extent to which the defendant's conduct departed from the proper standard of care incumbent upon him, involving as it must have done a risk of death to the patient, was such that it should be judged criminal.[18]

The House of Lords dismissed the defendant's appeal.

Thinking points:

- To establish gross negligence manslaughter, it must first be established that there is a duty of care. When will a duty of care be owed?

Under the principles of negligence, a person owes a duty of care to their neighbour. These are the people who are "so closely and directly affected by my actions that I ought reasonably to have them in contemplation as being so affected when I am directing my mind to the acts or omissions which are called in question".[19] There is a clear distinction between the aims of tort and criminal law, and a difference in the required standard of proof. Notwithstanding, this civil concept is applied when considering whether the defendant owes a duty of care in criminal law for his acts or omissions. Criminal law, however, takes a more limited approach to the situations in which a person will owe a duty to not fail to act. These are considered further below.[20]

As quoted above, Lord Mackay states that the ordinary principles of negligence apply. From this it can be assumed that all the rules of negligence are relevant. One such rule is the *ex turipi causa non oritur actio*, which means from a dishonourable cause an action does not arise. This reflects the policy aim that a person should not be able to profit from their crime. In *R v Wacker*[21] the defendant tried to

18 *R v Adomako* [1995] 1 AC 171 at 187.

19 *Donoghue v Stevenson* [1932] AC 562, 580.

20 See Chapter 4.4.

21 [2003] QB 1207.

rely on this rule to avoid liability for gross negligence manslaughter. Wacker had been hired to bring 60 Chinese illegal immigrants into the country across the channel in his lorry. To avoid detection, he had closed the only air vent to the refrigerated area where the immigrants were concealed. As a result, when the lorry was stopped at Dover, 58 of the immigrants were found to have suffocated to death. Wacker claimed that he owed the immigrants no duty of care as *ex turipi causa non oritur actio* rule meant that a duty relationship did not exist between the parties involved in a joint criminal enterprise. In dismissing the appeal, and holding that to interpret *Adomako* so this rule did not apply would be incorrect, Lord Justice Kay stated:

> Why is then, therefore, this distinction between the approach of the civil law and the criminal law? The answer is that the very same public policy that causes the civil courts to refuse the claim points in a quite different direction in considering a criminal offence. The criminal law has as its function the protection of citizens and gives effect to the state's duty to try those who have deprived citizens of their rights of life, limb or property. It may very well step in at the precise moment when civil courts withdraw because of this very different function. The withdrawal of a civil remedy has nothing to do with whether as a matter of public policy the criminal law applies. The criminal law should not be disapplied just because the civil law is disapplied. It has its own public policy aim which may require a different approach to the involvement of the law.
>
> Further the criminal law will not hesitate to act to prevent serious injury or death even when the persons subjected to such injury or death may have consented to, or willingly accepted, the risk of actual injury or death. By way of illustration, the criminal law makes the assisting another to commit suicide a criminal offence and denies a defence of consent where significant injury is deliberately caused to another in a sexual context.[22] The state in such circumstances has an overriding duty to act to prevent such consequences.
>
> Thus, looked at as a matter of pure public policy, we can see no justification for concluding that the criminal law should decline to hold a person as criminally responsible for the death of another simply because the two were engaged in some joint unlawful activity at the time or, indeed, because there may have been an element of acceptance of a degree of risk by the victim in order to further the joint unlawful enterprise. Public policy, in our judgment, manifestly points in totally the opposite direction.[23]

Accordingly, the Court of Appeal looked at the policy behind the law when interpreting Lord Mackay's words from *Adomako*, which stated that the normal rules of negligence should be applied. This consideration of policy led the Court of Appeal to conclude, in *Wacker*, that the normal rules of negligence relating to owing a duty of care to other parties in a joint enterprise did not apply in this case. Reed criticises this, stating "ad-hocery now reigns supreme with public policy operating as a judicial divining rod to meet hard cases. Flexibility has prevailed over certainty."[24] The way that Lord Mackay's words in *Adomako* were easily brushed aside, and not applied in *Wacker*, means that Reed's statement is true. One thing is certain though, the civil law policy concern that criminals should not be able to sue their fellow parties to a crime to profit from their criminal enterprise was not applicable in this case. In *Wacker*, there was no question of the Chinese immigrants profiting from the situation, they had paid the ultimate price of losing their lives. Therefore, instead the policy aim in criminal law, of protecting the vulnerable from harm, was

---

22 Brown [1994] 1 AC 212.
23 *R v Wacker* [2003] QB 1207, [33]–[35].
24 Alan Reed, "Ex Turpi and Gross Negligence Manslaughter" [2005] J Crim L 132, 139.

applied.[25] This may not have achieved certainty but did result that could be concluded as morally acceptable in a civilised society.[26]

- According to *Adomako*, the second requirement for a conviction of gross negligence manslaughter is that there must be a breach of the duty of care. How is this assessed?

Whether there has been a breach of duty is judged objectively, meaning that someone who may not appreciate the nature of the duty they have undertaken. or what is required from them in response to this duty, can be found in breach of it.[27]

Moreover, in *Adomako* Lord Mackay referred to the breach creating a risk of death. In subsequent cases the courts have, however, appeared to modify this. In *R v Singh (Gurphal)*[28] the Court of Appeal described the trial judge's direction to the jury that the breach "must be such that a reasonably prudent person would have foreseen a serious and obvious risk not merely of injury, even serious injury, but of death," as a model direction.[29] Thus, it appears that there must be a serious and obvious risk of death.

This requirement has again more recently been examined by the Court of Appeal in *R v Rose*,[30] who determined that this risk must be considered prospectively, rather than retrospectively after the death had already occurred. The defendant, an optometrist, had failed to carry out a statutory check as part of a routine eye test on a 7-year-old boy. This led to the victim's condition of an abnormality of the optical nerve, for which there were at the time no obvious symptoms, going unnoticed. The condition eventually led to the victim's death some five months later. In court it was established that if the tests had been carried out, the condition could have been diagnosed and treated. The defendant successfully appealed against her conviction. The Court of Appeal held that when directing the jury on whether it was reasonably foreseeable that the defendant's breach of duty gave rise to a serious and obvious risk of death, the reasonably prudent professional is to be endowed with the knowledge the defendant had at the time of the breach of duty. This is not the knowledge the defendant would, could, or should have had available, had the breach not occurred.[31] This outcome could be considered somewhat surprising as the defendant was under a duty pursuant to the Opticians Act 1989, section 26(1) to acquire this knowledge from the statutory tests she was required to carry out. Furthermore, it seems to suggest that the more incompetent a person is at acquiring the required knowledge to effectively make decisions about another's care, the more likely they will not be deemed in breach. It can perhaps be explained by reference to the policy ideal of protecting medical professionals from liability, but surely no policy wants to protect those who do not carry out their job in line with statutory minimum requirements.

- According to Adomako, the third requirement for a conviction of gross negligence manslaughter, is that the defendant's actions must be grossly negligent. What does it mean to be "grossly" negligent?

In *R v Bateman*[32] a test for what is grossly negligent was set out:

---

25 See Chapter 1.3.2 for a discussion of policy in criminal law.
26 *R v Wacker* [2003] QB 1207, [30].
27 *R v Stone and Dobinson* [1977] QB 354.
28 [1999] Crim LR 582.
29 *R v Singh (Gurphal)* [1999] Crim LR 582.
30 [2017] EWCA Crim 1168.
31 *R v Rose* [2017] EWCA Crim 1168, [77]–[78].
32 (1925) 19 Cr App R 8.

> In order to establish criminal liability, the facts must be such that, in the opinion of the jury, the negligence of the accused went beyond a mere matter of compensation between subjects and showed such disregard for the life and safety of others as to amount to a crime against the state and conduct deserving punishment.[33]

In *R v Sellu*[34] the Court of Appeal reiterated that the jury should be directed that conduct of the defendant must have been "truly exceptionally bad"[35] and thus regarded as criminal.[36] This definition is not without problems. As noted by the House of Lords, for example, the circularity of someone being deemed a criminal if their actions are criminal.[37] Also, that the defendant's conduct does not need to be so bad as to amount to manslaughter, but just has to amount to a crime. Moreover, this definition incorporates a question of morality by asking the jury not only to make a judgment of the facts but to make a value judgment of whether the conduct was deserving of punishment. Thus, the decision of who will meet this third requirement, and resultingly be convicted of gross negligence manslaughter, is question of morals.

- The final requirement for gross negligence manslaughter is that the defendant's conduct must cause the victim's death. How do you establish that someone's failure to act has caused a particular outcome?

As discussed in Chapter 3, causation is not always easy to establish. If someone has failed to act, then it would be easy to see how they had not altered the current state of affairs. So, in literal terms, could not be said to have caused the death. This raises the question of when an omission can be said to have caused the victim's death. In *R v Bawa-Garba*[38] the Court of Appeal had to consider whether the doctor's negligent treatment of a seriously ill six-year-old boy caused his death. The court refused the defendant's appeal. They held that the judge had correctly directed the jury that they had to ask themselves whether her failure to treat him properly significantly contributed to the boy's death or led to him dying significantly sooner than he would have done otherwise. On the facts the jury found that the doctor's failure to diagnose or treat the septic shock, or consult with a more senior colleague, fulfilled the requirements of causation for a conviction of gross negligence manslaughter. Thus, if the failure has a significant impact on the resulting consequence, it can be said to be the cause.

4.4 Omission Duty Situations

In the above discussion of gross negligence manslaughter, it can be seen that medical professionals have a duty of care to their patients, which can be breached through an act or an omission. Liability for an omission while restrictive is not, however, limited to the situation of a doctor's failure to act to prevent harm to their patient. Unlike many other countries,[39] English law does not impose a general duty to act in situations when it would be easy to prevent harm to another without incurring harm to oneself. Moore argues that this is because generally omissions are not a proper subject of

---

33 *R v Bateman* (1925) 19 Cr App R 8, 11–12.

34 [2017] 4 WLR 64.

35 [2017] 4 WLR 64, [153].

36 See also, *R v Kuddas* [2019] EWCA Crim 837.

37 *R v Adomako* [1995] 1 AC 171, 187.

38 [2016] EWCA Crim 1841.

39 For example, in France there is a duty to render assistance to a person in danger under Articles 223–226 of the French Criminal Code and Article 135 of the Brazilian Penal Code requires that a person provides medical assistance or calls the public authority for help for those in peril.

criminal liability and, therefore, liability should only be imposed in limited duty situations.[40] This is referred to as the conventional view of omissions. Williams supports this conventional view and argues that liability for omissions should only be imposed in exceptional circumstances, and that these circumstances should be clearly stated by Parliament.[41] This conventional view can be attributed to the idea that criminal law should only impose on us the duty to not do certain actions that we are informed of in advance of their implementation.[42] These restrictions are limited in number and ideally are framed so as to have the least impact on personal autonomy. Imposing a general duty to not fail to act, however, would mean that society would no longer have a free choice to decide how to act at any given time. It would mean that if a certain situation arose, a person would be compelled to act in a prescribed way or face criminal punishment. Therefore, to protect the right of self-determination and personal autonomy, the situations when a duty to act can exist should be limited.

Alternatively, it can be argued that English law should be widened to adopt a social responsibility view of omissions. This would place a more general duty on people to help others who are in immediate danger. Ashworth argues that the conventional view is too individualistic to be a basis for morality and criminal liability.[43] He promotes a social responsibility view based on the fact that all human's existence is interdependent, and therefore by helping others we are ensuring autonomy for everyone.[44] Currently, however, there is no criminal liability for failing to act, unless a duty situation imposes a duty to act.

The established duty situations in English law are summarised in the following sections.

4.4.1 Statutory Duty

Acts of Parliament can contain provisions that make a failure to act a crime. Section 170(2) of the Road Traffic Act 1988, for example, sets out the duty that following an accident the driver of a mechanically propelled vehicle must stop and, if required to do so by any person having reasonable grounds for so requiring, give their name and address.

Another example can be seen under section 1 of the Children and Young Person Act 1933, which makes it an offence for a parent or legal guardian to fail to appropriately care for a child under 16. Therefore, in the scenario at the start of the chapter, Danielle could face a criminal conviction for her failure to feed her child.

Furthermore, section 5(1)(d)(ii) of the Domestic Violence, Crimes and Victims Act 2004 states that: A member of the household can be guilty of causing or allowing a child or vulnerable adult to die, or suffer serious physical harm, when they failed to take such steps as they could reasonably have been expected to take to protect the victim from the risk of serious physical harm. In 2006 Rebecca Lewis was one of the first to be charged and convicted of this offence, labelled familial homicide, after allowing her 13-month-old son's death, by leaving him with her partner who she knew to be violent. While this duty situation covers members of the household who have regular contact with the child or vulnerable person, but do not necessarily live in the home, it is unlikely to cover Edgar in the scenario set out at the start of the chapter. This is because although he has knowledge of the child's emancipation, he is a neighbour rather than a member of the household. Therefore, while there is arguably a moral duty to notify the appropriate authorities in this situation, there is no legal requirement.

---

40 Michael S Moore, *Act and Crime: The Philosophy of Action and its Implications in Criminal Law* (Clarendon Press 1993) 350.

41 Glanville Williams, "Criminal Omissions – The Conventional View" [1991] LQR 86.

42 See Chapter 2.3.3 for a discussion of the importance of avoiding retrospective law.

43 Andrew Ashworth, "The Scope of Criminal Liability for Omissions" [1989] LQR 424, 430.

44 Andrew Ashworth, "The Scope of Criminal Liability for Omissions" [1989] LQR 424, 431.

In 2016 the Government considered whether there should be a mandatory reporting duty to report known or suspected child abuse or neglect for those who work with children in England, but in 2018 the Government announced that it had decided against imposing such a duty. The matter was reconsidered again in October 2022, with the final report of the Independent Inquiry into Child Sexual Abuse stating that: Children had suffered as a result of "a marked absence of a cohesive set of laws and procedures in England and in Wales that require individuals working with children to report child sexual abuse".[45] This means, currently while guidance promotes the reporting of child abuse, there is no legal duty to do so. Again, making this a matter of morals rather than law.

4.4.2 Contractual Duty

Except for in statutory duty situations, the courts are left to decide when a duty will be imposed – and thus when a person will be held to be criminally blameworthy. The court, therefore, plays a filtering role in retrospectively deciding what omissions will be considered criminal. Fletcher terms this the "constitutional argument" and questions on what basis the court decides when a duty should be imposed.[46]

One accepted duty situation, is a duty to act in a way that has been agreed through a contract. A case that illustrates this duty situation is *R v Pittwood*.[47] The defendant was employed by a railway company as a crossing gate keeper. He had gone to lunch, forgetting that he had left the crossing gate propped open. During this time a horse and cart were hit by a train on the crossing, and as a result the cart driver died. Pittwood claimed that he had no duty of care to the victim, as his contractual duty was only to his employer. The court held that he did have a duty to act as the railway company had assumed a duty to protect the public whenever they used the road that crossed the railway. Ashworth notes that under the conventional view of omissions, Pittwood would have only owed a contractual duty to his employer, but was held to have a duty to common humanity. This illustrates a social responsibility view of omissions.[48] As such, Pittwood was convicted of gross negligence manslaughter. A similar approach can be seen in *R v Dytham*,[49] when a on-duty police officer was convicted of misconduct for his failure to intervene when he saw a man kicked to death outside a nightclub. The court held the "misconduct impugned was calculated to injure the public interest so as to call for condemnation and punishment".[50] Therefore, despite not being the one responsible for kicking the victim to death, the police officer could be held criminally liable for his failure to protect.

In the scenarios given at the start of the chapter, Gertrude, an on-duty lifeguard, will have a contractual duty of care and thus a duty to act in the situation. Consequently, her seeing a child drowning in the sea and doing nothing to help could lead to a charge of gross negligence manslaughter. Alternatively, Cerise who sees a child drowning in a paddling pool but does nothing to help, under the conventional view of omissions, will not be criminally responsible for the child's death as no contract exists. This raises a question of whether a social responsibility approach, where a duty to common humanity would more generally exist, would be more morally acceptable.[51]

This raises the further question of when a person can be found criminally liable for the breach of a civil law contract. Ashworth states that "undertakings related to welfare and safety

---

45 Alexis Jay, Malcolm Evans, Ivor Frank, and Drusilla Sharpling, "The Report of the Independent Inquiry into Child Sexual Abuse" (2022) HC 720.

46 George P Fletcher, *Rethinking Criminal Law* (Oxford University Press 2000) 628–629.

47 (1902) 19 TLR 37.

48 Andrew Ashworth, "The Scope of Criminal Liability for Omissions" [1989] LQR 424, 445.

49 [1979] QB 722.

50 *R v Dytham* [1979] QB 722, 728.

51 See Chapter 4.5 below.

would be a more appropriate basis for criminal liability".[52] Both of the cases given above show that the defendant's breach of their contractual employment duties led to harm of another. Does this mean, however, that if a person contracts with another to prevent their property from criminal damage and then purposely fails to do this, that they can be liable for the criminal damage or that there is only an action in civil law for breach of contract? The lack of case authority on this point means that the law is unclear as to when criminal liability for breach of a civil contractual duty starts and stops.

4.4.3 Duty Arising from a Relationship

The courts have held that a defendant can owe the victim a duty of care, and thus be under a duty to act in certain situations, through their relationship. As Fletcher notes, the relationship does not need to be a formal legal one, the important issue is whether the relationship is one of interdependence.[53] It has previously been established, for example, that a father can owe a duty to their child,[54] a husband can owe a duty to his wife,[55] and a man to his partner.[56]

In *R v Gibbins and Proctor* the court held that the father's duty of care for his seven-year-old daughter went beyond providing funds to support her, but as he lived in the same house he had a duty to act to prevent the neglect she was suffering at the hands of his partner. Their omission, coupled with the intent to for the daughter to suffer at least serious harm, led to a conviction of murder.[57] Such a duty, of an over 16-year-old not to neglect a child in their care or custody, has since become a statutory duty under the Children and Young Person Act 1933.[58] This demonstrates the view of society that children are vulnerable and should be protected by their parents or guardians.

In *R v Hood* the defendant appealed against his sentence of four years imprisonment for the gross negligence manslaughter of his wife.[59] He was her sole carer and had failed for a number of weeks to seek medical help after she had sustained several broken bones. By the time she was admitted to hospital she was in a debilitative state and died from an infection that her poor care had contributed to. On trial the defendant was convicted of gross negligence manslaughter due to his neglect. On appeal, however, the sentence was reduced to 30 months due to the wife's own reluctance to receive medical help, and that his neglect was not the only cause of her death. In comparison, in *R v Broadhurst*[60] the defendant's application to appeal against his sentence for 3 years and 8 months imprisonment was refused. He had been in a loving relationship with his partner, Natalie Connolly, but when she fell after drinking and taking cocaine, he failed to summon help and instead went to bed. The court held that "he had shown a blatant disregard for Miss Connolly's obvious injuries and for the obvious need to summon medical assistance".[61]

4.4.4 Voluntarily Assuming a Duty

In *R v Evans* the courts have held that a duty can arise when "a voluntary assumption of risk by the defendant has led the victim, or others, to become dependent on him to act".[62] It has long been

---

52 Andrew Ashworth, "The Scope of Criminal Liability for Omissions" [1989] LQR 424, 445.
53 George P Fletcher, *Rethinking Criminal Law* (Oxford University Press 2000) 613.
54 *R v Gibbins and Proctor* (1919) 13 Cr App R 134.
55 *R v Hood* [2003] EWCA Crim 2772.
56 *R v Broadhurst* [2019] EWCA Crim 2026, [10].
57 *R v Gibbins and Proctor* (1919) 13 Cr App R 134.
58 Section 1.
59 [2003] EWCA Crim 2772.
60 *R v Broadhurst* [2019] EWCA Crim 2026.
61 *R v Broadhurst* [2019] EWCA Crim 2026, [28].
62 *R v Evans* [2009] 1 WLR 1999, [36].

established that this is based on moral obligation. As seen in *R v Instan*,[63] when the defendant failed to feed or care for her elderly aunt, with whom she lived, when she became ill. Lord Coleridge stated:

> It would not be correct to say that every moral obligation involves a legal duty; but every legal duty is founded on a moral obligation. A legal common law duty is nothing else than the enforcing by law of that which is a moral obligation without legal enforcement . . . The prisoner was under a moral obligation to the deceased from which arose a legal duty towards her; that legal duty the prisoner has wilfully and deliberately left unperformed, with the consequence that there has been an acceleration of the death of the deceased owing to the non-performance of that legal duty.[64]

Instan's failure to care for her aunt or seek medical assistance led to a conviction for manslaughter. A similar outcome can be seen in *R v Stone and Dobinson*,[65] when the defendants were held to have assumed responsibility for the care of Stone's sister when she came to live with them.

While it seems morally acceptable to hold someone responsible for the risks they have voluntarily undertaken, this does cause an issue when the person accepting the risk is not fully aware of what responsibility they are undertaking. For example, Stone and Dobinson willingly accepted responsibility for the adult sister by allowing her to live with them. They were not, however, equipped to manage her eating disorder nor were they capable of appreciating what level of care was required of them. Nonetheless, as they were charged with gross negligence manslaughter, their breach of duty, from their failure to act, was judged by the standards of what a reasonable person would have done. Similarly, if two friends are voluntarily consuming drink or drugs, one can be found criminally liable should the other overdose and die. Attempts to help an overdosing friend will amount to an assumption of a duty, even when their attempts to help might be hindered by their own intoxication.[66] Resultingly, a person can be criminally liable for undertaking a duty that they are unable to fulfil. The law requires a standard based on what society would find acceptable, not what a certain individual could achieve.

4.4.5 Creating a Dangerous Situation

The final situation in which the courts have determined that a duty to act can arise is when the defendant has created a dangerous situation. This is seen in *R v Miller*[67] when the defendant was convicted of arson. He had inadvertently started a fire but did nothing to address this once he became aware. The issue was that the *actus reus* and *mens rea* did not coincide.[68] When Miller dropped a lit cigarette, the actions which started the fire, he did this without the required intent or recklessness needed for a charge of arson, as he was asleep. When he decided to do nothing about the fire, and thus formed the *mens rea*, the *actus reus* had already occurred. While Miller's actions could have been viewed as a continuing act, as they were by the Court of Appeal, the House of Lords preferred the duty theory as being simpler for jurors and held:

> [T]he accused is guilty of the offence under section 1 (1) of the Criminal Damage Act 1971 if, when he does become aware that the events in question have happened as a result of

63 *R v Instan* [1893] 1 QB 450.
64 *R v Instan* [1893] 1 QB 450, 453–454.
65 [1977] QB 354
66 *R v Ruffell* [2003] EWCA Crim 122.
67 [1983] 2 AC 161.
68 See Chapter 2.3.4.3.

> his own act, he does not try to prevent or reduce the risk of damage by his own efforts or if necessary by sending for help from the fire brigade . . .[69]

This duty situation has been applied beyond preventing damage belonging to another, as seen in *R v Bowler*.[70] The defendant successfully appealed against the length of his sentence for gross negligence manslaughter. The victim died after being wrapped by the defendant in cling film and PVC as part of a consensual sexual act. The defendant had left air holes in the cling film, but not the PVC. Nonetheless, the cause of death was not suffocation. The victim had taken drugs before his death and this alongside the sex and wrapping had increased his body temperature, which resulted in heart failure. The court stated that the defendant's culpability for gross negligence manslaughter was based on him leaving the victim helpless and "in a situation which was obviously dangerous".[71] This dangerous situation was one that the defendant had created despite the victim's consent and encouragement. Regardless, the defendant was liable for the resulting death.

Therefore, it can be seen that there is a wide range of situations in which a person can be under a duty to act. These come from statute, or from the defendant entering into an agreement to act through a contract, relationship, or voluntarily assuming responsibility for another. These duty situations are not without difficulty, for example, as discussed, the scope of a contractual duty might be unclear, or a person may voluntarily undertake a duty they cannot fulfil. Moreover, the duty from creating a dangerous situation increases the scope of liability even further. A person could be liable without prior notification from a statute of the expected standards of behaviour, and without voluntarily agreeing to the duty. Nonetheless, there is still no general duty to act unless one of these duty situations is established. There is no "Good Samaritan" law, which would place a duty on people to act to help others in easy rescue situations.

4.5 A Good Samaritan Law?

In 2015 Parliament introduced the Social Action, Responsibility and Heroism Act. Section 4 provides that if a person acts heroically to intervene in an emergency to assist an individual in danger, then the court must have regard to this when assessing any alleged negligence or breach of statutory duty. This does not require that an individual acts but gives some protection from a civil claim if they do. English criminal law does not require a person to act unless they fall within one of the recognised duty situations above. So why, in situations such as that of Cerise at the start of the chapter – allowing a child to drown in a paddling pool – does the law not require a person to act, when arguably our morals require that we do? Ashworth argues that a general duty should be imposed when: "(a) there is a threat of harm to another citizen who is in sudden peril, and has not voluntarily entered that condition, and (b) a citizen is in a position to prevent the harm or its continuance or to take steps towards the enforcement of the law (as by summoning the police or the emergency services)".[72] This raises the question of whether it is the law's function to promote higher moralistic standards, or to just prevent wrongdoing.[73] Ashworth's proposals would create a "Good Samaritan" law. Williams disagrees, and argues that the proper function of the law is just to prevent wrongdoing. He justifies this by stating that prisons are full of people committing acts, and it would

69 *R v Miller* [1983] 2 AC 161, 179.

70 [2015] EWCA Crim 849.

71 *R v Bowler* [2015] EWCA Crim 849, [20].

72 Andrew Ashworth, "The Scope of Criminal Liability for Omissions" [1989] LQR 424, 453.

73 See further discussion in Chapter 1.3.1.

exceed the bounds of possibility to criminalise people for not promoting higher standards.[74] Thus, according to this conventional view of omissions, in the scenario at the start of the chapter where Hermione goes out drinking and drunkenly swimming with her friend Ian in the sea, she would not be criminally liable. Hermione does not fall under any of the recognised duty situations as she does not have a statutory duty, is not under a contract, does not necessarily have the required relationship nor assumed responsibility, and has not created the dangerous situation. Therefore, under English law she is not responsible for Ian's death. Or is she?

R v Bowditch

In *R v Bowditch* the defendant was charged with murder, but pled guilty to a charge of gross negligence manslaughter. Bowditch had met Becky Morgan at a party. They went to the Port of Ramsgate and were messing around at the harbour. Somehow Becky Morgan ended up in the water. Instead of providing the help she asked for, Bowditch left to go clubbing. Hours later he called the police saying that he had seen someone drown. Sentencing Bowditch to five and a half years in prison, Judge Jeremy Carey said: "You did not try in any way to help a drowning girl – not by throwing her a life buoy, not by going to her aid as some would have done, not by calling for help, not by contacting the rescue or emergency services. In other words, you left her to drown."[75]

Thinking points:

- Bowditch failed to summon help for Becky Morgan after she fell in the water. The conventional view of omissions means that he would only have a duty to act if he fell into one of the recognised duty situations. Which duty situation did he fall under?

Bowditch did not know Becky Morgan before the night of her death; he had only just met her, so there was no relationship duty between them. There was also no statutory or contractual duty for him to act, and there was no evidence that he had created the dangerous situation by pushing her into the water. This case can be contrasted to *R v Ruffell*[76] where the defendant created a dangerous situation by leaving the victim, his friend who he knew to be overdosing from drugs, outside in the cold. While *Adomako* confirms that for gross negligence manslaughter the normal rules of negligence apply, so that we have a duty of care to our neighbours to prevent our actions from causing foreseeable harm, this does not necessarily mean that there is a duty to act. Unlike the cases of *Instan* or *Stone and Dobinson*, Bowditch was not living in the same household as the victim and arguably had not voluntarily accepted a duty to look after her. Without clearly establishing a duty to act this case appears to go against the conventional view of omissions.

- If it is accepted that Bowditch did not fall under the established duty situations, then how can his conviction for Gross Negligence be explained?

74 Glanville Williams, "Criminal Omissions – The Conventional View" [1991] LQR 86, 87–89.

75 R v Bowditch (Michael) unreported, 26 January 2017 (Crown Ct (Maidstone)).

76 *R v Ruffell* [2003] EWCA Crim 122.

Crosby argues that this case shows the emergence of a "Good Samaritan" law and goes on to state: "In recent years, it appears that the courts have been combining moral duties with existing categories of recognised legal duties to impose criminal responsibility in an uncertain and haphazard way in omissions cases to meet the moral exigency of the moment in the effort to do justice".[77] This suggests a move away from the conventional view of omissions towards one of social responsibility. As such, the courts can keep extending liability for omissions in a drive to uphold moral values and achieve justice, with the result of undermining the principle that criminal law should be certain and not have retrospective effect.[78]

- Can Bowditch be said to have caused the victim's death as required for a conviction of gross negligence manslaughter?

If it can be established that Bowditch had a duty of care, which he breached in a grossly negligent way so as to create a serious and obvious risk of death, it would still need to be established that his omission caused the victim's death in fact and law. As discussed above, it can be difficult, if not impossible, to determine when a failure to act has caused an outcome.[79] In *R v Bowditch* if it is asked "but for" the defendant's actions would the victim still have died, the answer could well be "yes", as his physical actions made no difference to her falling from the harbour wall into the sea. In *R v Bawa-Garba*[80] the Court of Appeal considered that the doctor could be the cause of the patient's death if her failure to treat him properly significantly contributed to his death. Even if Bowditch had called for help straight away the result may have stayed the same, so it is questionable to say that he significantly contributed. Furthermore, the appeal in *R v Broughton*[81] was allowed, as it was held that to prove the defendant's negligence had caused the death, the prosecution would have to exclude realistic or plausible possibilities that the victim would have died anyway even if medical help had arrived promptly. In *Broughton* this could not be shown even though expert medical evidence provided that the victim would have had a 90% chance of survival if the defendant had not been negligent when he summoned medical help. This suggests that when applying the rules of causation, Bowditch would not be considered the cause of Becky Morgan's death. She had fallen into the cold sea at night. There was a chance that even if Bowditch had immediately summoned medical help, it would not have arrived in time to save her. Crosby, therefore, argues that Bowditch being guilty of gross negligence manslaughter goes against the established rules of causation.[82] The distinction between the cases appears to be that in *Broughton* he negligently summoned help, for example by struggling to give the correct location of where he and the victim were to others trying to send medical help, whereas in *Bowditch* the defendant failed completely to summon medical help at the time. This distinction appears to be a fine one, that enabled punishment to be imposed on Bowditch for his failure, without establishing the "but for" test in causation in the normal way.

The numerous situations in which a duty to act can exist, and the ability of the courts to construct when a duty will be owed in-line with moral values, seems to suggest a move towards a "Good Samaritan" law. There are, however, many arguments why the law should not impose a general duty to act. Dressler sums these up as follows: (i) the cost of investigating and prosecuting bystanders might be prohibitive; (ii) a statute imposing a general duty to act would have to be drafted narrowly to avoid injustice and as a result prosecutions would be rare; (iii) the person trying to help might cause harm to the person they are trying to help, others, or themselves; (iv) laws

---

77 Cath Crosby, "Gross Negligence Manslaughter by Omission: The Emergence of a Good Samaritan Law" [2018] J Crim L 127, 130.
78 See Chapter 2.3.3.
79 See Chapter 4.3.1.
80 [2016] EWCA Crim 1841.
81 *R v Broughton* [2020] EWCA Crim 1093.
82 Cath Crosby, "Gross Negligence Manslaughter by Omission: The Emergence of a Good Samaritan Law" [2018] J Crim L 127, 136.

requiring a person to act do not require the person to prevent the harm from being caused, and so a minimal effort to assist that has no practical effect could fulfil the duty requirement and; (v) positive duties to act restrict human liberty to a greater degree than laws that prohibit certain actions.[83] Incremental development of duty situations by the courts does not allow this issues to be considered and debated in Parliament in overarching manner. Therefore, while it might seem morally desirable that Cerise should have a duty to stop a child from drowning in a paddling pool, currently she is under no duty to do so. If the law was to change to introduce a "Good Samaritan" law, which would place her under a duty, careful consideration would need to be taken of how the law is formulated to avoid the pitfalls that Dressler identifies.

4.6 Conclusion

Gross negligence manslaughter occurs when the defendant has a duty of care, breaches that duty to create a serious and obvious risk of death, causes death, and is grossly negligent. This crime has been defined by common law, which enables continual development of the definition. The requirement of "gross" negligence also enables jurors to apply their own moral judgment in determining who shall be held blameworthy. While the criteria for gross negligence manslaughter can be fulfilled through the defendant's actions, it is one of many crimes that can be committed by omission. This means that the defendant can be held criminally responsible for their failure to act.

According to the conventional view of omissions, liability will only be imposed in clearly defined duty situations. This protects an individual's right to determine their own behaviour and exercise autonomy over their actions. Statute defines numerous duty situations. These are supplemented by the common law, which imposes a duty through a contract, a relationship, voluntary assumption, and creating a dangerous situation. Again, enabling the courts to develop the situations of when liability can be imposed. Morals and policy have helped to shape when there will be a duty to act with the aim of achieving justice in individual cases. The result is that there is a lack of certainty as to when a duty will be imposed. The continued expansion by the courts of when a duty will be owed suggests a move towards a social responsibility view of omissions, and the introduction of a "Good Samaritan" law, without thorough consideration of the matter by Parliament.

4.7 Further Reading

Ashworth A, "The Scope of Criminal Liability for Omissions" [1989] LQR 424.
Ashworth A, "Manslaughter by Omission and the Rule of Law" [2015] LQR 563.
Crosby C, "Gross Negligence Manslaughter by Omission: The Emergence of a Good Samaritan Law" [2018] J Crim L 127.
Dressler J, "Some Brief Thoughts (Mostly Negative) about 'Bad Samaritan' Laws" (2000) 40 Santa Clara Law Review 971.
Honore A, "Are Omissions Less Culpable?" in P Cane and J Stapleton (eds) *Essays for Patrick Atiyah* (Oxford University Press 1991).
Williams G, "Criminal Omissions – The Conventional View" [1991] LQR 86.

83 Joshua Dressler, "Some Brief Thoughts (Mostly Negative) about 'Bad Samaritan' Laws" (2000) 40 Santa Clara L Rev 971, 981–989.

Chapter 5

Murder, *Mens Rea*, and Blameworthiness

Chapter Contents

DOI: 10.4324/9781003408383-6

5.1 Chapter Aims and Objectives

This chapter will examine the concept of *mens rea* as a tool to determine the defendant's level of blameworthiness and correct label. To do this it will provide an overview of the principles of intention, recklessness and negligence, and a discussion of the difference between intention and motive. It will consider the offence of murder and the case of *R v Woollin*.[1]

By the end of this chapter, you should be able to:

- Define murder.
- Outline the concepts of intention, recklessness and negligence.
- Discuss the relevance of motive in apportioning blame.
- Identify and discuss the key issues raised by *R v Woollin*.

> The issues that will be examined in this chapter can be illustrated through the following scenarios. Before starting the chapter, consider who in these situations, is most blameworthy.
>
> - Lucy accidentally trips and falls into Lillie, causing Lillie to fall over and hit her head. As a result of the fall, Lillie dies.
> - Caitlin, a doctor, wants to end her terminally ill patient's suffering. So, she gives the patient a lethal dose of pain medication and the patient dies.
> - Alfie pushes into Matilda while in a rush to catch a bus. This causes Matilda to fall over and hit her head on the pavement. As a result of the fall, she dies.
> - Beth pushes Chris hard while they are arguing at the top of a flight of stairs. Due to the push, Chris falls down the stairs and consequently dies.
> - Morgan wants to kill Ellie. He fires his gun at her, but misses and kills Tia, who is stood next to Ellie.
> - Ayo wants to seek revenge on Henry. He finds Henry and attacks him, intending to seriously hurt him. Henry dies because of his serious injuries.
> - Eva wants to seek revenge on Millie. She finds Millie and attacks her, intending to kill her. Millie dies because of the attack.
> - Debbie wants to kill Jess. She acquires a gun but has no idea how to use it. She points the gun towards Jess, who is quite some distance away, and pulls the trigger thinking it is very unlikely to fire, and that it is even more unlikely that she will hit and kill Jess. Unexpectedly, the bullet does hit Jess and she dies as a result.

5.2 *Mens Rea*

As discussed in Chapter 2, before a person can be found guilty of a crime, it is generally required that the prosecution prove beyond reasonable doubt that they have committed the *actus* reus with the required *mens rea* for the crime with which they are charged.[2] Therefore, *mens rea* acts as a vehicle to ensure that punishment is only given to those who are deserving of it; those who are at fault. It ensures that those, such as Lucy in the scenario at the beginning of the chapter, are not punished

---

1 [1999] 1 AC 82.

2 See Chapter 2.3.4.1 for more discussion on the requirement of *actus reus* and *mens rea*.

for accidentally fulfilling the *actus reus* of a crime. As a result, this implements the principle that there should be no punishment without just cause.[3]

Sayre examines how historically *mens rea* was synonymous with moral blameworthiness, rather than *mens rea* indicating a specified state of mind.[4] Now, different levels of *mens rea* are used to represent different levels of blameworthiness. This can lead to the defendant being tried for different levels of offence. For example, when a person under a duty of care kills due to their gross negligence, the correct charge would be manslaughter, but when a person intentionally causes the death of another the correct charge would be murder. Therefore, the blameworthiness of the defendant is assessed through their mental state when committing the crime, and as a result they are given the appropriate corresponding label.[5] Also, a person who intentionally commits a crime is arguably more in need of deterrence than someone who has acted negligently. The person who intentionally kills is, therefore, more deserving of the harsher punishment that is associated with the more serious offence of murder.

5.3 The Relevance of Motive

A person's motives for acting may make them seem more or less blameworthy. For example, a person who steals to feed their starving children may seem morally less blameworthy than someone who steals for the entertainment of it. Equally, a doctor who kills out of mercy may seem less morally blameworthy than someone who kills out of contempt for the victim. The problem is that legal principle requires certainty rather than a moral judgment on a case-by-case basis. Therefore, blameworthiness is judged on the existence of *mens rea* rather than the examination of the morality of the defendant's motive.

This means there is no distinction between those who act for good or bad reasons. The assessment of whether the defendant has the required *mens rea* for a particular crime is value neutral, and so can arguably lead to individual injustice. This is because when someone has acted intentionally it does not automatically mean that they are morally more blameworthy than someone who has acted recklessly or negligently. For example, a doctor who kills their patient out of mercy, such as Caitlin in the scenarios at the start of the chapter, may be deemed less morally blameworthy than a parent who negligently starves their child to death. Nonetheless, the former will attract a charge of murder whereas the latter will be gross negligence manslaughter. There is no assessment of the defendant's character or motives in assessing liability. This, however, produces clearer lines of what we can and cannot do. Moreover, the harshness that may occur from such an approach is softened by the fact that motive may still be relevant in assessing whether the defendant can claim a defence, or in the mitigation of punishment.

This suggests that using the principle of *mens rea*, rather than examining the moral blameworthiness of each defendant, creates certainty in the law. However, the way judges interpret the requirements of *mens rea* may not adhere to such strict legal principle, and instead it could be argued that morals and policy have a role in defining the law. For example, in *R v Cox*[6] a doctor was convicted of attempted murder after administering a dose of medication to his patient intending to kill him to relieve him of his pain, whereas in *R v Adams*[7] Devlin held that if administering the medication was for pain relief, even though it was enough to advance death, then the intent was lawful.

3 See Chapter 2.3.7 for further discussion of the principle of no punishment without just cause.
4 F Sayre, "The Present Signification of *Mens Rea* in Criminal Law" (1934) Harvard Legal Essays 399.
5 See Chapter 2.3.2 for a discussion of fair labelling.
6 (1992) 12 BMLR 38.
7 [1957] Crim LR 365.

Thus, it appears that cannot be certain how motive and intention will be interpreted to determine whether there is criminal liability.

A similar approach was taken in *R v Steane*.[8] In this case the British defendant was acquitted of doing an act likely to assist the enemy with intent to assist the enemy contrary to Regulation 2A of the Defence (General Regulations) 1939, after he had entered the service of the German broadcasting system in 1940. The defendant had acted under threats of harm to himself and his family. In allowing the appeal the court acknowledged that there was a difference between intent and motive,[9] however, it held that the defendant's reasons for acting had to be considered when establishing if he had the necessary intent.[10] As such, Wilson comments that this case illustrates "allowing a formal concept (intention) to do a moral job of work".[11] The result is that such an approach, while achieving a morally desired outcome in this case, undermines certainty within the law.

5.4 Intention

Intention is the most blameworthy type of *mens rea* and therefore associated with the most serious types of crimes, such as murder. Intention can take different forms, which includes direct intent, indirect (or oblique) intent, transferred intent (otherwise known as transferred malice), and conditional intent.

5.4.1 Direct Intention

Direct intention was defined in *R v Mohan*[12] as "a decision to bring about, in so far as it lies within the accused's power, the commission of the offence which it is alleged the accused attempted to commit, no matter whether the accused desired that consequence of his act or not".[13] In the case of Caitlin, from the scenario at the start of the chapter, she acted to bring to fruition her desire to kill the patient. Regardless of her motives, it can be said that she has direct intention to kill.

5.4.2 Indirect Intention

Indirect intention, otherwise known as oblique intention, occurs when the defendant decides to act to bring about one consequence but as a result of this another foreseeable outcome occurs. For example, a footballer who lines up just outside the penalty box to take a free kick in front of a five-man wall, may have the direct intent to score a goal, but it is foreseeable that the ball could hit an opposing player instead. He does not want this, but by kicking the football at them it is a foreseeable consequence.

There are two contrasting views of whether indirect intent can be said to amount to intention. The *identity view*, as advanced by Williams, states that a defendant who foresees that an action will cause a result can by definition be said to intend such a result.[14] He argues that: "There is no morally relevant distinction between acting with the purpose of causing a particular result and acting with the foresight that one is virtually certain to cause that result."[15] Both intention and virtually certain

8 [1947] KB 997.
9 *R v Steane* [1947] KB 997, 1004.
10 *R v Steane* [1947] KB 997, 1005.
11 William Wilson, *Central Issues in Criminal Theory* (Hart Publishing 2002) 152.
12 [1975] QB 1.
13 *R v Mohan* [1975] QB 1, 11.
14 Glanville Williams, "Oblique Intention" [1987] CLJ 417.
15 Glanville Williams, "Oblique Intention" [1987] CLJ 417, 423.

foresight of a consequence will amount to intention. Thus, this is a matter of law that does not need to be decided by the jury.

In contrast, the *inference view*, as promoted by Finnis maintains that intention is distinct from foresight. As such, foresight is only factual evidence of intention from which a jury may infer a defendant's intention.[16] Kaveny, goes even further to argue no degree of foresight should be equated with intention.[17] The inference view, has however, been identified by the Court of Appeal as the correct approach to use.[18] Nonetheless, the area that has caused much judicial consideration is the level of foresight that is required before the jury can infer intention. In a succession of cases the courts have tried to resolve the relationship between foresight and intention.

In *DPP v Smith*[19] the House of Lords held that the correct approach was not to ask what the defendant foresaw as a natural and probable outcome of his actions, but instead what an ordinary person would have contemplated to be the natural and probable result in those circumstances.[20] This was problematic as it did not require the defendant themselves to appreciate the outcome of their actions, and so a person could be liable for a crime that they did not mean or foresee. This objective approach was then changed by section 8 of the Criminal Justice Act 1967, which states:

> Proof of criminal intent.
>
> A court or jury, in determining whether a person has committed an offence, –
>
> (a) shall not be bound in law to infer that he intended or foresaw a result of his actions by reason only of its being a natural and probable consequence of those actions; but
> (b) shall decide whether he did intend or foresee that result by reference to all the evidence, drawing such inferences from the evidence as appear proper in the circumstances.

Thus, demonstrating that a subjective approach was to be taken in asking what the defendant intended or foresaw, but still providing little guidance on how probable the outcome needed to be before it could be inferred by the jury that the defendant intended it.

The matter was considered in *DPP v Hyam*[21] when the House of Lords confirmed that even when the defendant's desire was not to bring about the result, she could justifiably be said to intend it if it was "highly probable".[22] The matter was then confused in *R v Moloney*[23] when the House of Lords stated that the jury had to be directed as to whether the outcome was a natural consequence of the defendant's voluntary act, and whether he foresaw it as such.[24] While this maintained the subjective standard as required by the Criminal Justice Act 1967, no reference was made to probability. Fortunately, the House of Lords were presented with a chance to correct their mistake shortly afterwards in *R v Hancock and Shankland*,[25] when the *Moloney* guidelines were deemed "unsafe and misleading".[26] The court held that juries needed to be directed that, "the greater the probability of a consequence the more likely it is that the consequence was foreseen and that if that

16 John Finnis, "Intention and Side Effects" in RG Frey and Christopher W Morris (eds) *Liability and Responsibility: Essays in Law and Morals* (Cambridge University Press 1991).
17 M Cathleen Kaveny, "Inferring Intention from Foresight" [2004] LQR 81.
18 *R v Moloney* [1985] AC 905; *R v Matthews and Alleyne* [2003] EWCA Crim 192.
19 [1961] AC 290.
20 *DPP v Smith* [1961] AC 290, 327.
21 [1975] AC 55.
22 *R v Hyam* [1975] AC 55, 82.
23 [1985] AC 905.
24 *R v Moloney* [1985] AC 905, 929.
25 [1986] AC 455.
26 *R v Hancock and Shankland* [1986] AC 455, 473.

consequence was foreseen the greater the probability is that that consequence was also intended".[27] Notwithstanding that the *Moloney* guidelines had been deemed unsafe, the judgment had set out that an Inference View should be taken and that a subjective approach was right.[28] *Hancock and Shankland* confirmed this as remaining a correct statement of the law.[29]

The trial of *R v Nedrick*[30] was heard before the publication of the judgments in *R v Moloney* and *R v Hancock and Shankland*. The change in the law that these cases effected meant that the jury direction as to intention given by the trial judge in *Nedrick* was "plainly wrong",[31] and Nedrick's appeal was allowed. Lord Lane stated that:

> Where the charge is murder and in the rare cases where the simple direction is not enough, the Jury should be directed that they are not entitled to infer the necessary intention, unless they feel sure that death or serious bodily harm was a virtual certainty (barring some unforeseen intervention) as a result of the defendant's actions and that the defendant appreciated that such was the case.[32]

This gave rise to the "virtual certainty" test for indirect intention, which is discussed below in Chapter 5.7 in the examination of *R v Woollin*.[33] Applying the virtual certainty test to the scenarios at the start of the chapter it is unlikely that Alfie will be convicted of the murder of Matilda. The prosecution would need to prove that he foresaw her death or serious bodily harm as virtually certain when he was just rushing to get a bus. In contrast, Beth pushes Chris hard at the top of a staircase. In this situation the jury might find it easier to infer that Beth intended death or serious injury if the prosecution make them sure that Beth foresaw the fall down the stairs, and resulting injury, as a virtual certainty. Moreover, it could even be established that Beth had direct intention to cause serious harm from the hard push regardless of the fall, which would satisfy the *mens rea* for murder.

5.4.3 Transferred Malice

Transferred malice occurs when the defendant intends to commit a crime, but then fulfils the crime against an alternative victim to the one meant. This is demonstrated in *R v Latimer*,[34] and more recently in *R v Gnango*.[35] Furthermore, the rules of accessorial liability[36] mean that a person can be convicted of a crime, such as murder, when not only has an unintended victim died but when it was not the defendant who fired the fatal shot.[37] Malice cannot, however, generally be transferred from one crime to fulfil the intent of another crime[38] (unless crime allows the *mens rea* to be constructed).[39] This holds with legal principle that states that there should be a correspondence of *actus reus* and *mens rea* for the crime charged.[40] In the scenarios at the start of the chapter, Morgan wants to kill Ellie but instead kills Tia. The intention that Morgan forms to kill Ellie can be transferred to Tia to fulfil the required *mens rea* for murder.

---

27 *R v Hancock and Shankland* [1986] AC 455, 473.
28 *R v Moloney* [1985] AC 905, 917.
29 *R v Hancock and Shankland* [1986] AC 455, 473
30 [1986] 1 WLR 1025.
31 *R v Nedrick* [1986] 1 WLR 1025, 1027.
32 *R v Nedrick* [1986] 1 WLR 1025, 1028.
33 [1999] 1 AC 82.
34 (1886) 17 QBD 359.
35 [2012] 1 AC 827.
36 See Chapter 11 for more discussion of accessorial liability.
37 For example, see *R v Morgan* [2021] EWCA Crim 895 and *R v Seed* [2024] EWCA Crim 650.
38 *R v Pembliton* (1874) 2 CCR 119.
39 For example, see the discussion of Unlawful Act Manslaughter at Chapter 3.4.1.
40 See Chapter 2.3.4.2.

5.4.4 Conditional Intention

Conditional intention refers to the situation when a defendant only intends something if certain conditions are met. This can be seen, for example, in the context of property offences, when the defendant only intends to steal something if they find something worth stealing. In *R v Walkington*[41] the Court of Appeal held that conditional intention was sufficient for a charge of burglary under section 9 of the Theft Act 1968, as to interpret the law otherwise would make a nonsense of the Act.[42] The Act only required that the defendant enter the property or part of the property as a trespasser with the intention to steal. Walkington's actions of going behind the till area in a department store with the intention of taking money from an open till drawer, if money was present, fulfilled the requirements of burglary. Conditional intention will not, however, always be sufficient for a crime. This will depend on the requirements of the crime charged. For example, the offence of theft requires that the defendant has an intention to permanently deprive.[43] In *R v Easom*[44] it was held that an intention to take valuables if any were found in a bag, was not an intention to permanently deprive. The defendant had replaced the bag back where he found it, when it was found to contain nothing of value. This means, while a conditional intention to steal under section 9 of the Theft Act 1968 is sufficient for burglary, conditional intention does not amount to an intention to permanently deprive under section 6 of the Theft Act 1968.[45] Thus, such distinctions means that it can be difficult to determine when conditional intention will be enough for the crime charged.

5.5 Recklessness

When a person is said to have acted recklessly this denotes that they still hold some form of blame, but that they are not as culpable as a person who intended an outcome. If it is accepted that Alfie, in the scenario at the start of the chapter, does not intend to kill Matilda, then he cannot be guilty of murder. This does not mean, however, that like Lucy he should be absolved of all responsibility. Arguably, Alfie has acted recklessly by pushing Matilda, and this has led to her death. Thus, potentially making him responsible for manslaughter. This is why it is important to establish what level of foresight is required before indirect intention can be inferred. Anything less than the outcome being foreseen as a virtual certainty will lead to manslaughter and a discretionary life sentence and anything more could mean murder and mandatory life.

While recklessness will be examined in the context of different offences throughout this book, here, due to the important distinction between murder and manslaughter identified above, the issues in determining what recklessness means will be considered. Similarly, to intention, the courts have struggled with assessing the culpable level of foresight required for determining when a person is reckless. In *R v Cunningham*[46] the Court of Appeal determined that the word malicious, in a charge contrary to section 23 of the Offences against the Person Act 1861, meant either an intention of the defendant to do that particular kind of harm, or that he foresaw the possibility of that particular type of harm and carried on recklessly with the actions regardless.[47] Thus, demonstrating a subjective approach to determine the defendant's foresight.[48] This approach meant the blameworthiness,

---

41 [1979] 1 WLR 1169.
42 *R v Walkington* [1979] 1 WLR 1169, 1178–1179.
43 Theft Act 1968, section 6.
44 [1971] 2 QB 315.
45 See Chapter 6.3 for the definitions, and discussion, of theft and burglary.
46 [1957] 2 QB 396.
47 *R v Cunningham* [1957] 2 QB 396, 399.
48 *R v Stephenson* [1979] QB 695.

or moral culpability, of the defendant could be assessed. If the defendant was incapable of appreciating the risk that they were taking, then the law would not hold them to account.

This subjective approach, however, ignored the situation when the defendant through their own failures, did not foresee a risk that they could have done and should have done. Applying the *Cunningham* definition of recklessness, a jury would have no choice but to find a defendant not guilty in such a situation. This problem was highlighted in *R v Parker*.[49] To address this the Court of Appeal stretched the *Cunningham* meaning of recklessness to include the situation when the defendant deliberately acted, knowing of all the circumstances, but closed his mind to the obvious resulting risk of damage.[50]

The leniency of the subjective approach was considered again in *R v Caldwell*.[51] The House of Lords held that recklessness under the Criminal Damage Act 1971 encompassed failure to give any thought to the risk where, if thought had been given to the risk, it would have been obvious.[52] This took an objective approach which judged the defendant's culpability on what they should have foreseen, not considering what they were capable of foreseeing.[53] This allowed a defendant to fulfil the *mens rea* of a crime by inadvertently taking an unjustified risk, which appears to move the definition of recklessness more towards the remit of negligence.[54] Lord Diplock justified this approach by stating that a person who took an inadvertent risk was as blameworthy as someone who took an advertent risk.[55] The *Caldwell* definition also created the potential problem of what was known as the "Caldwell Lacuna". This occurred when the defendant does give thought to the risk but decides one does not exist so goes ahead anyway. Under the definition given in *Caldwell* the defendant would not be reckless even if the risk was obvious to an ordinary person. Such reasoning was not, however, accepted in *Chief Constable of Avon and Somerset v Shimmen*,[56] when the court held even a minimal appreciation of the risk could render the defendant reckless.

The matter was again considered by the House of Lords in *R v G and R*.[57] Similarly to *Caldwell*, the case involved a charge contrary to the Criminal Damage Act 1971. It involved two boys aged 11 and 12, who had been charged with arson. They claimed that they had set fire to a newspaper without the appreciation that the fire could spread and cause damage to nearby buildings. The defendants argued that there was a clear moral distinction between advertence and inadvertence and as they had acted inadvertently, they should not be to blame as this meant they did not have the required *mens rea*.[58] Lord Bingham, basing his reasoning on morals and policy, held that:

> It is neither moral nor just to convict a defendant (least of all a child) on the strength of what someone else would have apprehended if the defendant himself had no such apprehension . . . I cannot accept that restoration of the law as understood before *R v Caldwell* [1982] AC 341 would lead to the acquittal of those whom public policy would require to be convicted.[59]

49 [1977] 1 WLR 600.
50 *R v Parker* [1977] 1 WLR 600, 604.
51 [1982] AC 341.
52 *R v Caldwell* [1982] AC 341, 353.
53 *Elliot v C* [1983] 1 WLR 939.
54 Glanville Williams, "Offences and Defences" (1982) 2 LS 233, 241.
55 *R v Caldwell* [1982] AC 341, 352.
56 (1976) 84 Cr App R 7.
57 [2004] 1 AC 1034.
58 *R v G and R* [2004] 1 AC 1034, 1038.
59 *R v G and R* [2004] 1 AC 1034, 1057.

Thus, *R v G and R* heralded a return to a subjective assessment of foresight, determining that a person will not be reckless if, due to his age or personal characteristics, he genuinely did not foresee a risk. Although, the precise risk does not necessarily need to be foreseen.[60] This achieves justice for the individual who is not punished for a risk they were incapable of foreseeing. Moreover, Lord Bingham asserts that such an approach does not offend public policy. Despite this claim, this case was decided in the context of two young boys who were perhaps undeserving of punishment. There is a significant difference between those who are incapable of appreciating an obvious risk and those who are capable but choose not to consider it. In the latter case, it is questionable whether public policy or society's morality would deem it appropriate to acquit the defendant. While the person may not be as blameworthy as someone who advertently takes the risk, this does not necessarily mean they are blameless for failure to consider a risk that they could and should have considered. *R v G and R* addresses this by stating:

> In a contested case based on intention, the defendant rarely admits intending the injurious result in question, but the tribunal of fact will readily infer such an intention, in a proper case, from all the circumstances and probabilities and evidence of what the defendant did and said at the time. Similarly with recklessness: it is not to be supposed that the tribunal of fact will accept a defendant's assertion that he never thought of a certain risk when all the circumstances and probabilities and evidence of what he did and said at the time show that he did or must have done.[61]

This means that, as with intention, it will be left the magistrates or jury to determine on the facts of the case whether they believe that the defendant honestly did not foresee the risk in the circumstances.

5.6 Negligence

A less blameworthy state of mind than intention and recklessness, is negligence. Negligence is a concept normally associated with civil law where the aim is compensation, rather than the criminal aim of retribution. This has led revered academics to suggest that it is improper for criminal law to use negligence.[62] When a person has been negligent it denotes that they have been careless when they should not have been. Thus, because their actions have fallen below the standard that can reasonably be expected in the circumstances, they are at fault. This is an objective assessment, comparing the person's actions to what could be expected of an ordinary person. As such, being negligent is not to say that the defendant intended the outcome or even that they foresaw the risk of it. Therefore, it could be said that there is a lack of moral blameworthiness. This has led some commentators to argue that this should not be a form of *mens rea*.[63] Despite this, in certain circumstances negligent actions attract culpability.

Negligence as sufficient *mens rea* for a crime is normally associated with regulatory offences that carry little stigma. This may assuage concerns about punishing those for their inadvertent actions. One area of criminal law, however, where a negligent state of mind will suffice to fulfil

---

60 *R v Brady* [2007] EWCA Crim 2413.

61 *R v G and R* [2004] 1 AC 1034, 1057.

62 For example, Larry Alexander and Kimberly Kessler Ferzan, with Stephen J. Morse, *Crime and Culpability: A Theory of Criminal Law* (Cambridge University Press 2009).

63 For example, JW Cecil Turner, *Kenny's Outlines of Criminal Law* (Cambridge University Press 1962) 34.

the *mens rea* of the crime is gross negligence manslaughter. As discussed in Chapter 4, this is when the defendant's actions are so bad to have gone beyond a mere matter of compensation as to amount to a criminal offence. Other serious crimes that can be satisfied through negligence include corporate manslaughter. As discussed further in Chapter 14, this offence is defined under section 1 of the Corporate Manslaughter and Corporate Homicide Act 2007. The offence requires that the way in which an organisation's activities are managed or organised causes a person's death, and amounts to a gross breach of a relevant duty of care owed by the organisation to the deceased. While both gross negligence manslaughter and corporate manslaughter require the defendant's negligence to be "gross", this is not a prerequisite before a serious crime can be completed with negligence.

There appears to be different degrees of negligence. For example, the offence of dangerous driving under section 2A of the Road Traffic Act 1988 requires that the way a person drives falls far below what would be expected of a competent and careful driver, and it would be obvious to a competent and careful driver that driving in that way would be dangerous. This offence has a maximum sentence of two-years imprisonment. Whereas the offence of careless and inconsiderate driving under section 3 of the Road Traffic Act 1988, only requires driving without due care and attention or without reasonable consideration of others. This crime, which does not require the same level of negligence, only has a non-custodial maximum sentence of an unlimited fine.

A policy argument can be used to explain the punishment of negligent actions. While it may seem unjust to punish those who are not intentionally, recklessly or even knowingly breaching the law, one accepted function of the law is to protect the public.[64] Thus, if a person is failing to drive with due care and attention, which could cause harm to others or property, then a criminal sanction such as a driving penalty may act as a deterrent and encourage the driver to be more careful in the future.

5.7 Murder

So far, this chapter has been discussing the types of *mens rea*. Murder is one example of a crime that requires intention to be established before the defendant can be found guilty. This next section will discuss the elements of murder and analyse the importance of the *mens rea* principles set out above in examining the case of *R v Woollin*.[65]

Murder is considered one of the most serious offences. Until the Homicide Act 1957, all persons convicted of murder were sentenced to death. Since the Murder (Abolition of Death Penalty) Act 1965 all murderers will be sentenced to life imprisonment. Schedule 21 of the Sentencing Act 2020 sets out the starting points that can be recommended by the judge before parole is considered. These are: a whole life order for exceptionally serious offences, 30 years for the most serious cases, 25 years for murder committed with a knife or other weapon taken to the crime scene, or 15 years (if the offender is over 18) or 12 years (if the offender is under 18) for anything else. Certain aggravating and mitigating factors can be considered. Aggravating factors include planning and premeditation, and abuse of a position of trust. Mitigating factors include intention to cause serious harm, rather than death, and a belief by the offender that the killing was an act of mercy.

64 See Chapter 1.3.2.
65 [1999] 1 AC 82.

R v Stewart

In 2021 Wayne Couzens was sentenced to a whole life order for the kidnapping, rape, and murder of Sarah Everard after pleading guilty:

> The circumstances of Couzens' crimes are notorious. He was a serving police officer in the Metropolitan Police. On the evening of 3 March 2021, when the country was in lockdown because of the Covid pandemic, Couzens kidnapped Sarah Everard from the street in London. She was walking home after seeing a friend. He then transported her 80 miles, restrained in handcuffs, and took her to a remote location in Kent. There he raped and murdered her. Over the course of the next two days, he disposed of and burned her body.[66]

Couzens appealed against the imposition of a whole life order, arguing that the killing was not exceptional within the meaning of Schedule 21. Furthermore, that his remorse demonstrated by an early guilty plea should have been considered as a mitigating factor to balance out the aggravating factor of him being a serving police officer.[67]

In its discussion of Couzens's sentencing at the Old Bailey, the Court of Appeal noted that the circumstances of this case were not within the categories stated in Schedule 21, which would normally be of exceptionally high seriousness and lead to a whole life order. As a single murder involving sexual conduct, this case fell at first sight within one of the categories of cases that would normally have a starting point of a minimum term of 30 years.[68] The court, however, stated that Schedule 21 must be applied in a flexible and not rigid way to achieve a just result.[69] In dismissing Couzens's appeal they held that admitting guilt was not the same as showing remorse.[70] Moreover, the extensive and extreme aggravating features of this case, which included Couzens using his knowledge and status as a police officer to commit these appalling crimes with cold-blooded planning and premeditation, meant that a whole life order was appropriate.[71]

Murder is a common law offence defined by Lord Coke as:

> when a man of sound memory, and of the age of discretion, unlawfully killeth within any county of the realm any reasonable creature in rerum natura under the King's peace, with malice aforethought, either expressed by the party or implied by law, [so as the party wounded, or hurt, etc die of the wound or hurt, etc within a year and a day after the same].[72]

In 1996, due to medical advances, the Law Reform (Year and a Day Rule) Act abolished the rule that the death must occur within a year and a day from the *actus reus* being committed. There is now no time limit, but if more than three years has passed the consent of the Attorney General is needed

66 *R v Stewart* [2022] 4 WLR 86, [53].
67 *R v Stewart* [2022] 4 WLR 86, [74].
68 *R v Stewart* [2022] 4 WLR 86, [79].
69 *R v Stewart* [2022] 4 WLR 86, [82].
70 *R v Stewart* [2022] 4 WLR 86, [76].
71 *R v Stewart* [2022] 4 WLR 86, [84].
72 Edward Coke, *The THIRD PART of the Institutes of the LAWS of England: CONCERNING HIGH TREASON, and OTHER PLEAS of the CROWN, and CRIMINALL CAUSES* (Printed by M. Flesher, for W. Lee, and D. Pakeman, 1644) 47.

for prosecution. All the other elements as stated by Lord Coke nearly 400 years ago are still relevant today and can be summarised as follows:

- **Unlawfully killing**. Murder can be committed by the commission or omission[73] of an act. The requirement that the killing is unlawful means that certain killings will not amount to murder. For example, if someone kills another in self-defence then this may not amount to murder.[74]
- **King's peace**. Under section 9 of the Offences against the Persons Act 1861 murder can be committed by a British Citizen anywhere in the world, however, killing in the heat of war is not murder.[75] In *R v Adebelajo*,[76] the defendant tried to claim that killing was in the course of war, but his argument was rejected by the court. The defendant could not rely on the fact that he believed he was a soldier of Islam at war with the UK when he killed British soldier Lee Rigby.
- **Human being**. For a conviction of murder the person killed must be a human being. This means that a foetus killed in the womb cannot be a victim of murder.[77] A baby is considered a human being once it has been fully expelled from the womb and taken its first breath, but the umbilical cord does not have to be cut or the afterbirth delivered. The baby must just have existence independent from the mother.[78] A person can also not be convicted of murdering a person who is already dead. Conventionally, it could be considered that death occurs when the victim's heartbeat and breathing stop. The current medical view is that the test for death is brainstem death, however, there is currently no legal definition of when a person is no longer considered a human being. The courts have, nonetheless, held that when a person is diagnosed brain dead but is being kept alive through artificial life-support systems, doctors can turn off life support without breaking the chain of causation between the defendant's acts of assault and the victim's death.[79]
- **Malice aforethought**. Malice aforethought simply means to kill or cause serious harm.[80] The intent to kill is known as express malice. From the intention to cause serious harm, the intention to kill can be constructed in what is termed implied malice. There is no need for premeditation or for the killing to be committed maliciously. The *mens rea* required for murder has evolved through a series of case judgments. These culminated in the House of Lords' decision in *Woollin*,[81] discussed in more detail below, when it was confirmed that the direction in *Nedrick* for intention was correct. Thus, intention for murder can be found by the jury if the defendant foresees death or serious injury as virtually certain. In the scenarios at the start of the chapter, Ayo only wants to seriously harm Henry. Nonetheless, the law deems that this means he has the required *mens rea* for murder, as it can be implied from his intentions. Alternatively, Eva expressly wants to kill Millie. As such, it could be argued that her state of mind is morally more culpable than Ayo's. The law, however, does not draw this distinction and both defendants will receive the same label and mandatory life sentence.

The above elements of murder and the distinction between direct and indirect intention and implied and express malice can be seen through an examination of the case of *R v Woollin*.[82]

---

73 *R v Gibbins and Proctor* (1919) 13 Cr App R 134.
74 *R v Beckford* [1988] AC 130.
75 *R v Page* [1954] 1 QB 170.
76 [2014] EWCA Crim 2779.
77 *Attorney General's Reference* (No 3 of 1994) [1998] AC 245.
78 *R v Handley* (1874) 13 Cox CC 79.
79 *Malcherek* [1981] 1 WLR 690, 697.
80 *R v Cunningham* [1982] AC 566.
81 [1999] 1 AC 82.
82 [1999] 1 AC 82.

R v Woollin

In *Woollin*, the defendant was charged with murder after he threw his 3-month-old son against a hard surface. It was accepted by both the prosecution and defence that his aim was not to harm the baby, but his action caused his son's skull to fracture, and the baby died as a result. Woollin was convicted of murder at trial and on appeal to the Court of Appeal. The case was then appealed to the House of Lords on the matter of when indirect intention could be inferred. The appellant argued that indirect intention could only be inferred from the defendant's actions when the outcome was virtually certain. Moreover, the trial judge's reference to the defendant needing to foresee a "substantial risk" of the outcome occurring made the conviction unsafe. The prosecution argued that in such a case as this there is no need to refer to virtual certainty, as foresight is just a point of evidence for the jury to decide. Furthermore, if the test of virtual certainty, as set out in *Nedrick*, was correct, it should only have limited application. It should not be used when there was other evidence to consider. The House of Lords, in allowing the appeal, held that in departing from the *Nedrick* direction and using the phrase "a substantial risk", the judge had blurred the distinction between intention and recklessness and thus between murder and manslaughter.[83] The defendant's conviction was quashed for being unsafe and murder was replaced with manslaughter.

Thinking points:

- Both the prosecution and defence agreed that the defendant did not intend to kill his baby. Furthermore, that he had no direct intention to cause serious harm. How then, was he initially convicted of murder?

There was no question in this case of whether the defendant had fulfilled the *actus reus* of murder; he had unlawfully killed a human being under the king's peace by throwing his baby onto a hard surface. The matter of the appeal surrounded what was sufficient *mens rea* for murder. The requirement of malice aforethought can be fulfilled in several ways, which while leading to the same result, are not necessarily as equally blameworthy. These include:

1. The defendant directly intends to kill the victim (direct intent, express malice).
2. The defendant indirectly intends to kill the victim (indirect intent, express malice).
3. The defendant directly intends to cause the victim serious harm (direct intent, implied malice).
4. The defendant indirectly intends to cause the victim serious harm (indirect intent, implied malice).

In *Woollin* it was accepted that none of the first three categories applied. Based on the directions given by the judge, as to what could amount to indirect intention, the jury found that the defendant had indirect intention to cause serious harm. This meant a conviction for murder could be achieved.

- What was the correct test for establishing indirect intent?

83 [1999] 1 AC 82, 95.

The House of Lords approved the direction set out in *Nedrick* and held that a jury are not entitled to find intention for murder unless they feel sure that the prosecution has shown that the defendant foresees the outcome of death or serious injury as a virtual certainty.[84] The court decided that for clarity, the word "infer" used in the *Nedrick* direction should be replaced with "find".[85] This raises the question of whether the House of Lords were promoting an *identity view* of intention,[86] whereby as a matter of substantive law foresight of a virtually certain outcome amounted to intention. The matter was later considered by the Court of Appeal in *R v Matthews and Alleyne*.[87] The court clarified that the trial judge had gone beyond the existing law by directing the jury to find intent provided that they were satisfied that the defendant appreciated a virtual certain risk of death.[88] They held that they did "not regard *Woollin* as yet reaching or laying down a substantive rule of law".[89] Thus, reinforcing an *inference view*, whereby inferring intention is a rule of evidence for the jury to consider on the facts of the case. The result of this is, that although a jury may consider the consequence a virtual certainty, they are still entitled to find that that defendant did not intend it.

The requirement of virtual certainty raises a further question of whether the same level of foresight is required when death or serious injury is the defendant's direct intent. In the scenario at the start of the chapter, Debbie's direct intention is to kill Jess. She takes actions to achieve this but does not see the outcome as a virtual certainty, or even a high probability, due to her lack of skill and experience. Does this mean that Debbie has the required *mens rea* for murder? *Woollin* leaves this question unanswered as the direction set out in this case only applies to establish if the defendant has indirect intention where a simple direction as to intent would not suffice. Thus, a person with direct intention could be convicted of murder for a result that they did not think there was a high foreseeability of happening. This can be justified by the fact that it is the person's aim to kill and they have achieved this result, so regardless of the probability, morally they should face punishment. Moreover, policy would dictate that people who want to commit serious harm need to prevented from being free to be able to do this.

- What issues does the *Woollin* definition of intention potentially cause with fair labelling and the correspondence theory?

As discussed in Chapter 2,[90] it is a fundamental principle of criminal law that the label given to the defendant should match the seriousness of the crime and the blameworthiness of the defendant. Arguably, a defendant whose aim is to kill is more blameworthy than a defendant who foresees the risk of serious injury, but this is not their desired objective. The label of murderer, however, is applied equally in both situations.

Furthermore, the defendant can be convicted and labelled as a murderer even though he did not intend or foresee death. As discussed in Chapter 2,[91] the correspondence theory of criminal law states that to establish blameworthiness the defendant should have the *mens rea* that corresponds to the *actus reus* they have committed. In the case of murder, the *mens rea* is implied from the defendant's intention to cause really serious harm. This is understandable if it is considered that "the outcome of intentionally inflicting serious harm can be so unpredictable that anyone prepared to act so

84 *R v Woollin* [1999] 1 AC 82, 96.
85 *R v Woollin* [1999] 1 AC 82, 96–97.
86 See above at Chapter 5.4.2.
87 *R v Matthews and Alleyne* [2003] EWCA Crim 192.
88 *R v Matthews and Alleyne* [2003] EWCA Crim 192, [44].
89 *R v Matthews and Alleyne* [2003] EWCA Crim 192, [43].
90 See Chapter 2.3.2.
91 See Chapter 2.3.4.2.

wickedly has little ground for complaint if, where death results, he is convicted and punished as severely as one who intended to kill".[92] This argument is justifiable when the defendant has intentionally caused really serious harm, but can the same be concluded when this is not the defendant's direct intent? Here, the intention to cause serious harm is firstly inferred from the defendant's foresight of the undesired consequence, and then it is implied that this intention is enough to fulfil the *mens rea* of murder. It could be argued that the judge's power to sentence up to life for manslaughter gives enough discretion for cases such as this, for it not to be considered murder.

One way to address the problem of inferred and implied intent being enough for murder, is to set a high bar for when intent can be inferred. Lord Steyn refers to the policy implications of setting the threshold of foresight for indirect intention so high with the result that the test for murder is narrow, but states: "I am satisfied that the *Nedrick* test . . . is pitched at the right level of foresight".[93] While such a limited definition for the *mens rea* of murder may reduce the deterrent effect of the law or the protection of the public, Lord Steyn justifies this lack of a policy based approach on the grounds that the offence of manslaughter, which sits immediately below that of murder, can attract a life sentence at the discretion of the court.[94] Therefore, the principle of fair labelling triumphs above an over-inclusive test for indirect intention, which would blur the line between murder and manslaughter.

- Lord Steyn gave the leading judgment in *Woollin*. How was his judgment influenced by morals and policy?

Lord Steyn provides an extensive review of the previous authorities in determining the level of foresight required for indirect intention. He states that the decision in *Woollin* is based on the law from *Nedrick*, which correctly followed the part of the judgment in *Moloney* that had not been overruled by *Hancock*.[95] Thus, clearly demonstrating that Lord Steyn is following the legal principles set out in previous precedent. In such a highly emotive case, Simester applauds Lord Steyn for resisting the *ad hoc* moral pull of the facts.[96] Many would consider that killing a baby through throwing it onto a hard surface was morally reprehensible, yet by following strict legal principle, and not morals, the appeal was allowed. Therefore, it can be concluded that morals had little weight in determining the outcome of this case.

At the start of the chapter, it was discussed how the adoption of differing levels of *mens rea* meant that a value neutral judgment of the defendant could be made. In assessing cases it becomes a question of fact as to whether the defendant intended the result or foresaw it as virtually certain, or whether they had been reckless by taking a foreseen unjustified risk. No moral assessment is made of the defendant *per se*, but culpability is determined by the choices the defendant makes with the intention or foresight they had. As concluded above, this moral neutral view is supported by the outcome of *Woollin*. Norrie, however, discusses that because a jury are entitled to find that a defendant did not intend a result, even when the outcome is virtually certain, this demonstrates that a decision is being made based on moral values.[97] Thus, the *inference view* gives the jury a degree of flexibility to apply a moral standard when the defendant has not directly intended the crime. This means that the line between intention and recklessness is not certain, leaving the division between murder and manslaughter unclear.

---

92 *R v Cunningham* [1982] AC 566, 582.
93 *R v Woollin* [1999] 1 AC 82, 95.
94 *R v Woollin* [1999] 1 AC 82, 94–95.
95 *R v Woollin* [1999] 1 AC 82, 93–94.
96 AP Simester, "Murder, Mens Rea, and the House of Lords – Again" [1999] LQR 17, 21.
97 Alan Norrie, "After Woollin" [1999] Crim LR 532, 538–539.

5.8 Conclusion

The concept of *mens rea* enables the law to make determinations about the blameworthiness of a defendant and their degree of culpability. Distinctions between crimes such as murder and manslaughter can be made based on a factual assessment of whether the defendant had the required intention or some lesser form of *mens rea*, such as recklessness or negligence. This then becomes a value neutral judgment. While this may suggest that morals and policy have a limited role to play in establishing the defendant's blameworthiness, it has been shown that these considerations are still essential in determining the definitions of these concepts and where the lines should be drawn. For example, moral considerations were employed in *R v G and R* to depart from the decision in *R v Caldwell*, and policy aims can be considered to explain why negligent behaviour attracts culpability. While the decision in *Woollin* was commended for not bowing to the moral pull of the facts, the jury are still entitled to find that there is no intention even when the outcome was a virtual certainty. The result is that when a jury does not think the case reaches the moral threshold to be deemed murder, they can conclude that the required intent is not present. Thus, demonstrating the relevance of morals and policy in rules of *mens rea*.

5.9 Further Reading

Cosby C, "Recklessness – The Continuing Search for a Definition" [2008] J Crim L 313
Finnis J, "Intention and Side Effects" in RG Frey and Christopher W Morris (eds) *Liability and Responsibility: Essays in Law and Morals* (Cambridge University Press 1991)
Kaveny C, "Inferring Intention from Foresight" [2004] LQR 81
Norrie A, "After Woollin" [1999] Crim LR 532
Simester AP, "Murder, Mens Rea, and the House of Lords – Again" [1999] LQR 17
Stark F, *Culpable Carelessness* (Cambridge University Press 2017)
Williams G, "Oblique Intention" [1987] CLJ 417

Chapter 6

Defining Dishonesty

Chapter Contents

DOI: 10.4324/9781003408383-7

6.1 Chapter Aims and Objectives

This chapter will examine the concept of dishonesty, which is an essential *mens rea* element that must be proved before someone can be convicted of property offences such as theft and fraud. To say someone is dishonest requires a factual assessment and a morally weighted judgment. As Baroness Hale states, when a jury or magistrate is determining whether a person is dishonest this goes beyond their normal remit of determining the facts of the case, as it "is a moral question".[1] The issue is whether in determining dishonesty, a jury should judge the defendant's actions subjectively, considering whether they realise that their actions are dishonest. Alternatively, whether an objective approach should be taken, therefore punishing someone whose actions do not meet the standard of honesty set by ordinary people, regardless of whether the defendant themselves appreciates this. Thus, is the moral judgment to be made of whether a person is dishonest, that of the defendant themselves or that of a reasonable honest person?

By the end of this chapter, you should be able to:

- Define dishonesty and related property offences.
- Discuss the problem of defining dishonesty in relation to the perceptions of a reasonable person or that of the defendant.
- Examine how legal principle was influenced by morals and policy in the decision of *R v Ghosh*.[2]
- Examine how legal principle was influenced by morals and policy in the decision of *Ivey v Genting Casinos (UK) Ltd t/a Crockfords*.[3]

> The issues that will be examined in this chapter can be illustrated through the scenarios below. Consider whether the following people are dishonest.
>
> - Amber mistakenly thinks that Ben has taken her pen. In fact, he has one that is exactly the same as hers. Amber takes the pen when Ben is not looking.
> - Bertram takes £5 from his mum's purse to pay for his bus fare to university without asking.
> - Claire finds a £20 note blowing in the wind while walking in the countryside. There is no one else around so she puts it in her purse.
> - Dominic is using a notepad at work. When he gets home, he finds that he has unconsciously put it in his bag. Despite feeling bad about taking it, he does not return it.
> - Emma asks her friend to donate to charity. They refuse, so she takes £10 from her friend's purse without them knowing. She gives the money to charity as she thinks that this is OK to do, as her friend has plenty, and it is for a good cause.

6.2 The Relevance of Dishonesty

There are many situations in day-to-day life where a person may intentionally take property belonging to another. For example, you see a pile of flyers advertising the village fete at the checkout of the local shop, and so you take one. This, however, does not amount to an offence unless the essential

---

1 Baroness Hale of Richmond, "Dishonesty" (2019) 48 Common Law World Review 5, 14.

2 [1982] QB 1053.

3 [2017] UKSC 67.

mens rea element of dishonesty is present. This requires a factual and moral enquiry that necessitates the jury or magistrates to determine whether the defendant's conduct or state of mind was sufficiently blameworthy.[4] Dishonesty is an essential element in establishing liability for offences such as theft and fraud. These are not insignificant offences, with data from the Crime Survey for England and Wales for the year ending June 2024 estimating that there were 2.8 million instances of theft and 3.6 million fraud offences committed.[5] Despite the importance of dishonesty in determining someone's culpability, it has never been fully defined by Parliament.

6.3 Defining Dishonesty in Section 2 of the Theft Act 1968

Theft is one property offence that requires the element of dishonesty. To be found guilty of theft under section 1(1) of the Theft Act 1968, the prosecution must prove beyond reasonable doubt that a person has dishonestly appropriated property belonging to another with the intention to permanently deprive. Each of the subsequent sections, two to six of the Theft Act 1968, further define these elements. The discussion in this chapter, however, is centred around the requirement for the defendant to act dishonestly, as this element raises the opportunity for significant dispute and value judgment.

Parliament made the Theft Act 1968 based on the recommendations of the Criminal Law Revision Committee.[6] This introduced the term "dishonestly" to replace the term "fraudulently" that was used in the previous law; the Larceny Act 1916. The Criminal Law Revision Committee stated that there was no need to define dishonesty: "'Dishonesty' is something which laymen can easily recognise when they see it."[7] It is an ordinary word that is in common use.[8] Therefore, the Theft Act 1968, section 2, only gives a partial definition of dishonesty by stating when someone will not be dishonest:

> 2(1) A person's appropriation of property belonging to another is not to be regarded as dishonest –
> (a) if he appropriates the property in the belief that he has in law the right to deprive the other of it, on behalf of himself or a third person; or
> (b) if he appropriates the property in the belief that he would have the other's consent if the other knew of the appropriation and the circumstances of it; or
> (c) (except where the property came to him as a trustee or personal representative) if he appropriates the property in the belief that the person to whom the property belongs cannot be discovered by taking reasonable steps.
>
> 2(2) A person's appropriation of property belong to another may be dishonest notwithstanding that he is willing to pay for the property.

This section is not without its difficulties. First, it requires the jury to consider what the defendant's belief was. In *R v Holden*[9] the court held that this should be judged subjectively, considering what the defendant honestly believed. The defendant had taken scrap tyres from Kwik Fit. He had previously worked at several branches of the company, and while not employed at the time of taking the tyres,

4 Law Commission, *Fraud* (Law Com No 276, 2002) para 5.1.
5 "Crime in England and Wales: Year Ending June 2024", 24 October 2024, www.ons.gov.uk/peoplepopulationandcommunity/crimeandjustice/bulletins/crimeinenglandandwales/yearendingseptember2022#theft-offences, accessed 28 November 2024.
6 The Criminal Law Revision Committee, *Theft and Related Offences* (Eighth Report, Cmnd 2977, 1966).
7 The Criminal Law Revision Committee, *Theft and Related Offences* (Eighth Report, Cmnd 2977, 1966) para 39.
8 *R v Feely* [1973] QB 530, 537.
9 [1991] Crim LR 478.

he was due to start work with them again. The defendant claimed that he had seen others taking the tyres and that a supervisor had granted permission for the tyres to be taken. Holden, therefore, claimed that he was not dishonest under the provisions of section 2(1)(a) of the Theft Act 1968, as he believed he had a legal right to the tyres. The depot manager, however, said that taking the tyres or allowing others to do so, was a sackable offence and that there was no right to take them. The defendant was convicted, but the appeal was allowed as the trial judge had directed the jury to consider whether the defendant had a reasonable belief in the legal right to take the tyres. The Court of Appeal held that the correct test was whether the defendant had, or might have had, an honest belief in the right to take the tyres.[10] This does not need to be a reasonable belief, but it does need to be a belief in the right to deprive the other of the property in law.

A further application of section 2(1)(a) of the Theft Act 1968 can be seen in *R v Robinson*,[11] so that the defendant could not be guilty of robbery. The definition of robbery, as set out in section 8(1) of the Theft Act 1968, states:

> A person is guilty of robbery if he steals, and immediately before or at the time of doing so, and in order to do so, he uses force on any person or puts or seeks to put any person in fear of being then and there subjected to force.

The prerequisite that the defendant steals means that all the elements of theft, including dishonesty, must be established alongside the additional requirements for robbery. In *Robinson* the defendant honestly believed that he was owed £7 by the victim's wife. During a struggle the victim dropped £5, which the defendant took in part satisfaction of the debt he believed to be owed. Following the precedent set in *R v Skivington*,[12] the appeal in *R v Robinson* was allowed. In opposition to what the judge had directed the jury, it did not need to be shown that the defendant had an honest belief in taking the property in the way that he did. It was enough that he had an honest belief in the right to take the property. Therefore, as the dishonesty requirement had not been satisfied for theft his conviction for robbery was quashed. As such, referring to the scenarios at the start of the chapter, Amber, would not be guilty of theft if she honestly believes the pen is hers, even though it is not.

A moral belief in the right to deprive, however, will not suffice. This applies even if the morally held belief is popularly shared. To take the example of a modern-day Robin Hood: If a person stole from the rich to distribute this wealth to the poor, while this might be deemed morally acceptable, it would still be dishonest if they knew that they did not have a right in law to take the money. Therefore, Emma in the scenarios at the start of the chapter will unlikely to be able to claim that her actions were honest under section 2(1)(a). If she knew what she was doing was legally wrong, even if she believed it was morally justified, she is not deemed honest.

Section 2(1)(b) holds that the defendant is not dishonest if they honestly believe they would have the other's consent to the appropriation if they knew of the circumstances. There is no need to establish that the other would have consented, just that the defendant believes they would have. Therefore, applying this section to the scenarios at the start of the chapter, it is unlikely that Bertram would be convicted of theft.

This section becomes problematic when the defendant has received the victim's consent to have the property, but the victim does not have the mental capacity to give this consent, or the defendant has exploited some vulnerability to obtain the consent.[13] In *R v Hinks*[14] it was established

10 *R v Holden* [1991] Crim LR 478, 479.
11 [1976] 10 WLUK 112.
12 [1967] 2 WLR 665. The defendant in this case was charged of robbery under section 23 of the Larceny Act 1916; the predecessor to the Theft Act 1968.
13 *R v Barton* [2021] QB 685, 736–739.
14 [2001] 2 AC 241.

that theft can occur even when the property had been given as a gift. Hinks had been a carer for the victim, a man of low intelligence. Over a period of months, the defendant had accompanied the victim to his building society where he withdrew sums of money to the total of approximately £60,000; money which he had inherited from his father. The money was deposited into the defendant's bank account. A colour television set was also transferred from the victim to the defendant. By a majority of three to two, the House of Lords dismissed the defendant's appeal on the certified question of whether the acquisition of an indefeasible title to property was capable of amounting to an appropriation of property belonging to another for the purposes of section 1(1) of the Theft Act 1968. They held that appropriation of the property had occurred within the meaning of section 3(1) of the Theft Act 1968, which requires "any assumption by a person of the rights of an owner". Lord Hutton, dissenting, also took the opportunity to consider how appropriation by means of a gift related to section 2(1)(b). He argued that the jury should have been asked to consider the validity of the gift, because while a valid gift might amount to appropriation of the property, it should not fulfil the requirements of acting dishonestly no matter how morally reprehensible they thought the defendant's conduct was.[15] On this reasoning, if a defendant wrongly, but genuinely, believes they would have had the owner's consent to appropriate the property if asked, they are not dishonest under section 2(1)(b). This would mean that they could appropriate property without the owner's actual consent and not be guilty of theft. Alternatively, if the defendant receives a gift from the owner of the property, but does not adequately investigate or consider the validity of the gift, they could be deemed dishonest. This leads to the paradoxical position where someone who takes property without express consent can avoid conviction, but someone who has been given express consent to have the property – such as *Hinks* – is deemed dishonest as they have not sufficiently checked the mental state or vulnerability of the giver of the gift.

Section 2(1)(c) again requires that the defendant must hold an honest belief. For this section, the belief must be that the property was abandoned. In *R v Small*[16] the defendant was charged with the theft of a car. He claimed that he honestly believed that the car was abandoned as it had sat unlocked in the same position on the corner of a road for two weeks, with the keys in the ignition, no fuel, a flat tyre and battery, and broken windscreen wipers. The Court of Appeal held that an honest belief, albeit an unreasonable one, was all that was required to fulfil section 2(1)(c).[17]

Therefore, in the scenario at the start of the chapter, Claire will not be dishonest if she honestly believes the £20 note is abandoned. The matter is not quite so simple though, as there is then an extra requirement that the defendant needs to take reasonable steps to find the owner. This adds an objective value judgment of what amounts to reasonable steps to find to whom the property belongs. Claire would have to honestly believe the £20 is abandoned and then take the steps that any other reasonable person would have taken to find the owner of such a sum of money in those circumstances. This means that if Claire honestly thinks the property is abandoned and takes steps to find the owner that she thinks are inadequate, but are reasonable by the assessment of an ordinary person, she would not be dishonest. Equally, if Claire honestly thought she had taken the necessary steps to find the owner, but an ordinary person would think the steps taken were unreasonable, she then could be dishonest. It would seem hard to separate these two elements as how can it be said that a person honestly thinks that the property is abandoned if they have not taken the steps that they think are suitable to find the owner? Requiring reasonable steps to be taken, means the defendant's honest belief can be set aside and instead a value judgment is made of how the defendant ought to have acted.

15 *R v Hinks* [2001] 2 AC 241, 258–260.
16 (1988) 86 Cr App R 170.
17 *R v Small* (1988) 86 Cr App R 170, 173–174.

Section 2(1)(c) was considered in relation to burglary in *R v Wood*, when the conviction depended on it being established that the defendant had stolen property.[18] Burglary is defined in section 9 of the Theft Act 1968, which states:

> (1) A person is guilty of burglary if –
> (a) he enters any building or part of a building as a trespasser and with intent to commit any such offence as is mentioned in subsection (2) below; or
> (b) having entered any building or part of a building as a trespasser he steals or attempts to steal anything in the building or that part of it or inflicts or attempts to inflict on any person therein any grievous bodily harm.
> (2) The offences referred to in subsection (1)(a) above are offences of stealing anything in the building or part of a building in question, of inflicting on any person therein any grievous bodily harm therein, and of doing unlawful damage to the building or anything therein.

In *Wood*[19] the defendant and his friend entered a business premises that had stood empty for 6 months and become dilapidated. They emptied the shop of all the stock, electronical equipment, and furniture that was present. The defendant admitted that he was a trespasser but claimed that he genuinely believed everything in the shop had been abandoned. The appeal was allowed as the judge had failed to direct the jury that they would have to acquit the defendant if he had, or might have had, an honest belief that the appropriated property was abandoned.[20] As the question of dishonesty was not adequately considered, the ulterior offence of theft was not complete, and therefore the defendant's conviction for burglary was quashed.

Should none of the sections set out in section 2(1) of the Theft Act 1968 apply, the jury will then be asked to consider the common law test for dishonesty. Lord Lane in reviewing the previous authorities in *R v Ghosh*[21] considered that there was not one single test for determining dishonesty in property offences, with an objective approach seen in relation to theft and a more subjective approach taken in fraud-based offences.[22] As will be discussed below, the case of *Ghosh* introduced a standard test for dishonesty that required an objective and subjective assessment of dishonesty. This test was used until 2017, when once again the common law test for dishonesty was reformulated in *Ivey v Genting Casinos (UK) Ltd t/a Crockfords*.[23] In *Ivey* it was held that the standard for dishonesty was an objective one and had always been until *Ghosh* set a precedent that did "not correctly represent the law".[24]

6.4 Defining Dishonesty in Fraud

Until the Fraud Act 2006 there were many different deception-based offences, which required that dishonesty was established. These offences were contained in the common law of conspiracy to defraud, the Theft Act 1968, the Theft Act 1978, and the Theft (Amendment) Act 1996. These deception-based offences included those that were the subject of the appeal in *R v Ghosh*.[25]

18 [2002] EWCA Crim 832.
19 *R v Wood* [2002] EWCA Crim 832.
20 [2002] EWCA Crim 832, [24].
21 [1982] QB 1053.
22 *R v McIvor* [1982] 1 WLR 409, 417.
23 [2017] UKSC 67.
24 [2017] UKSC 67, 74.
25 [1982] QB 1053.

> **R v Ghosh**
>
> In *R v Ghosh* the defendant was a surgeon acting as a locum tenens consultant at a hospital. He claimed fees for operations he had not performed or for those that had been carried out under the National Health Service. He was tried for one count of attempting to procure the execution of a security by deception contrary to section 20(2) of the Theft Act 1968,[26] and three counts of obtaining, or attempting to obtain, money by deception contrary to section 15(1) of the same Act. The defendant argued that he had not been dishonest as the money he claimed was owed to him in unpaid consultancy fees. The Court of Appeal dismissed his appeal but took the opportunity to review the previous case authority and devise a standard test for dishonesty in property offences. This led to the *Ghosh* test for dishonesty which asked the jury to consider:
>
> 1 whether the conduct complained of was dishonest by standards of ordinary reasonable and honest people (the "objective test"); and, if yes,
> 2 whether the defendant realised that ordinary honest people would so regard his behaviour as dishonest ("the subjective test").

Applying the *Ghosh* test to the scenarios at the start of the chapter, Dominic may not have been guilty of stealing the notepad if ordinary and honest people would not find his actions dishonest.[27] The first limb of the test allowed the jury to apply their own moral standards of what is acceptable in society, and so despite Dominic taking the notebook and not returning it he could avoid liability if anyone else would have done the same. Comparatively, Emma has taken £10 from her friend's purse without their consent. Under the *Ghosh* test she would have most probably been dishonest by the standards of ordinary and honest people. Therefore, it would have needed to be considered whether she realised her behaviour was dishonest by these standards. This is when the test became more problematic as Emma thinks her behaviour, which society would judge as unacceptable, is not dishonest by those standards. If Emma could convince the jury of this, then she would not be liable for theft. The second limb of the test was aimed at preventing the defendant from running a "Robin Hood" defence,[28] but this depends on the defendant knowing that ordinary and honest people would think their actions are dishonest. In a society, for example, where the poor are starving and the rich are exploiting them to become even richer, this might be difficult to establish. A person may argue that they thought the no one would think their actions dishonest in those circumstances. Moreover, under the *Ghosh* test there was no requirement that the defendant themselves did not identify their behaviour as dishonest. Just that they believe that they are not dishonest by the standards held by honest and reasonable people.

Thinking points:

- The defence in *Ghosh* argued that a subjective approach should be taken to assessing whether the defendant was dishonest.[29] The Crown argued that an objective yardstick should first be applied before judging what the defendant's state of mind was.[30] Why is this distinction important?

26 Repealed by the Fraud Act 2006.
27 See the discussion below of why assessing the standards of ordinary and honest people may be problematic.
28 *R v Ghosh* [1982] QB 1053, 1064.
29 *R v Ghosh* [1982] QB 1053, 1055–1056.
30 *R v Ghosh* [1982] QB 1053, 1056.

As explained in Chapter 5, when judging if a defendant has acted intentionally or recklessly a subjective approach is taken. This ensures that a person is only found blameworthy when the result is their desired aim, or they advertently take the risk of the consequence occurring. Similarly, a subjective definition of dishonesty would ensure that only those who knew they were being dishonest would be found guilty. In *Ghosh* the defendant argued that he did not think he was dishonest as despite him not being owed the money he claimed for operations, he maintained that he was owed the money for consultations carried out. If a subjective approach had been taken, and the jury believed his version of events, he could have been found not guilty. This does not necessarily mean a defendant could escape liability just by claiming that he thought his actions were not dishonest. It is still a question for the jury to decide. As seen in *R v Gilks*[31] even when a subjective assessment of dishonesty is made, the jury can reject the defendant's claims that they were acting in a way they thought was honest and return a guilty verdict.[32]

Alternatively, an objective approach would assess the defendant by the standards of honest and reasonable people. Rather than judging the defendant by his own moral values, he would be judged by the collective moral standard of society – or at least this standard as viewed and applied by the jury in each case. Thus, a defendant could be found to be dishonest even when they did not think they were. Regardless, in *Ghosh* the court found that once the jury had rejected his account of events no jury could have concluded, by any test, other than that he was dishonest.[33]

- The defendant claimed that he believed he had a legal right to the money as it was owed to him for consultancy work done. If he had been charged with theft, rather than obtaining property by deception, could he have claimed he was not dishonest under section 2(1)(a)?

Theft, which is defined under section 1(1) of the Theft Act 1968 requires that a person dishonestly appropriates property belonging to another with the intention to permanently deprive. Before it was repealed, section 15(1) of the Theft Act 1968 defined obtaining property by deception as when a person who by any deception dishonestly obtains property belonging to another, with the intention of permanently depriving the other of it. There were many similarities between the offences of theft and obtaining property by deception. For example, section 3 of the Theft Act 1968 defines appropriation as assuming the rights of the owner, but in *R v Gomez*,[34] when the defendant was convicted of theft after deceiving the owner of the property to sell it in return for stolen cheques, the court held that appropriation under the offence of theft could include when the property had been obtained by deception. Money was taken in *Ghosh*, which would fulfil the definition of property for theft[35] and for obtaining property by deception. Furthermore, Section 15(3) of the Theft Act 1968 stated that the same definition of intention to permanently deprive as set out in section 6 of the Theft Act 1968 for theft, also applies to obtaining property by deception. Due to the overlaps between the offences, it has been stated that virtually all section 15 offences could also amount to a section 1 theft offence.[36] Therefore, *Ghosh*, could have been charged with the alternative offence of theft.

When a person is charged with theft the exceptions of when a person will not be dishonest under section 2 can be applied. Consequently, as discussed above,[37] when a person honestly believes that they have a legal right to the property they will not be dishonest under section 2(1)(a).

---

31 *R v Gilks* [1972] 1 WLR 1341.
32 *R v Gilks* [1972] 1 WLR 1341.
33 *R v Ghosh* [1982] QB 1053, 1064–1065.
34 [1993] AC 442.
35 As set out in section 4(1) of the Theft Act 1968.
36 David Ormerod and Karl Laird, *Smith and Hogan's Criminal Law* (16th edition, Oxford University Press 2021) 870–871.
37 See chapter 6.2.

This is a wholly subjective test which does not depend on the reasonableness of the defendant's belief. Section 1(3) of the Theft Act 1968 appears to imply that the section 2 exceptions of when the defendant will be deemed honest only apply to theft offences committed contrary to section 1 of the Theft Act 1968. Unlike Robbery and Burglary (when the ulterior offence is theft), obtaining property by deception is not contingent on establishing theft. Therefore, as *Ghosh* was charged with obtaining property by deception under section 15, strictly viewed the section 2 exceptions would not apply. Had he been charged with the alternative offence of theft; however, he could claim that he legally thought he was owed the money he obtained and could have been found not guilty.

The applicability of section 2 was not considered on appeal in *Ghosh*, but in the year following *Ghosh* the Court of Appeal were given the opportunity to consider whether section 2(1)(a) of the Theft Act 1968 could apply to the offence of obtaining property by deception.[38] The Crown conceded that section 1(3) prevented the application of section 2(1)(a) to section 15 but argued that this section could be read into the law due to the common law claim of right.[39] The court agreed.[40] As a result, the claim of right, coupled with the common law doctrine of mistake, means that if the defendant honestly but mistakenly thought that they had a right to the property, this would negate their *mens rea*.[41] This would apply equally to theft and fraud type cases that require dishonesty.[42] This approach of determining the facts of the situation as the defendant believed them to be is reflected in the current test for dishonesty as adopted in *Ivey*, discussed below.[43]

- In *Ghosh*, Lord Lane rejects that *R v Feely*[44] definitively establishes an objective standard for assessing dishonesty. He argues that such an approach would be inconsistent with the wholly subjective approach taken under section 2 of the Theft Act 1968. Furthermore, it could penalise "conduct to which no moral obloquy could possibly attach".[45] Why is this important?

Lord Lane in *Ghosh* refutes a purely objective approach, expressing that a state of mind such as dishonesty cannot be established independently of the knowledge and belief of the accused.[46] He gives the example of a man who comes from a country where public transport is free, who thinking these same rules apply uses public transport in this country without making the required payment. Objectively he would be dishonest as ordinary people know that a payment must be made, however, in his mind he is honest. Lord Lane asserts that Parliament cannot have intended such a person to be dishonest.[47] Thus, ensuring a just outcome for a defendant was of paramount importance in the judicial reasoning in *Ghosh*. Not penalising those who are not blameworthy respects the principle of fair labelling,[48] and protects those who are incapable of appreciating that their actions are dishonest. Lord Lane did, however, restrict the application of the *Ghosh* test by making it clear that a person cannot avoid liability because they believe their actions are morally justified, but knows that ordinary people would consider them legally dishonest.[49]

---

38 *R v Woolven* (1983) 77 Cr App R 231.
39 *R v Woolven* (1983) 77 Cr App R 231, 235.
40 *R v Woolven* (1983) 77 Cr App R 231, 235.
41 Bo Wang, "Mistaking Theft: Dishonesty 'Turns Over a New Leaf'" [2022] J Crim L 3, 10.
42 Bo Wang, "Mistaking Theft: Dishonesty 'Turns Over a New Leaf'" [2022] J Crim L 3, 8.
43 See Chapter 6.5.
44 [1973] QB 530.
45 *R v Ghosh* [1982] QB 1053, 1063–1064.
46 *R v Ghosh* [1982] QB 1053, 1063.
47 *R v Ghosh* [1982] QB 1053, 1063.
48 See Chapter 2.3.2 for further discussion of fair labelling.
49 *R v Ghosh* [1982] QB 1053, 1064.

- There was substantial academic criticism of the two-part *Ghosh* test for dishonesty.[50] What were the key concerns raised?

The first limb of the *Ghosh* test assesses the defendant by the standards of ordinary and honest people. Thus, the aim is to provide a normative judgment of the defendant's actions. The problem is that there is no standard understanding of dishonesty. Furthermore, as the Law Commission recognises, "people's moral standards are surprisingly flexible".[51] For example, in the scenario given at the start of the chapter, many people might admit that like Dominic they have taken stationery from work. Thus, the ordinary person is not necessarily an honest one. Additionally, it does not follow that conduct being a regular occurrence means that it is a morally accepted norm. If sat on a jury and asked to judge whether this behaviour was dishonest by the standards of society, evidence shows that many people will apply a standard of honesty that is greater than their own.[52] Thus, the defendant is judged against some fictional higher standard that does not represent the conduct of the ordinary person sat on the jury.

Another key criticism of the second limb of the *Ghosh* test was that the further detached a person was from understanding what behaviour is acceptable in society, the more likely that they will not be found dishonest. For instance, take the example of a Member of Parliament who claims expenses that they are not entitled to. An ordinary and honest person would most likely think this was dishonest. But, what if the Member of Parliament could claim that they did not think what they were doing was dishonest as it was an accepted practice in that context. If the jury were to believe that the defendant honestly did not think their actions were dishonest by the standards of ordinary people, they would be obliged to acquit.[53] While the subjective limb ensured those who are not meaning to be dishonest are not found to be dishonest, thus ensuring individual justice and fair labelling, it does not uphold the moral standards of society. It also does not communicate what behaviour is acceptable, nor does it achieve the policy aim of deterrence. Therefore, although Lord Lane wanted to ensure that no culpability was attached to actions where there was no moral obloquy, the result is that actions that have moral obloquy could go unpunished.

This problem was demonstrated in *DPP v Gohill*.[54] The defendants had been charged with theft and false accounting. They worked at a tool hire company and hired tools to customers without charging the set fee. They changed the computer records to indicate the tool had not been hired, when in fact it had. Often in return they were given a small tip from the customer. The defendants argued that even though they knew this was not allowed, they had acted as they did because the hires were only for very short periods of time and that this amounted to good customer service for the benefit of the company. The Magistrates, in applying the *Ghosh* test acquitted the defendants on the ground that they were not convinced beyond reasonable doubt that the defendants were acting dishonestly by the standards of ordinary and honest people.[55] The prosecution appealed the case and, despite the Magistrates applying what assumingly they considered a normative standard of dishonesty, the High Court allowed the appeal, finding that the decision was perverse.[56]

---

50 For example, see Kenneth Campbell, "The Test of Dishonesty in *R v Ghosh*" [1984] The Cambridge Law Journal 349; E Griew, "Dishonesty: The Objections to Feely and Ghosh" [1985] Crim LR 341; David Ormerod and Karl Laird, *Smith and Hogan's Criminal Law* (16th edition, Oxford University Press 2021) 913–914.

51 Law Commission, *Fraud* (Law Com No 276, 2002) para 5.9.

52 Law Commission, *Fraud* (Law Com No 276, 2002) paras 5.9–5.10.

53 In practice, convincing a jury might be quite challenging, as seen in the case against the former MP Jim Divine. He was found guilty by a jury of false accounting under section 17(1)(b) of the Theft Act 1968 despite claiming that he thought what he had done was accepted practice. See "Former MP Jim Devine Jailed for 16 Months Over Expenses", 31 March 2011, www.bbc.co.uk/news/uk-politics-12918742, accessed 28 November 2024.

54 [2007] EWHC 239.

55 *DPP v Gohill* [2007] EWHC 239 [8].

56 *DPP v Gohill* [2007] EWHC 239 [10]–[11].

When Parliament reformed the law of deception-based offences, with the passing of the Fraud Act 2006, three new fraud offences were introduced under section 1 of that Act:

> (1) A person is guilty of fraud if he is in breach of any of the sections listed in subsection (2) (which provide for different ways of committing the offence).
> (2) The sections are –
> (a) section 2 (fraud by false representation),
> (b) section 3 (fraud by failing to disclose information), and
> (c) section 4 (fraud by abuse of position).

Each of these offences require the defendant to act dishonestly. Additionally, section 11 of the Fraud Act 2006 also contains the offence of obtaining services dishonestly. The introduction of such offences provided the opportunity for the definition of dishonesty to be put on a statutory footing. The Law Commission report that led to the enactment of these offences did not, however, define dishonesty. They stated, "if an exhaustive definition of . . . 'dishonesty' were incorporated into the law, there would inevitably be examples of behaviour which were legally dishonest, but which the fact-finders would characterise as morally blameless".[57] Thus, a preferred approach was one where the jury decides on moral blameworthiness of the defendant, rather than having stringent legal rules. The Law Commission concluded that despite the academic criticisms that had been raised, the *Ghosh* test was unproblematic in practice.[58] Therefore, even with this opportunity to enact a statutory definition of dishonesty, the common law remained unchanged. This was until the case of *Ivey v Genting Casinos (UK) Ltd t/a Crockfords*.[59]

6.5 Reformulating Dishonesty

Ivey v Genting Casinos (UK) Ltd t/a Crockfords

In the civil case of *Ivey v Genting Casinos (UK) Ltd t/a Crockfords*,[60] the claimant attempted to recover £7.7 million in winnings from Crockfords Casino. The claimant had accumulated the amount by playing the game Punto Banco over two days in August 2012. The casino refused to pay out the winnings after their investigation had shown that the claimant had used an edge sorting technique, which they said meant the game had been compromised.[61] The claimant argued that the technique was legitimate gamesmanship.[62] At the trial the claimant lost the case, with Mitting J stating that the claimant's actions amounted in fact and law to cheating despite the claimant's belief.[63] The matter was appealed to the Civil Division of the Court of Appeal, who dismissed the appeal. Ivey subsequently appealed to the Supreme Court, where *obiter dicta* the meaning of dishonesty was considered. Ivey's appeal was once again dismissed, but the test for dishonesty was reformulated.

---

57 Law Commission, *Fraud* (Law Com No 276, 2002) para 5.5.
58 Law Commission, *Fraud* (Law Com No 276, 2002) para 5.18.
59 [2017] UKSC 67.
60 [2017] UKSC 67.
61 *Ivey v Genting Casinos (UK) Ltd t/a Crockfords* [2017] UKSC 67, [26].
62 *Ivey v Genting Casinos (UK) Ltd t/a Crockfords* [2017] UKSC 67, [27].
63 *Ivey v Genting Casinos (UK) Ltd t/a Crockfords* [2017] UKSC 67, [27].

Thinking points:

- The decision in *Ivey* was made in the context of a civil appeal case. Why might this be problematic for criminal law?

Deciding the criminal test for dishonesty in a civil case may be problematic on a theoretical level. The theoretical underpinning of criminal law differs from that of civil law. For example, criminal law aims to punish criminal behaviour and deter future wrongdoing. Civil law on the other hand aims to compensate for the loss suffered. Thus, with such different objectives it could be claimed that a civil case was not the right forum to establish the test for dishonesty for use in criminal offences.

On a practical level, as *Ivey* was a civil case about cheating, there was not the opportunity during the appeal hearing for legal debate on the merits of retaining the *Ghosh* test for dishonesty. The decision was made to reformulate the test for dishonesty, which was not central to the appeal, without counsel presenting arguments on this matter.

The decision in *Ivey* has, however, meant an adoption of a standard of dishonesty that is the same in both civil and criminal law. This was the explicit intention of the court.[64] This is helpful when the same set of facts could lead to a criminal case, and a claim in civil law. It reduces the possibility of the defendant's actions being found honest in one course of action and dishonest in the other, although inconsistent outcomes are still possible due to the differing standards of proof. Nonetheless, this consistency between civil and criminal law in the definition of dishonesty does not address that other elements of property offences have differing meanings depending on what type of action is brought. For example, the judgment in *Hinks*[65] demonstrates that receiving a gift can amount to appropriation, and thus theft, under section 1 of the Theft Act 1968. Lord Steyn, in the majority in *Hinks*, acknowledges, however, that this conflicts with principles of civil law.[66] Another example can be seen in the criminal offence of burglary under section 9 of the Theft Act 1968. This requires that a person enters a building, or part of a building, as a trespasser. The person cannot later become a trespasser for the purposes of burglary in an area they have entered lawfully.[67] This can be compared with the tort of trespass where a person can later become a trespasser under the doctrine of *ab initio*.[68] Legal guidance from the Crown Prosecution Service clearly states "[t]he civil doctrine of '*trespass ab initio*' . . . does not apply in criminal law".[69] Therefore, while there may be consistency between civil and criminal law in the definition of dishonesty, there remains clear distinctions in other elements of property offences, which has the ability to undermine the benefit of having a standard dishonesty definition.

As *Ivey* was a civil case, it would normally only be persuasive in future criminal cases. The appeal to the Supreme Court asked three questions: (1) the meaning of the concept of cheating in gambling, (2) the relevance to it of dishonesty, and (3) the proper test for dishonesty if such is an essential element of cheating.[70] The court held that dishonesty was not a relevant element for cheating and therefore had no reason to consider the third question. Accordingly, the discussion of dishonesty was *obiter dicta*. Again, this would normally only hold persuasive authority for future cases. The Supreme Court, however, made it clear that this was the definition of dishonesty to be adopted in future criminal cases. This left the law in a state of uncertainty, when it was unclear

64 *Ivey v Genting Casinos (UK) Ltd t/a Crockfords* [2017] UKSC 67, [63].

65 [2001] 1 AC 241.

66 *R v Hinks* [2011] 2 AC 241, 253.

67 *R v Laing* [1995] Crim LR 395.

68 *The Six Carpenters Case* (1610) 1 SMLC 134.

69 "Theft Act Offences", 9 September 2022, www.cps.gov.uk/legal-guidance/theft-act-offences accessed, 28 November 2024.

70 *Ivey v Genting Casinos (UK) Ltd t/a Crockfords* [2017] UKSC 67, [1].

whether the lower courts would follow this persuasive precedent or follow the binding precedent in *Ghosh*. The matter was resolved in *R v Barton*,[71] when the Court of Appeal adopted the *Ivey* definition of dishonesty in a criminal case.

The first defendant, *Barton*, owned a luxury nursing home that was managed by the second defendant, *Booth*. The particulars of the case were that the defendants had targeted and befriended wealthy and vulnerable elderly residents of the nursing home to profit from them. At trial *Barton* was convicted of four counts of common law conspiracy to defraud, three counts of theft contrary to section 1 of the Theft Act 1968, one count of false accounting contrary to section 17 of the same Act, fraud contrary to section 1 of the Fraud Act 2006, and transferring criminal property contrary to section 327 of the Proceeds of Crime Act 2002. These crimes all included dishonesty as one of the elements. Booth was convicted of three counts of common law conspiracy to defraud. The trial judge directed the jury as to the *Ivey* definition of dishonesty. The defendants claimed that the *Ghosh* test for dishonesty was binding and according to the rules of precedent should have been applied.[72] The Court of Appeal in *Barton* acknowledged that "[t]he rules of precedent exist to provide legal certainty which is a foundation stone of the administration of justice and the rule of law. They ensure predictability while allowing for the development of the law in well-understood circumstances".[73] Despite this, they held that the decision in *Ivey* meant that "the ordinary rules of precedent (or *stare decisis*) have been modified . . . this limited modification is confined to cases in which all the judges in the appeal in question in the Supreme Court agree that to be the effect of the decision".[74] Thus, while the Supreme Court did not itself acknowledge in *Ivey* that they were modifying the rules of precedent, this effect has been achieved by the Court of Appeal in *Barton* by deciding to follow the *obiter dicta* statement in the civil decision of *Ivey* rather than the binding decision in *Ghosh*.

- The definition of dishonesty stated in *Ivey* is that when determining whether someone is dishonest it first must be established what the facts of the situation are as the defendant honestly believed them to be. It must then be asked whether the defendant's actions in the situation as they believed it to be, were dishonest by the standards of an honest person. Does this definition of dishonesty better uphold society's moral values?

In *Ivey*, Lord Hughes recognised that the principal objection to the second limb of the *Ghosh* test was that "the less the defendant's standards conform to what society in general expects, the less likely he is to be held criminally responsible for his behaviour".[75] He discusses the problem that people who are acting dishonestly have the capacity to persuade themselves that their actions are not wrong, and so would not be caught under the *Ghosh* definition of dishonesty.[76] As discussed above,[77] this means that defendants such as Emma, in the scenario at the start of the chapter, could avoid being found criminally liable. The removal of the second limb of the *Ghosh* test resolves this problem as there is no longer a determination of whether the defendant knows that they are dishonest by the standards of ordinary and honest people. As reiterated in *Barton*: "This results in dishonesty being assessed by reference to society's standards rather than the defendant's understanding of those standards."[78] Thus, despite the Supreme Court in *Ivey* stating that the test of dishonesty is an assessment of the

71 [2021] QB 685.
72 *R v Barton* [2021] QB 685, 692.
73 *R v Barton* [2021] QB 685, 728.
74 *R v Barton* [2021] QB 685, 728.
75 *Ivey v Genting Casinos (UK) Ltd t/a Crockfords* [2017] UKSC 67, [58]. See discussion above at Chapter 6.4.
76 *Ivey v Genting Casinos (UK) Ltd t/a Crockfords* [2017] UKSC 67, [59].
77 See Chapter 6.4.
78 *R v Barton* [2021] QB 685, 728.

defendant's state of mind,[79] it means that a person can be found criminally liable even though they do not think they have been dishonest. Lord Hughes justifies this approach by stating:

> The law does not, in principle, excuse those whose standards are criminal by the benchmarks set by society, nor ought it to do so. On the contrary, it is an important, even crucial, function of the criminal law to determine what is criminal and what is not; its purpose is to set the standards of behaviour which are acceptable.[80]

This suggests that the purpose of the law is to set a standard that reflects society's moral values. While this appears to better uphold behaviour that is deemed acceptable, this moralist view of the law[81] presumes there is a consensus as to what standards of behaviour are acceptable. By not considering the defendant's subjective state of mind, individual justice is not achieved because a person can be punished without appreciation of their own wrongdoing. This is contrary to the approach taken to assess other forms of *mens rea*.[82] These subjectively ask, for example, whether the defendant foresaw the outcome as virtually certain to infer intent, or whether the defendant foresaw an unjustified risk to establish recklessness.

The *Ivey* test for dishonesty is not, however, wholly objective. The Supreme Court stated that in determining whether the defendant has been dishonest it must first be subjectively established what the "actual state of the individual's knowledge and belief as to the facts" was.[83] The Court of Appeal in *Barton* further developed this to state that the Supreme Court was "referring to all the circumstances known to the accused and not limiting consideration to past facts . . . That will include consideration, where relevant, of the experience and intelligence of the accused".[84] Thus, unlike the concerns that were presented when a solely objective approach was taken to recklessness,[85] the law of dishonesty would not punish someone who was incapable of appreciating that their actions were dishonest.

The subjective requirement in the *Ivey* test for dishonesty is different to the subjective limb of the *Ghosh* test. This is because it is not assessing whether the defendant is aware of the standards of honesty held by ordinary people. It is instead assessing the defendant's perception of the facts of the situation they found themselves in. Thus, to give the example provided in *Ghosh*, the court justified the inclusion of the subjective limb to ensure censure would not be placed on "a man who comes from a country where public transport is free. On his first day here he travels on a bus. He gets off without paying. He never had any intention of paying. His mind is clearly honest; but his conduct, judged objectively by what he has done is dishonest."[86] This man would not know his actions were dishonest by the standards of ordinary honest people and thus he would fail the second limb of the *Ghosh* test and be found not guilty. Applying the *Ivey* test for dishonesty, this man could still avoid criminal liability as he had made a mistake to the facts, honestly believing no payment was due. Judging his actions by the standards of an honest and reasonable person in this situation, he is still likely to not be deemed dishonest. Thus, the subjective limb of the *Ghosh* test, which allows those whose moral values are divergent from the rest of society, is not needed to protect those such as the man on the bus in the stated scenario.

79 *Ivey v Genting Casinos (UK) Ltd t/a Crockfords* [2017] UKSC 67, [60].
80 *Ivey v Genting Casinos (UK) Ltd t/a Crockfords* [2017] UKSC 67, [59].
81 See Chapter 1.3.1.
82 See Chapter 5.
83 *Ivey v Genting Casinos (UK) Ltd t/a Crockfords* [2017] UKSC 67, [74].
84 *R v Barton* [2021] QB 685, 730.
85 See Chapter 5.5.
86 *R v Ghosh* [1982] QB 1053, 1063.

Given the same outcome is achieved in practice, it appears there is little difference between the *Ghosh* and *Ivey* test. This, however, is not so. Returning to the scenarios at the start of the chapter, the change in the definition of dishonesty is unlikely to have any impact on the outcome of the case against Dominic. The question was, and remains, whether an ordinary and honest person would think taking and keeping the notepad was dishonest. The *Ivey* test requires that it is first established what the facts of the situation are as the defendant believed them to be. Therefore, if Dominic had mistakenly thought the notepad was his, or that it was complimentary for employees, he would not be dishonest. This reflects the provisions in section 2 of the Theft Act 1968.[87] In relation to Emma, the situation changes. She can no longer claim that she thought her actions of taking £10 from her friend were honest. She knows that she does not have her friend's consent to take the money, and thus her actions would be judged against the standards of an honest and ordinary person with this knowledge. Consequently, a person can make an honest mistake about the facts of the situation they find themselves in, but their own assessment of society's required standards of honesty will not be the decisive factor.[88] Thus, it could be argued that the *Ivey* test does bring the law more in line with society's moral values. Furthermore, it achieves the policy aim of deterrence, by not enabling people to avoid liability due to their misguided notion of what others would find acceptable.

While Lord Hughes in his judgment in *Ivey* identified several problems with the second limb of the *Ghosh* test,[89] the court did not give consideration of the problems caused by the first objective limb of the test. As discussed above, the concept of what is dishonest by the standards of an ordinary and honest person can be problematic.[90] Removing the second limb of the *Ghosh* test means that the focus is now solely on the objective assessment, which could further exacerbate the identified issues. Therefore, while the definition of dishonesty may now better uphold society's moral values, what will be deemed honest remains ambiguous.[91]

6.6 Conclusion

Dishonesty is an essential element in property offences that provides the dividing line between conduct that will be considered criminal and non-criminal. Despite the high volume of offences committed requiring dishonesty, the concept has not been defined by Parliament. While section 2 of the Theft Act 1968 sets out circumstances when the defendant will not be deemed dishonest, beyond that the jury is left to make a moral judgment of the defendant's actions. In directing the jury on how to do this the courts have tried to achieve a delicate balance. Treading a fine line between not convicting those who are incapable of determining what is honest or genuinely but mistakenly thinking they were acting honestly, and ensuring that the standards of honest and reasonable people in society are upheld. The *Ivey* test addresses the concerns raised by the subjective limb of the *Ghosh* test. It brings the law more in line with moral values and aligns the definition of dishonesty in both civil and criminal law. As such, it provides a greater deterrence against acting dishonestly. It sets an objective-based standard for determining dishonesty but leaves unanswered the unanswerable question of what a reasonable and ordinary person would deem is honest.

---

87 See Chapter 6.3 above for a discussion of the provisions set out in section 2 of the Theft Act 1968.

88 See David Ormerod and Karl Laird, "The Future of Dishonesty – Some Practical Considerations" [2020] 6 Arch Rev 8, 9–10, who discuss that the defendant's belief as to the accepted standards of dishonesty could be a relevant circumstance in relation to subjectively assessing the defendant's belief as to the facts.

89 *Ivey v Genting Casinos (UK) Ltd t/a Crockfords* [2017] UKSC 67, [57].

90 See Chapter 6.4.

91 Emily Finch, "The Elephant in the (Jury) Room: Exploring Mock Jurors' Understanding of Different Approaches to Dishonesty" [2012] Crim LR 513.

6.7 Further Reading

Finch E, "The Elephant in the (Jury) Room: Exploring Mock Jurors' Understanding of Different Approaches to Dishonesty" [2012] Crim LR 513
Griew E, "Dishonesty: The Objections to Feely and Ghosh" [1985] Crim LR 341
Ormerod D and Laird K, "The Future of Dishonesty – Some Practical Considerations" [2020] 6 Arch Rev 8
Wang B, "Mistaking Theft: Dishonesty 'Turns Over a New Leaf'" [2022] J Crim L 3

Chapter 7

Consent and the Restriction of Personal Autonomy

Chapter Contents

DOI: 10.4324/9781003408383-8

7.1 Chapter Aims and Objectives

This chapter will consider the issue of consent and the freedom of people to make their own choices about what happens to them. Consent allows an individual to give permission for the invasion of their bodily integrity. Valid consent means that actions that would otherwise be criminal are not. The issue that will be addressed is whether there should be limits on a person's autonomy to grant permission for harm against themselves, and if so, where the line for this limit should be drawn. To reach this conclusion the cases of *R v Brown*[1] and *R v BM*[2] will be considered.

By the end of this chapter, you should be able to:

- Recognise the importance of consent and when it can be used to avoid criminal liability.
- Discuss personal autonomy versus the harm principle.
- Define consent and different non-fatal offences.
- Examine how legal principle was influenced by morals and policy in the decisions of *R v Brown* and *R v BM*.
- Discuss the offence of non-fatal strangulation and suffocation.

> The issues that will be examined in this chapter can be illustrated through the following scenarios. Before starting this chapter, consider who would be entitled to the defence of consent and thus avoid criminal liability:
>
> - Andrea is disabled from the neck down. She asks her husband to help her die as she cannot bear to live anymore.
> - Barry is rushing to get to his class and pushes past Celeste in order to get to class on time.
> - Danni has always wanted to be a nurse but does not have the qualifications. She goes into a hospital in a uniform borrowed from her friend and starts treating patients.
> - Edward is playing football. He breaks one of Frank's ribs when they crash into each other when they are both going for the ball.
> - Graham and Hakam are messing around at college. Hakam is rocking on his chair while holding onto the desk for balance. Graham moves the desk, which causes Hakam to fall to the floor and break his arm.
> - Ian is found unconscious and is taken to hospital, where he is found to need surgery. The doctors operate without realising that his religion means that he would not consent to such a procedure.

7.2 The Importance of Consent

Consent is said to be morally significant as its presence can change criminal behaviour into justified actions. As such, it has been described as "morally transformative",[3] and even as "moral magic".[4] As discussed in the previous chapter, consent, or belief in consent if the victim knew the

1 [1994] 1 AC 212.
2 [2019] QB 1.
3 Alan Wertheimer, *Consent to Sexual Relations* (Cambridge University Press 2003).
4 Hedi Hurd, "The Moral Magic of Consent" (1996) 2 Legal Theory 121.

circumstances, can result in the action of appropriating property belonging to another as being honest and thus not criminal. Equally, the presence of consent has an important role to play in determining blameworthiness in sexual offences and non-fatal offences against the person.

For example, compare:

- A defendant intentionally stabs someone in an unprovoked and unwanted attack, cutting them open.
- A surgeon cuts open a patient with their consent as part of a medical procedure.

The first situation is criminal, as the person has not given consent to be wounded. The law will penalise the defendant for their invasion of the victim's right to have their bodily integrity protected. In the second situation, no crime has occurred. The patient's autonomy means that they have the right to choose to undergo an invasive medical procedure.

The lack of consent can also change otherwise non-criminal actions into a crime.

For example, compare:

- Two people over the age of 16 are having consensual sex.
- A defendant forces someone to have sex without their consent.

In the first situation, assuming the consent is valid, no crime has been committed. In the second situation, the lack of consent forms a definitional element of the offence of rape.[5] Thus, making what would otherwise be innocent actions, criminal.[6]

7.3 Personal Autonomy

Personal autonomy was defined in a speech given at the Royal Athenaeum of Paris in 1819 by Benjamin Constant as:

> the right of everyone to express their opinion, choose a profession and practice it, to dispose of property, and even to abuse it; to come and go without permission, and without having to account for their motives or undertakings. It is everyone's right to associate with other individuals, either to discuss their interests, or to profess the religion which they and their associates prefer, or even simply to occupy their days or hours in a way which is most compatible with their inclinations or whims.[7]

Personal autonomy refers to the freedom to make our own choices, and live our lives in the way we please. The question is whether this freedom is unlimited, and if not, what justifiable restrictions can be placed on our liberty.

Philosopher Berlin considered this in 1958 when delivering his inaugural lecture at the University of Oxford titled the "Two Concepts of Liberty".[8] This seminal lecture divided the notion of liberty into negative and positive freedom. Positive freedom, which Berlin rejected, is based on the premise that a person is free, or has personal autonomy, when their actions are internally

---

5 Section 1 of the Sexual Offences Act 2003.

6 See further discussion of sexual offences in Chapter 7.

7 The transcript of this speech was the essay entitled, "The Liberty of Ancients Compared with that of Moderns", 1819, https://oll.libertyfund.org/title/constant-the-liberty-of-ancients-compared-with-that-of-moderns-1819, accessed 29 November 2024.

8 See a printed version of this lecture in I Berlin, *Four Essays on Liberty* (Oxford University Press 1969).

self-directed.[9] Conversely, negative freedom holds that a person is only free to the extent that they can do what they please when unobstructed by external interference.[10] Berlin acknowledges that this freedom cannot be limitless as this would lead to "social chaos in which . . . the liberties of the weak would be suppressed by the strong",[11] but equally "there ought to exist a certain minimum area of personal freedom which must on no account be violated".[12] The problem is where this line should be drawn between allowing people to do as they please and regulating behaviour to protect the vulnerable.

The civil liberties system of law in the UK, reflects the negative concept of freedom. A person is free to do what they please so long as their actions have not been deemed illegal. To protect civil liberties and personal autonomy, as Simester states, there are limits to the criminalisation of behaviours:

> The criminal law is not a tool to be deployed wherever someone may do wrong. As a regulatory device, it is a bluntly coercive and morally loaded tool, something to be used sparingly and with care . . . It represents the most severe infringement of a person's liberty and, as such should be available only where there is clear social justification.[13]

In terms of consent, this means a person would be free to make their own decisions of what they can consent to, with minimal restriction placed upon them by the law. The right to bodily integrity enables a person to do what they want with their own body within limits, but this is not unfettered personal autonomy that could be exercised with the risk of harm to others.

7.4 Consent and the Harm Principle

One way to determine the proper place, or extent, of state interference to restrict personal autonomy is with reference to the harm principle.[14] Famously articulated by Mill, the harm principle states that there should only be external interference with personal autonomy to prevent harm to others.[15] This is distinct to legal paternalism, which allows the state to make laws based on what it deems is in a person's best interest regardless of their own wishes or desires. The harm principle suggests that if a person consents to the harm against themselves, then no wrongdoing has been caused by the harm inflicted, and so there is no justification for state interference. Mill recognises, however, that no person is always so isolated that their actions will not cause harm to others. He gives the example of a person injuring his body having an affect on the happiness of those who depend on him, of him not being able to render his services to society, and the potential for that person to become a burden to society.[16] This is not a question of morals, but a neutral judgment of whether harm has been caused to the degree that the person is permanently impaired and so will need to be maintained by the state. Feinberg, also in promoting the harm principle and rejecting legal paternalism, gives further guidance on when the state should be able to intervene. He discusses that when a person has not chosen harm voluntarily, for example, due to lack of understanding of what they are agreeing to, then they are not actually exercising free will. Therefore, state interference

9 Isaiah Berlin, *Four Essays on Liberty* (Oxford University Press 1969) 22–23.
10 Isaiah Berlin, *Four Essays on Liberty* (Oxford University Press 1969) 15–16.
11 Isaiah Berlin, *Four Essays on Liberty* (Oxford University Press 1969) 17.
12 Isaiah Berlin, *Four Essays on Liberty* (Oxford University Press 1969) 17.
13 AP Simester, JR Spencer, F Stark, GR Sullivan and GJ Virgo, *Simester and Sullivan's Criminal Law: Theory and Doctrine* (7th Edition, Hart Publishing 2022) 745.
14 See Chapter 2.3.6.
15 John Stuart Mill, *On Liberty* (first published 1859, Oxford University Press 2015) 12–13.
16 John Stuart Mill, *On Liberty* (first published 1859, Oxford University Press 2015) 78.

to prevent the harm being caused is not an infringement on personal autonomy.[17] Instead, Feinberg argues that if a person is making a fully informed, voluntary choice to have harm inflicted against themselves then the state cannot intervene. He argues that if the state could intervene: "As a principle of public policy, it has an acrid moral flavour, and creates serious risks of governmental tyranny."[18] Therefore, according to Feinberg, while there is a responsibility to ensure that the person's choices are voluntary, beyond this the state should allow people to choose how they treat their own bodies.

In opposing Mill, legal moralist Devlin states that behaviour can be criminalised for being immoral if it goes against the common good.[19] This is even when it causes no direct harm or offence. Devlin argues that this enforcement of moral principles is not a legal paternalistic approach, as it is not the law trying to dictate what is best for us. Instead, it is a utilitarian view that is trying to achieve what is best for society as a whole.[20] Therefore, the state can interfere with an individual's liberty, when necessary, as to not do so would lead to the disintegration of society.[21] This means that if causing harm to another, even with their consent, would be deemed immoral by society then the law can intervene to prevent such behaviour.

In distinction to both Mill and Devlin, Hart discusses that the law does take a paternalistic approach but that this is not based solely on morals. He states that: "The rules excluding the victim's consent as a defence to charges of murder or assault may perfectly well be explained as a piece of paternalism, designed to protect individuals against themselves".[22] He further discusses that, even though a person consents to harm, they may not know what is in their own best interest.[23] Therefore, the role of the criminal law is to protect individuals.

These differing opinions demonstrates the difficulty the law faces when trying to allow people to live their lives in the way they choose without overbearing state interference, and protecting people from harm.

7.5 Consent in Non-Fatal Offences

There is some lack of clarity about the relationship between consent and non-fatal offences. On the one hand it can be argued that as a non-fatal offence requires the unlawful causing of harm to another, the *actus reus* of the offence is not made out if the harm is caused lawfully due to consent. Alternatively, consent can be viewed as a defence to be applied separately to negate blameworthiness after it has been established that the *actus reus* and *mens rea* of the offence have been fulfilled.[24] This debate caused some consternation in *R v Brown*, as discussed below.[25]

There is also a question of whether consent must actually exist, or whether the defendant just has to believe it does. This can be split into two separate issues. First, if the victim explicitly gives consent then it has to be determined that this consent was real, non-fraudulently obtained and informed. Second, where consent has not been explicitly obtained, then it must be determined whether it can be implied from the situation and whether an honest, but unreasonable, belief that

17 Joel Feinberg, *Rights, Justice, and the Bounds of Liberty: Essays in Social Philosophy* (Princeton University Press 1980) 119.

18 Joel Feinberg, *Rights, Justice, and the Bounds of Liberty: Essays in Social Philosophy* (Princeton University Press 1980) 121.

19 Patrick Devlin, *The Enforcement of Morals* (Oxford University Press 1970) 117–118. See Chapter 1.2.1 for more discussion of natural law and Devlin.

20 Patrick Devlin, *The Enforcement of Morals* (Oxford University Press 1970) 104.

21 Patrick Devlin, *The Enforcement of Morals* (Oxford University Press 1970) 13–14.

22 HLA Hart, *Law, Liberty and Morality* (Stanford University Press 1963) 31.

23 HLA Hart, *Law, Liberty and Morality* (Stanford University Press 1963) 32–33.

24 In *R v Meachen* [2006] EWCA Crim 2414 the Court of Appeal held that in addition to the *actus reus*, the *mens rea* need to be established notwithstanding of the issue of consent.

25 See Chapter 7.5.4.5.

the consent existed is sufficient. As has been shown in the previous chapter,[26] an honest belief held by the defendant that they have consent to take property, even when this belief is unreasonable, is enough to deem that the defendant is not dishonest in relation to a theft offence.[27] The situation with non-fatal offences differs. A defendant may be able to rely on a mistaken belief that there was valid and informed consent, but, as will be examined below, this seems to depend on the situation.[28]

7.5.1 The Nature of Consent

Before consent can be considered in relation to non-fatal offences, it must be determined that when consent is given whether the consent was real. In *Burrell v Harmer*[29] the defendant was convicted of assaulting two boys aged 12 and 13 after tattooing their arms. The court held that as the boys were unable to appreciate the nature of the act their apparent express consent was no consent.[30]

The consent must also be obtained non-fraudulently. In *R v Richardson*[31] the defendant was a registered dentist who was convicted of six counts of actual bodily harm contrary to section 47 of the Offences against the Person Act 1861, after treating patients following her suspension. Section 47 requires that the defendant has caused an assault or battery that occasions actual bodily harm[32] and that they intended or where reckless as to such an assault or battery.[33] On appeal the Crown argued that Richardson's suspension meant the patients had made a mistake as to the true identity of the defendant, which negated their consent. The Court of Appeal, in rejecting this argument and allowing the appeal, stated that there had been no fraud as to the nature or quality of the acts undertaken nor to the identity of the person carrying out the treatment.[34]

This can be compared with *R v Tabassum*,[35] whose conviction for three counts of indecent assault was upheld. The defendant's deception of three women, who thought he was medically qualified for the purpose of demonstrating how to conduct a breast examination, changed the quality of the act so that there was no consent.[36] Further doubt has been placed on the extent that *Richardson* will apply following *R v Melin*.[37] The defendant was convicted of two counts of grievous bodily harm contrary to section 20 of the Offences against the Person Act 1861. The defendant caused serious harm to two women by injecting them with Botox for cosmetic purposes. Section 20 requires that the defendant has inflicted serious harm[38] or a wound,[39] with intent or recklessness as to some harm.[40] Both women claimed that their consent was dependent on their belief that the defendant had medical qualifications, something that is not a perquisite for administrating Botox injections. It was held in *Melin* the defendant's identity was inextricably linked with the claimed professional status, and therefore as the victims had been deceived as to the defendant's identity, this was a

26 See Chapter 6.3.
27 Theft Act 1968, section 2(1)(b).
28 As will be further discussed in Chapter 8, the situation again differs in for determining what amounts to consent in sexual offences.
29 [1967] Crim LR 196.
30 *Burrell v Harmer* [1967] Crim LR 196.
31 [1999] QB 444.
32 *R v Donovan* [1934] 2 KB 498.
33 *R v Savage* [1992] 1 AC 699.
34 *R v Richardson* [1999] QB 444, 450.
35 [2000] 2 Cr App R 328.
36 *R v Tabassum* [2000] 2 Cr App R 328, 337.
37 [2019] QB 1063.
38 *DPP v Smith* [1961] AC 290.
39 *C v Eisenhower* [1984] QB 331.
40 *R v Mowatt* [1967] 3 WLR 1192.

ground on which consent could be vitiated.[41] A fine distinction was made from *Richardson* whereby the defendant had deceived the patient's as to her license status with the regulatory body, not as to her medical qualifications and consequently not her identity.[42]

Thus, in the scenario at the start of the chapter, where Danni goes into a hospital in a uniform borrowed from her friend and starts treating patients without the relevant qualifications, this could amount to an offence. If she lied about her identity by actively impersonating her friend, there would be fraud as to her identity which would vitiate the consent. Even if she did not actively impersonate her friend, it could be found that holding herself out to have medical qualifications would be intrinsically linked to her identity as in *Melin*, or that the failure to have these qualifications could change the nature and quality of the acts undertaken as in *Tabassum*. Either way, consent would not operate as a defence as it would be fraudulently obtained.

R v Paterson[43] developed the law a step further. The defendant, a surgeon, was charged with 17 counts of wounding with intent under section 18 of the Offences against the Person Act 1861 and three counts of under section 20 of the same Act. He had carried out breast surgery of multiple women, which no responsible body of breast surgeons would have carried out, and he was aware of this.[44] The defendant argued that his actions fell under the medical exemption of reasonable surgical interference, which would allow a person to inflict serious harm on another.[45] The Court of Appeal refused his appeal. While the court did not directly address the question of whether the medical exception could apply, they held that his deception of exaggerating the need for surgery had meant that the consent given by the patients had been vitiated.[46] This goes beyond the decisions in *Richardson*, *Tabassum*, and *Melin*, as the defendant had not deceived the victim as to the nature or the quality of his actions, nor his identity or qualifications.

In addition to consent being real and non-fraudulent, it must also be informed. In *R v Dica*[47] the defendant appealed against his conviction for two counts of grievous bodily harm contrary to section 20 of the Offences against the Person Act 1861. He had unprotected sex with two women knowing that he had HIV, but without informing them. Both women contracted HIV. The Court of Appeal held that consent to having sex was not the same as consenting to the risk of a consequent disease.[48] Consent to the risk of HIV could not be an honest belief by the defendant inferred from consent to unprotected sex. The consent had to be willing and informed.[49]

7.5.2 The Scope of Consent

Consent is limited according to the severity of the harm committed. Consent cannot be a defence to deliberate killing of another. While suicide is no longer an offence in this country, a person can be charged under section 2(1) of the Suicide Act 1961 for aiding and abetting another's suicide.[50] Thus, in relation to the scenarios at the start of the chapter, it can be determined that despite Andrea providing consent for her husband to assist her dying, if he did so, this could still amount to an offence under section 2(1) of the Suicide Act 1961.

---

41 *R v Melin* [2019] QB 1063, 1071.

42 *R v Melin* [2019] QB 1063, 1072.

43 [2022] EWCA Crim 456.

44 *R v Paterson* [2022] EWCA Crim 456, [33].

45 See discussion below at Chapter 7.5.2.4.

46 See Mark Thomas and Samantha Pegg, "'Proper Medical Purpose': Reviewing Consent and the Medical Exemption to Offences against the Person" [2022] J Crim L 281, for an interesting discussion of whether an alternative approach could have been taken by the court.

47 [2004] EWCA Crim 1103.

48 *R v Dica* [2004] EWCA Crim 1103 [59].

49 *R v Kanzani* [2005] 2 Cr App R 14 [44]–[45].

50 *Pretty v DPP* [2001] UKHL 61.

The term non-fatal offences, however, refers to the situation when the defendant's actions or omissions have caused personal harm to the victim, short of death. There are different levels of seriousness of non-fatal offences depending on the harm caused and the *mens rea* of the defendant at the time. Contingent on the seriousness of the non-fatal offences caused, consent may be available to negate the defendant's criminal liability. This applies, even when the non-fatal offence caused by the defendant then goes on to unintentionally cause the victim's death.[51]

Consent can always be used as a defence to least serious non-fatal offences of assault and battery.[52] Both of these offences are categorised under section 39 of the Criminal Justice Act 1988 as summary offences. An assault occurs when the prosecution prove that that defendant has intentionally or recklessly caused the victim to apprehend immediate unlawful personal violence.[53] Unlike assault, battery requires contact between the defendant and the victim. It is defined as any conduct by which the defendant intentionally or recklessly applies unlawful force,[54] however trivial, upon the victim.[55] When the charge is one of assault or battery, consent need not be explicit as it can be inferred, for example, touching in the course of the jostling of everyday life.[56] Therefore, in the scenario that the start of the chapter, while Barry has most likely committed a battery against Celeste by pushing past her this may not amount to an offence. As this is not a serious offence, the defence of consent would be available. Even though Celeste has not expressly given consent, this could be implied in the jostling of everyday life.

Public policy determines that consent is not a defence to more serious non-fatal offences. As stated by the Court of Appeal in *Attorney General's Reference (No 6 of 1980)*, "it is not in the public interest that people should try to cause, or should cause, each other actual bodily harm for no good reason".[57] Therefore, a crime is committed regardless of whether the person wanted to be subjected to that harm.

There are, however, limited exceptions to this rule. As stated in *Attorney General's Reference (No 6 of 1980)*:

> Nothing which we have said is intended to cast doubt upon the accepted legality of properly conducted games and sports, lawful chastisement or correction, reasonable surgical interference, dangerous exhibitions, etc. These apparent exceptions can be justified as involving the exercise of a legal right, in the case of chastisement or correction, or as needed in the public interest, in the other cases.[58]

Adopting an approach that considers public policy, the courts have held there can be a defence of consent to actual bodily harm contrary to section 47 of the Offences against the Person Act 1861 and grievous bodily harm contrary to sections 20 and 18 of the Offences against the Person Act 1861. This is in the situations outlined in *Attorney General's Reference (No 6 of 1980)*, and other limited circumstances, as examined below.

7.5.2.1 Lawful Chastisement

Lawful chastisement is listed above in the judgment of *AG's Ref (No 6 of 1980)*, as a situation when harm can be caused to another. This is not on the grounds that the victim has consented to the

---

51 *R v Slingsby* [1995] Crim LR 570.

52 D Ormerod and K Laird, *Smith, Hogan, and Ormerod's Criminal Law* (Oxford University Press 2021) 709. Although, see *Marland v DPP* [2023] EWHC 1046 when allegedly acting under in the victim's best interest under the presumption of implied consent, did not overrule the victim's non-consent to the battery.

53 *Fagan v Commissioner of the Police of the Metropolis* [1969] 1 QB 439, 444.

54 *R v Venna* [1976] QB 421, 429.

55 *R v Nelson* [2013] 1 WLR 2861, 2863.

56 *Collins v Wilcock* [1984] 1 WLR 1172, 1177.

57 *Attorney General's Reference (No 6 of 1980)* [1981] QB 715, 719.

58 *Attorney General's Reference (No 6 of 1980)* [1981] QB 715, 719.

harm but on the basis that such behaviour was deemed acceptable for the good of the individual. Due to lawful chastisement not strictly being a typical consent-based defence, and because the applicability of the defence has changed somewhat since the statement was made in *AG's Ref (No 6 of 1980)*, the defence of lawful chastisement will be addressed first before moving onto the more central instances of when consent is raised as a defence to causing harm.

Common law has long held that parents, or a person in *loco parentis*, are entitled to administer physical punishment to their children, or children in their charge, as a means to correct the child's behaviour.[59] The common law ambiguously required that this punishment was reasonable and not excessive for the purpose.[60] Thus, the law allowed a defence to those who had inflicted harm on another.

Societal views on lawful chastisement are not, however, static. When the Government was reviewing the law in this area in 2000, it noted that a commissioned report by the Office for National Statistics Omnibus Survey in 1998 found that 88% of respondents agreed that it was sometimes necessary to smack a naughty child.[61] While there was overwhelming support to retain a defence for a person who chastised, there was little support in allowing serious harm to be caused to children. Fewer than 1% of respondents agreed that punishment was "reasonable" if it left marks and bruises which lasted for more than a few days.[62] Shortly after, in September 2003 the Government published a Green Paper on Every Child Matters, alongside its official response to the Victoria Climbié Inquiry.[63] The proposals made, included that the law should be changed to restrict the degree of harm that could be caused through lawful chastisement. This became law under section 58 of the Children Act 2004. This states that any harm, amounting to an offence under sections 47, 20 or 18 of the Offences against the Person Act 1861, will not be deemed reasonable under the defence of lawful chastisement. This did, however, mean that assault and battery could still be lawfully carried out against children.

A more recent YouGov poll published in March 2023 suggested that two thirds of the 3497 people surveyed across England thought that physically disciplining a child was not acceptable.[64] While lawful chastisement currently still provides a defence to assault and battery in England, since the enactment of the Children Act 2004 both Scotland[65] and Wales[66] have made any form of chastisement unlawful. Thus, giving children in these parts of the UK the same level of protection against an assault or battery, that they did not consent to, as would be afforded to an adult.

7.5.2.2 Sport

In situations when harm is caused during sport, the public policy aim of not allowing harm to be caused to another for no good reason needs to be weighed against the desirability and entertainment value of people participating in sport. In *R v Barnes*[67] the defendant appealed against his conviction for unlawfully and maliciously inflicting grievous bodily harm contrary to section 20 of the Offences against the Person Act 1861. During a game of football, the defendant's tackle on the victim had caused a serious leg injury. The Court of Appeal made it clear that when there had not been explicit consent to the injury, public policy would limit the defence of consent to harm that was reasonably

59 *R v Hopley* (1860) 2 F & F 202.

60 *A v UK* (1999) 27 EHRR 611.

61 Department of Health, Protecting Children, Supporting Parents (2000) 5.

62 Department of Health, Protecting Children, Supporting Parents (2000) 5.

63 Department for Education and Skills, Cm 5860 (September 2003).

64 NSPCC, "Survey Results", March 2023, https://docs.cdn.yougov.com/r174szdh2m/NSPCC_PhysicalPunishment_230302_W.pdf, accessed 5 February 2025.

65 Children (Equal Protection from Assault) (Scotland) Act 2019.

66 Children (Abolition of Defence of Reasonable Punishment) Wales Act in 2020.

67 [2005] 1 WLR 910.

implied through agreement to play the sport.[68] This suggests that a mistaken and unreasonable belief in consent would be insufficient. The court, however, allowed the appeal stating that within the realms of sport, "a criminal prosecution should be reserved for those situations where the conduct is sufficiently grave to be properly categorised as criminal".[69] This inserts a moral value judgment in assessing when a consent defence will be available. In determining whether the conduct was sufficiently grave, it had to be considered what risks the victim had consented to by agreeing to play the game. This considers matters such as the type of sport, the level at which it is played, and whether the injury had occurred within the rules of the sport.[70] As such, *Barnes* can be contrasted to the earlier case of *R v Billinghurst*,[71] when the defendant punching an opposing player and fracturing his jaw in a game of rugby, outside the rules of the game, did amount to grievous bodily harm.

Thus, referring back to the scenario at the start of the chapter where Edward is playing football and breaks one of Frank's ribs, it is likely that the defence of consent would be available. The incident occurs when they crash into each other when they are both going for the ball. Therefore, this would be considered an "on the ball" incident within the rules of the game, and is unlikely to meet the sufficiently grave threshold to be deemed criminal.

7.5.2.3 Horseplay

In the extreme example of *R v Aitkens and Others*,[72] the appeals of three defendants against their convictions for section 20 grievous bodily harm were allowed. The court held that setting the victim alight as part of a RAF celebratory party could amount to horseplay. As such, this amounted to one of the recognised exceptions of when the victim could consent to serious harm, although in this case he had not expressly done so. Similarly, in the earlier case of *R v Jones*[73] the Court of Appeal held that despite explicit consent being absent, if the defendants genuinely believed that the victims were consenting to rough and undisciplined play, then they were entitled to be acquitted even if the held belief was unreasonable.[74] Therefore, this seems to contradict the requirement of reasonableness imposed in a sporting context.

In the scenario at the start of the chapter, Graham and Hakam are messing around at college. Hakam is rocking on his chair while holding onto the desk for balance. Graham moves the desk, which causes Hakam to fall to the floor and break his arm. Graham could argue that he honestly believed he had Hakam's consent as the actions were part of their horseplay, thus absolving him of liability despite the unreasonableness of his belief (and actions). But, as was commented in *Jones*,[75] it may well be that if a jury had been given the opportunity of considering the defence of consent in such a situation, they would have had little difficulty in rejecting that the defendant did honestly believe that the victim consented to such harm.

7.5.2.4 Reasonable Surgical Interference

A person can consent to serious harm caused in the course of a surgical operation for a purpose recognised as valid by the law. An adult of sound mind can also withdraw consent to medical treatment, even if the treatment is required to preserve their life or when such a decision seems "morally repugnant".[76] But, what if the doctor honestly believes that the patient consents, when

68 *R v Barnes* [2005] 1 WLR 910, 913.
69 *R v Barnes* [2005] 1 WLR 910, 911–912.
70 *R v Barnes* [2005] 1 WLR 910, 913–914.
71 [1978] Crim LR 553.
72 [1992] 1 WLR 1006.
73 (1986) 83 Cr App R 375.
74 *R v Jones* (1986) 83 Cr App R 375, 378.
75 (1986) 83 Cr App R 375, 379.
76 *St George's Healthcare NHS Trust v S* [1998] 3 WLR 936, 957.

in fact they do not? For example, an adult with capacity can make an advance decision to refuse treatment.[77] This means that if a doctor treats this person then, in addition to any action in tort, they could be criminally liable for assault. In the scenario at the start of the chapter, Ian is found unconscious and is taken to hospital where he is found to need surgery. The doctors operate without realising that his religion means that he would not consent to such a procedure. In this situation, the doctors will not incur liability unless they are satisfied that an advance directive exists which is valid and applicable to the treatment.[78] This is a subjective judgment considering the evidence available to them. Therefore, if they honestly, but mistakenly, believe there is no withdrawal of consent, they will not face criminal liability as they are acting out of necessity. Alternatively, if the question was one of withholding or withdrawing treatment, then the doctors' belief must be an objectively reasonable one.

Even when the victim clearly consents there are limits to what surgical interference can be consented to. This is considered below in the examination of *R v BM*.[79]

R v BM

In *R v BM*[80] the defendant was a registered tattooist and body piercer convicted of three counts of grievous bodily harm with intent, contrary to section 18 of the Offences against the Person Act 1861. To be liable for this offence the prosecution must prove that the defendant caused a wound or grievous bodily harm, with the intent to cause grievous bodily harm[81] or with intent to resist or prevent the lawful apprehension or detainer of any person.[82] The defendant had openly carried out body modifications on three people with their consent. The body modifications consisted of removal of a customer's ear, removal of a customer's nipple, and splitting a customer's tongue to resemble a reptile's tongue. He appealed against the convictions on the basis that consent was an available defence. He argued that while the procedures were not medical or surgical, they should be viewed as akin to body adornment. Body adornment is widely accepted, and is a natural extension of tattooing and piercing, which do not attract criminal liability. The court dismissed the appeal, stating that body modification of this kind did not fall under the accepted categories of when a victim can consent to serious harm.

Thinking points:

- Why were the body modifications carried out in *R v BM* treated differently from cosmetic surgery?

A person can choose to undergo any number of procedures for purely cosmetic reasons. This respects the concept of personal autonomy; giving a person having the power to make their own decisions about their body. These procedures, such as breast enlargements or reductions, nose reshaping, or eyelid surgery, will often include intentionally causing grievous bodily harm. In *BM* there was evidence that the victims wanted the procedures that they had undergone. Furthermore,

---

77 Mental Capacity Act 2005, section 24.
78 Mental Capacity Act 2005, section 26.
79 [2019] QB 1.
80 [2019] QB 1.
81 *R v Belfon* [1976] 1 WLR 714.
82 *R v Morrison* (1989) 89 Cr App R 17.

under law there were no training or qualifications required to be undertaken before performing body modification procedures, and no requirement of registration with a regulatory body. This differs from cosmetic surgery where all independent clinics and hospitals that provide cosmetic surgery in England must be registered with the Care Quality Commission. Moreover, all doctors carrying out cosmetic surgery must, as a minimum, be registered with the General Medical Council. This regulation of cosmetic surgery could justify why a person is allowed to intentionally harm another. The regulation ensures the safety of those undergoing the treatment. Therefore, despite there being no regulatory measures for body modification this does not mean people should be unlimited in the harm they can cause to others.

- Why were the body modifications in *R v BM* not considered to be an extension of tattooing or ear-piercing?

It is hard to explain where the line falls between legal tattooing and piercing, compared to body modification. For example, the legal practice of stretching piercings could be deemed akin to body modification. The defendant in *BM* did not claim that he was conducting medical procedures, but that the work undertaken was an extension of his existing licensed tattooing and piercing business. In the appeal, the Court of Appeal made passing reference to *R v Wilson*.[83] In *Wilson* the defendant was successful in his appeal against a charge of actual bodily harm contrary to section 47 of the Offences against the Person Act 1861. He had branded his initials on his wife's buttocks at her request. The Court of Appeal found that despite the husband not being registered, or his activities regulated in any way, that there was no "logical difference between what the appellant did and what he might have done in the way of tattooing".[84] Moreover, the law allows for ritual circumcision to be carried out by non-medical professionals towards those who are too young to consent for themselves.[85] This would seem to be a clear example of permanent body modification. Thus, if unregulated activity such as this, and the branding in *Wilson*, can be consented to, this opens the debate as to why body modification is also not acceptable.

Lord Burnett considered this issue in the judgment of the Court of Appeal in *R v BM* when he stated:

> There is a general interest of society in limiting the approbation of the law for significant violence, albeit inflicted with consent. There is some need to protect from themselves those who have consented, most particularly because they may be vulnerable or even mentally unwell. Moreover, serious injury, even consented to, brings with it risk of unwanted injury, disease or even death and may impose on society as a whole substantial cost . . . Yet there is a need to reflect the general values of society which have long accepted tattooing and piercing (not just of ears) as acceptable . . .[86]

Thus, while society generally accepts tattooing and ear-piercing, policy dictates that people (and society as a whole) need to be protected from themselves for the above stated reasons. This is especially so when they are vulnerable or mentally unwell. This policy approach suggests that all people are unable to decide what is in their own best interest. It adopts the paternalistic approach promoted by Hart, which rejects the personal autonomy approach advocated by Mill.[87]

83 [1996] 2 Cr App R 241.
84 [1996] 2 Cr App R 241, 244.
85 *R v BM* [2019] QB 1, 12.
86 *R v BM* [2019] QB 1, 11–12.
87 See Chapter 7.4 for more discussion of Hart and Mill.

Lord Burnett claims that the law should reflect the views of society, thus inserting a moral judgment into the determination of what body modification or adornment will be acceptable. There is, however, an issue in determining what the general values of society are in an area that attracts such a wide range of views.[88] Moreover, this would mean that should body modification become increasingly popular, the courts would have to change their approach to allow such activity even if it remained unregulated by Parliament. This idea of popular morality deciding the law also means that the views and desires of the minority are ignored, and that body modification cannot be consented to even when there is no unwanted disease, injury or cost to society.

7.5.2.5 Sexual Activity

One area that has caused much debate and discussion is that of harm caused within the wider context of sexual activity. When the defendant has caused an assault or battery that was consented to during sexual activity the defendant has a defence available. This is even when the defendant's actions in committing an assault or battery then unintentionally lead to the victim's death.[89] When the defendant has caused greater harm than an assault or battery during sexual activity, consent will not automatically operate as a defence, as considered by the House of Lords in *R v Brown*.[90]

R v Brown

In *R v Brown* a group of men carried out consensual sado-masochistic activities for sexual pleasure. This included, inserting a fishhook through another's penis, branding, nailing of the other's scrotum or foreskin to a board, insertion of hot wax into the urethra, and the burning of another's penis with a candle. The defendants were charged with actual bodily harm and grievous bodily harm offences contrary to sections 47 and 20 of the Offences against the Person Act 1861. In their defence they argued that the *actus reus* of these offences was not made out due to consent. Moreover, that the Offences against the Person Act 1861 was made with the purpose of preventing people from attacking each other, not for consensual acts. Furthermore, that everyone should have the right to deal with their body as they please.[91] On appeal, the matter of general public importance that the Court of Appeal put to the House of Lords was:

> Where A wounds or assaults B occasioning him ABH in the course of a S and M encounter, does the Prosecution have to prove lack of consent on the part of B before they can establish A's guilt under section 20 or section 47 OAPA 1861?[92]

The majority in the House of Lords decided that the prosecution does have to prove lack of consent for a mere assault, but for more serious injury, consent would provide no defence unless the harm caused was for good reason. The court deemed that the satisfying of sado-masochistic desires did not constitute a good reason, and dismissing the appeals upheld the convictions.

---

88 See Chapter 1.3.1.

89 *R v Slingsby* [1995] Crim LR 570.

90 *R v Brown* [1994] 1 AC 212.

91 *R v Brown* [1994] 1 AC 212, 235.

92 *R v Brown* [1994] 1 AC 212, 230.

Thinking points:

- Lord Templeman, as part of the majority judgment, stated that policy and principle need to be considered when deciding if consent should provide a defence.[93] What policy reasons are there for denying a defence to those who willingly cause harm to each other as part of sado-masochistic activities to enhance sexual pleasure?

In a free society people should be free to choose how they live their lives, and the activities that they choose to undertake. In conflict with this is the policy consideration that people should not be able to cause each other serious injury for no good reason. In *Brown* the House of Lords were required to decide what amounted to a "good reason", and where the line should fall in restricting a person's autonomy to live their life as they please. Lord Templeman, in rejecting the defence of consent, referred to the dangers of transmitting aids. He also considered that the appellants were middle-aged men and the victims were youths. Some of which had been introduced to the sado-masochistic activities before they attained the age of sexual consent.[94] These perceived policy considerations of acting to protect the wider public health and to protect vulnerable members of society seem to have influenced Lord Templeman's decision to deny the defence.

- Lord Jauncey, as part of the majority judgment, makes many similar points to Lord Templeman. He further discusses that "the possibility of proselytisation and corruption of young men is a real danger".[95] Do you agree?

Proselytisation is the process of trying to change another's way of life or beliefs to your own. Therefore, Lord Jauncey is arguing that the defendants involved were trying to convert and corrupt young men into their way of thinking. It is somewhat naïve to suggest that a young man can be induced into deriving pleasure from homosexual sado-masochistic activities, which he had no interest or predilection for before.

Alternatively, it could be argued that these younger men, one who was allegedly 15-years-old at the time he was first approached by the defendants, did not truly desire to participate in these homosexual sado-masochistic activities. Instead, this could be viewed as a situation akin to grooming, whereby the consent given was not truly free or informed. While the defendants claimed that they never coerced anyone into participating, the evidence disclosed showed that drink and drugs were employed to obtain consent and increase enthusiasm.[96] Even considering the dictum of Mill, who promoted minimal state interference to uphold individual liberty, it can be conceded that this type of harm could justify state intervention. As Mill states, a person should be compelled to control his vices and follies that the sight or knowledge of might corrupt or mislead others.[97] Thus, the fact that the group recruited members, rather than remaining private, impacts on what state interference could be justified. Recruiting members of the public could be said to have caused indirect harm or offence to society. Moreover, Mill argues that state interference does not restrict individuality if it prevents actions that have always been condemned and are not suitable or useful to any person's individuality.[98] This interpretation requires that there is mutual agreement in society that inducing others to participate in sado-machoistic practices has always, and is still, condemned. If

93 *R v Brown* [1994] 1 AC 212, 234–235.
94 *R v Brown* [1994] 1 AC 212, 235.
95 *R v Brown* [1994] 1 AC 212, 246.
96 *R v Brown* [1994] 1 AC 212, 236.
97 John Stuart Mill, *On Liberty* (first published 1859, Oxford University Press 2015) 78.
98 John Stuart Mill, *On Liberty* (first published 1859, Oxford University Press 2015) 78–79.

this could be established, it would be imperative to not allow a defence to this type of unregulated behaviour, whereby it could be deemed only a matter of luck that no one was seriously injured.

- Lord Mustill, dissenting, argues that there is no established legal principle to state that public interest requires the penalisation of actual bodily harm inflicted for sexual gratification. He considers the role of morals in determining how the law of consent should be interpreted. What role should morals play?

As legal moralists such as Devlin[99] would deem is right, moral considerations seem to have played a role in the majority judgment. For example, at the end of Lord Templeman's judgment he states: "Society is entitled and bound to protect itself against a cult of violence. Pleasure derived from the infliction of pain is an evil thing. Cruelty is uncivilised".[100] Lord Lowry further states, "Sado-masochistic homosexual activity cannot be regarded as conducive to the enhancement or enjoyment of family life or conducive to the welfare of society".[101] Therefore, demonstrating that the defence of consent could be denied as allowing it in this situation would have conflicted with what they believed were public moral values.

Opposingly, Lord Mustill considers that just because something is considered morally unacceptable by many, does not mean it is necessarily criminal.[102] Instead, he approaches the appeal, not by asking when actual bodily harm and grievous bodily harm can be consented to, but from the starting point that these crimes can always be consented to unless there is just cause for them not to be. Consequently, while the majority in this case considered that consensual acts causing bodily harm are, *prima facie*, unlawful unless they fall within one of the exceptions recognised at common law that allow consent to be applied as a defence to negate blameworthiness, Lord Mustill took an alternative approach. He considered consent is an element of the offence, and therefore that the *actus reus* of the offence is not made out if the harm is caused lawfully due to consent. Thus, he considered that it is not for judges to determine the moral question of what behaviours are acceptable and as such provide a good reason to allow actual bodily harm and grievous bodily harm to be consented to. Instead, in allowing the appeal he argues that it is for Parliament to determine when there is no good reason for consent to negate liability.

- This leads onto a further question, of whether it is the role of judges to decide when there is good reason for consent to negate criminal liability for serious harm?

One of the pillars on which the United Kingdom's unwritten constitution is founded, is the principle of the separation of powers.[103] This states that to avoid concentration of power, and to protect individual liberty, there should be a division of power between the executive, legislature, and judiciary. In the English legal system this means that Parliament as the legislature makes the law, the executive administers the law, and the judiciary applies the law. Judicial independence requires that the judiciary is free from outside pressure or political influence in the way that it interprets and applies the law. Lord Slynn, dissenting, argued that it is not for the courts to introduce new crimes in the interests of "paternalism". In other words, it is not for the courts to make crimes just to protect individuals from themselves. This leads Lord Slynn to the conclusion that whether consent can be a defence in *R v Brown* is a question of policy "in an area where social and moral factors are

99 See above at Chapter 7.4 for more discussion of Devlin.
100 *R v Brown* [1994] 1 AC 212, 237.
101 *R v Brown* [1994] 1 AC 212, 255.
102 *R v Brown* [1994] 1 AC 212, 273.
103 Montesquieu, *L'Esprit des Lois*, book 11 (1748) ch. 6.

extremely important and where attitudes can change",[104] and as such he states: "In my opinion it is a matter of policy for the legislature to decide".[105] Thus, making it clear that in his opinion where the line should be drawn of what can be consented to is not a matter for judges. This, however, was not the opinion of the majority in the case, who did exactly that, by denying the appeal.

- Another consideration in *R v Brown* was whether judges should be able to dictate the conduct between individuals in private?

In *Attorney General's Reference (No 6 of 1980)*[106] Lord Lane stated, "in our judgment, it is immaterial whether the act occurs in private or in public; it is an assault if actual bodily harm is intended and/or caused".[107] Thus, suggesting that no distinction in criminality will be drawn between what happens in a person's private home or in public. In the later case of *R v Wilson*,[108] however, Russell LJ states: "Consensual activity between husband and wife, in the privacy of the matrimonial home, is not, in our judgment, normally a proper matter for criminal investigation, let alone criminal prosecution".[109] This suggests that matters that occur consensually between two individuals in private are not the proper domain for criminal law. So, what is the proper place for criminal law in these situations?

Lord Slynn, dissenting and allowing the appeal in *R v Brown*, stated that:

> Neither the applicants nor anyone else complained as to what was done. The matter came to the attention of the police "coincidentally"; the police were previously unaware that the accused were involved in these practices though some of them had been involved for many years. The acts did not result in any permanent or serious injury or disability or any infection and no medical assistance was required.[110]

Thus, he argued that the fact that the acts were conducted in private is of importance.[111]

Lord Lowry, also considered whether "to place a restriction on sado-masochism is an unwarranted interference with the private life and activities of persons who are indulging in a lawful pursuit and are doing no harm to anyone except, possibly, themselves".[112] In dismissing the appeal, he concluded that because the individuals were not indulging in a lawful activity to begin with, as "there is no legal right to cause actual bodily harm in the course of sado-masochistic activity",[113] the courts are not placing a restraint on the right to a private life. This reasoning seems a little circular, at best. It is claiming that the actions are illegal as the consent defence does not apply, and the consent defence does not apply as the actions are illegal. This enabled judges through their interpretation of the law to dictate the consensual conduct of adults in private.[114]

The appellants in *Brown* also asserted their right to a private life in the European Court of Human Rights.[115] The Court, however, unanimously held that the prosecution, conviction, and sentence in *R v Brown* did not contravene Article 8 of the European Convention on Human Rights.

---

104 *R v Brown* [1994] 1 AC 212, 282.
105 *R v Brown* [1994] 1 AC 212, 282.
106 *Attorney General's Reference (No 6 of 1980)* [1981] QB 715.
107 *Attorney General's Reference (No 6 of 1980)* [1981] QB 715, 719.
108 *R v Wilson* [1997] QB 47.
109 *R v Wilson* [1997] QB 47, 50.
110 *R v Brown* [1994] 1 AC 212, 281.
111 *R v Brown* [1994] 1 AC 212, 280.
112 *R v Brown* [1994] 1 AC 212, 356.
113 *R v Brown* [1994] 1 AC 212, 356.
114 See also *R v Emmett* [1999] EWCA Crim 1710.
115 *Laskey v UK* (1997) 24 EHRR 39.

Therefore, while there are numerous activities which will meet the criteria of being a good reason to cause harm to another, this does not include actual or grievous bodily harm caused for the purpose of pain during sexual activity.

7.5.3 Legislative Reform

Several years after the Judgment in *R v Brown*, Parliament has reformed the law. The Domestic Abuse Act 2021 section 70 amended the Serious Crime Act 2015. It introduced two new sections; section 75A and 75B. These created a new and specific criminal offence of non-fatal strangulation and suffocation, with a maximum sentence of 5 years. Prior to the legal change, strangulation was notoriously difficult to prosecute, given there was often no or very few physical marks. This meant that when strangulation was prosecuted, it was frequently charged as a battery rather than the more serious offence of actual bodily harm. Meaning that, following the common law, consent would be available as a defence.

The offences of non-fatal strangulation and suffocation enables a charge to be brought that has the same maximum sentence as actual bodily harm, without the same physical evidence difficulties. Under this offence consent will be no defence when the victim suffers serious harm and the defendant intended or was reckless as to serious harm. Serious harm for the purpose of this Act, is defined under section 75A(6) of the Serious Crime Act 2015 as grievous bodily harm, wounding and actual bodily harm.

Moreover, section 71 of the Domestic Abuse Act 2021 provides that consent to serious harm for sexual gratification is not a defence to charges under section 47, 20 and 18 of the Offences against the Person Act 1861. Thus, providing a legislative framework for the common law principles set out in *R v Brown*.

7.6 Conclusion

This chapter has considered the issue of consent in non-fatal offences. For consent to be valid it must be real, non-fraudulent, and informed. Establishing when these criteria will be fulfilled is not necessarily easy. Especially in medical situations, for example, as seen by the fine distinctions drawn between *R v Richardson*, *R v Tabassum*, *R v Melin*, and *R v Paterson*.

The availability of the defence also hinges on the severity of the harm caused. The defence will not be available when a person has intentionally assisted in the death of another. Non-serious harm caused by means of an assault or battery will mean that a defendant would have the defence of consent available to them. Serious harm, short of intentional death, can be consented to in certain situations as decided by statute or the courts. In these situations, personal autonomy allows an individual to choose what harm to subject themselves to without state interference. These situations, when serious harm caused will be deemed to have occurred for a good reason, includes lawful chastisement, sport, surgery, and sexual activity. Thus, what actions are morally acceptable is decided by the state.

Implied, or mistaken, consent will also be accepted to non-fatal offences. This means a defendant could avoid liability for inflicting serious harm, even when the victim has not expressly agreed to it. On the contrary, when a person has expressly agreed to serious harm, this consent may not be adequate, if the law has decided that the harm caused is not for a good reason. Thus, the defence of consent will be denied to the person who has inflicted the harm on the person requesting it. As shown in this chapter, this means that a person cannot choose to have certain body modifications, or have harm inflicted against themselves by another for sexual pleasure. In other words, desiring such serious harm, for no good reason means that the state needs to protect the person from their own choices. They lose their personal autonomy. The justification for this legal paternalism is that it protects those who are vulnerable or mentally unwell. This blanket ban on certain kinds of harm being caused, however, assumes that no one with capacity would make the choices these people have.

As the law already requires that consent is real, non-fraudulent and informed, it is questionable whether further restraints are needed to restrict what harm a person can have inflicted upon themselves. The only way this infringement of the right to personal autonomy can be explained is with reference to policy. For example, concerns about the cost to society of people requiring medical treatment, or from allowing people to maim themselves, provides a justification for not allowing people to seriously harm each other.

Ultimately, people do not have complete personal autonomy to decide what happens to their own body. Society lives under a system of legal paternalism where what is morally acceptable, or for the benefit of the majority, is decided by the state not the individual.

7.7 Further Reading

Falsetto B, "Crossing the Line: Morality, Society, and the Criminal Law" [2009] CSLR 182
Pegg S, "Not So Clear Cut: The Lawfulness of Body Modifications" [2019] Crim LR 579
Thomas M and Pegg S, "'Proper Medical Purpose': Reviewing Consent and the Medical Exemption to Offences against the Person" [2022] J Crim L 281.
Williams R, "Body Modification and the Limits of Consent to Injury" [2019] LQR 17

Chapter 8

Consent, Sexual Offences, and Strict Liability

Chapter Contents

DOI: 10.4324/9781003408383-9

8.1 Chapter Aims and Objectives

This chapter continues to consider the issue of consent, but within the context of sexual offences. There will be examination of the infamous case of R v R[1] on the subject of marital rape, followed by discussion of how the Sexual Offences Act 2003 defines consent. Finally, the interplay between consent and strict liability will be considered through the examination of R v G.[2]

By the end of this chapter, you should be able to:

- Examine how legal principle was influenced by morals and policy in the decision in R v R.
- Discuss the definition of consent within the Sexual Offences Act 2003, and compare this to the common law definition of consent provided for non-fatal offences.
- Discuss consent in cases of strict liability as seen in R v G.

The issues examined in this chapter can be illustrated through the following scenarios. Before starting the chapter, consider whether the following people are blameworthy for any potential crimes they may have committed.

- Ron and Cecil are married. Ron forces Cecil to have sex without her consent.
- Jake is asleep. His girlfriend, Monica, wakes him up by kissing him.
- Audrey is intoxicated. Nick takes advantage of this and has sex with Audrey without her consent.
- Sven impersonates a famous actor to induce women to have sex with him.
- Jenna is 15 years old and agrees to have sex with her boyfriend, Kane, who is also 15.

8.2 Consent and Sexual Offences

Chapter 7 considered the meaning of consent and when consent can act to negate blameworthiness for non-fatal offences. This Chapter continues to develop this discussion of consent by considering the relevance of consent in relation to sexual offences, and how the defence operates when the crime is one of strict liability.

First, the infamous case of R v R[3] will be considered to highlight the issues faced when defining consent in relation to sexual offences.

8.2.1 Marital Rape

R v R

In 1991, the House of Lords considered the case of *R v R*.[4] The appellant and the victim married in 1984. In 1989, as a result of matrimonial difficulties, the wife left the matrimonial home with their son and returned to live with her parents. A month later, while the

1 [1992] 1 AC 599.
2 [2008] UKHL 37.
3 [1992] 1 AC 599.
4 [1992] 1 AC 599.

parents were out, the appellant forced his way into the parents' house and attempted to have sexual intercourse with the wife against her will. The appellant pleaded guilty at trial to attempted rape contrary to section 1(1) of the Sexual Offences (Amendment) Act 1976 by having "unlawful sexual intercourse with a woman who at the time of the intercourse does not consent to it".

On appeal, the question which the court had to decide was whether the wife must be deemed by the fact of marriage to have consented, despite the wife's refusal to consent to sexual intercourse. In other words, did the marriage mean the wife provided permanent consent to sex that could not be removed while the marriage was in place.

In 1736 Sir Matthew Hale wrote, what was an accepted statement of the law:

> But the husband cannot be guilty of a rape committed by himself upon his lawful wife, for by their mutual matrimonial consent and contract the wife hath given up herself in this kind unto her husband which she cannot retract.[5]

In *R v R*, the House of Lords rejected this defence of consent and in upholding the defendant's conviction for attempted rape, overturned the principle set out by Hale.

Thinking points:

- In R v R the word "unlawful" in the Sexual Offences (Amendment) Act 1976 caused an issue. Why might this word have been problematic?

The inclusion of the word "unlawful" in the Sexual Offences (Amendment) Act 1976 suggested that there could be occasions when sexual intercourse, with a woman who at the time of the intercourse does not consent to it, can be "lawful". In the earlier case of *R v Chapman*[6] it was held that "unlawful sexual intercourse" under section 19 of the Sexual Offences Act 1956 meant "'illicit' i.e. outside the bond of marriage".[7] Thus, giving further support to Sir Matthew Hale's proposition that there could not be rape between a husband and wife. In examining the words of Hale in R v R, Lord Keith, stated:

> It may be taken that the proposition was generally regarded as an accurate statement of the common law of England. The common law is, however, capable of evolving in the light of changing social, economic and cultural developments. Hale's proposition reflected the state of affairs in these respects at the time it was enunciated. Since then the status of women, and particularly of married women, has changed out of all recognition in various ways which are very familiar and upon which it is unnecessary to go into detail. Apart from property matters and the availability of matrimonial remedies, one of the most important changes is that marriage is in modern times regarded as a partnership of equals, and no longer one in which the wife must be the subservient chattel of the husband. Hale's proposition involves that by marriage a wife gives her irrevocable consent to sexual intercourse with her husband under all circumstances and irrespective of the state of her health or how

5 Sir Matthew Hale, *Historia Placitorum Coronae* 1736 (Classical English Law Texts 1971) 629.
6 [1959] 1 QB 100.
7 [1959] 1 QB 100, 105.

> she happens to be feeling at the time. In modern times any reasonable person must regard that conception as quite unacceptable.[8]

Therefore, Lord Keith considered that the changes in society and the values held, meant that the common law needed to change. Thus, the majority moral standards of society were used to inform the judges' interpretation of the statute.[9] This led to his conclusion that "there is now no justification for the marital exception in rape".[10] As such, despite the word "unlawful" being included in the 1976 Act, the House of Lords stated that "it should be treated as being mere surplusage in this enactment".[11] Meaning that the judges had decided to interpret the Act in a way that ignored the inclusion of this word. This judicial activism can perhaps be rightly not criticised, as shortly afterwards this interpretation was reflected in parliamentary reform when the Criminal Justice and Public Order Act 1994 revised the Sexual Offences Act 1956 with the effect that the word "unlawful" was removed.

- As discussed in Chapter 2,[12] certainty and avoidance of retrospective law making are essential to the Rule of Law. *R v R* can be said to offend these principles. How might this be justified?

Prior to *R v R* it was commonly believed that a man could not be guilty of raping his wife.[13] This rule had been considered in numerous cases, whereby the courts had restricted its application. For example, in *R v Clarke*[14] the defendant was convicted of raping his wife, as the justices had previously made an order providing that the wife was no longer bound to cohabite with the husband. Thus, she had withdrawn her consent to sexual intercourse.[15] Similarly, in *R v O'Brien*[16] the courts held that a *decree nisi* signalled that the wife had withdrawn her consent, and in *R v Roberts*[17] a formal separation agreement had the same effect.[18] In *R v R* none of these previously established exceptions applied, as although the couple had separated and had talked about divorce, no formal proceedings had begun. Therefore, it could be argued that as the law stood at the time the defendant could not be guilty of rape as he had his wife's consent through marriage. In *R v Rimmington and Goldstein*[19] Lord Bingham highlighted the importance of prospective and certain law, when he stated:

> There are two guiding principles: no one should be punished under a law unless it is sufficiently clear and certain to enable him to know what conduct is forbidden before he does it;

---

8 *R v R* [1992] 1 AC 599, 616.

9 Not all of society holds this same view. A YouGov survey in 2018 showed that nearly a quarter of the population thought that sex without consent within marriage was not rape: "End Violence Against Women Coalition: Attitudes to Sexual Consent", December 2018, www.endviolenceagainstwomen.org.uk/wp-content/uploads/2018/12/1-Attitudes-to-sexual-consent-Research-findings-FINAL-1.pdf, accessed 2 December 2024.

10 *R v R* [1992] 1 AC 599, 618.

11 *R v R* [1992] 1 AC 599, 623.

12 See Chapter 2.3.3.

13 For example, see *R v Clarence* (1888) 22 QBD 23 when the proposition seems to have been accepted by the majority of judges. See also, *R v Miller* [1954] 2 QB 282, 291–292 when the defendant was convicted for the assault of his wife and not rape. The husband used force to have sex with his wife but the judge held that a wife could not refuse her consent and so even if the act was against her will it would not amount to rape.

14 [1949] 2 All ER 448.

15 *R v Clarke* [1949] 2 All ER 448, 449.

16 [1974] 3 All ER 663.

17 [1986] Crim LR 188.

18 This can be compared to *R v Sharples* [1990] Crim LR 198, when it was held that a family protection order issued under the Domestic Proceedings and Magistrates' Court Act 1978 did not infer that the wife had withdrawn her consent to sexual intercourse.

19 [2005] UKHL 63.

> and no one should be punished for any act which was not clearly and ascertainably punishable when the act was done.[20]

In concluding in *R v R* that the defendant could be guilty for the rape of his wife, it appears there is a lack of certainty in the law, and that the defendant is being convicted of something that was not a crime when the actions were undertaken. This is further demonstrated in the later case of *R v C*,[21] when in 2004 the defendant appealed against his conviction for the rape of his wife in 1970. He argued that the marital exemption for rape was not removed until 1991 in *R v R*, and thus he should not have been convicted for his actions that had been carried out 20 years earlier. The court, however, rejected his appeal.

This further raises issues under Article 7(1) of the European Convention of Human Rights, which states that "no one shall be held guilty of any criminal offence on account of any act or omission which did not constitute a criminal offence under national or international law at the time when it was committed". This was considered in *SW v UK*.[22] The European Court of Human Rights agreed with the reasoning of Lord Lane in the Court of Appeal in *R v R*, which had been approved on appeal by the House of Lords.[23] In deciding that a husband could be guilty of raping his wife, this was not creating a new offence, as the offence of rape was already established under the law.[24] Instead, the outcome was one that was reasonably foreseeable considering the development of the common law,[25] and was "removing a common law fiction which had become anachronistic and offensive".[26] Therefore, there was no breach of Article 7. Moreover,

> the abandonment of the unacceptable idea of a husband being immune against prosecution for rape of his wife was in conformity not only with the civilised concept of marriage but also, and above all, with the fundamental objectives of the Convention, the very essence of which is respect for human dignity and human freedom.[27]

The outcome in *R v C* was also justified in light of Article 7(2), which states: "This Article shall not prejudice the trial and punishment of any person for any act or omission which, at the time when it was committed, was criminal according to the general principles of law recognised by civilised nations." Applying this Article, the Court of Appeal held that:

> Article 7(2) provides ample justification for a husband's trial and punishment for the rape of his wife, according to the general principles recognised by civilised nations. Indeed, as it seems to us, it would be surprising to discover that the law in any civilised country protected a woman from rape, with the solitary and glaring exception of rape by the man who had promised to love and comfort her.[28]

Thus, while the Rule of Law requires that there is certainty and not retrospective law-making, it can be argued that the outcome of *R v R* was a predictable one when looking at the development of the

---

20 *R v Rimmington and Goldstein* [2005] UKHL 63, [33].
21 [2004] 1 WLR 2098.
22 (1995) 21 EHRR 363.
23 *R v R* [1992] 1 AC 599, 623.
24 *SW v UK* (1995) 21 EHRR 363, [41].
25 *SW v UK* (1995) 21 EHRR 363, [43].
26 R v R [1991] 2 WLR 1065, 1074.
27 *SW v UK* (1995) 21 EHRR 363, [44].
28 [2004] 1 WLR 2098, 2105.

law and changing social attitudes.[29] Furthermore, that the law had not been changed retrospectively as rape was already illegal under the Sexual Offences Act 1956 (and later amendments), all that had changed was the removal of an historic and increasingly restricted unacceptable fictional exception.

Returning to the scenarios at the start of the Chapter, when Ron forces Cecil to have sex without her consent, this would amount to an offence of rape under section 1 of the Sexual Offences Act 2003. He rightly would not be able to rely on the existence of the marriage to provide a defence.

8.2.2 Consent and the Sexual Offences Act 2003

In Chapter 7 it was identified that consent in relation to non-fatal offences could be seen as an additional element to consider after the *actus reus* and *mens rea* of the offence had been established.[30] In sexual offences, consent is relevant to establishing both *actus reus* and *mens rea* of the offences set out in sections 1 to 4 of the Sexual Offences Act 2003. This Act took huge strides to updating the law of sexual offences. For example, by acknowledging that rape could occur through penetration of the mouth or anus in addition to the vagina, and that body parts referred to throughout the Act include those that have been surgically constructed.[31] The Sexual Offences Act 2003, section 1 defines the offence of rape, section 2 provides for assault by penetration, section 3 sets out sexual assault, and section 4 proscribes causing a person to engage in sexual activity without consent. In these sexual offences, the victim has to not consent, which forms part of the *actus reus*. Additionally, the defendant has to reasonably believe that the victim does not consent, which forms part of the *mens rea*. This takes a qualified objective approach to assessing the defendant's *mens rea*. It considers whether the defendant's belief is reasonable having regard to all the circumstances, including any steps taken to ascertain whether there is consent. This means that the defendant is not judged against what a reasonable person would do, but the defendant's belief must be reasonable in the circumstances known to them.

Prior to the Sexual Offences Act 2003 in the Government review, Setting the Boundaries: Reforming the Law on Sexual Offences,[32] there was acknowledgement of the conflicting views of whether a subjective or objective approach should be taken in assessing whether there was consent, with reference to the divided approach taken in other common law jurisdictions.[33] Numerous policy considerations were weighed against each other to come to the recommendation that there should be a reasonable belief in consent. These included considering that a subjective approach would ensure that the law did not punish people just for what they did but for what they intended to do, and whether it was correct to apply an objective standard to a defendant for a serious crime who may not have the capacity to appreciate that there was no consent.[34] This was contrasted to not wanting to undermine sexual autonomy of an individual who should be able to say no and for it to mean no, and acknowledges that this is a situation where it is easy to seek consent and that the cost to the victim of forced penetration is very high.[35] The adoption of an objective approach was a change from the previous law.[36] It also contrasts to the approach to consent taken in section 2(1)(b) of the Theft Act 1968[37] and to consent in horseplay, which take

29 For an illuminating discussion of how this change was brought about, see Maddy Travis and Katie Hunt, "The Road to *R v R*: How Feminist Campaigners Abolished the Marital Rape Exemption" [2024] Crim LR 154.

30 See Chapter 7.5.

31 See Jennifer Temkin and Andrew Ashworth, "The Sexual Offences Act 2003: (1) Rape, Sexual Assaults and the Problems of Consent" [2004] Crim LR 328, for a detailed discussion of the changes made.

32 Home Office, *Setting the Boundaries: Reforming the Law on Sexual Offences*, vol. 1 (Home Office 2000).

33 Home Office, *Setting the Boundaries: Reforming the Law on Sexual Offences*, vol. 1 (Home Office 2000) 2.13.3.

34 Home Office, *Setting the Boundaries: Reforming the Law on Sexual Offences*, vol. 1 (Home Office 2000) 2.13.6.

35 Home Office, *Setting the Boundaries: Reforming the Law on Sexual Offences*, vol. 1 (Home Office 2000) 2.13.7.

36 *DPP v Morgan* [1976] AC 182.

37 See Chapter 6.3.

a subjective approach to consent.[38] Under the Sexual Offences Act 2003, this means that if the defendant makes a mistake about whether the victim is consenting, this mistake would need to be reasonable. A genuine belief would not be sufficient.[39] The courts have demonstrated their adherence to this objective approach, for example, in *R v M(M)*[40] when the defendant's bi-polar disorder could not be used to render an objectively manifestly unreasonable belief in consent as reasonable in the circumstances.[41] This is in stark contrast to the subjective direction taken to the *mens rea* requirements of intention and recklessness that establish criminal blameworthiness in a range of other offences.[42] It does, however, reflect the policy aims of public protection trying to be achieved within the Sexual Offences Act 2003.

The Sexual Offences Act 2003 also introduced a legislative definition of consent for sexual offences. The broadly phrased section 74 of the Act states that a person consents if he agrees by choice, and has the freedom and capacity to make that choice. Little further guidance is given as to what this means in the explanatory notes accompanying section 74 of the Act. These simply state: A person might not have sufficient capacity because of his age or because of a mental disorder. There is no further guidance as to the form consent must take or when consent must occur. In case law it has long been established that submission is not the same as consent,[43] and where the victim consents reluctantly the matter of consent should still be put to the jury to decide whether there was actual consent.[44] The operation of section 74 can be seen in *R v Lawrance*.[45] A lie about fertility was not sufficiently closely connected to the performance of sexual intercourse so as to be able to negate consent under section 74 of the Sexual Offences Act 2003. Consent can, however, be negated if the defendant fails to meet the conditions that the consent was based on, for example, the use of a condom.[46] Consent can also be negated if the defendant deceives the victim as to their gender.[47] Again, the Act offers little guidance on these situations of deception, which fall outside of the remit of section 76, as discussed below.

Section 74 applies after it has first been considered whether there are any evidential or conclusive presumptions about consent under sections 75 and 76 of the Sexual Offences Act 2003.

Section 75(2) of the Sexual Offences Act 2003 sets out the circumstances in which it is presumed that the victim has not consented. The presumption applies unless the defendant can provide sufficient evidence to raise an issue as to whether the victim did consent or whether the defendant reasonably believed that they did. As stated in *R v Ciccarelli*, this means that before the issue of consent can be left to the jury, "some evidence beyond the fanciful or speculative had to be adduced to support the reasonableness of his belief in her consent".[48]

The circumstances in which it is presumed the victim has not consented are that:

(a) any person was, at the time of the relevant act or immediately before it began, using violence against the complainant or causing the complainant to fear that immediate violence would be used against him;
(b) any person was, at the time of the relevant act or immediately before it began, causing the complainant to fear that violence was being used, or that immediate violence would be used, against another person;

38 See Chapter 7.5.2.3.
39 *R v B (MA)* 1 Cr App R 36, [36].
40 [2011] EWCA Crim 1291.
41 *R v M(M)* [2011] EWCA Crim 1291, [50].
42 See Chapter 5.
43 *R v Olugboja* [1981] 3 All ER 443.
44 *R v W* [2015] EWCA Crim 559.
45 [2020] EWCA Crim 971.
46 *Assange v Swedish Prosecution Authority* [2011] EWHC 2849.
47 *R v McNally* [2013] EWCA Crim 1051.
48 *R v Ciccarelli* [2012] 1 Cr App R 15, 194.

(c) the complainant was, and the defendant was not, unlawfully detained at the time of the relevant act;
(d) the complainant was asleep or otherwise unconscious at the time of the relevant act;
(e) because of the complainant's physical disability, the complainant would not have been able at the time of the relevant act to communicate to the defendant whether the complainant consented;
(f) any person had administered to or caused to be taken by the complainant, without the complainant's consent, a substance which, having regard to when it was administered or taken, was capable of causing or enabling the complainant to be stupefied or overpowered at the time of the relevant act.

This is a finite list, which leads to some consternation. For example, section 75(2)(a) includes that if violence was used against the victim, this would amount to a rebuttable presumption against consent. This suggests there are situations when a person can give valid consent despite being subjected to violence. On the contrary, *R v Brown*,[49] and its consolidation in section 71 of the Domestic Abuse Act 2021, suggest that violence beyond assault and battery in sexual activity cannot be consented to. Therefore, if, as discussed in Chapter 7,[50] violence in sex is undesirable in both morals and policy, this presumption needs to be more stringently phrased or treated as a conclusive presumption where the violence exceeds assault or battery.

Section 75(2)(a) also covers causing the victim to fear that immediate violence would be used against them. In considering this as compared to the offence of assault this raises further questions. For a charge of assault the victim does not need to be in fear, they just have to apprehend violence.[51] Section 75(2)(a) takes a narrower approach. Therefore, actions that could amount to an assault would not necessarily lead to a presumption against consent. Furthermore, the section specifies that there must be a fear of immediate violence. The requirement of immediacy has been interpreted widely for the offence of assault, as meaning some time not excluding the immediate future,[52] but this definition of immediacy has not been adopted in the statutory language of section 75(2)(b). Thus, again, providing a narrower definition in the Sexual Offences Act 2003 than that found for the offence of assault.

Equally problematic is the inclusion of the complainant being asleep or unconscious as a rebuttable presumption under section 75(2)(d). This places sleep with being unconscious, when they are two very different states. A person can normally be easily awoken from sleep but not unconsciousness. Thus, a person in a state of unconsciousness is far more vulnerable than a person who is asleep, as they cannot regain consciousness to withdraw consent. As this is a rebuttable presumption, this also suggests that there can be occasions when a person could consent while not conscious. This seems absurd as it is clearly impossible to provide instantaneous consent if unconscious. The only logical explanation, is that the law deems a person can provide prior, or ongoing, consent. This, however, undermines the concept of personal autonomy, and as Lady Hale states: "One does not consent to sex in general. One consents to this act of sex with this person and this time and in this place."[53] An alternative, would be to adopt the approach taken in Scotland. Section 14(2) of the Sexual Offences (Scotland) Act 2009 states that a person is incapable of consenting to any conduct while asleep or unconscious. This suggests that Scotland has a conclusive presumption regarding the lack of consent when a person is asleep. Thus, making it easier to establish that an offence has been committed.

---

49 *R v Brown* [1994] 1 AC 212. See Chapter 7.5.4.5.
50 See Chapter 7.5.4.5.
51 *R v Lamb* [1967] 2 QB 981.
52 *R v Constanza* [1997] 2 Cr App R 492.
53 *R v Cooper* [2009] UKHL 42, [27].

In the scenario at the start of the chapter, Monica wakes up Jake by kissing him. The action of kissing him could amount to an offence of sexual assault under section 3 of the Sexual Offences Act 2003. This requires an intentional touching of another person, that the touching is sexual, that the other person does not consent to the touching, and the defendant does not reasonably believe that the other consents. If Jake claimed that he did not consent to being awoken this way, it would need to be considered whether the presumption under section 75(2)(d) of the Sexual Offences Act 2003 was rebutted. Monica would have to raise evidence to show that Jake was either not asleep and consented, or that she reasonably believed that Jake consented. If she was unsuccessful, the presumption would apply and she could be found guilty. If she successfully raises evidence to put the issue of consent into dispute, the jury would be left to decide under section 74 whether Jake agreed by choice, and has the freedom and capacity to make that choice. This then raises a question of the timing of the consent.[54] Jake will not have the capacity to consent while asleep, but if he has requested before he falls asleep to be awoken in this manner or is regularly awoken in this manner without complaining, can Monica rely on this previous express or implied consent? The words from Lady Hale in *R v Cooper* suggest that this will not amount to actual consent. Therefore, it will be a question for the jury to decide whether it amounts to Monica having a reasonable belief that Jake consents, having regard to all the circumstances.

As a final example of some of the issues raised by the evidential presumptions, section 75(2)(f) provides a presumption against consent when the victim is involuntarily intoxicated. Many cases considering whether the victim has consented relate to capacity to consent when the victim is voluntarily intoxicated. In this situation, the matter of whether the victim consented is left to the jury to decide with direction on whether the self-induced intoxication meant that the victim had the capacity to make a choice under section 74.[55] This includes situations short of the victim being unconscious but when the victim cannot remember if they consented or not.[56] The defendant is under an obligation to assess the validity of the consent, even when it has been expressly given.[57] When the victim has had alcohol or drugs administered to them without their consent, the defendant has the burden of producing evidence to raise the issue that the victim did consent to the sex or sexual activity. Temkin and Ashworth criticise the distinction between voluntarily and involuntary intoxication, stating that it introduces a moral standard into the concept of consent.[58] In other words, it could be perceived, and by the wider public such a perception is held, that a victim who drinks is partly to blame for the resulting sexual offence committed against them.[59] Consequently, the categorising of one situation under section 74 and one under 75, despite the victim perhaps having the same (in)ability to consent to the sexual activity, makes moral judgment on the blameworthiness of the victim and therefore the culpability of the defendant.

In the scenario stated at the start of the chapter, Nick takes advantage of Audrey's intoxicated state to have sex with her without her consent. The presumption in section 75(2)(f) means that it will be presumed that Audrey did not consent if she is involuntarily intoxicated. It does not need to be shown that the intoxicant caused Audrey to be stupefied or overpowered at the time of the relevant act, only that the substance given was capable of engendering this effect. This would place the burden on Nick to raise evidence to show that Audrey did consent, or that he reasonably believed that she did. The matter would become further complicated if Audrey had willingly been

---

54 For an interesting discussion of this issues, see Paul Jarvis, "The Timing of Consent" [2019] Crim LR 394.

55 *R v Bree* [2007] EWCA Crim 804.

56 *R v Hysa* [2007] EWCA Crim 2056.

57 This echoes the law relating to dishonesty in property offences when the defendant is given a gift under section 2(1)(b) of the Theft Act 1968. As considered in Chapter 6.3 the defendant in this situation is also under an obligation to assess the validity of the consent.

58 Jennifer Temkin and Andrew Ashworth, "The Sexual Offences Act 2003: (1) Rape, Sexual Assaults and the Problems of Consent" [2004] Crim LR 328, 339–340.

59 Bethany Simpson, "Why Has the Concept of Consent Proven So Difficult to Clarify" [2016] J Crim L 97, 110–117.

consuming an intoxicant and then had her drink spiked. In this situation, applying the wording of section 75(2)(f), that requires a substance to be administered, it could be assumed that the presumption would still apply. If, however, Audrey has chosen to become intoxicated, the presumption will not apply. Then the prosecution will have to establish beyond reasonable doubt that Nick did not reasonably belief that Audrey consented, using the definition of consent under section 74. Without the evidentiary presumption, this may make it harder to achieve a conviction.

Section 76 of the Sexual Offences Act 2003 sets out the very limited conclusive (non-rebuttable) presumptions about consent that exist in England and Wales:

> (1) If in proceedings for an offence to which this section applies it is proved that the defendant did the relevant act and that any of the circumstances specified in subsection (2) existed, it is to be conclusively presumed –
> (a) that the complainant did not consent to the relevant act, and
> (b) that the defendant did not believe that the complainant consented to the relevant act.
>
> (2) The circumstances are that –
> (a) the defendant intentionally deceived the complainant as to the nature or purpose of the relevant act;
> (b) the defendant intentionally induced the complainant to consent to the relevant act by impersonating a person known personally to the complainant.

The courts have made it clear that section 76(2)(a) will only apply in rare cases, when the defendant has deceived the victim as to the nature or purpose of the act committed rather than the surrounding circumstances that the act took place under.[60] This restrictive approach reflects the common law in *Tabassum*,[61] when the victims had been deceived as to the purpose of the act. The courts have made it clear that the word "purpose" under section 76(2)(a) should have a narrow interpretation.[62] This narrow approach means that if a person has consensual unprotected sex with another, without informing them of any sexually transmitted disease they have, this would not fall under the section 76(2)(a) conclusive presumption.[63] Thus, while sexually transmitting a disease in this manner could amount grievous bodily harm,[64] as the harm caused would not be consensual, it would not necessarily make the actions that led to the transmission of the disease criminal. Unlike the approach taken by the House of Lords in *R v Brown*,[65] the Court of Appeal considered in *R v B* that this was a matter of public and social policy that impacts personal autonomy in relationships. The court thereby concluded that as such, this required public debate outside a court of law.[66]

Section 76(2)(b) seems to have an even more restrictive approach. Deception as to identity on its own will not suffice. The wording of the Act means that the defendant has to intentionally cause the victim to consent through their impersonation, showing a high *mens rea* requirement and the need to establish a causal link. Moreover, the requirement that the person being impersonated is personally known to the victim makes it hard to think of many circumstances when this section would apply. Thus, this appears to be a more restrictive approach than that taken in *R v Melin*[67] for non-fatal offences, which held that not knowing a person's medical qualifications, even when not required for the procedure being undertaken, would amount to a deception as to identity.[68]

---

60 *R v Jheeta* [2007] EWCA Crim 1699, [24].
61 [2000] 2 Cr App R 328. See Chapter 7.5.1.
62 *R v Bingham* [2013] 2 Cr App R 29, [19].
63 *R v B* [2007] 1 WLR 1567.
64 *R v Dica* [2004] EWCA Crim 1103.
65 See Chapter 7.5.4.5.
66 *R v B* [2007] 1 WLR 1567, 1571–1572.
67 [2019] QB 1063.
68 See Chapter 7.5.1.

Thus, in the scenario at the start of the chapter, when Sven impersonates a famous actor to induce women to have sex with him, it is unlikely that the conclusive presumption under section 76(2)(b) will apply. It would have to be shown that his claimed fame was the cause of the women having sex with him. Assuming the normal rules of causation applied, the alleged fame would not need to be the sole factor but would have had to significantly contributed to the women's decision to consent to sex. Moreover, it would need to be shown that Sven was personally known to the women. It is unclear what "personally known" equates to, but assumingly if the women knew Sven well they would be less likely to believe that he was a famous actor. If they did not really know him, which would make the deception easier to pull off, then the section would not apply.

This limited approach to section 76 ensures that the defendant is provided with some protection from a provision which could be overly punitive, while still providing a measure of justice to the victim who can rely on section 74 if section 76 does not apply. Therefore, it can be concluded that this compromise, while not entirely satisfactory, achieves a balance.

8.3 Sexual Offences and Strict Liability

As discussed in Chapter 2,[69] the maxim *actus reus non facit reum nisi mens sit rea* requires that the prosecution prove the defendant has both the *actus reus* and *mens rea* for the crime with which they are charged.[70] This is especially true for more serious offences when a person's liberty could be at stake. Crimes of strict liability, however, do not require the prosecution to prove *mens rea* for one or more aspects of the *actus reus*.[71] These crimes tend to be regulatory in nature, and can be justified through the aim of raising standards in areas of social concern.[72] Generally, these offences are created through acts of Parliament, although sometimes the courts are left to interpret the provisions of the Act to determine if the crime is one of strict liability.[73] In this situation, the courts start with the presumption that *mens rea* is required.[74] This presumption can be rebutted, for example, when it is of clear or necessary implication to give effect to the statute.[75] The Sexual Offences Act 2003, despite dealing with serious offences, rather than those of a more regulatory nature, does create crimes of strict liability.

The Sexual Offences Act 2003 provides for a number of sexual offences against children. For example, sections 5 to 8 of the Act deal with rape and other offences against children under 13, and sections 9 to 15 regulate child sex offences. These offences consider the age of the victim in relation to the requirements of the offence as it is deemed that a child cannot consent to sexual activity even if they appear to desire it. Thus, like with the rules relating to consent for serious injury,[76] a legal paternalistic approach is adopted to protect those who are vulnerable. While the actions undertaken need to be done with the requisite *mens rea* for the differing offences, liability is strict in regard to the victim's age when they are under 13. This means that if the defendant intentionally has sex with a child who is between the age of 13 and 15 they can avoid liability if they reasonably believed the victim was over the age of 16 and thus of an age of being able to consent. If, however, the defendant has sex with a child who is under 13, then regardless of what age they believed the child to be, and

---

69 See Chapter 2.3.4.

70 *R v Woolmington* [1932] UKHL 1.

71 See Chapter 14.3 for more discussion of Corporate Liability for strict liability offences.

72 For example, section 5A of the Road Traffic Act 1988 legislates against driving or being in charge of a motor vehicle with a concentration of specified controlled drug above the specified limit. This section aims to improve road safety by deterring potential drug drivers.

73 *Gammon (Hong Kong) Ltd v Attorney General of Hong Kong* [1985] 1 AC 14.

74 *Sweet v Parsley* [1970] AC 132.

75 For example, see *Pharmaceutical Society of GB v Storkwain* [1986] 2 All ER 635; *James and Son Ltd v Smee* [1955] 1 QB 78; *Sheppard and Sheppard* [1981] AC 394.

76 See the conclusion drawn in Chapter 7.6.

regardless of what age they are themselves, they would be guilty of an offence that has the maximum penalty of life imprisonment. Such a situation is demonstrated in *R v G*.[77]

R v G

In *R v G* the defendant was a 15-year-old boy who had sex with a 12-year-old girl. The girl had reported the incident to her friends saying that she had not wished to partake in the sexual activity. The matter was brought to the police's attention and the defendant was charged with rape of a child under 13 under section 5 of the Sexual Offences Act 2003. This section states that a person commits an offence if (a) he intentionally penetrates the vagina, anus, or mouth of another person with his penis, and (b) the other person is under 13. The victim later changed her story and stated that she had agreed to have sexual intercourse and that she had told the defendant that she was 15 years old. The defendant pled guilty to rape of a child under 13, contrary to section 5 of the Sexual Offences Act 2003. He was sentenced to a 12-month detention and training order. The defendant appealed to the Court of Appeal against his conviction and sentence. His appeal against his conviction was dismissed but the appeal against his sentence was successful and it was reduced to a 12-month conditional discharge.

The Court of Appeal certified two questions as being of general public importance, namely:

(i) Whether a criminal offence of strict liability could violate the right to a fair trial under the European Convention on Human Rights, article 6(1) or article 6(2) and
(ii) Was it compatible with a child's right to respect for a private and family life under the European Convention on Human Rights, article 8, to convict him of rape contrary to section 5 of the Sexual Offences Act 2003, in circumstances where the agreed basis of the plea established that his offence fell properly within the ambit of section 13 (child sex offences committed by children or young persons).

On a majority of three to two, the House of Lords respectively answered the certified questions "no" and "yes", and dismissed his appeal.

Thinking points:

- Counsel for the defendant in *R v G* argued that the creation of strict liability would always engage a consideration of article 6(2) of the European Convention on Human Rights. This article states that everyone charged with a criminal offence shall be presumed innocent until proven guilty according to the law. The House of Lords in *R v G* found that there was no breach of the right to a fair trial under article 6(2). Why was this?

As discussed in Chapter 2,[78] justice is a fundamental principle of criminal law. The idea of substantive justice considers the content of the law, whereas procedural justice is about ensuring the methods adopted to administer justice are fair and impartial. In *R v G*, Lord Hoffman identified that article 6(2) "does not say anything about what the mental or other elements of the offence should

77 [2008] UKHL 37.
78 See Chapter 2.3.1.

be".[79] Therefore, he concluded that article 6 referred only to procedural justice.[80] Consequently, section 5 of the Sexual Offences Act 2003 being a crime of strict liability did not breach article 6. Lord Hope further considered that offences of strict liability will not breach article 6(2) "as long as the prosecution bears the burden of proof of all the elements that constitute the offence".[81] In *R v G* the prosecution had the burden of proving that the defendant had intentionally had sex with a child under 13, and so it could not be claimed that imposition of strict liability had led to a reversal of the presumption of innocence.

- The House of Lords were, however, divided in their judgment regarding the application of article 8 of the European Convention of Human Rights. Why was the application of this article divisive?

Article 8 states:

1 Everyone has the right to respect for his private and family life, his home and his correspondence.
2 There shall be no interference by a public authority with the exercise of this right except such as is in accordance with the law and is necessary in a democratic society in the interests of national security, public safety or the economic well-being of the country, for the prevention of disorder or crime, for the protection of health or morals, or for the protection of the rights and freedoms of others.

The argument was not being made that the law should not interfere when children are having sexual relations in the privacy of their own home. What instead was being argued was that by not reducing the charge to one of section 13 of the Sexual Offences Act 2003, when the victim changed her story to say that she had agreed to the sexual intercourse, was an unnecessary interference under article 8. In *R (S) v Director of Public Prosecution*,[82] when again a 15-year-old boy had sex with a 12-year-old girl, the prosecution did abandon the charge under section 5 of the Sexual Offences Act 2003 and replaced it with section 13.

Section 13 of the Act legislates against child sex offences committed by children or young persons. It states: (1) A person under 18 commits an offence if he does anything which would be an offence under any of sections 9 to 12 if he were aged 18.

The actions of the defendant in *R v G* would have fallen under section 9, sexual activity with a child, which states:

(1) A person aged 18 or over (A) commits an offence if –
  (a) he intentionally touches another person (B),
  (b) the touching is sexual, and
  (c) either – (i) B is under 16 and A does not reasonably believe that B is 16 or over, or (ii) B is under 13.
(2) A person is guilty of an offence under this section, if the touching involved –
  (a) penetration of B's anus or vagina with a part of A's body or anything else,
  (b) penetration of B's mouth with A's penis,
  (c) penetration of A's anus or vagina with a part of B's body, or
  (d) penetration of A's mouth with B's penis.

79 *R v G* [2008] UKHL 37, [4].
80 *R v G* [2008] UKHL 37, [4]–[6]. See also, Lord Hope, [27]–[31].
81 *R v G* [2008] UKHL 37, [30].
82 [2006] EWHC.

In *R v G* the prosecution was invited to abandon the case altogether once the victim changed her story, but they declined to do so. Counsel for the defendant argued that imposing a conviction under section 5, and the stigma attached to this as well as the lifelong consequences of such a conviction, was not necessary in a democratic society.[83] Lord Hope, dissenting from the House of Lords majority, agreed with the defence counsel. He concurred that despite the sentence being reduced by the Court of Appeal, convicting the defendant of rape under section 5 "was wholly disproportionate to any legitimate aim sought to be achieved".[84] This led Lord Hope, as well as Lord Carswell, to the conclusion that on the basis of article 8 the appeal should be allowed, as the offence should have properly been brought under section 13 of the Sexual Offences Act 2003.[85]

The legitimate aims being referred to under article 8(2) require consideration of both morals and policy. The Sexual Offences Act 2003 takes a paternalistic approach and aims to protect the rights and freedoms of others, by creating offences of strict liability to safeguard children under 13. As Lady Hale states, there is "long term and serious harm, both physical and psychological, which premature sexual activity can do".[86] Similarly to Lord Hoffman,[87] she concludes that *R v G* does not engage the article 8 rights of the defendant, but even if it did, the interference would be rational and proportionate in pursuit of the aims of protection of health and morals and the freedom of others.[88] While this reasoning is sound in achieving the aims of the harm principle,[89] and as Lady Hale enunciates the harm caused to the victim does not change with the age of the person who causes it,[90] it perhaps places little weight on considering that the defendant is also a child who may need protecting.[91]

- Does convicting the defendant of rape under section 5 of the Sexual Offences Act 2003 offend the principle of fair labelling?

As discussed in Chapter 2,[92] one of the underpinning principles of criminal law is that of fair labelling. This requires that the label the defendant receives reflects the seriousness and blameworthiness of the crime they have committed. This is especially important in a situation such as the one in *R v G*, when there is vast moral condemnation associated with the label placed n the defendant. In *R v G* the defendant was labelled as a child rapist, despite being a 15-year-old child who had sex with a 12-year-old girl with her agreement. As Lord Hope acknowledges, "the creation of an unqualified offence of this kind carries with it the risk of stigmatising as rapists children who engage in a single act of mutual sexual activity".[93] Lord Carswell in his dissenting judgment argues that rape is not the correct label, stating that: "It certainly does not reflect the reality of an act of the kind of that which was the subject of the defendant's guilty plea."[94] Thus, a conviction under section 13 would have led to the more appropriate, and less stigmatic, label of child sex offences committed by children or young persons.

---

83 *R v G* [2008] UKHL 37, [35].
84 *R v G* [2008] UKHL 37, [34]–[35].
85 *R v G* [2008] UKHL 37, [39]–[40] and [60].
86 *R v G* [2008] UKHL 37, [49].
87 *R v G* [2008] UKHL 37, [9]–[10].
88 *R v G* [2008] UKHL 37, [54]–[55].
89 See Chapter 2.3.6 for discussion of the harm principle.
90 *R v G* [2008] UKHL 37, [49].
91 This can be compared to *R v G and R* [2004] 1 AC 1034, 1057 when Lord Bingham stated that it is not moral or just to convict a child who did not appreciate the risk of the offence occurring. See Chapter 5.5 for further discussion.
92 See Chapter 2.3.2.
93 *R v G* [2008] UKHL 37, [14].
94 *R v G* [2008] UKHL 37, [60].

On the contrary, Lady Hale as part of the majority argues that rape is the correct label. She highlights that Parliament had legislated this offence with this label for the activity that the defendant undertook,[95] namely having sex with a child under 13. Moreover, even though the label rape connotes a lack of consent, that is still appropriate in *R v G* as a child under 13 is disabled by the law from giving consent.[96] She argues that the lack of blameworthiness is properly reflected in the lenient sentence given.[97] Equally, Lord Mance states that even though there are many negative long-term consequences for a conviction as a rapist, these same concerns would exist if the defendant had instead been convicted contrary to section 13 of the Sexual Offences Act 2003.[98] He argues that the stigma attached to being labelled a rapist would still exist, even if not to quite the same extent, for the label of sexual activity with a child.[99] Therefore, undermining the defendant's argument that conviction of section 5 of the Sexual Offences Act 2003 was disproportionate and should have been substituted with section 13.

In the scenario given at the start of the chapter, Jenna who is 15 years old agrees to have sex with her boyfriend Kane. As we have seen in Chapter 7, consent to non-fatal offences can act to negate criminal liability when it is real, non-fraudulent, and informed.[100] In sexual offences, to help ensure that consent is valid, the law places a minimum age bar of 16 on who can consent to sexual activity. In *R v G* the fact that the victim was under 13 meant liability was strict. This meant she could not give valid consent due to being under 16, and the defendant had no defence of believing that she was older. Therefore, it was irrelevant that the defendant thought she was 15. Consequently, the defendant was labelled and convicted as a rapist under section 5 of the Sexual Offences Act 2003, failing in his appeal that this breached his human rights. Thus, showing that once someone has reached the age of criminal responsibility of 10 years-old,[101] they can be found blameworthy for their actions while still a child, while at the same time a child under 16 does not have the legal capacity to consent to sexual activity.

In the scenario, the fact that Jenna is 15, changes matters. Kane could not be convicted under section 5 of the Sexual Offences Act 2003 due to Jenna's age. Kane would still fulfil the requirements of section 9, which would apply to him as a 15-year-old under section 13 of the Act. However, because Jenna is over 13 this is no longer a crime of strict liability. Section 9(1)(c)(i) means that if Kane reasonably believes Jenna is over 16 then he could avoid liability, as he could claim that he thought she was old enough to provide valid consent. This belief would still need to be a reasonable belief, which in the circumstances of him being her boyfriend might be difficult to establish.

Alternatively, Kane could be charged with rape under section 1 of the Sexual Offences Act 2003. As discussed above, this is one of the sections of the Act where it is required to establish a lack of consent and lack of reasonable belief that the victim consents. Despite sections 9 to 13 of the Act making it clear that a child under 16 cannot consent to sexual activity, there is no mention in section 1, or sections 74–76 dealing with consent, that the victim being under 16 means there is no consent or that there is a presumption against consent. The explanatory notes that accompany section 74 just state that a person may not have capacity to consent due to their age, but do not specify at what age this will apply. Furthermore, the Crown Prosecution Service guidance states: "If there are difficulties proving the non-consensual offence, then an offence under section 9 may be

95 *R v G* [2008] UKHL 37, [54].
96 *R v G* [2008] UKHL 37, [54].
97 *R v G* [2008] UKHL 37, [55].
98 *R v G* [2008] UKHL 37, [68]–[69].
99 *R v G* [2008] UKHL 37, [70].
100 See Chapter 7.5.1.
101 Section 34 of the Crime and Disorder Act 1998.

appropriate (where the elements can be proved)".[102] Therefore, unlike the defendant in *R v G*, it may be that Kane can avoid the stigma and label of a rape conviction.

8.4 Conclusion

This chapter has shown how the law relating to sexual offences has developed. A woman is no longer considered the property of her husband, and her marriage to him does not provide irrevocable consent to sex. The decision in *R v R* shows how the law can advance according to public morality.

Section 74 of the Sexual Offences Act 2003 provides a statutory definition of consent, which applies when the presumptions in sections 75 and 76 do not. These presumptions are not without their problems and seem to introduce a moral hierarchy that finds that impersonating a person is worse than having sex with someone unconscious, or having sex with someone who chooses to get drink without their consent is not as bad as having sex with someone without their consent who has not chosen to be intoxicated.

For clear policy reasons a child cannot consent to sex under the age of 16. The law assumes a paternalistic approach of safeguarding a child from sexual activity even if they believe they desire it. Moreover, if the child is under 13, the law assumes strict liability as to the victim's age, meaning that any belief by the defendant that the victim is older is irrelevant. Such an approach has obvious advantages in protecting children from harm, but does not consider that the perpetrator could also be a child as in *R v G*. This leaves a child over the age of 10, with the stigma of a serious sexual offence conviction when both parties thought they were acting consensually. Thus, the law can find a child criminally responsible for a crime that the law states they have the inability to consent to.

8.5 Further Reading

Jarvis P, "The Timing of Consent" [2019] Crim LR 394
Simpson B, "Why Has the Concept of Consent Proven So Difficult to Clarify" [2016] J Crim L 97
Temkin J and Ashworth A, "The Sexual Offences Act 2003: (1) Rape, Sexual Assaults and the Problems of Consent" [2004] Crim LR 328.
Travis M and Hunt K, "The Road to R v R: How Feminist Campaigners Abolished the Marital Rape Exemption" [2024] Crim LR 154
Wallerstein S, "'A Drunken Consent Is Still Consent' – or Is It? A Critical Analysis of the Law of Drunken Consent to Sex Following Bree" [2009] J Crim L 318

102 "Rape and Sexual Offences – Chapter 7: Key Legislation and Offences", 8 July 2022, www.cps.gov.uk/legal-guidance/rape-and-sexual-offences-chapter-7-key-legislation-and-offences, accessed 1 December 2024.

Chapter 9

Committing Crime while Intoxicated

Chapter Contents

DOI: 10.4324/9781003408383-10

9.1 Chapter Aims and Objectives

This chapter studies whether a person should avoid liability for a crime they have committed while intoxicated. It considers the blameworthiness of a person who has voluntarily chosen to become intoxicated compared to a person who has involuntarily become intoxicated. The leading case of *DPP v Majewski*[1] is examined, with consideration of the rules developed from this case for both basic and specific intent crimes. It will be shown that while there are moral and policy justifications for how the law of intoxication operates, the approach taken does not follow strict legal principle. A comparison of English law will be drawn to Scotland, as the geographically closest neighbours. There is also consideration of the law of intoxication in Australia, New Zealand, and Canada, to show that, despite these jurisdictions having a similar common law system to England, they have abandoned the *Majewski* approach. Finally, it will be considered how intoxication does not always occur in isolation from other defences. It will be shown how a strict stance has been taken on the applicability of allowing intoxication to be considered in association with other offences.

By the end of this chapter you should be able to:

- Discuss intoxication as a mitigating or aggravating factor.
- Discuss the policy laden nature of the rules relating to intoxication.
- Examine how legal principle was influenced by morals and policy in the decision of *DPP v Majewski.*
- Draw comparisons to approaches taken in Scotland, Australia, New Zealand, and Canada.
- Identify the interaction of intoxication with other defences, with examination of *R v Coley, McGhee and Harris.*

> The issues that will be examined in this chapter can be illustrated through the following scenarios. Before starting the chapter, consider whether the following are equally as blameworthy for the crimes they commit.
>
> - Alfie goes out with his friends and gets really drunk. He does not know what he is doing and on the train back home punches someone.
> - Beth goes out with her friends and takes some recreational drugs. As a result, she goes "on a trip" and during this, punches a stranger while thinking she is in an Olympic boxing match.
> - Caitlin goes out with her friends. They are all drinking but she is the designated driver, so does not drink. Someone spikes her drink. Not knowing what she is doing she punches one of her friends.
> - Debbie goes out with her friends. She has recently been ill and is taking prescribed medication. She only drinks diet cola but has an unusual reaction to the medication, which causes her to punch the barman. She does not know what she is doing.
> - Edwardo goes out with his friends. He has recently been diagnosed with clinical depression and is taking prescribed medication. He gets very drunk and punches a stranger in an unprovoked attack. Edwardo claims afterwards that he has no recollection of the events.
> - Fabian has a long history of drink and drug abuse. This results in him suffering episodes of paranoia. During one of these episodes he genuinely, but mistakenly thinks that a person directing traffic, is trying to attack him. He responds by punching the person in, what he believes is, self-defence.

1 [1977] AC 443.

9.2 Intoxication: An Aggravating or Mitigating Factor?

Historically, it was felt that being drunk was an aggravating factor that would increase the blameworthiness of the person who had committed the crime.[2] Arguably, if someone has chosen to get themselves into an intoxicated state, which increases their propensity to commit crime, then they deserve no concession to punishment under the law. Since the 1850's a more lenient approach has been taken. Intoxication, however, does not operate as a defence.[3] It is just evidence that can be used to show that the defendant did not form the *mens rea* of the offence with which they are charged. Apart from offences of strict liability, legal principle generally requires that the defendant has the corresponding *mens rea* and *actus reus* of the crime before they can be convicted.[4] If the defendant has formed the *mens rea* for the crime with which they are charged then they can be found guilty regardless of the fact that they were intoxicated.[5] As stated in *R v Sheehan*, "a drunken intent is nevertheless an intent".[6] If, however, the defendant has not formed the *mens rea* because of being intoxicated, then according to legal principle they should be acquitted. It does not need to be established that the defendant is incapable of forming the intention, which seemed to be suggested in *DPP v Beard*.[7] Instead, as per section 8(b) of the Criminal Justice Act 1967, the jury should be directed to consider all the evidence, including that relating to the intoxication, when drawing inferences as to the defendant's state of mind at the time of the offence.[8]

This, however, could be said to offend moral values. It may seem counterintuitive to allow a person who has chosen to become intoxicated to avoid liability for a crime they would not have committed unless intoxicated. Furthermore, policy reasons, such as protection of the public and the law acting as a deterrent, require that intoxication as a means to avoid liability should be restricted. As will be discussed below, the law has developed to provide a complex set of rules to compromise between the legal principle of not finding someone to blame when they do not have *mens rea*, and not allowing a person to use intoxication as an excuse for committing crime.

9.3 The Rules of Intoxication

The law makes no distinction on the means a person uses to become intoxicated. A person who has become intoxicated through the legal consumption of alcohol is treated in the same way as a person who has become intoxicated through illegal substances.[9] Therefore, while some might argue that Beth, who in the scenario at the start of the chapter punches someone after taking recreational drugs, seems more blameworthy than Alfie who has punched someone after becoming drunk, the rules of intoxication will apply to them both equally.

As discussed below a distinction is, however, drawn between those who have become voluntarily intoxicated and those who are involuntarily intoxicated. The law also operates differently depending on the type of crime that the defendant has committed while intoxicated, with a distinction drawn between basic and specific intent crimes.

---

2 See discussion in *DPP v Beard* [1920] AC 479, 494–495.
3 For further discussion see, AP Simester, "Intoxication Is Never a Defence" [2009] Crim LR 3.
4 See Chapter 2.3.4.
5 *R v Kingston* [1995] 2 AC 355.
6 *R v Sheehan* [1975] 1 WLR 739, 744.
7 *DPP v Beard* [1920] AC 479, 499.
8 *R v Sheehan* [1975] 1 WLR 739, 744.
9 *R v Lipman* [1970] 1 QB 152, 156.

9.3.1 Involuntary Intoxication

When a person has become intoxicated but this is not through their own choice, it is morally more agreeable to allow that person to rely on their intoxicated state to avoid liability. As with the scenario at the start of the chapter when Caitlin goes out with her friends and her drink is unknowingly spiked,[10] she is not at fault for her intoxicated state. Therefore, is arguably less blameworthy for the resulting battery that she commits. This was the argument made in *R v Kingston*, when the defence counsel stated: "If a man is surreptitiously given drink or drugs and as a result thereof he commits a criminal act the common law recognises that he should be excused liability."[11] This case revolved around the fact that involuntary intoxication had lowered the defendant's inhibitions to conduct paedophilic activity. While the House of Lords recognised that involuntary intoxication could be a defence to all crimes, when the defendant had not formed the requisite *mens rea* for the crime charged, the Lords rejected Kingston's appeal, stating that involuntary intoxication adds no further defence if the *mens rea* for the crime has been formed.[12] In coming to this conclusion a distinction was drawn between the lack of moral fault of the defendant and his intention with Lord Mustill stating: "I would therefore reject that part of the respondent's argument which treats the absence of moral fault on the part of the appellant as sufficient in itself to negative the necessary mental element of the offence."[13] Thus, in the given scenario Caitlin will only avoid liability if it can be established that she did not form the necessary *mens rea* for the battery. If the prosecution does establish that she had the necessary *mens rea* then the fact that she had not chosen to become intoxicated, or that she would not have conducted the battery were it not for her inhibitions being lowered due to the intoxication, will not act to remove her criminal liability for the offence.

A defendant will not be considered to be involuntarily intoxicated if they make a mistake about the strength of their drink. This was observed in *R v Allen* when the defendant's appeal was dismissed. The court held that the defendant drinking alcohol, ignorant of its precise strength, did not make the intoxication involuntary.[14] This demonstrates a strict policy approach to ensuring that a person can not use their self-intoxication to avoid liability.

9.3.2 Voluntary Intoxication

When a person has become voluntarily intoxicated, an assessment needs to be made as to whether it is right to hold them criminally liable for any criminal conduct they undertake while in an intoxicated state. The law views such a person less generously than a person who has become involuntarily intoxicated, due to the blame that can be placed on them for knowingly taking the risks associated with consuming drink or drugs. In *DPP v Beard* the House of Lords considered that if a person due to voluntary drunkenness could not form the specific intent required for the crime, in that case murder, then the defendant could instead be found guilty of manslaughter.[15] This, however, does not address the question of how intoxication operates if the defendant has been charged with a crime that does not require specific intent. This was considered by the House of Lords in *DPP v Majewski*.[16]

---

10 This is a colloquial term used to describe the situation when another substance has unexpectedly and without consent been added to a person's food or drink.

11 *R v Kingston* [1995] 2 AC 355, 358.

12 *R v Kingston* [1995] 2 AC 355, 358.

13 *R v Kingston* [1995] 2 AC 355, 366.

14 *R v Allen* [1988] Crim LR 698.

15 *DPP v Beard* [1920] AC 479.

16 *DPP v Majewski* [1977] AC 443.

9.3.3 The Majewski Rules

DPP v Majewski

On 19 February 1973 Majewski and another were involved in a fight in the Bull public house in Basildon. The Landlord tried to stop the fight, but he was prevented from doing so by Majewski and then attacked by him when he went to call the police. Majewski was finally ejected from the pub, but then fought his way back in. During these events Majewski was reportedly very violent and he cut the Landlord's hand with a piece of glass and cut another customer's finger. When the police arrived, the arresting officer was kicked and abused by Majewski, and another officer was kicked as Majewski was being transported to the police station. The following morning, Majewski attacked a police inspector who went to his cell at the police station. Majewski was charged and convicted of three counts of assault occasioning actual bodily harm contrary to section 47 of the Offences against the Person Act 1861, and three offences of assault on a police officer in the execution of his duty contrary to section 51(1) of the Police Act 1964. The Court of Appeal dismissed his appeal, but granted leave to appeal to the House of Lords a question of public importance. This was whether the judge had misdirected the jury by saying that a defence was not available and thus: "whether a defendant may properly be convicted of assault notwithstanding that by reason of his self-induced intoxication, he did not intend to do the act alleged to constitute the assault".[17] The Crown argued that for the policy reason of public safety a person should not be able to avoid liability when they had committed a crime when voluntarily intoxicated.[18] In reply the defence argued that strict legal principle requires that a person is not held to be blameworthy unless they have the required *mens rea* for the crime, and if being intoxicated means that they do not form the *mens rea* then they should not be guilty.[19] The House of Lords unanimously dismissed the appeal stating that intoxication was no defence to crimes where no specific intent was required.

Thinking points:

- The defendant in Majewski was found criminally liable even though he did not form the *mens rea* for the crimes that he committed. How can this be explained?

The context of the appeal is made clear by Lord Elwyn-Jones who, in quoting Lord Denning,[20] states it is the general principle of English law that subject to very limited exceptions, drunkenness is no defence to a criminal charge.[21] Thus, the problem remains that if drunkenness is not a defence, but the defendant does not have the requisite *mens rea* for the crime, how can a conviction be explained? Lord Elwyn-Jones discusses that the required *mens rea* for an assault is recklessness,[22] as stated in *R v Venna*.[23] While *Majewski* may not have foreseen the risk of an assault, Lord Elwyn-Jones determined that the recklessness of getting drunk and then using unlawful force, could constitute

17 *DPP v Majewski* [1977] AC 443, 447.

18 *DPP v Majewski* [1977] AC 443, 469.

19 *DPP v Majewski* [1977] AC 443, 470.

20 *Attorney General for Northern Ireland v Gallagher* [1963] AC 349, 380.

21 *DPP v Majewski* [1977] AC 443, 474.

22 *DPP v Majewski* [1977] AC 443, 474–475.

23 *R v Venna* [1976] QB 421, 429. See Chapter 7.5.2 for further definition of assault.

the recklessness for an assault.[24] This approach is supported by Lord Simon who stated that a person who, through voluntarily taking drink or drugs, is unaware of their prohibited acts or consequences has a state of mind as wrongful as someone who consciously contemplates the prohibited act or foresees its consequence.[25] Thus, meaning that someone who does not have the *mens rea* for the crime due to voluntary intoxication can be morally just as blameworthy as someone who does. As Lord Salmon further elaborates: "there is a very real distinction between someone who acts accidently and so is immune from prosecution and someone who does not know what they are doing because they are drunk".[26] Therefore, it may be justifiable from a moral standpoint to hold a person to account for the crimes they have unintentionally committed when voluntarily intoxicated.[27] Nonetheless, this does not follow strict legal principle of only punishing those with the required *mens rea* for the crime for which they are charged.

While many might agree that by becoming intoxicated a person takes the risk and the responsibility of any actions that might result, this is problematic as it offends the correspondence theory.[28] The defendant is being found guilty for the *actus reus* of assault occasioning actual bodily harm and assault of a police officer with the mismatched *mens rea* of getting drunk. In other words, the defendant is being found criminally liable for a crime they did not intend or foresee. Furthermore, equally as problematic is that the *actus reus* and *mens rea* do not coincide.[29] *Majewski* became intoxicated over a period of time, and the day before the final assault of the police inspector. This means that if deciding to drink is the recklessness for the crime, this *mens rea* was formed substantially before the *actus reus* took place. The two elements are not occurring at the same time.

A defendant choosing to become intoxicated does not, however, automatically mean that they are reckless. In the situation when the defendant has chosen to become intoxicated, they could still have a defence to both basic intent crimes if they have not formed the *mens rea* of the crime and have not been reckless in becoming intoxicated. For example, a defendant can avoid liability for basic intent crimes when they have chosen to take a substance but have had an unusual response to it. This is because they have not been reckless in taking the substance, and therefore the recklessness of becoming intoxicated cannot be used to form the *mens rea* of the crime. This was seen in *R v Hardie*, when the self-administration of the soporific drug Valium caused the defendant to set fire to a wardrobe, when there were two others in a nearby room.[30] The trial judge determined that the self-administration of the drug was irrelevant and as such the jury was directed to disregard any incapacity which resulted or might have resulted from the taking of the Valium. The defendant was convicted on an indictment containing a count of arson with intent to endanger life or being reckless as to whether life would be endangered contrary to section 1(2) and (3) of the Criminal Damage Act 1971. In allowing the appeal, the Court of Appeal held that the jury should have been directed to consider whether the defendant, because of the drugs, was unable to appreciate the risks to property and persons. They should then consider whether the taking of the Valium was itself reckless.[31] Thus, in the scenario at the start of the chapter, Debbie, would have a defence to the specific intent crime of section 18 grievous bodily harm, if she does not have the required intention. She could also have a defence to the basic intent offences of section 20 grievous bodily harm, section 47 actual bodily harm, or battery, if she has not been reckless. Therefore, the law upholds a moral approach so that

24 *DPP v Majewski* [1977] AC 443, 474–475.

25 *DPP v Majewski* [1977] AC 443, 479–480.

26 *DPP v Majewski* [1977] AC 443, 482.

27 *DPP v Majewski* [1977] AC 443, 292 per Lord Edmund-Davies, who refutes that it is unethical to convict someone of a crime that requires *mens rea* if the person does not have the *mens rea*.

28 See Chapter 2.3.4.2.

29 See Chapter 2.3.4.3.

30 [1985] 1 WLR 64.

31 *R v Hardie* [1985] 1 WLR 64, 70.

those who have chosen to take an intoxicant, but are not blameworthy or reckless in doing so, are not condemned.

- In concluding that becoming recklessly intoxicated could amount to the *mens rea* of the offence in *DPP v Majewski*, Lord Simon drew a distinction between basic and specific intent crimes. Why is this distinction problematic?

A person choosing to become intoxicated, is at worst reckless as to any resulting criminal offence that might occur. Therefore, if the criminal offence charged requires intention, the recklessness of becoming intoxicated cannot be substituted as the necessary *mens rea* as it is not sufficient. Consequently, the defendant can avoid liability for specific intent crimes. The problem is that this reasoning to allow a defence to specific intent crimes, and not basic intent crimes, is illogical. In neither situation the defendant had intended or foreseen the outcome of their actions due to intoxication.[32]

Furthermore, there is no clear distinction between basic and specific intent crimes. As Lord Simon acknowledges, the term "specific intent" is ambiguous.[33] He summarises its meaning as follows: "In short, where the crime is one of 'specific intent' the prosecution must in general prove that the purpose for the commission of the act extends to the intent expressed or implied in the definition of the crime".[34] This suggests that if the crime requires that the defendant form a certain intention, such as in the offence of murder when the prosecution are required to prove that the defendant intended death or serious injury, then the crime can be said to be one of specific intent.

The case of *R v Heard*,[35] however, illustrates that the distinction between basic and specific intent crimes is anything but clear.[36] The defendant, who was voluntarily intoxicated at the time of the offence, was convicted contrary to section 3 of the Sexual Offences Act 2003 for sexual assault. This crime requires intentional touching of another, which is sexual, without their consent. Before summing up, the trial judge had been asked whether this was a basic or specific intent crime and had ruled that it was basic intent, and therefore, that intoxication could not be used as a defence.[37] The defendant appealed, stating that *Majewski* meant that because the crime required intention, and the *mens rea* could not be fulfilled recklessly, this was a crime of specific intent and so the intoxication should have been considered. Hughes LJ in his judgment, stated: "The first thing to say is that it should not be supposed that every offence can be categorised simply as either one of specific intent or of basic intent".[38] Thus, indicating a worrying lack of certainty in the law with resulting inconsistency in the application of the rules of intoxication. The court noted that only the touching needed to be intended and that whether the touching was sexual and without consent were normative questions, to which intoxication would be irrelevant.[39] In reviewing the judgment of *Majewski*, Hughes LJ in *Beard* stated that a crime of specific intent was one when the defendant had to intend something beyond their actions, such as the consequence of their actions.[40] This meant that sexual assault could be classified as a basic intent crime. Intent was only required for the touching conduct element of the crime and not the

---

32 *DPP v Majewski* [1977] AC 443, 482.

33 *DPP v Majewski* [1977] AC 443, 478.

34 *DPP v Majewski* [1977] AC 443, 479.

35 *R v Heard* [2008] QB 43.

36 As the Law Commission, *Intoxication and Criminal Liability* (Law Com No 314, 2009) para 1.28 states, the distinction is "ambiguous, misleading and confusing".

37 *R v Heard* [2008] QB 43, 46–47.

38 *R v Heard* [2008] QB 43, 48.

39 *R v Heard* [2008] QB 43, 49.

40 *R v Heard* [2008] QB 43, 54–55.

conditions aspects of the *actus reus* (of the touching having to be sexual and without consent).[41] This reasoning seems to add further confusion as it means that crimes such as murder, could also be deemed to be ones of basic intent despite requiring intention. For example, a charge of murder requires that the defendant intends the consequence of killing or causing grievous bodily harm.[42] The other *actus reus* conditions of the crime (the need for the victim to be a human being and the actions to be under the King's peace) would be classified under the reasoning in *Heard* as normative questions to which intoxication was irrelevant. This draws the law to an illogical conclusion when it has long been accepted that murder is a specific intent crime.[43]

The classification of murder as a specific intent crime, and thus the intoxication being available to avoid liability when the defendant has not formed the relevant *mens rea*, has led to the adoption of the "fallback offence". This means that instead of the defendant avoiding conviction of a specific intent crime they are instead charged with a lesser basic intent crime, where the recklessness of becoming involuntarily intoxicated is enough to satisfy the *mens rea* requirements. This can be seen in *R v Lipman*.[44] The defendant killed the victim after they had both voluntarily taken hallucinogenic drugs (LSD). He claimed that he had no knowledge of what he was doing and no intention to harm her. The defendant was acquitted of the specific intent crime of murder but found guilty of the basic intent crime of manslaughter. It was deemed enough that "the acts complained of were obviously likely to cause harm to the victim" and no specific intent for manslaughter was needed.[45] *Lipman* was distinguished from *R v Lamb*.[46] In *Lamb*, the defendant's lack of *mens rea* for the unlawful act, that led to the victim's death, was sufficient to avoid liability as no intoxication was involved.[47] Unlike in *Lipman*, in *Lamb* it was held that *mea rea* was an "essential ingredient in manslaughter".[48] Thus, when a defendant commits an act without *mens rea* that leads to a person's death, there is no offence, but when a defendant commits an act without *mens rea* but has become intoxicated in the process, there is an offence to answer to.

While this may seem harsh it considers the prior fault of getting voluntarily intoxicated and taking the risk of what could occur, while still protecting the defendant from a charge of murder and a mandatory life sentence. In this way a compromise has been achieved. In the example of Beth, given at the start of the chapter, if she has caused serious injury she would not be charged with section 18 grievous bodily harm, as this is a specific intent offence to which her intoxication would be relevant to show she did not have the required *mens rea*. Instead, she would be charged with the "fallback offence" of section 20 grievous bodily harm, which can be committed recklessly and so can be classified as a basic intent crime. Her decision in becoming intoxicated would then amount to the necessary *mens rea* without it having to be established what outcome she actually intended or foresaw. The problem is, however, that not all offences have a relevant "fallback offence" that the defendant can be charged with. As seen above in *Heard*, this means that to uphold morals and policy aims, the only avenue left open to the courts in these situations is either an acquittal, or a reclassification of specific intent crimes as become basic intent so that the defendant cannot rely on intoxication.

In Canada, the problem has been approached in a slightly different way. While still acknowledging the law from *DPP v Majewski*, and allowing intoxication to be considered for specific intent crimes, a defendant can also rely on intoxication to negate *mens rea* for basic intent crimes, with one

41 *R v Heard* [2008] QB 43, 55–56.
42 *R v Cunningham* [1982] AC 566.
43 *DPP v Beard* [1920] AC 479.
44 *R v Lipman* [1970] 1 QB 152.
45 *R v Lipman* [1970] 1 QB 152, 159.
46 [1967] 2 QB 981.
47 *R v Lamb* [1967] 2 QB 981.
48 *R v Lamb* [1967] 2 QB 981. 988.

notable exception. The Canadian Criminal Code 1985, section 33.1(1) states that if the accused voluntarily reaches a state of objective extreme intoxication that means they departed markedly from the standard of care expected of a reasonable person in the circumstances, then they cannot rely on the intoxication to avoid criminal liability. Extreme intoxication is defined under section 33.1(4) as intoxication that renders a person unaware of, or incapable of consciously controlling, their behaviour. This means that a person can rely on intoxication to show that they have not formed the *mens rea* for the offence committed, but if they become so intoxicated that they cannot form the *mens rea* and then commit an offence that harms another they will be unable to rely on the intoxication. Thus, while providing a little more flexibility on when intoxication can be relied on to negate *mens rea*, the law in Canada imposes a normative standard on the acceptable levels of intoxication to ensure individual behaviour meets a standard acceptable to society.

Elsewhere the problem of how to classify offences is again approached differently. In the same year that *DPP v Majewski* was reported, the High Court of Justiciary in Scotland was also considering how to approach the issue of crime committed while intoxicated in *Brennan v HM Advocate*.[49] The defendant had consumed between 20 and 25 pints of beer and taken LSD before stabbing his father to death. The defendant was convicted of murder and appealed. While it is acknowledged that the Scottish crime of murder differs from the definition in England, the High Court of Justiciary made it clear that the distinction between basic and specific intent crimes was "illogical"[50] and "inappropriate".[51] Moreover, that: "There is nothing unethical or unfair or contrary to the general principle of our law that self-induced intoxication is not by itself a defence to any criminal charge".[52] Thus, demonstrating that intoxication will not provide a defence in Scotland regardless of whether the crime if one of basic or specific intent.

In *The Queen v O'Connor*,[53] the Australian High Court also decided not to follow the distinction made between basic and specific intent crimes in *DPP v Majewski*.[54] In a decision, which forms the law of the State of Victoria, the court held that such a distinction was "unhelpful".[55] Instead of intoxication being a substantive principle of law on which liability can be constructed for basic intent crimes, it is raised in evidence by the defence to cast doubt on whether they had the required *mens rea* for the crime.[56] This approach echoed that of New Zealand in the earlier case of *R v Kamipeli*, when it was stated that no distinction should be drawn between basic and specific intent crimes, and that evidence of intoxication was relevant to whether defendant acted "with the intention or recklessness required by the charge".[57] This shows an approach that adheres to strict legal principle of only condemning those who have the intention or recklessness for the crime charged, rather than drawing an arbitrary distinction between different types of offences. Consequently, the decision of whether the defendant had the required *mens rea* for the crime is left to be decided on the facts of the case, regardless of the type of crime committed. As discussed below, such an approach is not unwarranted. If a jury can be left to decide whether a defendant does not have *mens rea* for any crime if the intoxication is involuntary, or for a specific intent crime if the intoxication is voluntary, the same approach could be applied to basic intent crimes when the defendant is voluntary intoxicated.

---

49 [1977] JC 38.

50 *Brennan v HM Advocate* [1977] JC 38, 47

51 *Brennan v HM Advocate* [1977} JC 38, 51.

52 *Brennan v HM Advocate* [1977} JC 38, 51.

53 (1980) 146 CLR 64.

54 *The Queen v O'Connor* (1980) 146 CLR 64, 88.

55 *The Queen v O'Connor* (1980) 146 CLR 64, 82.

56 *The Queen v O'Connor* (1980) 146 CLR 64, 88. See AP Simester, "Intoxication Is Never a Defence" [2009] Crim LR 3, for a discussion of the substantive versus evidential nature of intoxication.

57 [1975] 2 NZLR 610, 616.

- In what way did policy concerns impact the judgment in *DPP v Majewski*?

In Lord Simon's judgment in *DPP v Majewski*, he makes it clear that one of the policy aims of criminal law is to protect the public from dangerous people.[58] This means that if Majewski were allowed to use intoxication as an excuse for his behaviour of harming others, a potentially dangerous person would avoid censure. From a policy point of view this would be unacceptable. Therefore, the House of Lords tried to find an approach that fulfilled the policy aim of protecting the public, while still respecting that a person should not be liable for a crime without the required *mens rea*. Virgo sums up the solution the House of Lords reached, stating:

> In *Majewski* the House of Lords acknowledged principle by allowing intoxication to be adduced to show that the mental element for specific intent offences did not exist but were swayed by policy objectives in convicting of basic intent offences despite intoxication. This compromise is defensible on policy grounds, but it fails to accord with accepted principles of the criminal law.[59]

Thus, when the crime is one of specific intent, which tend to be more serious offences, the legal principles of criminal law stand. Whereas, the principles of criminal law have been conceded to achieve the policy aim of protecting the public for basic intent crimes. This can be justified when considering the stigmatic labels and severe punishment associated with specific intent crimes such as murder and robbery. For basic intent crimes, however, it assumes that everyone is a potential risk to the public if they are reckless by becoming intoxicated. This assumption does not depend on an assessment of the individual's knowledge or experience. It is a blanket imposition of *mens rea* deduced from objective evidence of intoxication, based on the presumption that intoxication leads to violence.

The policy aims in *DPP v* Majewski can be seen as going beyond protecting the public from violence. The decision could also be said to impact society's view of the criminal justice system. As Lord Russell states:

> The ordinary citizen who is badly beaten up would rightly think little of the criminal law as an effective protection if, because his attacker had deprived himself of ability to know what he was doing by getting himself drunk or going on a trip with drugs, the attacker is to be held innocent of any crime in the assault.[60]

Consequently, in addition to the practical application of guaranteeing that members of society are protected, not allowing intoxication to excuse criminal liability ensures faith is maintained in the criminal justice system. It is important that the ordinary citizen, referred to by Lord Russell, feels that justice is being achieved. In the context of intoxication this means a utilitarian justice whereby the public can be satisfied that intoxication cannot be used readily utilised as an excuse, rather than justice for the individual who has committed a crime without the necessary *mens rea*. This means applying the *Majewski* rules even when it may appear unjust to the individual to have responsibility for a crime they neither intended nor were reckless to. In the extreme, if society does not feel that justice is being achieved, the risk is that more generally the criminal law will not be obeyed and the system will break down. This is based on the idea of the social contract

---

58 *DPP v Majewski* [1977] AC 443, 476. See Chapter 1.3.2 for further discussion of the general policy aims of criminal law.

59 Graham Virgo, "The Law Commission Paper on Intoxication and Criminal Liability: Part 1: Reconciling Principles and Policy" [1993] Crim LR 415.

60 *DPP v Majewski* [1977] AC 443, 498.

theory, which states that society obeys the law made by the state in return for protection from the state.[61] Therefore, if society does not feel that they are being protected by the law, then there is no motivation to obey it.

As discussed above, the State of Victoria in Australia and New Zealand make no distinction between basic and specific intent crimes. If this distinction is needed for the policy reason of protecting the public and upholding the criminal justice system, it suggests that these jurisdictions would face difficulties in meeting these policy objectives through the application of their intoxication rules. Research, however, shows that the intoxication rules in Australia and New Zealand have had little negative impact. This is because often the defendant is found to have the *mens rea* regardless of being intoxicated, and thus complete acquittal is rare.[62] As Orchard notes: "The argument from social protection is not borne out by experience in Australia and New Zealand."[63] The robustness of juries can be relied upon to dismiss unmeritorious claims without the *Majewski* requirement of drawing a distinction between basic and specific crimes, and constructing recklessness from becoming intoxicated for basic intent crimes.

9.4 Intoxication and the Interplay with Other Defences

The final part of this chapter gives an overview of the interplay between intoxication and other defences. This is in recognition that intoxication does not always occur in isolation, and there may be a number of other relevant factors. Considering the restrictive approach to intoxication formed through the *Majewski* rules, it will be unsurprising that this moral and policy-based approach is reflected in how intoxication interacts with other defences.

9.4.1 Lack of Capacity Defences

Intoxication is often compared to lack of capacity defences.[64] It differs from these because, as stated above,[65] it is not a defence. Intoxication does not provide a justification or an excuse for the defendant's behaviour. Instead, intoxication is used to argue that the defendant has not formed the *mens rea* of the crime charged. Whereas, lack of capacity defences rely on showing that the defendant was incapable of forming the necessary *mens rea*. Hart asserts that before determining that a person is criminally responsible, it needs to be established that they had capacity and fair opportunity to adjust their behaviour to the requirements of the law.[66] Thus, as Gross states, "criminal liability is unjust if the one who is liable was not able to choose effectively to act in a way that would avoid criminal liability, and because of that he violated the law".[67] A person who, for example, suffers from a mental illness may not have the capacity to adjust their behaviour and choice to act in a way that is compatible with the law. It would be unfair to hold someone to blame, who was faultless in this way. As discussed above, in cases of intoxication the law takes a restrictive approach to allowing culpability to be avoided for basic intent crimes when the defendant has become voluntarily intoxicated. The law assumes the defendant has prior fault for getting themselves into a state when

61 See Raymond Wacks, *Understanding Jurisprudence; An Introduction to Legal Theory* (6th edition, Oxford University Press 2020).

62 Law Commission, *Intoxication and Criminal Liability* (Law Com CP No 127, 1993), paras. 5.15–5.22.

63 Gerald Orchard, "The Law Commission Consultation Paper on intoxication and criminal liability: Part 2: Surviving without Majewski – a View from Down Under" [1993] Crim LR 426.

64 For a more detailed analysis of the interplay between intoxication, insanity and automatism, see Alan Reed and Michael Bolander, *General Defences in Criminal Law: Domestic and Comparative Perspectives* (Routledge 2020), ch. 8.

65 Chapter 8.2.

66 HLA Hart, *Punishment and Responsibility: Essays in the Philosophy of Law* (2nd edition, Oxford University Press 2008) 181–189.

67 Hyman Gross, *A Theory of Criminal Justice* (Oxford University Press 1979) 137.

there is an increased risk that they will commit crime. Policy does not intervene in the same way to restrict the application of lack of capacity defences, as it does with intoxication. On the contrary, when a defendant has been able to show that they lack the capacity of reason or control expected of a reasonable person, this provides a way for defendants to avoid liability through the application of a lack of capacity defence. Stark identifies two such situations that he summarises as "insane people (whose understanding of the nature and quality of their conduct, or its wrongfulness, is insufficient), and automatons (who lack adequate control over their actions)".[68]

Insanity is a Victorian defence defined by the *M'Naghten* rules, following the case of *R v M'Naghten*.[69] To establish the defence, the defendant must prove on a balance of probabilities that "at the time of the committing of the act, the party accused was labouring under such a defect of reason, from disease of the mind, as not to know the nature and quality of the act he was doing; or, if he did know it, that he did not know he was doing what was wrong".[70] A defect of reason means a deprivation of the power of reasoning,[71] and the disease of the mind must come from an internal cause.[72] The defendant must show that this causes them to not know the nature and quality of their acts,[73] or to not know that what they are doing is unlawful[74] and morally wrong by the standards of ordinary people.[75]

Alternatively, automatism is summarised in *Bratty v Attorney General for Northern Ireland* as "an act which is done by the muscles without any control by the mind . . . or an act done by a person who is not conscious of what he is doing, such as an act done while suffering concussion".[76] The defence is heavily restricted by the need for a total destruction of the defendant's voluntary control[77] from an external cause,[78] so that a person's mind is not controlling or directing their limbs.[79]

The relationship between intoxication, insanity, and automatism was considered by the Court of Appeal in *R v Coley, McGhee and Harris*.[80]

R v Coley, McGhee and Harris

R v Coley, McGhee and Harris involved three separate cases with the common feature of the interplay between voluntary intoxication and the law relating to insanity or automatism considered. In Coley the defendant entered into a neighbour's house in the night and repeatedly stabbed the neighbour's partner with a knife. The defendant claimed that he had blacked out at the time and had no memory of the attack. He was a regular heavy user of cannabis and medical evidence showed that this could have induced a brief psychotic episode, despite there being no underlying mental illness or personality disorder. The defendant argued that the defences of insanity and automatism should have been put to the jury, but the trial judge had declined to do so concluding that this was a case of voluntary intoxication. At trial, Coley was convicted of attempted murder.

68 Finlay Stark, "Prior Fault" [2014] CLJ 8, 8.
69 [1843] 8 ER 718.
70 *R v M'Naghten* [1843] 8 ER 718, 722.
71 *R v Clarke* [1972] 1 All ER 219, 228.
72 For example, see *R v Kemp* [1957] 1 QB 399; *R v Sullivan* [1984] AC 156; *R v Hennessy* [1989] 1 WLR 287; *R v Burgess* [1991] 2 QB 92.
73 *R v Codere* (1917) 12 Cr App R 21, 26–28.
74 *R v Windle* [1952] 2 QB 826, 832–834.
75 *R v Keal* [2022] EWCA Crim 341; *R v Usman* [2023] EWCA Crim 313.
76 *Bratty v Attorney General for Northern Ireland* [1963] AC 386, 409.
77 *Watmore v Jenkins* [1962] 2 QB 572, 586–587; *Attorney General's Reference (No 2 of 1992)* [1994] QB 91, 105.
78 *R v Quick* [1973] QB 910, 922–923.
79 *Broome v Perkins* [1987] RTR 321, 330.
80 [2013] EWCA Crim 223.

McGhee suffered from tinnitus for which he took medication. Despite being warned not to mix the medication with alcohol, he claimed that he had no choice but to drink to ease his symptoms. After drinking a lot, and going to an off-licence to buy more alcohol, he became aggressive and fought with another customer. He then later returned with a knife and stabbed the shop assistant. He claimed he had no recollection of the events. A drug expert gave evidence at trial that the prescription drugs combined with alcohol could reduce social restraint and lead to disinhibited behaviour. The judge rejected the claim that the defendant's drinking had not been voluntary, and ruled that there was no evidence of automatism. The jury found McGhee guilty of wounding with intent.

In Harris the defendant had started a fire in his own house, and was charged with aggravated arson through the reckless endangerment of his neighbours' lives. He suffered from clinical depression and previously had been hospitalised for episodes of alcohol psychosis or alcohol-induced hallucinosis following the sudden cessation of his excessive drinking. At the time of the fire he was suffering from such an episode. He knew what he was doing and that it was wrong, but claimed that he had not given any thought to the risk his actions would pose to others. The judge ruled that the drinking was not relevant to his recklessness, and consequently the defendant pleaded guilty.

Thinking points:

- In all three cases the defendants appealed because the directions the trial judges had given to the juries regarding the relevance of the defendants' lack of capacity. All three defendants were in altered mental states when they committed the crimes, but are their cases the same?

In the judgment of the Court of Appeal, Lord Justice Hughes made it clear that the cases: "Neither individually nor collectively do they provide an occasion for any wide-ranging general statement of the law of loss of capacity generally".[81] Thus, in the case of Coley, while the court confirmed that insanity, like intoxication, could be temporary,[82] there was a distinction between a disease of the mind that is required under the *M'Naghten* rules for insanity, and the effect on the mind that alcohol can cause.[83] Moreover, taking drink or drugs would amount to an external factor, which is inconsistent with the defence of insanity that requires the disease of the mind arises from an internal factor.[84] The defence of automatism was also examined. The court held that irrational behaviour did not necessarily amount to involuntary behaviour, as required by the automatism defence.[85] Furthermore, that the defence would not be available if the automatic state was induced by the fault of the defendant.[86] The court held that when an automatic state had been self-induced by something other than intoxicants, the jury would need to consider whether the defendant had been reckless in reaching this state. If we return to the scenario of Debbie at the start of the chapter, if her automatic state was caused solely by the diet cola then she potentially could have a defence of automatism if she did not know that she would react this way. She would, however, have no defence if this had

81 *R v Coley, McGhee and Harris* [2013] EWCA Crim 223, [1].
82 *R v Coley, McGhee and Harris* [2013] EWCA Crim 223, [15].
83 *R v Coley, McGhee and Harris* [2013] EWCA Crim 223, [18].
84 *R v Coley, McGhee and Harris* [2013] EWCA Crim 223, [19]–[20].
85 *R v Coley, McGhee and Harris* [2013] EWCA Crim 223, [23].
86 *R v Coley, McGhee and Harris* [2013] EWCA Crim 223, [24].

happened before and was thus reckless if she knew this was a possibility.[87] In Coley, however, as the automatic state was due to drugs, the question of whether he had been reckless did not need to be asked. Regardless of how he thought he would act, or had previously acted, when taking such drugs, the defendant was considered to be voluntarily intoxicated and consequently prior fault automatically was assumed. Therefore, the trial judge was correct in withdrawing both the insanity and automatism defences from the jury.[88]

In McGhee the defendant appealed against his conviction for the specific intent crime of wounding with intent. He argued that the defence of automatism should have been put before the jury. Similarly to Coley, the court held that the defendant's state was self-induced.[89] Despite the drugs being prescribed for their soporific effect, this case can be distinguished from that of *R v Hardie*, in which the defendant had an usual reaction to such drugs.[90] McGhee had been warned not to take the prescribed drugs with alcohol, but had chosen to do so. Thus, McGhee had accepted the risk, whereas Hardie had been unaware that there was one. Moreover, the court held that McGhee's actions could not rely on automatism as his actions were not involuntary. Even though they could have been caused by the interaction between his prescribed drugs and the alcohol, which led to a lowering of his inhibitions, this was insufficient for automatism.[91] Therefore, his appeal was also dismissed.[92]

In Harris, similarly to Coley, the defendant's altered mental state was induced due to the intoxicant that he had previously taken. Thus, the Crown argued that the mental illness from which he was suffering was bought on by his voluntary drinking. The court stated: "We agree that there is scope for the argument that an illness caused by his own fault ought as a matter of policy to be treated in the same way as is drunkenness at the time of the offence."[93] The court, however, did not apply this policy argument. Instead they held that because the defendant was not drunk at the time, he had stopped drinking some five or six days earlier, the *Majewski* rules of voluntary intoxication should not apply. Thus, the *Majewski* rules that assume prior fault should not be extended to cover mental illnesses that had been caused by past culpable conduct.[94] As such, the defendant's appeal was allowed.[95] It may seem difficult to reconcile this outcome with Coley, but perhaps one key difference was that the defendant was not intoxicated at the time but suffering from alcohol psychosis or alcohol-induced hallucinosis that was further complicated by depression.

The same approach to intoxication and prior fault as seen in *R v Coley, McGhee and Harris* can also be seen in the defence of diminished responsibility.[96] Similarly to the judgment in Coley that stated the effects of alcohol did not in themselves amount to a disease of the mind, diminished responsibility does not allow self-induced intoxication to amount to an abnormality of the mind.[97] Thus, the defendant cannot rely on their prior fault in becoming intoxicated to provide an excuse for killing. To rely on the defence, the defendant would need to show, like in Harris, that the alcohol had led to a recognised medical condition.[98] This includes allowing a defence when a pre-existing medical condition has been triggered by self-induced intoxication.[99] In the situation where the defendant

---

87 *R v Bailey* [1983] 1 WLR 760.

88 *R v Coley, McGhee and Harris* [2013] EWCA Crim 223, [27].

89 *R v Coley, McGhee and Harris* [2013] EWCA Crim 223, [47].

90 *R v Hardie* [1985] 1 WLR 64. See Chapter 9.3.3 above.

91 *R v Coley, McGhee and Harris* [2013] EWCA Crim 223, [46].

92 *R v Coley, McGhee and Harris* [2013] EWCA Crim 223, [48].

93 *R v Coley, McGhee and Harris* [2013] EWCA Crim 223, [59].

94 *R v Coley, McGhee and Harris* [2013] EWCA Crim 223, [59].

95 *R v Coley, McGhee and Harris* [2013] EWCA Crim 223, [60].

96 As defined under section 2 of the Homicide Act 1957 as amended by section 52 of the Coroners and Justice Act 2009. See further discussion of Diminished Responsibility in Chapter 13.4.1.

97 *R v Dowds* [2012] 1 WLR 2576.

98 For example, alcohol dependency syndrome. See, *R v Stewart* [2009] 2 Cr App R 30.

99 *R v Joyce and Kay* [2017] EWCA Crim 647.

suffers from a medical condition and is intoxicated, the courts must consider if, notwithstanding the intoxicant consumed and its effect, whether the abnormality of mental functioning substantially impaired their mental responsibility for their acts in doing the killing.[100]

In examining the scenarios at the start of the chapter, Edwardo is intoxicated but also suffering from a recognised medical condition when he punches a stranger. If Edwardo was to state that his voluntary intoxication meant that he did not form the required *mens rea*, then the *Majewski* rules would apply. It would need to be considered whether he had committed a basic or specific intent crime. The intoxication could be considered if he was charged with grievous bodily harm with intent contrary to section 18 of the Offences against the Persons Act 1861, as this is a specific intent crime. If he was charged with section 20 grievous bodily harm, section 47 actual bodily harm, or with battery then the *Majewski* rules would assume prior fault. The recklessness of becoming intoxicated would satisfy the *mens rea* for these basic intent crimes. Alternatively, Edwardo could consider the defence of automatism. This, however, would be problematic. It would be difficult to establish that Edwardo's actions were completely involuntary. The intoxication is self-induced, and therefore would not amount to automatism. He could try and argue that the reaction was a response to the mixture of his prescribed medication and the drinking, but if there was a warning to not drink alcohol while taking the medication, prior fault would still be assumed. Moreover, the clinical depression is an internal cause, and as such, would also not be considered as a cause of automatism. This leaves the defence of insanity. Edwardo may be able to argue that he has a defect of reason that means that he does not know what he is doing. He will, however, have to show that the defect of reason came from a disease of the mind. The intoxication on its own will not amount to a disease of the mind. Edwardo would need to show that drinking had caused some other diagnosable medical condition. If he was unable to do so, in an approach akin to the one taken for diminished responsibility, assumingly the intoxication would need to be disregarded. This would leave the clinical depression to be considered. Clinical depression could amount to an internal disease of the mind. But, if the alcohol is removed from consideration, Edwardo would need to prove on the balance of probabilities that the depression caused a defect of reason so that he did not know the nature and quality of his acts or that what he was doing was unlawful and morally wrong.

9.4.2 Intoxicated Mistake and Self-Defence

Intoxication can also lead to a mistake being made. In law it is no excuse to claim that you mistakenly believed that something was not a crime, which is. A drunken mistake can, however, provide a defence when the intoxication means that the defendant mistakenly believes that he is damaging property where the owner would consent to such damage.[101] This is due to the defendant's belief in the consent being assessed subjectively.[102] A drunken mistake to consent is not, however, a defence to sexual offences.[103] The belief in consent is judged objectively,[104] and so if it was unreasonable to make the mistake when sober the defendant will not avoid liability. Thus, demonstrating a clear policy decision to protect an individual's bodily integrity.

Similarly, Parliament has also made it clear that when a defendant mistakenly believes that they need to use force to defend themselves because they are voluntarily intoxicated then they will have

100 *R v Dietschmann* [2003] UKHL 10.

101 *Jaggard v Dickinson* [1981] QB 527.

102 Section 5(2)(a) of the Criminal Damage Act 1971 provides a defence of consent to criminal damage if the defendant honestly believes, "that the person or persons whom he believed to be entitled to consent to the destruction of or damage to the property in question had so consented, or would have so consented to it if he or they had known of the destruction or damage and its circumstances".

103 *R v Fotheringham* (1989) 88 Cr App R 206.

104 See Chapter 8.2.2 for further discussion of consent under the Sexual Offences Act 2003.

no defence of self-defence.[105] This policy-based provision, to not allow people to use intoxication as an excuse, was given a wide interpretation in *R v Taj*.[106]

R v Taj

In *Taj*, the defendant encountered the victim who was at the side of the road with his broken-down car. Due to psychosis and paranoia induced by historic drink and drug abuse, the defendant mistakenly thought that the victim was a terrorist and presented a bomb threat. The defendant notified the police, who arrived at the scene and confirmed there was no threat. The defendant remained concerned and later returned to the scene and attacked the victim with a tyre iron, causing substantial injuries. He was charged with attempted murder, but at trial tried to rely upon section 76(4)(b) of the Criminal Justice and Immigration Act 2008. This allows a defendant to rely on a genuinely held mistaken belief in the need to use self-defence. The court, however, concluded that because the defendant had a history of drink and drug misuse, the circumstances fell under section 76(5) of the Criminal Justice and Immigration Act 2008. This section does not enable the defendant to rely on any mistaken belief attributable to intoxication that was voluntarily induced. Thus, the defence of self defence was withdrawn from the jury and the defendant was convicted. The defendant appealed on the basis that this was a misdirection as he had not been voluntarily intoxicated on the day of the incident, similarly to the facts of Harris discussed above. The Court of Appeal, nevertheless, distinguished the case from *R v Coley, McGhee and Harris*,[107] which had not focussed on self-defence. They stated that there were strong policy reasons for giving a wide meaning to the word "attributable" used within section 76(5).[108] Therefore, because his mistaken belief in the need to use self-defence was due to his psychosis and paranoia that was a direct and proximate result of drink and drug abuse in the days and weeks prior to the incident, it was attributable to intoxication that was voluntarily induced.[109] Thus, this provided an application of the policy-based prior fault approach adopted in *DPP v Majewski*.[110] Consequently, Taj's appeal was dismissed.[111]

Returning to the final scenario at the start of the chapter, Fabian has mistakenly used force in self-defence as a result of substance abuse paranoia. Like in the scenarios discussed previously, Fabian would only be able to rely on self-induced intoxication for specific intent crimes to show a lack of the required *mens rea*, and this would only be relevant if he was intoxicated at the time of the incident. Similarly, he may also struggle to rely on the defences of automatism and insanity for the reasons previously considered in relation to the scenario involving Edwardo. This leaves the defence of self-defence. The court will be in a position of having to determine whether the mistake was attributable to a direct and proximate result of the voluntary intoxication, or whether it was a result of a long-term "mental illness precipitated (perhaps over a considerable period) by alcohol or drug misuse".[112] In the latter situation, self-defence would not be excluded

105 Section 76(5) of the Criminal Justice and Immigration Act 2008. See Chapter 12.3.1 for a more general discussion of self-defence.
106 [2018] EWCA Crim 1743.
107 *R v Taj* [2018] EWCA Crim 1743, [60].
108 *R v Taj* [2018] EWCA Crim 1743, [30].
109 *R v Taj* [2018] EWCA Crim 1743, [31], [57]–[60].
110 *R v Taj* [2018] EWCA Crim 1743, [57].
111 *R v Taj* [2018] EWCA Crim 1743, [65].
112 *R v Taj* [2018] EWCA Crim 1743, [60].

under section 76(5) of the Criminal Justice and Immigration Act 2008. Following the judgment of *Taj*, Fabian's substance caused paranoia, may mean that self-defence would not be open to Fabian. This is even if the force used was proportionate in the circumstances as Fabian mistakenly believed them to be.[113]

9.5 Conclusion

This chapter has shown how the law relating to intoxication is morally charged and driven by policy. It is generally accepted that a person should not be able to escape criminal responsibility due to not forming the required *mens rea* due to intoxication. While concession is given to those who commit crime while involuntarily intoxicated, due to moral necessity, the law holds to blame those who have become voluntarily intoxicated and commit crime despite having no *mens rea*. The apportionment of blame on those who are voluntary intoxicated operates on the principle of prior fault. The assumption is that it is well-known that taking drink or drugs can lead to dangerous behaviour. Thereby, from imbibing in such substances, even when legal to do so, a person is being reckless. This approach only applies to basic intent crimes, which causes complexity with no clear distinction between which crimes are those of basic intent and those that are specific intent. Moreover, it becomes a matter of arbitrary distinction of whether voluntary intoxication will be considered or rejected depending on whether the specific intent crime has a basic "fallback" offence.

The policy justification for the *Majewski* rules is that the law needs to protect the public from dangerous people and uphold faith in the criminal justice system. For basic intent crimes, this does not depend on any subjective evaluation of the defendant's intentions, nor an assessment of the risks they foresaw from becoming voluntarily intoxicated. The objective assumption is that they are reckless. Perhaps this is understandable as they would not be facing a criminal charge unless they had undertaken some form of criminal action while in their intoxicated state. Nonetheless, legal principle requires that a person should not face criminal sanction unless they have the *mens rea* for the crime committed. The *Majewski* rules ignore this, and as such undermine the correspondence and coincidence theories of *actus reus* and *mens rea*. Other common law systems, have abandoned the Majewski rules without seeing a compromise on the policy goals of protecting the public. As such, perhaps it is time that the *Majewski* rules were abandoned in England too.

The defendant is being punished for the decision they made to become intoxicated before the crime was committed. This differs to other defences when a defendant is in an altered state, but due to lack of capacity. In these situations, such as those of insanity or automatism, the defendant has not made a choice to impair themselves. As such, they are not blameworthy. This simple analysis does not however account for the complex situations that arise with the interplay between intoxication and other defences. Continual advancement in medical knowledge, understanding of substance abuse and its short and long-term effects, mean that intoxication has been recognised as inducing medical conditions. As such, it becomes increasingly harder to establish where to draw the line between those who are voluntarily intoxicated and those who should have an alternative offence available to them due to their lack of capacity.

9.6 Further Reading

Gough S, "Surviving without Majewski?" [2000] Crim LR 720
Law Commission, *Intoxication and Criminal Liability* (Law Com No 314, 2009)
Law Commission, *Criminal Liability: Insanity and Automatism* (Law Com DP, 2013)

113 As defined in section 76(6) of Criminal Justice and Immigration Act 2008.

Reed A and Bolander M, *General Defences in Criminal Law: Domestic and Comparative Perspectives* (Routledge 2020)

Simester AP, "Intoxication Is Never a Defence" [2009] Crim LR 3

Stark F, "Prior Fault" [2014] CLJ 8

Virgo G, "The Law Commission Paper on Intoxication and Criminal Liability: Part 1: Reconciling Principles and Policy" [1993] Crim LR 415

Williams R, "Voluntary Intoxication – a Lost Cause" [2013] LQR 264

Chapter 10

Protecting the Sanctity of Human Life

Chapter Contents

DOI: 10.4324/9781003408383-11

10.1 Chapter Aims and Objectives

This chapter will consider the moral requirement to protect the sanctity of human life in relation to the availability of the defences of duress and necessity. Through an examination of *R v Dudley and Stephens*[1] and *R v Howe*,[2] it will examine how the legal protection that these defences provide have been shaped by moral concerns and policy considerations.

By the end of this chapter, you should be able to:

- Recognise the difference between a justification and an excuse.
- Define necessity and duress of circumstance.
- Define the sanctity of human life.
- Examine how legal principle was influenced by the need to protect the sanctity of human life in the decisions of *R v Dudley and Stephens* and *R v Howe*.

The issues that will be examined in this chapter can be illustrated through the following scenarios. Before starting the chapter, consider whether the following people are blameworthy for their actions.

- Austin has nowhere to live. He sees a house standing empty and unlocked and so he moves in.
- Bridie has suffered a horrific motorcycle accident and is in constant pain. The only thing to relieve her pain is taking illegal drugs. She is found in possession of these drugs.
- Caleb works for MI5 and has signed the Official Secrets Act 1989. He discovers corruption that he fears is putting lives at risk. Caleb has reported this to his manager but nothing has been done. He feels the only way to protect lives is to leak the information to the press.
- Daria breaks into an international airport and glues herself to the runway to stop planes from deporting immigrants to Africa.
- Elijah is homeless and has no winter clothes. One night he sees a bag of donated clothes outside a charity shop, and takes a coat to keep warm.
- Freddie is on a boat that is sinking. He needs to climb a ladder to get off the boat but the person ahead of him has "frozen" from fear on the ladder. Freddie can only get passed them by throwing them off of the ladder into the rising water, where they drown.
- Gordon is driving home from collecting his daughter from nursery. While stopped at a set of traffic lights an armed gunman gets into the back of the car next to his daughter, and says that if Gordon does not run over a pedestrian up ahead he will kill Gordon's daughter. Gordon runs over and kills the pedestrian.

10.2 Justifications and Excuses

Before examining when the law will provide a defence when a person takes another's life, the theoretical underpinning of defences needs to be understood. Defences can be divided into justifications

1 (1884) 14 QBD 273.
2 [1987] AC 417.

or excuses. This distinction is important because it "is a fundamental one for moral judgement".[3] The distinction assumes that justified actions are morally right or permissible because the defendant has chosen the lesser of two evils. Conversely, excused actions can be excused even though they are wrong. In other words, when a person is justified in the actions they have undertaken, the actions are not in themselves blameworthy. Whereas, when a person is excused, the actions are blameworthy, but in the particular circumstances the individual is not to blame. As Colvin states, justifications modify criminal rules by making (unlawful) actions lawful and right in certain circumstances, while excuses leave the criminal rule intact but allow a defence because of the special context.[4]

As the distinction imposes a moral judgment, it has an important declaratory function. It means that the law signals to society what types of behaviour are right because they are justified, and which are wrong but excused. This may have limited practical effect due to the outcome of the case potentially being the same regardless of whether a justificatory or excusatory defence is successfully pleaded. It will, however, have an impact on the narrative given of the defendant's actions that is presented at trial and, as will be further discussed below, the availability of any defence pleaded.

10.2.1 Necessity and Duress of Circumstances

In the scenarios given at the start of the chapter, it could be said that the defendants have committed the crimes that they have out of necessity.

Necessity was defined by Lord Justice Brooke in *Re A (Children) (Conjoined Twins: Surgical Separation)*[5] as when:

(i) the act is needed to avoid inevitable and irreparable evil;
(ii) no more should be done than is reasonably necessary for the purpose to be achieved; and
(iii) the evil inflicted should not be disproportionate to the evil avoided.

Necessity, is considered a justificatory defence based on the fact that the defendant's actions are morally correct as the lesser of two evils.[6] As this means that the defendant's actions need to be the morally right course of conduct, the application of the defence is limited. The restriction of necessity is famously enunciated by Lord Denning in *Southwark London Borough Council v Williams and Another.*[7] In denying the defence of necessity to a homeless family in dire need of accommodation, who were squatting in an empty local authority house, Lord Denning stated: "If homelessness were once admitted as a defence to trespass, no one's house could be safe. Necessity would open a door which no man could shut."[8] So, in the scenarios at the start of the chapter, Austin will have no defence of necessity if he moves into the empty house. The individual value of him having shelter is deemed not to outweigh the moral imperative that the law protects people's property.

---

3 K Greenawalt, "The Perplexing Border between Justification and Excuse" (1984) 84 Col LR 1897, 1898.

4 E Colvin, "Exculpatory Defences in Criminal Law" (1990) 10 OJLS 381, 385.

5 [2001] Fam 147, 240 quoting from James Fitzjames Stephen, *History of the Criminal Law of England*, vol II (Macmillan 1883).

6 See, for example: Edward B Arnolds and Norman F Garland, "The Defence of Necessity in Criminal Law: The Right to Choose the Lesser Evil" (1974) 65 J Crim L Criminol 289, 290; Michael Bohlander "In Extremis – Hijacked Airplanes, 'Collateral Damage' and the Limits of Criminal Law" [2006] Crim LR 579; Eric Colvin, "Exculpatory Defences in Criminal Law" (1990) 10 OJLS 381, 387; Ian Dennis, "On Necessity as a Defence to Crime: Possibilities, Problems and the Limits of Justification and Excuse" (2009) 3 Crim L Phil 29, 33; Joshua Dressler, "Justifications and Excuses: A Brief Review of Concepts and Literature" (1986–1987) 33 Wayne L Rev 1155, 1164; Joshua Dressler, "Exegesis of the Law of duress: Justifying the Excuse and Searching for its Proper Limits" (1989) 62 S Cal L Rev 1331, 1352; George Fletcher, "The Individualization of Excusing Conditions" (1973–1974) 47 S Cal L Rev 1269, 1274–1280.

7 [1971] Ch 734.

8 *Southwark London Borough Council v Williams and Another* [1971] Ch 734, 744.

The restrictive nature of necessity can further be seen in *R v Quayle*[9] when necessity was denied to the charge of possession, cultivation, importation or supply of cannabis for the purpose of pain management. Additionally, in *R v Shayler*, a former employee of the security service was unable to use the defence of necessity in relation to his illegal disclosure of protected information. He thought disclosure was necessary to protect the public, but as he could not identify any specific external action that created an imminent threat to life of the general public his defence failed.[10] More recently in *R v Thacker*, the Court of Appeal held that the trial judge was right not to put the matter of necessity before the jury. Even though the defendants were successful in their appeal against a conviction for intentional disruption of services at Stansted Airport, following their breach of the perimeter to stop individuals being deported to West Africa, the Court disagreed that the necessity defence could be relied upon to take the law into one's own hands in a functioning state governed by the rule of law.[11] Therefore, in the scenarios at the start of the chapter the restrictive application of the necessity defence may make it unlikely that Bridie, Caleb and Daria will be able to plead necessity. Nonetheless, as Reed has acknowledged when discussing necessity: "This body of jurisprudence is so inconsistent and policy themed that it seems to have come about by judicial divining rod."[12] Thus, suggesting the outcome is anything but certain.

Alternatively, in the scenarios at the start of the chapter, it could be said that the defendants have committed the crimes due to duress from the circumstances they find themselves in.[13] Duress of circumstances as defined in *R v Martin*,[14] requires:

> [F]irst, was the accused, or may he have been, impelled to act as he did because as a result of what he reasonably believed to be the situation he had good cause to fear that otherwise death or serious physical injury would result? Second, if so, may a sober person of reasonable firmness, sharing the characteristics of the accused, have responded to that situation by acting as the accused acted?[15]

It can be seen that there are overlaps in the definitions of necessity and duress of circumstances. For example, in the case of Elijah in the scenarios at the start of the chapter, he could claim that he has taken the coat out of necessity to keep warm. Alternatively, it could be said that he has taken the coat under duress. That he has acted out of fear that he will die or become seriously injured by not being able to stay warm, and any other reasonable person would have done the same.

There has been much academic debate as to whether duress of circumstances and necessity are two names for the same defence or whether duress of circumstances is a separate defence.[16] This has been fuelled by the terms being used interchangeably during case judgments. For example, Lord Woolf in *Conway* stated that "whether duress of circumstances is called 'duress' or 'necessity' does not matter".[17] Moreover, the two terms were merged in *Quayle* with "necessity of circumstance"

---

9 (2005) 1 WLR 3642.

10 *R v Shayler* (2001) 1 WLR 2206.

11 [2021] EWCA Crim 97, [101]–[103].

12 Alan Reed, "Necessity: Supply of Cannabis for Medical Purpose" (2005) JCL 464, 464.

13 See Chapter 11 for further discussion of duress.

14 *R v Martin* (1989) 88 Cr App R 343.

15 *R v Martin* (1989) 88 Cr App R 343, 346.

16 Peter Alldridge, "Duress, Duress of Circumstances and Necessity" (1989) 139 NLJ 911; Keith J Smith, "Duress and Steadfastness: In Pursuit of the Unintelligible" [1999] Crim LR 363, 367–368; Glanville Williams, *Criminal Law: The General Part* (2nd edition, Stevens and Sons 1961) 740. The Court of Appeal also considered the matter at length in *R v Shayler* (2001) 1 WLR 2206, 2223–2239.

17 *R v Conway* (1989) QB 290, 297. See also *R v Hasan* [2005] UKHL 22 at [22], *R v Pommell* (1995) 2 Cr App R 607, 614; *R v Willer* (1986) 83 Cr App R 225, 228. Furthermore, in *DPP v Jones* [1990] RTR 33, 36 when in another driving case Tutor Evans refers to "duress/necessity".

referred to.[18] Smith claims states that duress of circumstances was the courts recognising a general defence of necessity by a "linguistic sleight of hand",[19] whereas Lord Hailsham in *Howe* stated that duress is a "species of the genus of necessity".[20] Alternatively, Lindsey states that necessity emerged from duress of circumstances.[21] If the two defences are in fact the same defence, it would suggest that similarly to necessity, duress of circumstances should also be designated as a justificatory defence. Horder disagrees. In comparing the theoretical underpinnings of necessity and duress, he states that necessity is a strong justificatory defence because the defendant has a moral imperative to act. He claims that duress, on the other hand, is an excuse because it only requires the defendant to make a personal sacrifice.[22] Gross further argues that duress operates as an excuse because the threat that the defendant faces means that he does not have a fair opportunity to make a choice. For that reason, Gross separates duress from the justificatory defence of necessity that operates when the defendant has the opportunity to choose and the choice made is justified as the lesser of two evils.[23] Thus, duress is only an excusatory defence as the defendant is not acting to objectively promote a greater moral good for the whole of society, but the lack of fair opportunity becomes the basis for allowing the defence. On the other hand, necessity means that the defendant's actions have fulfilled some objectively desired moral value.

If it is accepted that the necessity defence applies when the defendant's actions are morally correct, this raises the question of whether it can ever be morally acceptable to take another's life.

10.3 The Sanctity of Human Life

The focus of this next section is the sanctity of human life. This is a religious concept, which "seems to denote the fact that human life is related to God".[24] Gushee further defines that:

> Human life is sacred: this means that each and every human being has been set apart for designation as being elevated status and dignity. Each human being must therefore be viewed with reverence and treated with due respect and care, with special attention to preventing any desecration or violation of a human being.[25]

This shows that human life has a special status that needs to be protected. This is understandable when considering the irreversible and irrevocable nature of killing. While other crimes, such as theft or battery, are an invasion of a person's rights, bodily integrity, and safety, they do not have the same finality as death. This does not mean, however, that the sanctity of human life will always make the taking of life unlawful. For example, as will be further discussed in Chapter 12,[26] the taking of a human life can be justified when completed in self-defence. In very limited circumstances the use of deadly force could also be lawful when used out of necessity. For example, following the attacks of 11 September 2001, the House of Commons Select Committee on Defence discussed the legality of using lethal force to shoot down a civilian plane that had hostile intent. Evidence from the Ministry of Defence stated that in domestic and international law they were satisfied that such

18 *R v Quayle* (2005) 1 WLR 3644, 3666.
19 Keith J Smith, "Duress and Steadfastness: In Pursuit of the Unintelligible" [1999] Crim LR 363, 367.
20 *R v Howe* [1987] AC 417, 429.
21 Jaime Lindsey, "A New Defence of Necessity in the Criminal Law" [2011] UCL Juris Rev 122, 123.
22 Jeremy Horder, "Self Defence, Necessity and Duress: Understanding the Relationship" (1998) 11 CJLJ 143, 143.
23 Hyman Gross, *A Theory of Criminal Justice* (Oxford University Press 1979) 137, 279.
24 David Novak, Sanctity of Human Life (Georgetown University Press 2007) ix.
25 David P. Gushee, *The Sacredness of Human Life: Why an Ancient Biblical Vision is Key to the World's Future* (Eerdmans, 2013) 24.
26 See Chapter 13.3.1.

actions would be legal.[27] These exceptions, however, are few and far between. As will be examined below, the moral requirement of the sanctity of human life is strong validation for limiting when an individual can take the life of another.

10.3.1 Is it Better to Die than to Kill?

> **R v Dudley and Stephens**
>
> In the infamous case of *R v Dudley and Stephens*[28] four individuals, including Dudley and Stephens, found themselves stranded for 20 days on a lifeboat after being shipwrecked over 1000 miles from shore. They had little food or water, and went several days without either. One of the individuals was 17-year-old cabin boy, Richard Parker. He had become progressively weaker and was close to death. Dudley decided, and acted, to kill Parker, with Stephens's assent, so they could feed from his flesh. Four days later they were rescued. The question in the case was whether in the circumstances this amounted to murder. The court rejected the plea of necessity, found the defendants guilty of murder, and sentenced them to death.

Thinking points:

- In the judgment of *R v Dudley and Stephens* the writings of Sir Matthew Hale are referred to. He states that self-defence is a defence that can justify killing, but necessity is not generally an accepted defence as a person "ought rather to die himself than kill an innocent".[29] Lord Coleridge agrees that it is not to be regretted that necessity does not provide a defence to murder.[30] How can this distinction to self-defence be justified?

Lord Coleridge states that although law and morals are not the same, that a complete divorce of law from morals would be fatal. As such, in the circumstances outlined it is the defendant's moral duty to sacrifice his own life rather than preserve it at the detriment of another life. This upholds the ideal of the sanctity of human life. Lord Coleridge justifies this approach by referring to Christianity and how Jesus made the ultimate sacrifice to save mankind.[31] Despite Lord Coleridge implying that he is following legal principle when he states, "[t]here is no safe path for judges to tread but to ascertain the law to the best of their ability",[32] it is clear from this that morals have swayed Lord Coleridge's reasoning. This is perhaps unsurprising when the whole premise of justifications, and thus necessity, is to weigh potential evils against each other to achieve the morally right outcome. Woolrich further argues that Lord Coleridge has been swayed by the Victorian idea that Christianity was the safeguard against the degeneration of society and morals. Therefore, to maintain law and order, and a cohesive society, sinful tendencies and

---

27 Defence Committee, *Defence: Sixth Report* (HC 2001–02, 518-II), Air Defence.

28 (1884) 14 QBD 273.

29 Sir Matthew Hale, *Historia Placitorum Coronae 1736* (Classical English Law Texts 1971) 51 cited in *R v Dudley and Stephens* (1884) 14 QBD 273, 283.

30 *R v Dudley and Stephens* (1884) 14 QBD 273, 287.

31 *R v Dudley and Stephens* (1884) 14 QBD 273, 287.

32 *R v Dudley and Stephens* (1884) 14 QBD 273, 288.

afflictions needed to be kept in check and the defence of necessity denied to stop the downward spiral of morality.[33]

This same reasoning does not apply when considering a defendant who has acted in self-defence. A victim who has acted as an aggressor towards the defendant morally forfeits their right to protection from harm under the law.[34] When the defendant responds in self-defence they are not infringing the rights of the victim, but are instead upholding their own moral right to protect their individual bodily integrity. Therefore, acting in self-defence, even when someone dies, can be distinguished from the situation of killing an innocent cabin boy for self-survival.

- Lord Coleridge, in discussing necessity, states "but it is quite plain that such a principle once admitted might be made the legal cloak for unbridled passion and atrocious crime".[35] What policy concern does he seem to be discussing?

It appears from this quote that one concern in *R v Dudley and Stephens* was that if the defence of necessity were to be allowed it would open the floodgates. It would become unclear when a person could choose not to follow the law through an alleged moral imperative to go against it. As already discussed, this approach of restricting the defence is echoed by Lord Denning in *Southwark LBC v Williams*.[36] It seems this policy consideration has informed the restrictive development of a limited defence of necessity.

- Lord Coleridge states that the law can set standards that any other ordinary person may not satisfy in the same circumstances.[37] Do you think this is fair? Would it make a difference if the actions taken were thought to be acceptable custom at the time?

Holding people to a higher standard than can ordinarily be expected, is a moralistic view of the law.[38] Not only is it trying to ensure that the law enforces morals, but also that the law encourages an even higher moral standard. This is based on the view that the law can act to change societal behaviour by criminalising certain actions, even if they are felt to be reasonable by the ordinary person. However, the wider spread a belief, or the more readily it is adhered to, the less likely the law will be able to change it.[39] Simpson argues, that before the decision in *R v Dudley and Stephens*, it was accepted custom of the sea that survival cannibalism could be resorted to, even when preceded by deliberate killing.[40] Therefore, if this was a widely held view that made killing morally acceptable at the time, the pronouncement that it was not acceptable in *R v Dudley and Stephens* would have little effect on customary practice. Alternatively, in a Victorian era guided by religious condemnation of perceived evil, the judgment can be seen as having a declaratory function, as well as deterrent effect,[41] to communicate what the law actually deemed acceptable.

Lord Coleridge does consider the harshness of not allowing a defence of necessity. He identifies that any individual injustice can be mitigated by the Sovereign exercising the prerogative of mercy.

---

33 Malcolm Woolrich, "R v Dudley and Stephens: Degeneration, the Christian Mindset and Judicial Reasoning" (2020) 22 Ecc LJ 15.

34 For more discussion see, Joshua Dressler, "Justifications and Excuses: A Brief Review of the Concepts and the Literature" (1986–1987) 33 Wayne L Rev 1155, 1164.

35 *R v Dudley and Stephens* (1884) 14 QBD 273, 288.

36 [1971] 2 All ER 175.

37 *R v Dudley and Stephens* (1884) 14 QBD 273, 288.

38 See Chapter 1.3.1. for more discussion of morals.

39 For more discussion see, Paul Robinson and Robert Kurzban, "Concordance and Conflict in Institutions of Justice" (2007) 91 Minnesota L Rev 1829; Paul Robinson and John Darley, "Institutions of Justice: Implications for Criminal Law and Justice Policy" (2007) S Cal L Rev 1.

40 AW Brian Simpson, Cannibalism and the Common Law (University of Chicago Press 1984).

41 See Chapter 1.3.2 for more discussion of these policy aims of the law.

Ultimately, this is what occurred, with Queen Victoria pardoning Dudley and Stephen's death sentence and commuting it to a six-month prison sentence.

- How could a defence of necessity be available in the later case of *Re A*, when it was so restricted in the earlier case of *R v Dudley and Stephens?*

In the case of *Re A*,[42] twins Mary and Jodie were born conjoined. The parents were devout Roman Catholics and due to their religious beliefs opposed the suggested medical treatment to separate the twins. Separation of the twins was expected to result in the death of Mary, who depended on a shared artery with Jodie to receive sufficient oxygenated blood. Without the operation, medical professionals opined that both twins would die within three to six months. This was due to the increased pressure that was being put on to Jodie's heart. Alternatively, if the twins were separated, Jodie would have a strong chance of survival. The Court granted a declaration so that the separation operation could be carried out. The parents appealed to the Court of Appeal. This case poses an issue in terms of the sanctity of human life. If the operation is not carried out then both Mary and Jodie would have died. Thus, offending the protection of the sanctity of human life. Alternatively, if the operation is carried out then the life of Jodie is being chosen over that of Mary, which once again offends the sanctity of human life principle. Both the cases of *R v Dudley and Stephens* and *Re A* involve a life being sacrificed to save that of another. As discussed above, in *R v Dudley and Stephens* a defence of necessity was rejected as a person ought rather to die themselves than kill an innocent. In *Re A*, however, the Court of Appeal held that the operation could be carried out. This led to the death of Mary and the survival of Jodie.

The significant difference between *R v Dudley and Stephens* and *Re A*, is perhaps the selection of the victim. In *R v Dudley and Stephens*, the defendants had discussed drawing lots to see who would die, but ultimately did not take this approach.[43] They selected Richard Parker as the one to die. In *Re A* the selection of Mary as the weaker twin was down to nature. Therefore, one of the key objections that prevented a necessity defence being available in *R v Dudley and Stephens*, of the defendants choosing who should live and who should die,[44] was not applicable in *Re A*.[45]

In the scenario at the start of the chapter, Freddie can only escape the sinking ship by throwing the "frozen" person from the ladder. In doing this he has chosen to save his own life, and those of anyone behind him, at the detriment of killing an innocent person. It could be argued that: (i) his act is needed to avoid inevitable and irreparable evil; (ii) he has done no more than is reasonably necessary for the purpose to be achieved; and (iii) the evil inflicted is not disproportionate to the evil avoided as he has sacrificed one life to potentially save many. Thus, as the definitely elements of the defence are successfully fulfilled, it should mean that Freddie has a defence for his actions. Notwithstanding this, the decision in *R v Dudley and Stephens*, and the requirement to protect the sanctity of human life, means, that despite fulfilling the defence requirements, no defence will be available to Freddie. A moral standard is applied that requires Freddie, and all those who are trapped behind him, die. Alternatively, as has been argued by Smith in the fortieth series of the Hamlyn Lectures, this situation could be distinguished from *R v Dudley and Stephens*. This is because, like in *Re A*, the defendant has not selected the victim.[46] In reality, it may be that prosecutorial discretion to not prosecute would need to be exercised in such a situation, to prevent Freddie being labelled a murderer when doing what many others would have done.

---

42 [2001] Fam 147.

43 *R v Dudley and Stephens* (1884) 14 QBD 273, 273.

44 *R v Dudley and Stephens* (1884) 14 QBD 273, 287–288.

45 [2001] Fam 147, 239.

46 This fictional example is based on the *Herald of Free Enterprise* disaster in Zeebrugge. For further discussion, see JC Smith, *Justification and Excuse in Criminal Law* (Stevens and Sons 1989) 73–79.

10.3.2 Sanctity of Human Life and Duress

Unlike the defence of necessity, duress does not require that the defendant does the right thing. Therefore, if there is no requirement that the defendant's actions be deemed as morally acceptable, does this mean duress can be a defence to murder by excusing the defendant for their wrongful actions in killing another?

R v Howe

This case considered the conjoined appeals of Howe and Banister, and Burke and Clarkson.[47] In the first case the two appellants, with an intended victim and another man called Bailey, were driven to an isolated area by a man called Murray. Murray was an older man with 25 previous convictions, including convictions for violence. The appellants assaulted the victim, and then Bailey killed him through strangulation. On a second similar occasion, at the direction of Murray, the appellants jointly strangled a victim with Bannister's shoelace. On a third occasion, the intended victim escaped before he could be killed. The four men were tried on indictment of two counts of murder and one of conspiracy to murder. During the trial, Murray and Bailey pleaded guilty. The appellants, Howe and Bannister, put forward a defence of duress. They argued that they feared for their own lives if they did not do as Murray directed. The judge left the issue of duress to the jury in respect of the first murder and the conspiracy to murder the third victim, but not for the second count of murder when the victim was strangled by the appellants. The appellants were convicted on all three counts.

In the second appeal, Burke, dressed as a police officer had shot the victim at Clarkson's direction. This was to prevent the victim from giving evidence against Clarkson. The appellants, Burke and Clarkson, were tried on a single count of murder. Burke's defence was that he had agreed to shoot the victim under duress because he feared that Clarkson would kill him if he did not do so, but that the gun had then gone off accidentally. The judge directed the jury that Burke could not rely on duress as a defence to the charge of murder. He left the issue of duress to the jury for a charge of manslaughter, if they believed that the killing had been unintentional. The judge further directed the jury that if they found that Burke was guilty of manslaughter, correspondingly the most Clarkson could be convicted of was also manslaughter. The jury returned a verdict of murder for both appellants.

The four appellants appeals were dismissed by the Court of Appeal. In granting leave to appeal to the House of Lords, the Court of Appeal certified three questions of law of general public importance:

(1) Is duress available as a defence to a person charged with murder as a principal in the first degree (the actual killer)?
(2) Can one who incites or procures by duress another to kill or to be a party to a killing be convicted of murder if that other is acquitted by reason of duress?
(3) Does the defence of duress fail if the prosecution prove that a person of reasonable firmness sharing the characteristics of the defendant would not have given way to the threats as the defendant did?[48]

47 *R v Howe* [1987] AC 417.
48 *R v Howe* [1987] AC 417, 423.

In comparison to the situations outlined above, where the conditions had made the defendants feel the need to act from necessity or duress of circumstance, in this case the defendants acted from a direct threat. In *R v Howe* the House of Lords confirmed the definition of duress of threats provided by the Court of Appeal in *R v Graham.*[49] This requires that (i) the defendant was impelled to act due to a reasonable belief that otherwise they would suffer death or serious physical injury, and (ii) the prosecution has made the jury sure that a sober person of reasonable firmness would not have acted in the same way.[50] Furthermore, the House of Lords confirmed that duress could not be a defence to principals or secondary parties charged with murder.[51]

Thinking points:

- In *R v Howe*, Lord Hailsham stated: "I do not at all accept in relation to the defence of murder it is either good morals, good policy or good law to suggest . . . that a man of reasonable fortitude is not supposed to be capable of heroism if he is asked to take an innocent life rather than sacrifice his own".[52] What previous case authority did the House of Lords refer to in justifying this decision?

One case the House of Lords relied on to reach their judgment was *R v Tyler.*[53] This case involved two men who were charged and convicted of murder as principals after aiding and abetting another man to kill. Their plea of duress was rejected. Lord Denman went as far as to say, "that no man, from fear of consequence to himself, has a right to make himself a party to committing mischief on mankind".[54] This case is problematic in two key ways. First, it seems to suggest that duress is not available as a defence to any crime against a person, but at this point in history duress had already been accepted as a defence for a range of crimes including those as serious as treason.[55] Second, this case did not necessarily mean that duress could never be a defence to murder. Lord Denman stated that the defence is unavailable when the defendants are acting in apprehension of personal danger,[56] so this does not necessarily rule out the defence being available when the defendants fear death.

The House of Lords in *R v Howe* also relied on *R v Dudley and Stephens.*[57] As discussed above,[58] this case depended on the availability of the defence of necessity, whereas in *R v Howe* a defence of duress was used. As identified above,[59] the two defences have different theoretical underpinnings. Necessity is a justificatory defence and duress is excusatory. Thus, the outcome of *Dudley and Stephens* was at most only persuasive precedent on the outcome of *Howe.* As such, contrary to what Lord Hailsham states, the House of Lords could have chosen not to follow *Dudley and Stephens* due to its

49 [1982] 1 WLR 294, 300.
50 *R v Howe* [1987] AC 417, 459.
51 See Chapter 11 for more discussion of principals and secondary parties.
52 *R v Howe* [1987] AC 417, 432.
53 *R v Tyler* (1838) 8 C & P 616 cited in *R v Howe* [1987] AC 417, 439.
54 *R v Tyler* (1838) 8 C & P 616, 620.
55 See for example, *John de Culewen* (1331) Edward III Statute of the Realm 1333 cited in Sir Matthew Hale, *Historia Placitorum Coronae* 1736 (Classical English Law Texts 1971) 167–168; and *Oldcastle's Case* (1419) cited in Sir Matthew Hale, *Historia Placitorum Coronae* 1736 (Classical English Law Texts 1971) 50.
56 *R v Tyler* (1838) 8 C & P 616, 621.
57 *R v Dudley and Stephens* (1884) 14 QBD 273 cited in *Howe* [1987] AC 417, 439.
58 See Chapter 10.3.1.
59 See Chapter 10.2.1.

lack of applicability, without declaring it bad law.[60] Moreover, *Dudley and Stephens* was decided in the Queen's Bench Divisional Court. As a lower court, this again meant that the precedent established in *Dudley and Stephens* was only persuasive on the House of Lords in *Howe*, and as such, did not need to be followed.

Both the cases of *R v Tyler* and *R v Dudley and Stephens* were decided pre-1898. Relying on authorities pre-1898 is outdated. As Lord Wilberforce acknowledges in *Abbott v The Queen*,[61] it must be observed that there is little use in looking back at authorities that are earlier than 1898, as until then the accused could not give evidence on their own behalf. This would have meant that before 1898, putting forward a plea of duress would almost certainly be foredoomed to failure. The defendant would not be able to provide evidence of why they acted as they did. Despite these comments by Lord Wilberforce in 1977, relying on pre-1898 authorities is exactly what the House of Lords did in *R v Howe* in 1987 when they were persuaded to deny duress as a defence to murder.

In *R v Howe*, although the House of Lords did not follow Lord Wilberforce's statements in *Abbott v The Queen* about not relying on pre-1898 cases, they did rely on the precedent set by the majority in that case.[62] In *Abbott v The Queen* the defendant was charged with murder after assisting in the killing of a woman, in the commune where he lived in Trinidad, under threats of death to himself and his mother. The majority in the Privy Council decided that duress was not available to the principal in a murder case.[63] In 1982, five years after the judgment in *Abbott v The Queen*, but five years before *R v Howe*, the Court of Appeal was faced with determining the definition for duress in *R v Graham*.[64] The defendant was tried for murder as a principal after assisting his male partner to kill his wife. The Court of Appeal did not follow the precedent in *Abbott v The Queen* as the prosecution did not argue, nor did the Court of Appeal examine, that the defence was unavailable to a charge of murder when formulating the accepted definition of duress.

In *R v Howe* the House of Lords could have chosen to ignore the precedent in *Abbott v The Queen* as once again it was only persuasive authority. Instead, they chose to follow it to determine that duress could not be a defence to murder. Alternative persuasive precedent came from Lords Wilberforce and Edmund-Davies in their dissenting judgments in *Abbott v The Queen*, when their Lordships commented that duress should be a defence to principals who committed murder under duress.[65] Following this persuasive precedent would have meant that the duress defence would be available in *R v Howe*.

Further persuasive precedent came from the *obiter dicta* comments of the majority in the House of Lords in *DPP for Northern Ireland v Lynch*.[66] Duress had been allowed as a defence to a secondary party to murder,[67] with Lord Morris stating that "instinct and perhaps duty of self-preservation is powerful and natural".[68] Moreover, that to not allow the defence to secondary parties to murder would be "censorious and inhumane".[69] As part of the majority Lords Wilberforce and Edmund Davies again commented that duress should be a defence to principals who committed murder under duress.[70] The House of Lords chose not to follow this persuasive precedent.[71] This means even when a defendant fulfils the requirements for the duress defence, of having fear of death or

60 See *R v Howe* [1987] AC 417, 429 where Lord Hailsham states that by allowing the appeal it would mean that the House of Lords would have to say that *Dudley and Stephens* (1884) 14 QBD 273 was bad law.

61 *Abbott v The Queen* [1977] AC 755, 772.

62 *R v Howe* [1987] AC 417, 436.

63 *Abbott v The Queen* [1977] AC 755, 768.

64 *R v Graham* [1982] 1 WLR 294.

65 *Abbott v The Queen* [1977] AC 755, 770 (Lord Wilberforce and Lord Edmund-Davies).

66 [1975] AC 653.

67 See Chapter 11.5.

68 *DPP for Northern Ireland v Lynch* [1975] AC 653, 671.

69 *DPP for Northern Ireland v Lynch* [1975] AC 653.

70 *DPP for Northern Ireland v Lynch* [1975] AC 653, 680–681 (Lord Wilberforce) and 715 (Lord Edmund Davies).

71 *R v Howe* [1987] AC 417, 432.

serious injury and a reasonable person acting in the same way, no defence will be available for a charge of murder.

Therefore, despite the excusatory nature of the defence of duress, which does not require the defendant to do what is deemed the morally right thing, the defence is not available as the defendant is expected to act as a hero by not succumbing to the threat.[72]

- Denying duress as a defence to murder can be explained with reference to the sanctity of human life, but how does this explain why the defence is potentially available for manslaughter and not available to attempted murder?

The writings of Hale, discussed above,[73] were referred to repeatedly in *R v Howe* to argue that a person ought to die themselves rather than kill an innocent.[74] In an echo of the reasoning given by Lord Coleridge in *R v Dudley and Stephens*, to hold otherwise would divorce law from morals.[75] While this provides an explanation of duress not being a defence to murder it causes other issues.[76] First, if protecting innocent life is the fundamental reason for excluding duress as a defence to murder, then duress should also be denied to manslaughter. There has been no authority to suggest that duress cannot be used for manslaughter. This point is further complicated as there is a very fine line between the *mens rea* for murder and manslaughter. Intent for murder can be found when the defendant foresees the consequence of at least serious injury as a virtual certainty.[77] Anything less than this, for example, the consequence being highly probable, is insufficient for murder but could lead to a charge of manslaughter. This means that the jury's determination of what level of foresight the defendant has could mean the difference between a conviction for murder with a mandatory life sentence, or a complete acquittal if the defence of duress is accepted to a charge of manslaughter. If the sanctity of human life is the guiding moral principle, then the defence should not be available to either offence.

Second, a person can be convicted of murder with only intention to cause serious bodily harm. This means a defendant could kill and have the same *mens rea* as someone committing a grievous bodily harm offence.[78] As previously discussed, the *mens rea* of murder is as such, as it may only be a matter of luck or intervention that the person does not die when serious harm is intentionally inflicted.[79] The result is that a defendant who intends serious harm, and as a consequence the defendant dies, will have no defence of duress. Whereas, another defendant who intends the same harm, and carries out the same actions but the victim survives, will have a defence available to them. This anomaly between grievous bodily harm and the current definition of murder can be explained by the sanctity of human life argument. No life has been taken when the defendant's actions only amount to grievous bodily harm. This same rationale does not, however, apply to allow a duress defence to attempted murder. Similarly, to a charge of grievous bodily harm no one has died when the defendant has committed attempted murder. Yet, the defence of duress is still denied due to the defendant's intention to kill.[80] Thus demonstrating that the policy concern,[81] of not allowing people who want to kill to have a defence, provides justification for denying a defence even when the sanctity of human life has not yet been infringed.

---

72 For further discussion see, Conor Gearty, "Howe to be a Hero" (1987) Crim LJ 203.
73 See Chapter 10.3.1.
74 *R v Howe* [1987] AC 417 at 427, 449 and 451.
75 *R v Howe* [1987] AC 417, 430.
76 *R v Howe* [1987] AC 417, 445.
77 *R v Woollin* (1999) 1 AC 82.
78 Under section 18 of the Offences against the Person Act 1861.
79 See Chapter 5.8.
80 *R v Gotts* (1992) 2 AC 412.
81 See Chapter 1.3.2. for more discussion of policy.

- The denial of duress to a charge of murder means that a person who kills while under duress will be labelled and punished in the same way as someone who kills not under duress. This offends the principle of fair labelling. Furthermore, the law allows a partial defence to murder for those who kill out of anger,[82] but *R v Howe* provides that no defence is available to those who kill out of fear. How can this difference be reconciled?

A person convicted of murder faces a mandatory life sentence. There are different starting points for the minimum amount of years to be served depending on factors such as the age of the offender, the degree of premeditation or planning, and whether the crime was motivated by racial or religious hostility. Schedule 21(10)(e) of the Sentencing Act 2020 allows that a fear of violence can be considered as a mitigating factor, once the starting point for establishing the minimum amount of years to be served has been determined.[83] This, however, does not give a judge the discretion to sentence to less than a mandatory life sentence even when the defendant has acted under duress.

One way to address this would be to not require a mandatory life sentence for those who had killed out of fear for themselves or those they feel responsible for. In *R v Howe*, the House of Lords considered and rejected the authoritative writings of Stephen, which asserted that duress should only be considered as a mitigating factor in sentencing and not as an excuse for the crime.[84] Such an approach would respect the sanctity of human life, as not allowing a defence of duress would retain the declaratory function of signalling that killing (even when under duress) is unacceptable, but would give judges wider sentencing discretion to avoid the harshness of the uniform application of the mandatory life sentence.

Mitigation was the approach taken to sentencing by the trial judge in *Attorney General v Whelan*.[85] The defendant had been convicted of handling stolen goods. The judge held that duress was only relevant to the sentence to be imposed. On appeal the conviction was quashed and a full acquittal given, as it was held that duress should lead to a full acquittal and not just mitigate the punishment. As Lord Hailsham asserts in *R v Howe*, "duress, if available and made out, entitles the accused to a clean acquittal, without, it has been said, the 'stigma' of a conviction".[86] This demonstrates that even if the sentence could be mitigated for murder, this would be problematic as the defendant would still be labelled as a murderer. Therefore, an alternative approach is needed to balance the individual's right to be correctly labelled and the utilitarian need to protect the sanctity of human life.

One way of achieving this balance, without removing the mandatory life sentence for murder, would be to recognise duress as a partial defence that would reduce a charge of murder to manslaughter. It would seem anomalous that duress operates as a full defence, available to all crimes except murder, alongside other justificatory defences such as self-defence, necessity or consent. It could more easily be compared to special partial defences, such as loss of control, where the defendant has the *actus reus* and *mens rea* of murder but with a legal excuse. Yet, loss of control is not generally available to all crimes, whereas duress currently does provide an excuse to a range of crimes.

In reaching the decision in R v Howe, the House of Lords confirmed the judgment given by Lord Lane in *R v Graham*. As part of that judgment Lord Lane determined that an objective assessment of the reasonableness of the defendant's actions was required to ensure consistency with what was then provocation (now loss of control), as the two defences were analogous.[87] Despite the claim in

82 See Chapter 12 for more discussion of the defence of Loss of Control.

83 Schedule 21(7) of the Sentencing Act 2020.

84 James Fitzjames Stephen, *History of the Criminal Law of England*, vol II (Macmillan 1883) 108 cited in *R v Howe* [1987] AC 417, 428, 436, 439 and 445.

85 *Attorney General v Whelan* [1934] IR 518.

86 *R v Howe* [1987] AC 417, 435.

87 *R v Graham* [1982] 1 WLR 294, 300.

R v Howe that Lord Lane's judgment in *R v Graham* was "entirely correct",[88] the Lords in *R v Howe* did not agree that duress should provide a partial defence to murder. Instead, they drew distinctions between duress and provocation. Lord Hailsham stated that it would be contrary to principle, to treat duress and provocation in the same way. He asserted that provocation is based on an emotional loss of control, whereas under duress a conscious decision may be coolly undertaken to sacrifice an innocent life.[89] This suggests that under provocation the defendant has not made a rational choice so is not fully blameworthy, but under duress a rational choice has been made. Moreover, when acting under provocation the defendant kills the person who is the source of the provocation, whereas when acting under duress the defendant has killed an innocent third party. These differences demonstrate how a distinction can be made between the different defences.

Moreover, Lord Griffiths further identified that by allowing duress as a complete defence to most crimes, but only as a partial defence to murder, would create an anomaly in the law.[90] Thus, it if was deemed morally incorrect that someone who killed under duress was treated in the same way as someone who was not under duress, the only alternatives would be to make duress mitigation to all crimes, which is unappealing for the reasons stated above, or to introduce a new partial defence for murder for when a defendant kills out of fear. This, however, would be a matter for Parliament.[91]

The Law Commission, in making recommendations to Parliament on how the law should be reformed, has grappled with the issue of whether duress should provide a defence to murder. In the last consultation paper on the matter, "A New Homicide Act for England and Wales?",[92] it was proposed that homicide should be divided into first degree murder, second degree murder, and manslaughter.[93] In a significant change from its previous recommendations, that duress should be a full defence to murder,[94] the Law Commission proposed that duress would only provide a partial defence to murder by reducing it from first degree to second degree murder. The rationale for duress being a partial defence, rather than a full defence, was that duress is an excuse, not a justification.[95] The proposals aimed to achieve consistency between duress and the other partial defences to murder. Additionally, the proposals intended to prevent the unfairness, especially to younger defendants,[96] caused by no defence being available to murder.[97] These proposals, would, however, mean that the defendant was still labelled as a second-degree murderer. Despite the reduction in label from a first-degree murderer, this is still unjust for someone who has only acted due to duress.

In 2006 the Law Commission revised the suggestions they had made one year earlier.[98] Opinion was divided among consultees in response to the 2005 consultation paper as to whether duress should be a full or partial defence to first degree, second degree, and attempted murder. An overwhelming majority thought that duress should provide a defence to murder where

---

88 *R v Howe* [1987] AC 417, 459.

89 *R v Howe* [1987] AC 417, 435.

90 *R v Howe* [1987] AC 417, 445.

91 For example, as Lord Bridge in *R v Howe* [1987] AC 417, 437 states: "Not only is it for Parliament to decide whether the proposed reform of the law is socially appropriate, but it is also by legislation alone, as opposed to judicial development."

92 Law Commission, *A New Homicide Act for England and Wales?* (Law Com CP No 177, 2005).

93 Law Commission, *A New Homicide Act for England and Wales?* (Law Com CP No 177, 2005) part 2.

94 Law Commission, *Legislating the Criminal Code. Offences against the Person and General Principles* (Law Com No 218, 1993) and Law Commission, *Report on Defences of General Application* (Law Com No 83, 1977) para 2.43 where the Law Commission stated that it would be "unjust that the defendant should suffer the stigma of a conviction even for manslaughter. We do not think any social purpose is served by requiring the law to prescribe such standards of heroism."

95 Law Commission, *A New Homicide Act for England and Wales?* (Law Com CP No 177, 2005) para 7.7.

96 Law Commission, *A New Homicide Act for England and Wales?* (Law Com CP No 177, 2005) paras 1.72 and 1.78. This injustice leads the Law Commission to ask whether duress should be a full defence to murder and attempted murder (para 7.73).

97 Law Commission, *A New Homicide Act for England and Wales?* (Law Com CP No 177, 2005) para 7.32.

98 Law Commission, *A New Homicide Act for England and Wales?* (Law Com CP No 177, 2005).

the defendant felt threatened with death or life-threatening harm. A slight majority of those responses stated that duress should be a partial defence to murder rather than a full defence.[99] Notwithstanding this response, the Law Commission recommended that duress should be a full defence to murder.[100] One of the stated reasons for this change was that the Law Commission had overemphasised the importance of duress being treated consistently with the partial defences of diminished responsibility and provocation.[101] The Law Commission stated that it was inappropriate to categorise duress as an excusatory defence in the same way as other special partial defences, as they had done in 2005. Their reasoning was that in some instances, duress comes closer to being a justification for killing.[102] The Law Commission provided several reasons why duress should be a full defence to murder. These included that the defence has a moral basis. As such, if the jury think that the defendant has acted reasonably, then they should not be convicted. Moreover, that the sanctity of human life argument was not suitable in this context as a person should not be expected (and the criminal law should not promote) that it is better to save the life of a stranger rather than the life of your child.[103]

Therefore, as the law stands, judges feel unable to extend duress to provide a defence to murder as this is a matter best left to Parliament. Parliament, however, have not enacted the changes proposed by the Law Commission. This is perhaps unsurprising as there appears to be little consensus on how the law should be reformed. As a result, a person who kills out of fear is left with less legal protection than one who kills out of anger.

In the scenario at the start of the chapter, Gordon kills an innocent pedestrian to save the life of his daughter. The defence of duress firstly requires that Gordon genuinely and reasonably fears death or serious injury for himself or someone he feels responsible for.[104] In the scenario, this criterion is fulfilled. Secondly, to reject the defence the prosecution must make the jury sure that a reasonable person would not have done the same thing. This criterion could also be fulfilled. Many people may run over a stranger to save the life of their child. The decision in *R v Howe*, however, makes the assessment of what society thinks is morally acceptable behaviour irrelevant. Even if others would do the same, or would excuse Gordon for his wrongful actions, the law from *R v Howe* prevents the duress defence from being applied. Gordon is deemed to be just as blameworthy as the gunman, or any other cold bloodied killer, who kills while not under duress. No partial defence is open to Gordon and he is, therefore, labelled and punished as a murderer.

10.4 Conclusion

Necessity, as a justificatory defence, requires the defendant to do the right thing. In the case of killing, this means that under the law the defendant ought to die themselves rather than kill an innocent. This protects the sanctity of human life. This moral constraint of having to do the right thing, in addition to floodgate concerns, has meant the defence of necessity has developed in a restrictive manner making the defence hard to successfully plead.

The same justificatory theoretical underpinning for necessity does not necessarily apply to duress. But, as this chapter has shown, the defence of duress is an enigma. It is not clear whether duress and necessity are separate or species of the same defence, or whether duress can truly be said to be an excusatory defence. This lack of clarity has led to difficulties in the courts developing

99 Law Commission, *Murder, Manslaughter and Infanticide* (Law Com No 304, 2006) para 6.17.
100 Law Commission, *Murder, Manslaughter and Infanticide* (Law Com No 304, 2006) para 6.21.
101 Law Commission, *Murder, Manslaughter and Infanticide* (Law Com No 304, 2006) paras 6.39 and 6.40.
102 Law Commission, *Murder, Manslaughter and Infanticide* (Law Com No 304, 2006) para 6.61.
103 Law Commission, *Murder, Manslaughter and Infanticide* (Law Com No 304, 2006) paras 6.43–6.52.
104 *R v Wright* [2000] Crim LR 510.

a coherent defence, and Parliament has chosen not to enact a law to resolve the issues. In *R v Howe* the House of Lords had the opportunity to make a clear distinction between duress and necessity. Instead, they chose to follow the persuasive precedent from the necessity case of *R v Dudley and Stephens* to conclude that duress could not be a defence to murder. Moreover, they determined that a person faced with having to decide who should live and who should die is expected to act as a hero and sacrifice their own life, thus demonstrating that the law tries to hold us to a moral standard that we cannot reasonably be expected to achieve.

10.5 Further Reading

Bohlander M, "Of Shipwrecked Sailors, Unborn Children, Conjoined Twins and Hijacked Airplanes – Taking Human Life and the Defence of Necessity" [2006] J Crim L 147

Colvin E, "Exculpatory Defences in Criminal Law" (1990) 10 Oxford Journal of Legal Studies 381

Gearty C, "Howe to Be a Hero" (1987) Crim LJ 203

Elkington A, "The Historical Development of Duress and the Unfounded Result of Denying Duress as a Defence to Murder" [2023] J Crim L 161

Greenawalt K, "The Perplexing Border between Justification and Excuse" (1984) 84 Col LR 1897

Gushee D, *The Sacredness of Human Life: Why an Ancient Biblical Vision is Key to the World's Future* (Eerdmans 2013)

Novak D, *Sanctity of Human Life* (Georgetown University Press 2007)

Reed A, "Necessity: Supply of Cannabis for Medical Purpose" (2005) JCL 464

Simpson AWB, *Cannibalism and the Common Law* (University of Chicago Press 1984)

Woolrich M, "R v Dudley and Stephens: Degeneration, the Christian Mindset and Judicial Reasoning" (2020) 22 Ecc LJ 15

Chapter 11

Discouraging Gang Activity

Chapter Contents

DOI: 10.4324/9781003408383-12

11.1 Chapter Aims and Objectives

One policy aim within criminal law is to discourage gang activity. This chapter will consider how this policy aim has shaped the liability for secondary parties to a crime and for those who commit crime under duress. Through an examination of *R v Jogee*[1] and *R v Hasan*[2] it will be shown that developing the law to address this policy concern, can have undesired consequences. The application of the rules of accessorial liability have led to the over-penalising of black males, and the restrictions to the duress defence has left victims of domestic abuse with no defence.

By the end of this chapter, you should be able to:

- Define the different parties to a crime.
- Explain joint enterprise.
- Examine how legal principle was influenced by policy in the decision of *R v Jogee*.
- Examine how legal principle was influenced by policy in the decision of *R v Hasan*.

> The issues that will be examined in this chapter can be illustrated through the following scenarios. Before starting the chapter, consider whether the following people are blameworthy for their actions.
>
> - Adele knowingly helps Bert and his gang commit a murder by driving him to the victim's house.
> - Chad unknowingly helps Debbie and her gang commit murder, by driving her to the victim's house in his taxi.
> - Elspeth agrees to commit the burglary with Francine. Unbeknown to Elspeth the homeowner is at home. After they break into the house, Francine beats up the homeowner who dies from her injuries.
> - Grant joins a criminal gang. As part of the gang initiation, he is forced at gun point to drive Hettie to a house knowing that this is so Hettie can commit a burglary.
> - Ian joins a climate change protest group. Unbeknown to Ian it has been widely reported in the press that this group has caused serious criminal damage as part of their protests. During a protest Ian is asked to graffiti the group's slogan onto a building. He refuses and is threatened with serious harm unless he complies. He carries out the graffiti, thus causing criminal damage.
> - Janina is subject to a violent relationship by her husband Kane. He has control of all the finances and regularly threatens her with violence unless she does as he says. Janina has tried to leave, but Kane always finds her and the violence intensifies. Kane tells Janina to commit a theft. She does so under fear of serious violence.

11.2 Parties to a Crime

Crimes are not always committed by a single person. There can be multiple "parties" involved. These can be divided into:

- **Principal** – the primary or most direct cause of the crime with the necessary *mens rea*.

---

1 [2016] UKSC 8.
2 [2005] UKHL 22.

- **Joint principals** – when two or more people are the direct cause of the crime with the necessary *mens rea*.
- **Secondary parties** – a person who assists or encourages the commission of a crime but is not the direct cause.
- **Innocent agent** – when a principal conducts a crime with the use of a person who is not blameworthy for their actions.

These different parties to a crime can be illustrated through the following example.

> Jemma decides to rob a bank. She illegally purchases a gun from Kamal. Kamal knows she plans to use this gun for a robbery. Jemma, then carries out the robbery with Liam. They enter the bank together and while Jemma threatens the cashier, Liam takes the money. Throughout, Martin, Jemma's 8-year-old son, waits outside on the lookout for the police.

In this situation, Jemma and Liam are Joint Principals. Kamal is a secondary party, or accessory, to the crime. Martin, as a child, could be considered an innocent agent. Martin, would not be blameworthy for his actions, but the law would consider Jemma, Liam and Kamal as equally blameworthy for the robbery.

11.3 Accessories and Abettors Act 1861, Section 8 (as Amended)

Section 8 of the Accessories and Abettors Act 1861, as amended by schedule 12 of the Criminal Law Act 1977, states:

> Whosoever shall aid, abet, counsel, or procure the commission of any indictable offence, whether the same be an offence at common law or by virtue of any Act passed or to be passed, shall be liable to be tried, indicted, and punished as a principal offender.

This means that legally a secondary party who aids, abets, counsels, or procures is as responsible as the principal. It is questionable, however, whether they are as morally blameworthy as a principal offender, as they have not directly caused the consequence. Nonetheless, if they have agreed to participate in criminal activity, then they invited moral censure. As such, despite the Act making no reference to *mens rea*, the secondary party's moral blameworthiness will depend on their knowledge or intention in helping the crime to be committed. For example, in the scenarios given at the start of the chapter, Adele has knowingly aided Bert in killing by driving him to the victim's house. Adele could argue that she did not actually conduct the killing and that her actions did not have a causal effect as if she had not driven Bert the crime could have still occurred by him finding another mode of transportation. Nonetheless, the fact remains that Adele has knowingly made a choice, and therefore in law can rightly be held responsible for Bert's actions.

Due to the potentially wide scope of secondary liability, the courts have limited the application of section 8 of the Accessories and Abettors Act 1861. First, by requiring that the secondary party can only be criminally liable if they intend to do acts of assistance.[3] Therefore, if the secondary

3 *National Coal Board v Gamble* [1959] 1 QB 11.

party acts unknowingly or recklessly, this will not be sufficient. Second, if the crime requires a particular *mens rea*, the secondary party must intend to assist or encourage the principal to act with that *mens rea*.[4] Third, the secondary party must have knowledge of the circumstances which amount to the *actus reus* and *mens rea* of the offence.[5] This knowledge is judged subjectively.[6] Therefore, returning to the scenarios at the start of the chapter, Chad will not be responsible for the killing carried out by Debbie, whereas Adele will be responsible for the killing carried out by Bert. Chad has intentionally done acts of assistance by driving the taxi to the victim's house. He has not, however, intended to assist Debbie in intentionally killing the victim, and does not know of the circumstances that have led to this. Nonetheless, this application of the law is still problematic. If sufficient *mens rea* cannot be proved for Bert, there is nothing to stop Adele being found guilty of murder and Bert facing the lesser charge of manslaughter.[7] Moreover, Adele's conviction for murder is not dependent on Bert being convicted at all.[8] This means that the secondary party can receive a harsher label and longer sentence than the principal.

11.4 Joint Enterprise

The law relating to secondary parties has faced further difficulty when the secondary party intends to assist with the commission of one crime, but the principal goes beyond this to commit another crime. This is known as joint enterprise. It can be illustrated in the following example.

> Noah decides to rob a bank and asks Omar to help him. As they are entering the bank Noah shows Omar that he has a gun. Omar does not know if the gun is loaded, and Noah says it is just to scare the bank teller into handing over the money. Omar knows that Noah has a bit of an unpredictable streak and Omar is worried that Noah might fire his gun at someone, but Omar thinks the likelihood of this occurring is small. When they enter the bank, Omar stands watch by the door. Noah threatens the bank teller, who refuses to hand over the money. Noah shoots and kills the bank teller.
>
> Omar only has the intention to assist in Noah committing the robbery, not the killing. Thus, the question becomes whether Omar, alongside Noah, should be held responsible for murder. Alternatively, whether Omar should instead be charged with unlawful act manslaughter as the death occurred because of the crime of robbery. Or, whether Omar should just be charged for the robbery, which is the only crime he agreed to commit.

Joint enterprise is also known as "parasitic accessorial liability". This was a term coined by Smith.[9] It described a form of criminal liability, adopted by the Privy Council in *Chan Wing-Siu v The Queen*.[10]

4 *R v Jogee* [2016] UKSC 8, [9]–[10].
5 *R v Jogee* [2016] UKSC 8, [9] and [16].
6 *R v Webster* [2006] 2 Cr App R 6, [25].
7 *R v Howe* [1987] AC 417, 458.
8 For example, see *DPP v K and B* [1997] 1 Cr App R 36 where the principal of a rape was not apprehended but the two female accessories were convicted.
9 JC Smith, "Criminal liability of accessories: law and law reform" (1997) 113 LQR 453, 455.
10 [1985] AC 168. For an account of the historic development of parasitic accessorial liability see also Findlay Stark, "The Demise of 'Parasitic Accessorial Liability': Substantive Judicial Reform, Not Common Law Housekeeping" [2016] CLJ 550, who argues that the doctrine was not created by *Chan Wing-Siu* but had been in existence since the sixteenth century.

It arose when the defendants formed an agreed intent to commit crime A, but the principal then goes on to commit a different crime (crime B) that the secondary party did not intend. Regardless of *Chan Wing-Siu v The Queen* being persuasive precedent, the doctrine was adopted and developed by the House of Lords in *R v Powell and English*.[11] At this time, this meant that the secondary party would be liable for crime A and crime B. The requirement was simply that the secondary party foresaw that the principal might commit crime B with the *mens rea* for that offence, and that there was no "fundamental departure" in the principal's commission of that offence and what the accessory foresaw. Thus, Omar would be convicted of murder as he had foreseen a small risk of Noah firing his gun at someone. He would only be able to escape liability if he could show there had been a fundamental departure. For example, that he did not know that Noah had a gun, or that he believed the gun was unloaded.

The doctrine served a useful policy purpose in ensuring criminal liability could be imposed, especially when on the case facts it was not clear which party was the secondary party and which was the principal. It was also felt to be essential to protect the public through deterrence of gang activity.[12] It did, however, create problems. This included that the accessory could be convicted of the same crime as the principal, but with lesser *mens rea*. The principal would need to intend death or serious harm for a murder conviction, whereas the secondary party would only have to foresee that this might occur. This caused issues of fair labelling[13] and offended the correspondence theory.[14] The law was changed in the combined appeals of *Jogee* and *Ruddock*.[15]

R v Jogee and Ruddock

The case of *R v Jogee and Ruddock* was the combined appeals of two cases. In the first case, Jogee, with another man called Hirsi, entered a property where the victim was present. Jogee threatened the victim with a bottle, and Hirsi stabbed and killed him. In the second case, Ruddock, with another man called Hudson, planned to steal the victim's car. The victim was found tied up with his throat slit. Ruddock claimed that Hudson had killed the victim while he was not present, but admitted that he had bound the victim. At their original trials both Jogee and Ruddock were convicted of murder. Jogee appealed to the Court of Appeal, where his appeal was dismissed. The Court of Appeal of Jamaica refused to hear Ruddock's appeal. The Supreme Court and the Privy Council then granted permission for the appeals to be heard. The basis of the appeal was that the principle of parasitic accessorial liability was flawed and based on questionable policy grounds. The appellants argued that foresight that the principal might kill with intent to kill or cause serious harm, as established by the House of Lords in *R v Powell and English*,[16] should not be enough to convict the secondary party of murder. Both appeals were allowed and the defendant's convictions for murder were quashed.

11 [1999] 1 AC 1.
12 [1999] 1 AC 1, 26.
13 See Chapter 2.3.2.
14 See Chapter 2.3.4.
15 [2016] UKSC 8.
16 [1999] 1 AC 1.

Thinking points:

- In the judgment it was discussed that the correct approach, when a defendant has taken part in a violent activity that they foresaw might lead to the victim's death, would be to convict of manslaughter rather than murder.[17] Why would a manslaughter conviction be more appropriate?

As discussed above, one of the key issues with the principle of joint enterprise was that a secondary party could be convicted of murder without the intention to kill or cause serious harm. This meant that the secondary party would receive the same label and punishment as the principal, but with lesser *mens rea*. Instead, a conviction of manslaughter would be based on the defendant carrying out an unlawful act, with the requisite *mens rea* for that act, which was objectively dangerous and caused death.[18] This is perhaps problematic if it is considered that the defendant's actions, such as those in Ruddock, were not in themselves objectively dangerous and would not have caused death if it had not been for the principal's actions. The defendant would still be stigmatically labelled as a manslayer, even though they intended some other lesser crime. It would, however, provide a distinction to the principal who could still be labelled as a murderer. Moreover, a conviction for manslaughter would give the judge sentencing discretion. Thus, fair labelling and fair discrimination in sentencing could be better achieved.

- The judgment refers to the policy aim of joint enterprise to discourage gang activity. Is it agreed that this policy approach was needed?

In 2016 the Government released a cross-government policy paper entitled: Ending gang violence and exploitation.[19] Thus, acknowledging the large-scale problem that is gang crime. This has been followed by a number of strategies and interventions, for example, to reduce knife crime, and protect vulnerable adults and children.[20] As stated above, the decision in *R v Powell and English* to impose parasitic accessorial liability was thought to promote this aim of protecting the public from people operating in gangs.[21] In *R v Jogee and Ruddock*, however, it was stated that there was no evidence that the law failed to do this before the introduction of parasitic accessorial liability in *Chan Wing-Sui v The Queen*.[22] In other words, convicting people for crimes that they did not have the *mens rea* for, had no discernible impact on reducing gang violence. Therefore, without this justification it is logical, and morally correct, to conclude that "guilt of crime by mere association has no proper part in the common law".[23]

This is particularly important when considering that the law aims to protect vulnerable adults and children, and yet disproportionately those convicted under joint enterprise were children.[24] Moreover, the doctrine of joint enterprise could be seen to be discriminative with a disproportionate number of black males being convicted.[25] This led to a CPS monitoring pilot

---

17 *R v Jogee* [2016] UKSC 8, [74].

18 See Chapter 3.4.1 for a discussion of the elements of unlawful act manslaughter.

19 Home Office, "Ending Gang Violence and Exploitation", 13 January 2016, https://assets.publishing.service.gov.uk/media/5a7f970ced915d74e33f75dc/Ending_gang_violence_and_Exploitation_FINAL.pdf, accessed 26 July 2024.

20 For example, see: Home Office, "Criminal Exploitation of Children and Vulnerable Adults: County Lines", 11 July 2017, www.gov.uk/government/publications/criminal-exploitation-of-children-and-vulnerable-adults-county-lines/criminal-exploitation-of-children-and-vulnerable-adults-county-lines, accessed 26 July 2024.

21 *R v Powell and English* [1999] 1 AC 1, 25–26.

22 *R v Jogee* [2016] UKSC 8, [75].

23 *R v Jogee* [2016] UKSC 8, [77].

24 Helen Mills, Matt Ford, and Roger Grimshaw, *The Usual Suspects: Joint Enterprise Prosecutions Before and After the Supreme Court Ruling* (2nd edition, Centre for Crime and Justice Studies 2022) 11–12.

25 Helen Mills, Matt Ford, and Roger Grimshaw, *The Usual Suspects: Joint Enterprise Prosecutions Before and After the Supreme Court Ruling* (2nd edition, Centre for Crime and Justice Studies 2022) 14–16.

in 2023, which confirmed over 50% of those charged were under 25 and 30% were black.[26] Furthermore, the wide scope of joint enterprise meant that while women were not charged and convicted as often as men,[27] research shows that 90% of women convicted of homicide through joint enterprise use no violence.[28] In addition to the question that joint enterprise raises as to fair justice, there is also an economic impact. Research in 2024 by Manchester Metropolitan University has shown that the practice of imprisoning those under the principle of joint enterprise has a colossal cost to the taxpayer.[29]

Thus, while the policy aim of introducing joint enterprise was to discourage gang activity and to protect the public, this was not achieved. As stated by the Supreme Court, the introduction of joint enterprise was based on "generalised and questionable policy arguments".[30] The result was a discriminative practice, that disproportionately punished certain sectors of society for their mere association with others who did commit crime. This was done at a huge personal cost to them, and with an enormous financial cost to society.

- In *R v Jogee and Ruddock* the Supreme Court acknowledged that the law had taken a "wrong turn"[31] in its development. What was this error that had been made, and what impact has its rectification had?

In *R v Jogee and Ruddock* it is stated that the common law took a wrong turn in *R v Powell and English* by following the doctrine of joint enterprise established in *Chan Wing-Sui v The Queen*.[32] The error was to equate foresight that the principal might commit a crime with intention. Foresight should only have been evidence of intent.[33] Despite acknowledging this error, which impacted cases decided between 1999 and 2016, the Supreme Court stated:

> The effect of putting the law right is not to render invalid all the convictions which were arrived at over many years by faithfully applying the law as laid down in the Chan Wing-Siu case and in R v Powell; R v English . . . where a conviction has been arrived at by faithfully applying the law as it stood at the time, it can be set aside only by seeking exceptional leave to appeal to the Court of Appeal out of time. That court has the power to grant such leave, and may do so if substantial injustice be demonstrated, but it will not do so simply because the law applied has now been declared to have been mistaken.[34]

This means that those who had been convicted under this doctrine would not necessarily be able to have their cases overturned, as seen in *R v Johnson* when the conjoined appeals of 13 defendants were refused.[35]

---

26 "Crown Prosecution Service Joint Enterprise Pilot 2023: Data Analysis", 29 September 2023, www.cps.gov.uk/publication/crown-prosecution-service-joint-enterprise-pilot-2023-data-analysis, accessed 26 July 2024.

27 Helen Mills, Matt Ford, and Roger Grimshaw, *The Usual Suspects: Joint Enterprise Prosecutions Before and After the Supreme Court Ruling* (2nd edition, Centre for Crime and Justice Studies 2022) 11, discuss that men make up 90% of the joint enterprise convictions.

28 Becky Clarke and Kathryn Chadwick, "The Criminalisation of Women in Joint Enterprise Cases: Exposing the Limits to 'Serving' Girls and Women Justice" (2023) 12(4) Int J Crime Justice Soc Democr 80.

29 Becky Clarke and Patrick Williams, *The Mounting Costs of Injustice: Calculating the Economic Costs of Joint Enterprise* (The Justice Project, Manchester Metropolitan University 2024).

30 *R v Jogee* [2016] UKSC 8, [79].

31 *R v Jogee* [2016] UKSC 8, [87].

32 *R v Jogee* [2016] UKSC 8, [87].

33 *R v Jogee* [2016] UKSC 8, [87].

34 *R v Jogee* [2016] UKSC 8, [100].

35 [2016] EWCA Crim 1613. *R v Crilly* [2018] EWCA Crim 168 is, however, one example of a successful appeal.

Despite the change in law having little effect on those cases decided in the period between 1999 and 2016, it would be expected that a change would be seen in those cases decided post-*R v Jogee and Ruddock*. Research published by the Centre for Crime and Justice Studies, however, has shown that this is not so. This research asserts that: "The Supreme Court ruling had no discernible impact on the numbers of people prosecuted or convicted of murder and manslaughter in multi-defendant cases."[36] Thus showing, that even though the *mens rea* bar has been raised for convictions, this has not produced a decline in those who are guilty by association. Moreover, even though it would be expected that there would be a shift in the amount of secondary parties being convicted of manslaughter rather than murder, due to their lack of *mens rea*, this also has not occurred. Thus, the law seems to be continuing to operate unjustly to convict people of serious crimes when the are not necessarily sufficiently blameworthy.

- Another key change implemented by the decision in *R v Jogee and Ruddock was to* change the previous law whereby a defendant could avoid liability if the principal's actions were a fundamental departure from what had been agreed.[37] Instead, the House of Lords made reference to an overwhelming supervening act.[38] What impact has this had?

Before *R v Jogee and Ruddock*, in *R v Rahman* the House of Lords stated that if the principal used a deadlier weapon than the defendant had contemplated, this could amount to a fundamental departure.[39] This was replaced in *R v Jogee and Ruddock* when the Supreme Court stated, if the death is "caused by some overwhelming supervening act by the perpetrator which nobody in the defendant's shoes could have contemplated might happen and is of such a character as to relegate his acts to history; in that case the defendant will bear no criminal responsibility for the death".[40] This concept of an overwhelming supervening act seems to have created a more stringent approach than the "fundamental departure" law before *R v Jogee and Ruddock*. This can be seen in *R v Tas*.[41] The defendant, the principal, and another were involved in an intentional fight with the victim and two of his friends. Tas punched one of the victim's friends and then left the fight. After he had left the principal produced a knife, which Tas claimed he did not know he had, and the principal stabbed the victim to death. The principal then rejoined Tas and they drove away together. The facts seemingly amount to the situation that the House of Lords stated in *R v Rahman* would amount to a "fundamental departure" under the law before *R v Jogee*. The Court of Appeal, however, held in *R v Tas* that this did not amount to an overwhelming supervening act, as the defendant foresaw some harm by being involved in the fight.[42] The key difference being that before *R v Jogee and Ruddock* foresight that the defendant might kill would be enough for a conviction of murder, rather than manslaughter, thus a to offset this a more lenient approach to what would amount to a fundamental departure was justifiable. In *R v Tas* there was no departure from the agreed upon crime to harm the victim, and the court held that these actions caused the unlawful act manslaughter of the victim.

---

36 Helen Mills, Matt Ford, and Roger Grimshaw, *The Usual Suspects: Joint Enterprise Prosecutions Before and After the Supreme Court Ruling* (2nd edition, Centre for Crime and Justice Studies 2022) 16. At 18 the research continues: "there is no indication of a significant reduction in either the number or proportion of secondary suspects in murder and manslaughter cases".

37 See *R v Powell and R v English* [1999] 1 AC 1, 30.

38 *R v Jogee* [2016] UKSC 8, [98].

39 *R v Rahman* [2008] UKHL 45, [47] and [68].

40 *R v Jogee* [2016] UKSC 8, [97].

41 [2018] EWCA Crim 2603.

42 [2018] EWCA Crim 2603, [26].

The Court of Appeal went one step further in *R v Lanning and Camille*.[43] In following *R v Tas* to determine that that there was no evidence of an overwhelming supervening act, the Court stated that even though the defendant did not know about the knife, and had no history of carrying knifes, in today's social climate knives were produced with a degree of frequency. Therefore, the trial judge was correct to conclude that there was no evidential basis for determining that the defendant could not have contemplated this.[44] Resultingly, and perhaps alarmingly, it would seem almost impossible to claim that the production of a knife is an overwhelming supervening act, as society is supposed to expect this as a regular occurrence.

Thus, in the scenario at the start of the chapter where Elspeth agrees to commit the burglary with Francine, both are criminally liable for Burglary after entering the house with intention to steal. The question is whether Elspeth can be convicted of a further, or alternative offence, due to the actions undertaken by Francine in attacking and killing the homeowner. The principle of joint enterprise no longer applies so, unlike for Omar in the scenario given earlier in the chapter, the normal rules relating to secondary parties would apply.[45] It would need to be established that Elspeth had intentionally done acts of assistance. Moreover, Elspeth must intend her actions to assist or encourage Francine to act with the required *mens rea*, with knowledge of the circumstances which amount to the *actus reus* and *mens rea* of the offence. Elspeth can be convicted of unlawful act manslaughter, as although she only intends burglary, it is this offence that has led to the victim's death. For this it would need to be established that the offence of burglary was in itself objectively dangerous. Dangerous in this sense means "an act which all sober and reasonable people would inevitably realise must subject the victim to the risk of some harm resulting whether the defendant realised that or not".[46] In the law before *Jogee*, it may have been possible for her to argue that because she thought the house was unoccupied, and Francine then used unexpected force, this amounted to a "fundamental departure". Now she would need to demonstrate that there had be an overwhelming supervening act, which as shown from precedents such as *Tas* and *Lanning*, appears nearly impossible to establish.

11.5 Participating in Crime under Duress

As discussed above,[47] section 8 of the Accessories and Abettors Act 1861 means that a secondary party will be tried and convicted as the principal. This means that when a person threatens another to compel them to commit a crime, the duressor can be convicted as a secondary party. The principal, who is acting under a threat of death or serious violence, will avoid liability due to a defence being available.

It has been illustrated in *R v Jogee and Ruddock* has raised the bar for when a person can be convicted for aiding and abetting a crime that they had not agreed to commit, by removing the doctrine of joint enterprise.[48] This means that the necessary *mens rea* must be established before the defendant can be convicted. Part of the justification for this change was that the implementation of such a draconian principle had little impact on the policy aim of reducing gang violence. While such a change is to be welcomed, the same policy reason is still being used to restrict the defence to those who commit crime under duress.[49]

---

43 [2021] EWCA Crim 450.

44 *R v Lanning and Camille* [2021] EWCA Crim 450, [69]–[70].

45 See Chapter 11.3 above.

46 *R v Watson* (1989) 1 WLR 684, 686.

47 See Chapter 11.3 above.

48 See Chapter 11.4 above.

49 See Chapter 10 for more discussion of the definition of duress and duress of circumstances.

The complex inter-relationship between secondary liability and duress can be seen in *DPP for Northern Ireland v Lynch*,[50] and subsequent cases. In *DPP for Northern Ireland v Lynch* the defendant was charged with murder after aiding and abetting the killing of a police officer. He had not done any of the shooting that killed the police officer but had driven a car to the location where this occurred. He claimed that he had done this under threat from members of the IRA under gunpoint. The judge withdrew the issue of duress from the jury and the defendant appealed first to the Court of Appeal, where his conviction was upheld. He further appealed to the House of Lords. In allowing the appeal, the court relied on *R v Kray*[51] as persuasive precedent to allow the defence of duress. In *R v Kray*, the Court of Appeal gave brief consideration of one of the defendants, Anthony Barry. He had been charged with murder after supplying a gun that was planned to be used for the purpose of murder by the Kray twins, although consequently a different weapon was used. At trial he had been acquitted on the grounds of duress to a charge of murder in the second degree. Following this, the House of Lords in *DPP for Northern Ireland v Lynch* held that duress was available as a defence to the defendant as he was a secondary party to murder even though he had associated with the IRA. Lord Wilberforce recognised that there are different degrees of heinousness even in homicide offences, and that a secondary party to murder should not be treated in the same way as a murderer.[52] Thus, while the Accessories and Abettors Act 1861 allows a secondary defendant to be tried, indicted, and punished as the principal,[53] allowing the defence of duress to an accessory avoids the stigma and further repercussions of a conviction. This reflects the blameworthiness of what could be a minor role in a subsequent murder, in this case driving a car, conducted under duress.

The judgment in *DPP for Northern Ireland v Lynch* to allow a full defence to secondary parties to murder led to problems shortly after in *Abbott v The Queen*, when the Privy Council held that duress could not be a defence to principals who committed murder.[54] Lord Wilberforce, dissenting in *Abbott*, argued this would lead to a grave injustice in the common law.[55] It meant that there was a distinction in the availability of the defence between those who had aided and abetted in a killing, and those who could be said to be joint principals. The House of Lords resolved the inconsistency, in *R v Howe*, by deciding that duress could not be a defence to murder to principals or secondary parties. The House of Lords used their power under the Practice Statement 1966 to overrule *Lynch*, as it was decided that there was no valid distinction between primary and secondary parties and neither should have the defence available to them.[56] The justification was that the Lords identified that the secondary party can be just as blameworthy, if not more so, than the principal.[57] Thus, consistency in the law was held to be more important than determining the culpability of defendants based on how much or how little they had contributed under duress.

While *Howe* resolved, if somewhat unsatisfactorily, the consistency of application of the duress defence to primary and secondary parties to murder, the question still remained as to what extent the duress defence would be open to those who voluntarily associated with others that then made them commit crimes other than murder.

50 [1975] AC 653.

51 (1970) 1 QB 125.

52 *DPP for Northern Ireland v Lynch* [1975] AC 653, 680–681.

53 Section 8.

54 *Abbott v The Queen* [1977] AC 755.

55 *Abbott v The Queen* [1977] AC 755, 773. Lord Wilberforce argued that duress should be available to both the principal and secondary party. See Chapter 10.3.2 for further discussion.

56 *R v Howe* [1987] AC 417, 439.

57 *R v Howe* [1987] AC 417, 441 Lord Griffiths discusses the example of a contract killer being who contrivution to the death is no less significant than the principal.

R v Hasan

The defendant worked as a minder for Taeger, who ran an escort agency and was involved in prostitution. He went with her to the house of a client. The client later claimed that the defendant stole money from a safe. The defendant claimed that he had not stolen money at that point but had told Taeger and her boyfriend, a man called Sullivan with a reputation for violence, about the safe. The defendant went on to claim that under threats of harm and fear of death from Sullivan, he was forced to go back and steal the money several months later. The defendant was charged with two counts of aggravated burglary and tried to rely on the defence of duress. He was found guilty of the second count of aggravated burglary at trial, but then successfully appealed his conviction at the Court of Appeal. The Crown appealed to the House of Lords seeking clarification on the availability of duress when a defendant had voluntarily associated with others who they knew were likely to subject them to threats to commit a crime. The Crown argued that the correct formulation for this restriction was an objective standard, which denied the defence of duress when the defendant ought to have foreseen the risk of being subjected to any compulsion through threats of violence. The defence argued for a less stringent approach. They argued that the correct direction was whether the defendant foresaw or ought to have foreseen the risk of being subjected to compulsion to commit criminal offences and that the defendant foresaw offences of the same type (or gravity) of those he was forced to commit. The House of Lords allowed the Crown's appeal, confirming that the defence of duress was unavailable when the defendant foresaw or ought to have foreseen the risk of being subjected to any compulsion through threats of violence.

Thinking points:

- *R v Hasan* imposes a normative standard to what the defendant ought to have foreseen when voluntarily associating, and does not require foresight of being made to commit a crime. How does this judgment change the law from how it had previously been construed?

The defence of duress had previously been denied in *R v Fitzpatrick*, when the defendant had voluntarily joined the IRA.[58] This restriction did not, however, only apply to those who had joined terrorist organisations. In *R v Sharp* the Court of Appeal held that the defence of duress was not available to a charge of manslaughter, when the defendant had voluntarily associated with an organisation or gang which he knew might compel him to commit serious crimes similar to those with which he was charged.[59] When joining a gang of robbers Sharp knew that they used firearms. Therefore, when participating in a robbery under duress, in which the gang leader shot and killed the victim, the defence of duress was not open to Sharp. The court held that for the defence to be denied the defendant must have knowledge of the nature of the gang, which Sharp did have due to a previous incident of a similar nature.[60]This means that the defendant's knowledge is judged subjectively when assessing if he knew of the risk when voluntarily associating with others. Shortly after *R v Sharp*, in *R v Shepherd* the Court of Appeal considered the breadth of this voluntary association

58 [1977] NI 20.
59 *R v Sharp* [1987] QB 853.
60 *R v Sharp* [1987] QB 853, 861.

restriction.[61] Similarly to Sharp, Shepherd had voluntary associated with a criminal organisation. Unlike Sharp, however, it was not established that the defendant had contemplated violence when joining the organisation. Thus, the question of duress should have been put to the jury, and the defendant's conviction for burglary was quashed.

The courts continued to grapple with the question of when it was right to deny the defence of duress to those who had voluntary associated in *R v Baker and Ward*.[62] The defendants, who committed robbery, had not joined with a criminal organisation but had voluntarily associated with them through their business of drug dealing. The Court of Appeal decided that for the defence to be denied, the defendant must be aware that there was a risk of being forced to commit crimes of the type they are being tried.[63] This had the, perhaps unintentional, effect of reducing when the voluntary association restriction would apply. Thus, in the same year that *R v Powell and English* introduced the doctrine of joint enterprise into English law to effectively deal with those who join in criminal enterprise,[64] more protection was being offered to those who had participated in crime under duress as either a principal or secondary party.

This extension in the defence of duress being available to those who had voluntarily associated with criminals was short lived. Soon after the decision in *R v Baker and Ward*, the Court of Appeal again took the opportunity to clarify and confine the law in *R v Heath*.[65] In another case where the defendant had associated with drug dealers, the Court of Appeal stated that: "It is the awareness of the risk of compulsion which matters. Prior awareness of what criminal activity those exercising compulsion may offer as a possible alternative to violence is irrelevant."[66] The Court of Appeal went one step further in *R v Harmer* to not even require that the defendant foresee that they would be compelled to commit crime.[67] The defendant had voluntarily associated with, and become indebted to, a drug supplier. The defence of duress was excluded as even though he did not foresee that he may be required to commit crimes under the threat of violence, he recognised that he had exposed himself to the risk of unlawful violence.[68] These cases suggest a conscious move to restrict duress being used by those associating with drug dealers, in what could be a judicial policy decision to not allow a defence to those who commit offences to pay for drug-taking.

In *Hasan* the matter of voluntary association reached the House of Lords and the binding judgment was made that, "the defence of duress is excluded when as a result of the accused's voluntary association with others engaged in criminal activity if he foresaw, or ought reasonably to have foreseen, the risk of being subjected to any compulsion by threats of violence".[69] This changed the previous precedent by including an objective criterion. Furthermore, it clarified that foresight is only required as to being subjected to compulsion not to being made to commit a crime. Therefore, the decision in *R v Hasan* means that the defence of duress has become considerably restricted in its application. The rationale is that the defendant should not be able to rely on duress when they have freely accepted the risk of being subjected to threats when associating with criminals. This can clearly be seen in *Hasan* as the defendant had chosen to work for Taeger. When Taeger formed a relationship with Sullivan, who was known to be violent and intimated that he had killed people, Hasan foresaw or ought to have foreseen the risk of compulsion by threats of violence. Hasan had several months with this knowledge whereby he could have disassociated from Taeger and Sullivan, before being made to commit the burglary under duress.

---

61 *R v Shepherd* (1988) 86 Cr App R 47.
62 (1999) 2 Cr App R 335.
63 *R v Baker and Ward* (1999) 2 Cr App R 335, 346.
64 See discussion above at Chapter 11.4.
65 [1999] 10 WLUK 172.
66 *R v Heath* [1999] 10 WLUK 172, [6].
67 *R v Harmer* [2001] EWCA Crim 2930.
68 *R v Harmer* [2001] EWCA Crim 2930, [16].
69 *R v Hasan* [2005] UKHL 22, [39].

Lord Bingham favoured the inclusion of an objective assessment of what the defendant ought to have foreseen when joining, as he felt that this was in keeping with other elements of the defence that require the defendant's choice of action to be judged against what a reasonable person would do.[70] This hard-line approach means that it does not matter that the defendant did not foresee the risk of compulsion if it was one that they would be expected to have appreciated. While this prevents unwarranted claims of duress from those who are culpable due to voluntarily associating with violent criminals, it means that the defence is automatically barred. Consequently, none of the defendant's circumstances or characteristics are considered to see if a defence is warranted.

Returning to the scenario at the start of the chapter, Grant joins a criminal gang and is forced to participate in a burglary. Despite not burgling the house himself, he has fulfilled the requirements to be charged as a secondary party. He has intentionally done acts of assistance by driving. This is done with the intention that this act will assist Hettie in completing the burglary, with knowledge of the circumstances which amount to the *actus reus* and *mens rea* of the offence. Grant will not be able to avoid liability by arguing that these actions were only conducted under duress. *R v Howe* means that no distinction is drawn between primary and secondary parties when considering how the duress defence applies.[71] Although *Howe* was in the context of murder, it can be assumed that the same principle will apply to all offences to retain consistency. Thus, Grant cannot argue that he is less culpable as a secondary party and more deserving of a defence. Moreover, if Grant has voluntarily joined the organisation then no duress defence will be available to him. Even though he may not have wanted to carry out the crime, he has intentionally done it to avoid the alternative. The law following *R v Hasan* will hold that he is to blame for putting himself in that position by joining a criminal organisation. He would have been aware, or objectively should have been, that by voluntarily associating with such people he could be compelled to commit a crime through threats of violence. Grant's only hope for reprieve is if an ordinary person would not think that by joining the gang they would be at risk of being subjected to any compulsion by threats of violence.

The decision in *R v Hasan* was applied by the Court of Appeal in *R v Mohammed Hussain*.[72] The basis for appeal was the defendant's belief in the duressor's bad character should have been put to the jury to support his claim of duress. The defendant's appeal was dismissed. It was argued that even if this evidence had been put to the jury the defence would have been excluded, as the defendant had voluntarily associated with the duressor knowing of his bad character (and the defendant had time to alert the authorities).[73] Thus, knowledge of bad character seems to be equated with foresight of the risk of being subjected to compulsion through threats. In the same year the defence of duress was further restricted in *R v Ali*.[74] The Court of Appeal held that the defendant need not be aware that the organisation is involved in criminal activity. They just need to associate with others who they foresee, or ought to have foreseen, the risk of being subjected to any compulsion by threats of violence.[75] This widens the voluntary association restriction to an unacceptable level. For example, a defendant who is friends with a normally law-abiding person who makes an idle threat against a third party when aggrieved, could then be denied the defence if that person then makes what (the defendant reasonably believes) are real threats against him unless he commits a crime.

Returning again to the scenarios at the start of the chapter, Ian joins a climate change protest group not knowing that they have committed criminal acts. His lack of knowledge of their criminal nature is irrelevant as the availability of the duress defence is not based on his awareness of this. The

---

70 *Hasan* [2005] UKHL 22, [37]. Contrary to his approach taken in *Hasan*, Lord Bingham highlighted the importance of a subjective approach in his leading judgment in *R v G and R* [2003] 1 AC 1034. See Chapter 5.5.

71 *R v Howe* [1987] AC 417, 439.

72 [2008] EWCA Crim 1117.

73 *R v Mohammed Hussain* [2008] EWCA Crim 1117 [22].

74 [2008] EWCA Crim 716.

75 *R v Ali* [2008] EWCA Crim 716, [12].

question is just whether he foresaw, or ought to have foreseen, the risk of being subject to compulsion by threats of violence. Not knowing of their nature means that Ian may not have foreseen the risk of being subjected to compulsion by threats of violence. An ordinary person, however, might have foreseen this due to the wide-reaching reports of the group's criminal activity. Moreover, bad character appears to be enough to conclude that a risk of compulsion by threats could exist, so previous criminal activity would probably be more than enough to also reach this conclusion. Thus, Ian is unlikely to be able to claim duress in defence of causing criminal damage.

- In the judgment in *Hasan* Lord Bingham states that the policy of the law should be to discourage association with known criminals, and that the law should be slow to excuse the criminal conduct of those who do.[76] How can this policy approach to restricting the availability of the duress defence be justified?

Prior to *R v Hasan*, Lord Simon in *DPP for Northern Ireland v Lynch* said, in regard to the availability of the duress defence, "in my respectful submission your Lordships should hesitate long lest you be inscribing a charter for terrorists, gang leaders and kidnappers".[77] These comments are perhaps unsurprising in context of this case that saw IRA gunmen shoot a police officer. Correspondingly, in *R v Fitzpatrick* duress was denied as a defence to murder and robbery, which the defendant had committed as a member of the IRA. He had tried to leave the IRA, but had been forced to stay under threat. In dismissing his appeal, the Court of Appeal held that the defence of duress was not available when the defendant had initially chosen to associate himself with violent criminals, and so voluntarily exposed himself to the risk of compulsion to commit criminal acts.[78] This is unduly harsh when the defendant has tried to leave, but equally the defendant has undertaken the risk of not being able to leave when choosing to join.

This policy aim to discourage gang association, and ensure gang leaders are unable to indemnify their followers, was also seen in *R v Howe*[79] when denying the defence of duress to murder.[80] As Lord Griffiths states: "We face a rising tide of violence and terrorism against which the law must stand firm recognising that its highest duty is to protect the freedom and lives of those that live under it."[81] Such was the fear that duress would provide an excuse to those in gangs, that in 1993 the Law Commission recommended a reversal of the burden of proof when the defence was claimed. They justified this by stating that otherwise the defendant could, especially where he might be a member of a gang, concoct a story that the prosecution would find hard to disprove.[82] While the burden of proof has remained on the prosecution to disprove the defence, the availability of duress to those who have voluntarily associated with others was considerably restricted by the House of Lords in *R v Hasan*.[83]

Lord Bingham, in *R v Hasan*, makes it clear that policy has influenced his decision when he states: "I must acknowledge that the features of duress . . . incline me, where policy choices are to be made, towards tightening rather than relaxing the conditions to be met before duress may be successfully relied on."[84] This policy-based approach of reducing gang association meant that the defence of duress was not available and the defendant's conviction was restored. At the time that

---

76 *R v Hasan* [2005] UKHL 22, [34].
77 [1975] AC 653, 688 (dissenting).
78 [1977] NI 20.
79 *R v Howe* [1987] AC 417.
80 See Chapter 10.3.2 for discussion of the restriction of duress as a defence to murder.
81 *R v Howe* [1987] AC 417, 444–445.
82 Law Commission, *Legislating the Criminal Code. Offences against the Person and General Principles* (Law Com No 218, 1993), paras 33.10–33.12.
83 [2005] 2 AC 467.
84 *R v Hasan* [2005] UKHL 22, [22].

Hasan was decided the doctrine of joint enterprise was still in effect. Thus, while the restriction implemented in *R v Hasan* regarding voluntary association may be considered severe, it shows a uniform application of the law for a specific purpose. Joint enterprise imposed liability to discourage individuals from joining gangs, and the defence of duress does not provide an excuse to those who have committed crime while in a gang. This raises the question, however, that as the law has changed in *R v Jogee and Ruddock* to make it harder to convict those who assist or encourage crimes, should the law set out in *Hasan* excluding duress to those who voluntarily associate with criminals also be reviewed? In other words, was this another "wrong turn" that needs to be remedied? As stated above,[85] since *R v Jogee and Ruddock* it has been held that guilt by mere association has no place in the common law. Nevertheless, this is exactly what the law of duress is achieving. A defendant who commits a crime under threat of death or serious injury is denied a defence because of their earlier voluntary association.

This restrictive approach could be because duress is an excusatory defence. As discussed in Chapter 10,[86] this means that the law is not stating that the defendant has done the right thing by committing the crime. Instead, it is deemed that the defendant has done the wrong thing, but in certain situations can be excused. Seemingly, if the defendant has chosen to voluntarily associate, policy dictates that this takes them outside of the scope of what can be excused.

The same approach does not apply when considering the justificatory defence of self-defence. In *R v Gill* the defendant had voluntarily associated with others involved with drugs and serious crime.[87] He thought that these people were trying to break into his house, and so he intentionally stabbed and wounded one of them. In fact, the intruder was a police officer lawfully executing a search warrant. The trial judge withdrew from the jury the householder defence of self-defence,[88] stating that it could not have been Parliament's intention to allow a defence to a person who undertook criminal activity and associated with other criminals.[89] The Court of Appeal held that the jury had been misdirected, quashed the conviction, and a retrial was ordered.[90] This demonstrates that while the law is slow to excuse those who commit crimes under duress after voluntarily associating with others who may compel them to act out of fear, the law does not apply the same policy concerns for the justificatory defence of self-defence. Therefore, even though justificatory defences are supposed to signal that the defendant has done the morally right thing, a decision to associate with criminals will not outweigh the right to protect one's property even when acting out of mistake.

- Lady Hale raises a further concern in *R v Hasan* about restricting the defence of duress, what is this?

Lady Hale argues that by denying the defence to those who associate with gangs the defence could also be denied to those who lawfully associate with violent people. Thus, people such as victims of domestic abuse, who find it difficult to escape their abuser, will have no defence.[91] Moreover, Lady Hale, argues that the requirement that the defendant only needs to foresee or ought to have foreseen, being subjected to any compulsion by threats of violence goes too far in restricting the defence. Lord Bingham's formulation of the voluntary association restriction means that a person

85 See Chapter 11.4.
86 See Chapter 10.2.
87 [2023] EWCA Crim 259.
88 For further discussion of the householder defence see Chapter 12.3.1.
89 *R v Gill* [2023] EWCA Crim 259, [23]–[25].
90 *R v Gill* [2023] EWCA Crim 259, [40]–[42].
91 *R v Hasan* [2005] UKHL 22, [78].

who foresees that they could come under compulsion by their violent partner to do the washing or cooking, could then not rely on the defence if unforeseen to them, or a reasonable person, they are then forced to commit a criminal offence under duress. It could be argued that these criticisms are unwarranted and that a case such as this is unlikely to arise. The facts of *Graham*[92] and *Gotts*,[93] however, are similar to this hypothetical situation. In each of these cases the defendants were living with people who they knew to be violent. Following the judgment in *Hasan* both would be excluded from having a duress defence, as they knew, or ought to have known, they might be subjected to doing things that they did not want to do. In fact, both cases failed to successfully plead the duress defence on different grounds, which raises the question of whether an additional restriction for those who voluntarily associate is even required. More recently, in *R v Johnson* the Court of Appeal refused permission to appeal to a defendant who had been convicted of perjury.[94] She had given false evidence under fear from her abusive partner and his mother. Despite the coercive and controlling behaviour she suffered, the court held that because she had previously sought police assistance for the abuse she suffered, this showed that she was able to escape the threat of duress when compelled to commit a crime.[95] Applying the voluntary association restriction in domestic situations seems illogical, as the defendant's relationships with their duressor makes it harder for them to escape or resist the intensified threat.

According to Lady Hale the correct test for voluntary association should be that the defence is excluded when the defendant foresees or ought to have foreseen the risk of being subjected to compulsion to commit criminal offences.[96] This would mean that those who had previously been compelled to do non-criminal actions would not be automatically excluded from the duress defence. This would provide a little more protection for the numerous women who find themselves charged as accessories or conspirators to crimes committed by their abusive partners.[97] Such defendants are widely divergent from the defendant who has voluntarily joined a gang or terrorist organisation, who the restrictions are aimed at.

In the scenarios at the start of the chapter, Janina is subject to a violent relationship by her husband Kane. He has control of all the finances and regularly threatens her with violence unless she does as he says. Janina has tried to leave, but Kane always finds her and the violence intensifies. Kane tells Janina to commit a theft. She does so under fear of serious violence. The ruling in *R v Hasan* means that Janina will have no defence of duress available to her. This is because she has continued to voluntarily associate with someone she foresees, or ought to foresee, will subject her to compulsion through threats of violence. The fact that she has previously tried to leave will not assist her in her defence. As *R v Fitzpatrick* demonstrates, if you have initially voluntarily joined then the defence is not available even if you try to leave. Moreover, if she has previously sought police protection, following *R v Johnson*, this can be used against her as evidence to show that she is capable of avoiding the duress by seeking alternative protection. Therefore, both Janina and Kane will be equally tried and convicted for the theft.

92 [1982] 1 WLR 294.

93 (1992) 2 AC 412.

94 [2022] EWCA Crim 832.

95 For further discussion see, Vanessa Bettinson, Vanessa E Munro, Nicola Wake, and Paramjit Ahluwalia, "A One-Sided Coin? Attributing Agency and Responsibility in Contexts of Coercive Control" in Melissa Bone, JJ Child and Jonathon Rogers (eds) *Criminal Law Reform Now*, vol 2 (Bloomsbury 2024), 128.

96 *R v Hasan* [2005] UKHL 22, [79].

97 For further discussion, see Susie Hulley, "Defending 'Co-offending' Women: Recognising Domestic Abuse and Coercive Control in 'Joint Enterprise' Cases Involving Women and their Intimate Partners" (2021) Howard Justice J 580.

11.6 Conclusion

The law recognises that when multiple people are intentionally involved in a crime, each party will be equally blameworthy regardless of how large or small the part was that they played. This ensures that blame can be assigned even when it is not clear of exactly who did what. The law, however, does not ascribe to guilt by mere association. This was the effect of the joint enterprise doctrine. Joint enterprise had been introduced to discourage gang activity, but there was no evidence to suggest this was achieved, and so this policy aim could no longer be used to justify convicting those who did not have the *mens rea* for the crime committed. In *R v Jogee and Ruddock* the Supreme Court acknowledged that they had taken a wrong turn in adopting this form of liability, and that a person should not be convicted without the requisite *mens rea*. This, however, has had little impact on the number of convictions, and the disproportionate penalisation of black males.

Following *Hasan*, the defence of duress is also restricted to not allow a defence to those who voluntarily associate with those who they foresee, or ought to have foreseen, would subject them to compulsion under a threat of violence. Similarly, to joint enterprise, the policy aim of this restriction is to discourage gang activity. Gang leaders should not be able to indemnify their followers, and those who choose to join gangs should not be able to rely on the defence to excuse the crime they are then forced to commit. For these reasons this restriction is more justifiable than joint enterprise, which imposed liability without sufficient *mens rea*, but its wide formulation is problematic. The defence can be denied when a person has tried to leave the gang, thus they can be held responsible for their prior choices when they may not have fully realised the implications of what they were joining. Additionally, the defendant themselves does not have to foresee the risk of being subjected to compulsion, meaning that they are judged by the standard of an ordinary person without consideration of their individual circumstances or characteristics. Moreover, the restriction does not just apply to those who have joined gangs or terrorist organisations. It could operate to deny a defence of duress in domestic settings when a person is compelled to commit crime by their abuser. This goes beyond the policy aim of discouraging gang activity and unsatisfactorily means the law fails to provide a defence of duress when morally it should.

11.7 Further Reading

Bo Wang V, "A Normative Case for Abolishing the Doctrine of Extended Joint Criminal Enterprise" [2019] J Crim L 144

Hulley S, "Defending 'Co-offending' Women: Recognising Domestic Abuse and Coercive Control in 'Joint Enterprise' Cases Involving Women and their Intimate Partners" (2021) Howard Justice J 580

Ormerod D, "Duress: Foreseeability of Risk of Being Subjected to Compulsion by Threats of Violence" [2006] Crim LR 142

Reed A, "Duress: Voluntary Joining of Criminal Associations" (2005) Crim Lawyer 1

Wilson P and Ormerod D, "Simply Harsh to Fairly Simple: Joint Enterprise Reform" [2015] Crim LR 3

Chapter 12

Loss of Control and Sexual Infidelity

Chapter Contents

DOI: 10.4324/9781003408383-13

12.1 Chapter Aims and Objectives

One area of law that does not fail to be contentious is loss of control. This defence allows a person to have a partial excuse for killing out of anger. This chapter considers why the law allows a defence in such circumstances, and whether the defence is in line with current moral standards through an examination of *R v Clinton*.[1] Moreover, it will be considered to what extent, through the introduction of a qualifying trigger, the Coroners and Justice Act 2009 achieves its policy aim of enabling a defence that better protects women and children.

By the end of this chapter, you should be able to:

- Define loss of control under sections 54 and 55 of the Coroners and Justice Act 2009.
- Identify the character theory of excuses.
- Discuss the lack of moral basis for allowing a defence to those who have killed in anger and the role of qualifying triggers.
- Discuss the failure of the law to achieve the policy aim of providing a defence to abused women who kill.
- Discuss why the alternative of self-defence is generally not available to abused women who kill.
- Examine how legal principle was influenced by morals and policy in the decision of *R v Clinton*.

The issues that will be examined in this chapter can be illustrated through the following scenarios. Before starting the chapter, consider whether you would lose your self-control in the following situations and thus whether you think the people are fully blameworthy for their actions.

- Amari gets continually irritated by his co-worker whistling while he works. He has repeatedly asked his co-worker to stop, but he just continues. Amari loses his self-control and kills his co-worker.
- Batsheva is dating Cohen. Cohen regularly stays at Batsheva's house but does not have a key. One evening Cohen turns up at Batsheva's house, forces his way in, and attempts to sexually assault her. She grabs the nearest object, which is a heavy vase, and hits him over the head. As a result, Cohen dies.
- Dosia has been married to Edwin for 5 years. Edwin is often verbally and physically abusive towards Dosia. Dosia becomes more and more scared that Edwin will kill her, as the violence towards her increases in frequency and intensity. She waits until Edwin is asleep and kills him.
- Frona is married to Gavin and they have a shared savings account. Gavin inherits a large sum of money after his mother dies. Frona takes all this money and plans to leave Gavin. As she is leaving she tells him that she never really loved him and was only with him for the money. Gavin loses his self-control and kills her.
- Hia logs into her partner's social media account and in the private messages finds evidence that her partner, Irene, is having an affair and has been mocking her for not realising what has been going on. Hia goes to Irene's house, and finds Irene having sex with a man. Hia loses her control and kills Irene.

1 [2012] EWCA Crim 2.

12.2 Loss of Control

The defence of loss of control was introduced under section 54 of the Coroners and Justice Act 2009. This replaced the previous defence of provocation defined under section 3 of the Homicide Act 1957, and the common law that had existed for hundreds of years prior to that.[2] Loss of control provides a partial defence to those who have fulfilled the requirements of murder.[3] A successful plea reduces the crime of murder to one of manslaughter.[4] In Chapter 10 it was examined how the sanctity of human life is a highly regarded moral value. As such, in 2004 when the Law Commission were reviewing partial defences to murder, they asked the following question: "The defence of provocation elevates the emotion of sudden anger above emotions of fear, despair, compassion and empathy. Is it morally sustainable for sudden anger to found a partial defence to murder?"[5] For hundreds of years the law has allowed a defence when a person has killed in anger, but there are policy reasons for restricting the defence:

> Anger is a criminogenic emotion and one of the key deterrent tasks of the criminal law is to provide incentives for citizens to curb violent responses induced by their angry states. A person disposed to respond to frustrations and setbacks with an angry loss of control culminating in serious violence would thereby demonstrate a dangerous and deficient character and should not be accorded any form of condonation.[6]

Despite this, only a small number of those who responded to the Law Commission's consultation argued that provocation no longer had a place in law.[7] The rationale provided by the Law Commission for retaining the defence of provocation in a reformed form was that "the moral blameworthiness of homicide may be significantly lessened where the defendant acts in response to gross provocation in the sense of words or conduct (or a combination) giving the defendant a justified sense of being severely wronged".[8] The mandatory life sentence for murder means that any reduction in blameworthiness cannot be represented in the sentence given. Therefore, allowing a defence, that reduces murder to manslaughter, enables sentencing discretion and a more appropriate label.[9]

While it may be accepted that someone who acts out of anger is not as blameworthy as a cold-blooded killer, the theoretical underpinning of the defence remains elusive.[10] This could be because it is difficult to ascertain the culpability of the defendant. In response to a provoking incident a person can intend to kill in the moment, with no premeditation and planning, and this could amount to murder. Equally, a person could respond to provocation by killing and dependent on the circumstances this could amount to a justified killing in self-defence, for which the defendant would avoid liability. It is unlikely that a person could be said to be justified in their actions when they have killed out of anger. This would not fulfil the requirement of being the lesser of two evils, nor promote a morally acceptable standard. It could, however, be said that the defendant who kills

---

2 See, Law Commission, *Partial Defences to Murder* (Law Com 290, 2004) appendix G for an interesting discussion of the historical and sociological basis for the defence of provocation.

3 For a further discussion of murder see Chapter 5.8.

4 Coroners and Justice Act 2009, section 54(7).

5 Law Commission, *Partial Defences to Murder* (Law Com CP No 173, 2003) para 4.164.

6 AP Simester, JR Spencer, F Stark, GR Sullivan, and GJ Virgo, *Simester and Sullivan's Criminal Law: Theory and Doctrine* (8th edition, Hart Publishing 2022), 411.

7 Law Commission, *Partial Defences to Murder* (Law Com 290, 2004) para 3.33.

8 Law Commission, *Partial Defences to Murder* (Law Com 290, 2004) para 3.63.

9 See Chapter 2.3.2 for more discussion of fair labelling.

10 Law Commission, *Partial Defences to Murder* (Law Com 290, 2004) paras 3.20–3.21.

in anger is excused. Thereby, the defendant has not done the right thing but because of the circumstances they are not held fully to blame in the same way a cold-blooded killer might be.

In Chapter 10 it was discussed how a person could be provided an excusatory defence if they lacked the opportunity to make a free choice due to duress.[11] This could apply to when someone has killed from anger, if it is argued that the provocation removes the defendant's opportunity to freely make a decision in that moment. Alternatively, Dressler argues that the provoked anger reduces the defendant's capacity to be able to make a choice.[12] This means that the defendant is not fully to blame for their actions as the anger makes them less able to respond in a morally acceptable manner. This capacity-based approach to excuses is considered further in relation to diminished responsibility in Chapter 13.[13] Yet, another theory, that can be employed to explain why we excuse people who have killed from anger is the character theory. The character theory can be divided into two different approaches. The first approach states that a person should not be punished, or the sentence should be mitigated, where they are acting "out of character" due to being put into such a state from something beyond their control.[14] For example, when a person of normally good character kills in response to provocation, then we allow them a partial defence. The basis for the defence is that the defendant's behaviour in killing does not reflect their settled character. In other words, they would not normally act in the way they did, and only acted as such due to the provocation. Such a person is not a danger to society, and thus not (as) deserving of punishment. This does, however, raise the question of how easy it is to determine what a person's settled character is and whether the law should be making judgments based on the perceived nature of the person, rather than judging the defendant's character on actions that they have undertaken. The second approach to the character theory considers whether a person should be afforded a defence because they have acted "in character", but that their actions are considered objectively reasonable in the situation.[15] This means that the character approach is not about proving that the defendant acted in an abnormal way by killing in response to the provocation, but that they acted normally and that this action can be expected from any other ordinary person. This means that the law would reflect the standards that society expects.

There being such diverse views on the proper theoretical underpinning for allowing a defence to someone who kills in anger, means that there is difficulty in formulating a satisfactory defence. This difficulty was reflected in the Coroner and Justice Act's passage through Parliament. For example, as seen in the debate in House of Commons of the House of Lords amendment to allow sexual infidelity as a qualifying trigger that the defence could be based on.[16] Regardless of the theoretical approach adopted, to be morally defensible as providing an excuse to those who kill in anger, restrictions on the availability of the defence are required. These could include that the anger is not self-induced, or that to become angry was a reasonable response to the situation. Such considerations were at the forefront of the Law Commission's proposals:

> We consider that the essence of gross provocation is that it is words and/or conduct which caused the defendant to have a justifiable sense of being seriously wronged. The preferred moral basis for recognising a partial defence of provocation is that the defendant had legitimate ground to feel strongly aggrieved at the conduct of the person at whom his/her

11 See Chapter 10.2.

12 Joshua Dressler, "Rethinking Heat of Passion: A Defence in Search of a Rationale" (1982) 73 J Crim L and Crim 421, 463–464.

13 See Chapter 13.4.1.

14 For further discussion see Victor Tadros "The Character of Excuses" (2001) 21 Oxford J Legal Studies 495, 503–508.

15 For further discussion see Peter Arenella, "Character, Choice and Moral Agency: The Relevance of Character to our Moral Culpability Judgements" (1990) 7 Soc Phil Policy 59, 73.

16 HC Deb 9 November 2009, vol 499, cols 78–100.

> response was aimed, to the extent that it would be harsh to regard their moral culpability for reacting as they did in the same way as if it had been an unprovoked killing.[17]

The Law Commission's proposals[18] led to the Coroners and Justice Act 2009 being enacted with the defence of provocation being replaced with loss of control. Section 54 states:

> (1) Where a person ("D") kills or is a party to the killing of another ("V"), D is not to be convicted if –
>
> a) D's acts and omissions in doing or being a party to the killing resulted from D's loss of self-control,
>
> b) the loss of self-control had a qualifying trigger, and
>
> c) a person of D's sex and age, with a normal degree of tolerance and self-restraint and in the circumstances of D, might have reacted in the same or in a similar way to D.

12.3 Qualifying Trigger

One of the key changes, from the previous law, was the introduction of a qualifying trigger. This element is the focus for this chapter. It is defined under section 55 as:

> (1) This section applies for the purposes of section 54.
>
> (2) A loss of self-control had a qualifying trigger if subsection (3), (4) or (5) applies.
>
> (3) This subsection applies if D's loss of self-control was attributable to D's fear of serious violence from V against D or another identified person.
>
> (4) This subsection applies if D's loss of self-control was attributable to a thing or things done or said (or both) which –
>
> a) constituted circumstances of an extremely grave character, and
>
> b) caused D to have a justifiable sense of being seriously wronged.
>
> (5) This subsection applies if D's loss of self-control was attributable to a combination of the matters mentioned in subsections (3) and (4).
>
> (6) In determining whether a loss of self-control had a qualifying trigger –
>
> a) D's fear of serious violence is to be disregarded to the extent that it was caused by a thing which D incited to be done or said for the purpose of providing an excuse to use violence;
>
> b) a sense of being seriously wronged by a thing done or said is not justifiable if D incited the thing to be done or said for the purpose of providing an excuse to use violence;
>
> c) the fact that a thing done or said constituted sexual infidelity is to be disregarded.

The introduction of a qualifying trigger was one way in which the defence of loss of control is restricted.[19] Previously anything, including innocent behaviour,[20] could be the basis of the

---

17 Law Commission, *Partial Defences to Murder* (Law Com 290, 2004) para 3.68.

18 Law Commission, *Partial Defences to Murder* (Law Com 290, 2004); Law Commission, *Murder, Manslaughter and Infanticide* (Law Com 304, 2006).

19 See Simon Parsons, "The Loss of Control Defence – Fit for Purpose" [2015] J Crim L 94, 101 who concludes that the courts interpretation of the law means that the defence is "barely available".

20 For example, see *R v Doughty* (1986) 83 Cr App R 319 when a baby crying was the basis of the defence.

provocation defence. The provoking act now needs to be things done or said that are objectively[21] extremely grave.[22] Moreover, the requirement that the trigger must cause the defendant to have a justifiable sense of being seriously wronged, inserts a moral question into the test. It is asking for the situation to be judged against society's norms and values to assess whether the anger was justified. This means the defence will only be available in very limited situations.

In the scenarios at the start of the chapter, Amari kills his co-worker in a loss of self-control following his co-workers incessant whistling. While under the previous law of provocation this may have been considered for the defence, the same is unlikely under the current law. The whistling will amount to a thing done under section 55(4) of the Coroners and Justice Act 2009, but objectively will not be considered extremely grave, and will not give Amari a justifiable sense of being seriously wronged.[23] This seems a morally right result and meets the policy aim of ensuring that dangerous people, such as those who kill in response to whistling, are imprisoned.[24]

12.3.1 Fear of Serious Violence

In addition to the provoking act being things done or things said, the Coroners and Justice Act 2009 identifies that the loss of self-control can be attributable to defendant's fear of serious violence from the victim against the defendant, or another identified person.[25] The inclusion of this section was to provide a defence to those who had killed in self-defence but had used excessive force.

The common law defence of self defence allows a person to use fatal or non-fatal force in order to protect themselves (or their property). This can be deemed a justificatory defence as the defendant has an affirmative legal right to protect his bodily integrity against the unlawful invasion from another.[26] Equally, it could be claimed that this is a justificatory defence as the victim forfeits their right to protection from harm if they have acted as an aggressor towards the defendant.[27] This means that if a person threatens the life of the defendant then the defendant is justified in using deadly force to protect himself.[28]

Self-defence requires that the defendant subjectively believes it is necessary to use force.[29] If this is established then it has to be determined that the force used is objectively reasonable in the circumstances that the defendant believed them to be.[30] Section 76 of the Criminal Justice and Immigration Act 2008 consolidated the common law. It gives guidance on when the force used will not be reasonable and states that, the degree of force used by the defendant is not to be regarded as having been reasonable in the circumstances as the defendant believed them to be if it was disproportionate in those circumstances.[31] Before the Coroners and Justice Act 2009, when a defendant used excessive force, they would have no defence available to them.[32] Therefore, instead of receiving

---

21 *R v Clinton* [2012] EWCA Crim 2, [38]; *R v Dawes* [2013] 2 Cr App R 3, 40.

22 For example, see *R v Zebedee* [2012] *EWCA Crim* 1428 when the burden of caring for his ill and elderly father was not sufficiently grave.

23 See, for example, *R v Zebedee* [2012] EWCA Crim 1428, when the defence was denied to a defendant who claimed to have lost his self-control in part due to being triggered by his father's whistling.

24 See Chapter 1.3.2 for further discussion of this policy aim.

25 Coroners and Justice Act 2009, section 55(3).

26 Joshua Dressler, "Justifications and Excuses: A Brief Review of the Concepts and the Literature" (1986–1987) 33 Wayne L Rev 1155, 1164.

27 Joshua Dressler, "Justifications and Excuses: A Brief Review of the Concepts and the Literature" (1986–1987) 33 Wayne L Rev 1155, 1164.

28 Andrew Ashworth, "Self-Defence and the Right to Life" (1975) 34 Cambridge LJ 282, 283.

29 *R v Williams (Gladstone)* (1984) 78 Cr App R 276, 281.

30 *R v Owino* 2 Cr App R 128, 134, citing Criminal Law Revision Committee, *Fourteenth Report: Offences Against the Person* (1980) Cmnd 7844.

31 Criminal Justice and Immigration Act 2008, section 76(6).

32 For example, see *R v Clegg* [1995] 1 AC 482.

a full acquittal for acting in self-defence, they would face a mandatory life sentence for murder if they had killed when protecting themselves. The introduction of the fear of serious violence to the defence of loss of control, means that a defendant who acts excessively and kills in self-defence can have a partial defence available to them.[33] Thus, reaching a compromise between the two polar opposites that were previously available.

In setting out its proposals for reform, a key factor considered by the Law Commission was whether the law of self-defence adequately protected householders and those subjected to abuse who kill out of fear.[34] Following the well-known case of Tony Martin,[35] when a homeowner shot and killed a burglar, the law was changed to allow more use of force to householders who acted in self-defence. Section 43(2) of the Crime and Courts Act 2013 inserted a new section 76(5A) in to the Criminal Justice and Immigration Act 2008. This states that in a householder case, the degree of force used by the defendant is not to be regarded as having been reasonable in the circumstances as the defendant believed them to be if it was grossly disproportionate in those circumstances. Thus, the insertion of the word "grossly" gives the defendant extra latitude in the amount of force that can be used, to provide the defendant was greater legal protection in householder cases.

The Law Commission recognised that self-defence may be particularly problematic when the defendant and victim are not of comparable strength, highlighting the example of an abused woman or child who kills their abuser. Research shows that 71% of women who kill have suffered violence or abuse from the deceased.[36] The Law Commission acknowledged that in the situation of strength discrepancy the use of a weapon to defend oneself was more likely, which in turn may result in the force used being deemed excessive.[37] Research shows that in cases when women killed their abusive partner, in 71% of the cases women stabbed their violent partner, in 9% of the cases another type of weapon was used, and in 7% of the cases women had set fire to their partner or committed arson that resulted in the partner's death.[38] The Law Commission stated that the introduction of the fear trigger, in addition to removal of the requirement that the loss of control be sudden and temporary,[39] would provide protection for abused people who kill their abuser.[40]

Despite the claim that the defence of loss of control would provide protection for abused people who kill, the reality has been somewhat different. Section 55(3) of the Coroners and Justice Act 2009 requires a fear of serious violence. This means that anything less will not meet the minimum threshold. As Bettinson argues, "the fear trigger excludes the defendant abused by psychological coercive control, where there the threats are not of physical harm, but directed at psychological

33 In reality to rely on both defences may not be so straightforward. As Holroyde LJ recognises in *R v Islam* [2019] EWCA Crim 2419, [32]: "It is often difficult for a defendant charged with murder to rely both on the defence of self-defence and on the partial defence of a loss of control."

34 Law Commission, *Partial Defences to Murder* (Law Com 290, 2004) paras 4.17–4.24.

35 *R v Martin* [2001] EWCA Crim 2245.

36 Sophie Howes, "Women Who Kill: How the State Criminalises Women We Might Otherwise Be Burying" (Centre for Women's Justice, 17 February 2021) 25.

37 Law Commission, *Partial Defences to Murder* (Law Com 290, 2004) paras 4.20 citing Aileen McColgan, "In defence of battered women who kill" (1993) 13 Oxford J Legal Studies 508, 515 and 520; Susan Edwards, "Injustice that Puts a Low Price on a Woman's Life", The Times, 2 September 2003 Law Supplement 5; Susan Edwards, "Abolishing Provocation and Reframing Self-Defence-the Law Commission's Options for Reform" [2004] Crim LR 181.

38 Sophie Howes, "Women Who Kill: How the State Criminalises Women We Might Otherwise Be Burying" (Centre for Women's Justice, 17 February 2021) 23.

39 Section 54(2) of the Coroners and Justice Act 2009 states that the loss of self-control need not be sudden, thus changing the common law as stated in *R v Duffy* [1949] 1 All ER 932. The restriction had been seen to deny the defence of provocation in cases including *R v Thornton (no 2)* (1993) 96 Cr App R 112; *R v Ahulwalia* (1993) 96 Cr App 133; and *R v Challen* [2019] EWCA Crim 916.

40 Law Commission, *Partial Defences to Murder* (Law Com 290, 2004) para 4.24; Law Commission, *Murder, Manslaughter and Infanticide* (Law Com 304, 2006), paras 5.50–5.77.

injury".[41] Thus, while it is recognised that psychological injury can amount to serious harm,[42] it is not enough to trigger the defence of loss of control

Moreover, the Wade Review in 2023 recommended that the minimum starting point of a 25-year mandatory life sentence for murder, when a weapon has been taken to the scene with intent, should not apply to abused women. Wade argued that victims of abuse do not fulfil the policy aim of the 25-year starting point provision, as this was aimed at reducing young people from carrying and using knives on the street.[43] The provision contained in schedule 21, section 4(2) of the Sentencing Act 2020 in effect causes indirect discrimination, as it applies far more often to women than men due to the strength discrepancy.[44] Thus, the Wade recommendations meant that if a woman failed in her defence, she would not face such stringent sentencing requirements. The Government, however, rejected this proposal.[45] Therefore, it seems the policy aim of reducing knife crime outweighs the need to provide protection to women who have pre-emptively armed themselves with a knife to protect themselves and then killed.

The case of *R v Martin* in the box below provides an example of how the law of self-defence and loss of control, in the context of domestic violence, operates in practice.[46]

R v (Farieissia) Martin

Farieissia Martin killed her former partner, Kyle Farrell, by stabbing him in the heart with a kitchen knife. At trial Martin claimed that she had acted in self-defence, or alternatively that loss of control be considered from a fear of serious violence. During the trial the history of physical abuse, sexual violence, and coercive and controlling behaviour had not been explored, and a mental health assessment had not been carried out. This was in part due to a lack of understanding of the way victims of abuse present.[47] The jury rejected both defences and Martin was convicted of murder. In the hearing for permission to appeal, Lady Justice Simler, granting the application, described the account giving by Martin to the defence experts as a "paradigm case of coercive control".[48] The physical and sexual abuse she had suffered had resulted in post-traumatic stress disorder, and this was relevant to assessing the considering how a reasonable might have acted in those circumstances. In her subsequent appeal her conviction was eventually quashed and a plea of manslaughter accepted, with her sentence of 13 years for murder replaced with a 10-year sentence.

Even if the loss of control defence is accepted to those who kill their abusers, as can be seen with the case of Farieissia Martin, this still results in the label of a manslayer and the potential of a long

---

41 Vanessa Bettinson, "Aligning Partial Defences to Murder with the Offence of Coercive or Controlling Behaviour" [2019] J Crim L 71, 83.

42 See for example, *R v Burstow* [1998] AC 147. For more discussion of this case, see Chapter 13.3.

43 Clare Wade, "Domestic Homicide Sentencing Review", 17 March 2023, https://assets.publishing.service.gov.uk/media/6411ce52d3bf7f79df1aa9c4/domestic-homicide-sentencing-review.pdf, accessed 11 August 2024, para 4.3.7.

44 Clare Wade, "Domestic Homicide Sentencing Review", 17 March 2023, https://assets.publishing.service.gov.uk/media/6411ce52d3bf7f79df1aa9c4/domestic-homicide-sentencing-review.pdf, accessed 11 August 2024, para 7.1.13.

45 Ministry of Justice, "Government Response to the Domestic Homicide Sentencing Review", 17 March 2023, https://assets.publishing.service.gov.uk/media/6411ce52d3bf7f79df1aa9c4/domestic-homicide-sentencing-review.pdf, accessed 14 August 2024, 16.

46 *R v Martin* [2020] EWCA Crim 1798.

47 Sophie Elmhirst "'Intimate Terrorism': How an Abusive Relationship Led a Young Woman to Kill Her Partner", *The Guardian*, 31 October 2019, www.theguardian.com/society/2019/oct/31/intimate-terrorism-domestic-abuse-coercive-control-farieissia-martin accessed, 4 August 2024.

48 Sally Middleton "Fri Martin: A 'Paradigm Case of Coercive Control'", 4 December 2020, www.justiceforwomen.org.uk/news/2020/12/4/fri-martin-a-paradigm-case-of-coercive-control, accessed 4 August 2024.

sentence. One way to mitigate this, would be to make self-defence more available to those who kill their abusers. As set out above, in 2013 an amendment was made to self-defence to allow a more lenient test of reasonableness to be applied to householders.[49] This allows householders to use force that is not grossly disproportionate. The effect of this, as Edwards discusses, is that a householder could receive more protection under the law than an abused woman.[50] It has been proposed in Parliament that a provision should be enacted to allow the amount of reasonable force used by an abused woman to mirror the existing provisions in householder cases.[51] Despite recognition in the House of Lords that research shows that the current law of self-defence fails women,[52] no changes have been adopted. Therefore, an abused person can only have the benefit of the householder defence if they can show that they are a householder, and that they believed the victim was a trespasser. This may be somewhat difficult to prove in the context of a domestic relationship, as seen in the case of *R v Magson*.[53]

R v Magson

At trial Emma Jayne Magson was convicted of murder after stabbing and killing James Knight. Like, with the case of *Martin*, her pleas of self-defence and loss of control were rejected by the jury, and she was found guilty of murder. She was sentenced to a minimum term of 17-years imprisonment. Following a retrial being granted, she gave evidence that Knight had put his hand around the front of her neck so that she could not breathe, which was supported by evidence of bruising. She stated that she had grabbed a knife and stabbed him in self-defence. The householder defence was not put to the jury. Magson's conviction was upheld on appeal to the Court of Appeal. Despite there being evidence that she had tried to refuse him entry to the house on the evening of the incident, the court held that there was no evidential basis for the defence. Knight "had lived with her for months and . . . had a key to the house. It was his home."[54] Thus, the extra-legal protection that is afforded to householders, was not extended to Magson.

Returning to the scenarios at the start of the chapter, it can be seen that Batsheva may struggle to successfully plead self-defence when she kills Cohen. She has used a weapon and the jury might find that this use of force is excessive. Alternatively, because this is her house, and Cohen does not have a key, it may be that a distinction can be drawn from *R v Magson*. If it can be established that Batsheva believed that Cohen was a trespasser, then the householder defence can be put to the jury. This would mean that the amount of force used will be deemed unreasonable if it is grossly disproportionate. This would give her more chance of successfully pleading self-defence, which would lead to a full acquittal. Alternatively, if her plea of self-defence fails, she could claim loss of control from her fear of serious violence. This would reduce her conviction from murder to manslaughter.

By contrast, Dosia will struggle to plead self-defence. At the time of the killing there is no immediate threat, and so it would be hard to show that the force used was proportionate. The householder defence, even if it would make a difference, cannot be applied as she lives with her abuser. Therefore, Edwin is not a trespasser.

---

49 Section 43(2) of the Crimes and Courts Act 2013 inserted section 76(5A) into the Criminal Justice and Immigration Act 2008, which added "grossly disproportionate".

50 Susan SM Edwards, "Recognising the Role of the Emotion of Fear in Offences and Defences" [2019] J Crim L 450, 465–468.

51 Domestic Abuse Bill Deb 17 June 2020, cols. 436–437 and the Criminal Justice Bill Deb 15 May 2024, cols. 284 and 317.

52 HL Deb 21 April 2021, vol 811, col 1892.

53 [2022] EWCA Crim 1064.

54 [2022] EWCA Crim 1064, [23].

Alternatively, Dosia, as in *R v Magson*, may try to plead loss of control. Her loss of self-control does not need to be sudden.[55] This means that Dosia may be able to establish that she lost her self-control. This is judged subjectively,[56] but there has to be a loss of self-control.[57] This cannot be cumulatively assumed from circumstantial evidence.[58] Next, Dosia would need to show that this loss of self-control came from a qualifying trigger. Doria could say that she feared serious violence, which would amount to a qualifying trigger under section 55(3) of the Coroners and Justice Act 2009. Alternatively, she could claim that the domestic abuse she has suffered amounts to things done and things said under section 55(4). This would need to constitute circumstances of an extremely grave character, and have caused Dosia to have a justifiable sense of being seriously wronged. Herring argues that "properly understood domestic abuse should readily be regarded as a very serious wrong".[59] Whether Cohen's actions were sufficient to amount to a qualifying trigger would be objectively decided by the jury.

Nonetheless, even if a qualifying trigger could be established, the final requirement for the loss of control defence would still need to be met.[60] This is that a person of Dosia's sex and age, with a normal degree of tolerance and self-restraint and in the circumstances of Dosia, might have reacted in the same or in a similar way she did. The problem is that this is judged objectively. Therefore, while the history of abuse could be a relevant circumstance,[61] any impact the abuse has had on her mental health will not be relevant.[62] Furthermore, as shown, for example, in the case of Farieissia Martin, people who have spent years hiding abuse may find it very difficult to expose these relevant circumstances. Moreover, because Dosia has killed Edwin through a loss of control while he is asleep, this may not convince a jury that at the time of killing they would have feared serious violence and reacted in the same way. The law is expecting a standard that is morally acceptable to society, rather than considering what can be expected from that specific defendant. Therefore, objectively, it may be difficult for the jury to understand Dosia's response, and thus the defence would fail. Moreover, the defence can be denied if it is thought she waited until Edwin is asleep to act out of revenge in retaliation for the abuse he has metered on her.[63]

It is acknowledged that the law in this area is not satisfactory, as there are questions over whether the defences available in domestic situations achieve just outcomes.[64] As such, in 2023 the Law Commission was asked by the Government to launch a new review of Domestic Homicide in response to the Wade Report.[65] This review has now become part of a larger review of homicide.[66]

12.3.2 Sexual Infidelity

Another of the key changes introduced by the Coroners and Justice Act 2009 was the restriction of the defence when the loss of control had been triggered by sexual infidelity.[67] Despite this restriction

55 Coroners and Justice Act 2009, section 54(2).

56 *R v Jewell* [2014] EWCA Crim 414.

57 *R v Goodwin* [2018] EWCA Crim 2287.

58 *R v Cheng* [2024] EWCA Crim 1400.

59 Jonathon Herring, "The Serious Wrong of Domestic Abuse and the Loss of Control Defence" in Alan Reed and Michael Bohlander (eds), *Loss of Control and Diminished Responsibility Manslaughter: Domestic, Comparative and International Perspectives* (Ashgate 2011), 73.

60 *R v Gurpinar* [2015] EWCA Crim 178, [13], confirms that the third question will only need to be considered if sequentially it has already been established that there has been a loss of control and that this is from a qualifying trigger.

61 *R v Thornton (no 2)* (1993) 96 Cr App R 112.

62 *R v Rejmanski and Gassman* [2017] EWCA Crim 2061, [29] and [82].

63 Coroners and Justice Act 2009, section 54(4).

64 See further discussion in Chapter 13.

65 "Law Commission to Review Defences in Cases of Domestic Homicide", 29 November 2023, https://lawcom.gov.uk/law-commission-to-review-defences-in-cases-of-domestic-homicide, accessed 6 August 2024.

66 See https://lawcom.gov.uk/project/revisiting-the-law-of-homicide.

67 Coroners and Justice Act 2009, section 55(6)(c).

not being considered by the Law Commission, the House of Commons felt that it was not a proper basis for the defence.[68] One of the first cases to be heard on appeal after the enactment of the Coroners and Justice Act 2009 was *R v Clinton*.[69] As there was no previous precedent to apply, the Court of Appeal had to decide the limits of the sexual infidelity restriction.

R v Clinton

Clinton and his wife had separated. He bludgeoned and strangled his wife to death after hacking into her social media account and finding evidence of her having an affair with another man. Evidence was provided that she had boasted about having sexual relationships with other men too, and that she had mocked the defendant for considering suicide. The judge ruled that there was insufficient evidence of loss of control for the defence to be put before the jury, as the basis for the defence was sexual infidelity. Clinton also tried to plead the parallel defence of diminished responsibility,[70] but he was convicted by the jury of murder. Clinton appealed to the Court of Appeal. The court held that although sexual infidelity could not be considered as a sole trigger for loss of control, that it could be considered in the context of other features of the case which did amount to permissible qualifying triggers.[71] Clinton's appeal was allowed and a retrial ordered. Clinton, however, pleaded guilty to murder on the first day of the retrial and was sentenced to 20 years in prison.

Thinking points:

- In the judgment, Lord Judge refers to how public opinion has changed over time, and how this is represented in the law.[72] What is he referring to?

Historically, one ground for the defence of provocation was adultery. In *R v Mawgridge* it was stated, "when a man is taken in adultery with another man's wife, if the husband shall stab the adulterer, or knock out his brains, this is bare manslaughter: for jealousy is the rage of a man, and adultery is the highest invasion of property".[73] Therefore, as at that time a wife was the husband's property, the law held that the husband was entitled to kill the man that had invaded his property. The husband's honour could be vindicated by acts of retaliatory violence. In today's society this view is clearly outdated. Lord Judge explains how the law now has to respect individual autonomy. Wives no longer belong to their husbands, so sexual infidelity cannot be used as an excuse for men defending their property.

Section 55(6)(c) of the Coroners and Justice Act 2009 recognises this change in society and so disregards sexual infidelity from the defence of loss of control. This means the judge can refuse to put the issue of loss of control to the jury, and thus has a filtering role in these types of cases. While this may sound like a positive step forward, it is not without problems. For example, the Act does not automatically exclude other honour-based killings or betrayals of trust. Therefore, if a father

68 HC Deb 9 November 2009, vol 499, cols 78–100.
69 [2012] EWCA Crim 2.
70 See Chapter 13.4.1.
71 *R v Clinton* [2012] EWCA Crim 2, [21].
72 *R v Clinton* [2012] EWCA Crim 2, [16].
73 *R v Mawgridge* [1707] Kel J 119, 135–137.

killed his daughter, because in opposition to his religious beliefs she had become pregnant outside of wedlock, this could be considered. It would then become a matter for the jury to decide whether such a trigger met the bar of being of an extremely grave character and causing the defendant to have a justifiable sense of being seriously wronged. While the jury may reject the defence, and so the outcome would be the same as if the judge had excluded the defence from consideration, this does not address the issue that honour-killing can still be put before the jury. Moreover, other types of betrayal that some may argue seem less severe than sexual infidelity can also be considered by the jury. Take the example given in the scenario at the start of the chapter. Frona has betrayed Gavin by taking his money. Their whole marriage is based on a fallacy. When Gavin kills Frona, he could argue that he has lost control from the things done and said. Again, it would be a matter for the jury to decide whether this objectively amounted to a qualifying trigger, but this breach of trust can be considered whereas if she had broken his trust through sexual infidelity this could not.

The problem of what can and cannot be put to the jury is further exacerbated by there being no definition of sexual infidelity within the Act.[74] The word "sexual" could encapsulate many different degrees of physical or non-physical engagement between individuals. The Act makes no reference to what kind of betrayal is needed before the exclusion is applied. For example, if a husband finds that his wife is "sexting" with another man, would this amount to sexual infidelity? The word "infidelity" creates just as many problems. It is unclear whether there has to be an existing relationship, and what type of relationship this needs to be. In *R v Clinton* the defendant and his wife were separated. Therefore, some may argue that her relationship with other men did not amount to infidelity, as there was no longer an expectation for her to be faithful.

- In deciding the case Lord Judge needed to decide what could be included for a qualifying trigger within things done and things said.[75] How did he interpret this section?

As discussed in Chapter 1, a positivist view of the law is that the law is the rules made by Parliament and applied objectively by judges.[76] This would mean giving the words of the Act their plain and ordinary meaning with no further interpretation. As discussed above, the wording of the Act states that the qualifying trigger can come from things done or things said[77] (or both together),[78] but that a thing done or said that constituted sexual infidelity is to be disregarded.[79] If these words are given their literal interpretation, this would suggest that the sexual infidelity should have no bearing on the qualifying trigger. In an approach, more akin to legal realism,[80] Lord Judge seems to have given the words a meaning beyond what is written. He concludes that "things 'said' includes admissions of sexual infidelity (even if untrue) as well as reports (by others) of sexual infidelity".[81] Allowing admissions of sexual infidelity, but not the act of sexual infidelity itself, is stretching the literal meaning of the Act.

Lord Judge recognises that in passing the Act, Parliament had made a policy decision to exclude sexual infidelity to prevent misuse of the defence by those who kill out of jealousy.[82] Despite this, Lord Judge holds that by allowing admissions of sexual infidelity, rather than the infidelity itself, to be considered as a qualifying trigger of things said he is giving effect to Parliament's intentions

74 *R v Clinton* [2012] EWCA Crim 2, [17]–[20].
75 *R v Clinton* [2012] EWCA Crim 2, [21]–[26].
76 Chapter 1.2.2.
77 Coroners and Justice Act 2009, section 55(4).
78 Coroners and Justice Act 2009, section 55(5).
79 Coroners and Justice Act 2009, section 55(6)(c).
80 For a discussion of legal realism, see Karl Llewellyn, "Some Realism about Realism" (1931) 44 Harv L Rev 1222.
81 *R v Clinton* [2012] EWCA Crim 2, [26].
82 *R v Clinton* [2012] EWCA Crim 2, [35]–[36].

in making the Act.[83] In criticising the judgment, Baker and Zhao state that: "It is clear Parliament did not intend sexual infidelity to be used in this way."[84] The chosen interpretation of the sexual infidelity exclusion goes against the Rule of Law,[85] as it does not provide a clear and predictable interpretation of the words of the Act.

Lord Judge further compounds the confusion that his interpretation has caused, by stating that sexual infidelity could also be considered as a relevant circumstance when considering if an ordinary person might have responded in the same way.[86] He justifies this by stating that it would be difficult and unrealistic to compartmentalise the sexual infidelity when it is integral to the facts as a whole.[87] While this observation may be true, the words of the Act mean this is exactly what Parliament intended should be done. It would be illogical for sexual infidelity to be disregarded as a qualifying trigger, to then allow it to be considered when judging how an ordinary person may have responded. Especially when the aim of the law was to not allow killing in such circumstances to provide a defence.

Lord Justice explains his approach to interpreting the law with reference to avoiding injustice.[88] As explained in Chapter 2,[89] justice is a complex principle that is based on the idea of achieving fairness within the law. Lord Judge suggests that if he follows the literal meaning of the Act, that this would lead to injustice. He holds that this was not what Parliament intended. This, however, ignores that it is for Parliament to decide what would amount to an injustice. As Baker and Zhou conclude: "The decision completely ignores the feminist aims behind the legislation."[90] The exclusion of sexual infidelity was not an oversight in the Parliamentary process that judges had been left to address. It was specifically considered in Parliament and enacted for the purpose of achieving justice for women in a modern society.

In the scenarios at the start of the chapter, Hia loses her control and kills Irene. Hia could claim that she has lost her self-control due to things said, which have arisen from reading about her partner's affair and the mocking comments. Following *R v Clinton*, this would not be disregarded. Moreover, as there is no definition of infidelity in the Act this may not even be defined as infidelity, if Hia and Irene are not married, or depending on the expectations of the relationship. When Hia arrives at Irene's home and observes the sexual infidelity, this is when section 55(6)(c) comes into operation. The sexual relations that she witnesses would need to be disregarded for the purposes of determining whether there was a qualifying trigger. This means that the things said, on their own, would need to be extremely grave and have caused Hia to have a justifiable sense of being seriously wronged. Nonetheless, if this criterion was fulfilled, according to *R v Clinton*, evidence of her partner having an affair with another man would be a relevant circumstance when judging what an ordinary person might do. Thus, potentially giving an increased likelihood of the defence being available than what Parliament intended.

12.4 Conclusion

Killing out of anger has been recognised as less blameworthy than killing in cold blood for hundreds of years. While there is no real agreement on the theoretical underpinning for the defence,

83 *R v Clinton* [2012] EWCA Crim 2, [44].

84 Dennis Baker and Lucy Zhao, "Contributory Qualifying and Non-qualifying Triggers in the Loss of Control Defence: A Wrong Turn on Sexual Infidelity" [2012] J Crim L 254, 271.

85 See Chapter 2.3.3 for more discussion of the Rule of Law.

86 *R v Clinton* [2012] EWCA Crim 2, [30]–[32].

87 *R v Clinton* [2012] EWCA Crim 2, [39].

88 *R v Clinton* [2012] EWCA Crim 2, [39]–[40].

89 See Chapter 2.3.1.

90 Dennis Baker and Lucy Zhao, "Contributory Qualifying and Non-qualifying Triggers in the Loss of Control Defence: A Wrong Turn on Sexual Infidelity" [2012] J Crim L 254, 275.

it can be explained by reference to loss of capacity or the character theory. This chapter has shown that the change in the law from provocation to loss of control was designed to make the law more fitting with current moral values. The introduction of a qualifying trigger was designed to restrict the law so only those who were not fully morally blameworthy would be provided an excuse for killing. In addition to this moral consideration, policy required a restriction in the law to not allow dangerous people to use their anger as an excuse for killing.

One qualifying trigger is the fear of serious violence. The inclusion of such a trigger was designed to enable vulnerable women or children, who used excessive force in response to a fear of serious violence, to have a defence. This is because the use of a weapon due to strength discrepancies may be deemed excessive force, and thus prevent them from successfully pleading self-defence. The introduction of the fear trigger did not, however, recognise that not all feared harm is physical violence, and that there are still barriers to victims of domestic abuse successfully accessing a defence due to the way they may present during questioning and trial.

The other type of qualifying trigger is things done or things said, or a combination of both. One of the restrictions placed on the qualifying trigger is that sexual infidelity should be disregarded. This was in recognition that it is no longer acceptable for a man to reclaim his honour by killing after another man is found to have had an affair with his wife. Nonetheless, the judgment in *R v Clinton*, means that this aim has not been fully realised. Sexual infidelity can still be considered as part of things said, and as a relevant circumstance for evaluating what an ordinary person might do.

Therefore, the introduction of a qualifying trigger has had mixed success in achieving the policy aims that Parliament set out to accomplish. As such, it comes as no surprise that this area of law is currently once again under review by the Law Commission.

12.5 Further Reading

Arenella P, "Character, Choice and Moral Agency: The Relevance of Character to our Moral Culpability Judgements" (1990) 7 Soc Phil Policy 59

Baker D and Zhao L, "Contributory Qualifying and Non-qualifying Triggers in the Loss of Control Defence: A Wrong Turn on Sexual Infidelity" [2012] J Crim L 254

Clough A, "Sexual Infidelity: The Exclusion that Never Was?" [2012] J Crim L 76

Edwards SM, "Women Who Kill Abusive Partners: Reviewing the Impact of s55(3) 'Fear of Serious Violence' Manslaughter" [2021] N I Legal Q 245

Law Commission, *Partial Defences to Murder* (Law Com 290, 2004)

Law Commission, *Murder, Manslaughter and Infanticide* (Law Com 304, 2006)

Parsons S, "The Loss of Control Defence – Fit for Purpose?" [2015] J Crim L 94

Tadros V, "The Character of Excuses" (2001) 21 Oxford J Legal Studies 495

Chapter 13

Domestic Homicide and Coercive Control

Chapter Contents

DOI: 10.4324/9781003408383-14

13.1 Chapter Aims and Objectives

In Chapter 12 the defence of loss of control was considered, and whether it meets the policy aim of providing a defence to victims of abuse who kill their abuser. This chapter will further consider what is meant by domestic abuse, and how the law has changed to reflect society's changing understanding of what amounts to domestic abuse. It then discusses, with examination of *R v Challen*,[1] how women who kill their abuser are compelled to utilise the defence of diminished responsibility to avoid a conviction for murder due to the lack of any suitable alternative.

By the end of this chapter, you should be able to:

- Recognise the government policy to reduce domestic abuse.
- Define domestic abuse.
- Define coercive and controlling behaviour.
- Define diminished responsibility.
- Identify the capacity theory of excuses.
- Examine how legal principle was influenced by morals and policy in the decision of *R v Challen*.

The issues that will be examined in this chapter can be illustrated through the following scenarios. Before starting the chapter, consider whether the people are fully blameworthy for their actions.

- Azael suffers from a diagnosed personality disorder. This causes him to become paranoid and suspicious of others. As a result, he wrongly believes he is being persecuted by Bodie, who he then kills.
- Celeste has suffered years of physical abuse at the hands of her abusive husband, Demetri. One night he threatens to kill her. She responds by grabbing a knife, and stabbing and killing him.
- Eliana has suffered years of abuse at the hands of her abusive husband, Fitz. As a result, she suffers from severe depressive illness. One night, fearing for her life, she waits until Fitz is asleep and then kills him.
- Gail has suffered years of coercive and controlling behaviour from her husband, Hector. She feels trapped and unable to leave. In desperation Gail kills Hector.
- Itzel has suffered years of coercive and controlling behaviour from her husband James. She suffers from severe depression, but because she is isolated and James will not allow her to go to the doctor, there is no evidence of this. She hides the way she feels from everyone as she is ashamed, and James gets angry when she expresses her feelings. She feels trapped and unable to leave. In desperation Itzel kills James. Following her arrest, it becomes apparent that Itzel is unable to form a rational judgment because of her severe depression caused by the years of psychological abuse she has suffered.

1 [2019] EWCA 916.

13.2 Tackling Violence against Women and Girls

In 1993 the United Nations made the Declaration on the Elimination of Violence against Women.[2] This recognised that:

> violence against women is a manifestation of historically unequal power relations between men and women, which have led to domination over and discrimination against women by men and to the prevention of the full advancement of women, and that violence against women is one of the crucial social mechanisms by which women are forced into a subordinate position compared with men.[3]

Violence against women and girls can take many forms, including domestic homicide, domestic abuse, sexual assault, honour-based abuse, and stalking. While violence is not only a crime against women and girls, the gender specificity of domestic abuse can be seen in England and Wales through data provided by the Office for National Statistics. The police recorded 851,062 domestic abuse-related crimes in the year ending March 2024.[4] It is felt, however, that this does not reflect the true number, with the Crime Survey for England and Wales estimating that 2.3 million people aged 16 years and over experienced domestic abuse in the year ending March 2024.[5] In the year ending March 2024, the victim was female in 72.5% of domestic abuse-related crimes. Moreover, between the year ending March 2021 and the year ending March 2023, 65.4% of victims of domestic homicide were female compared with 12.3% of victims of non-domestic homicide.[6]

For years, tackling domestic abuse has been high on the Government agenda, with the acknowledgement that abuse has a significant and long-lasting effect on a range of issues including mental health and homelessness.[7] "Tackling Violence against Women and Girls Strategy" was published in July 2021. The policy aim was to increase access to support for victims and survivors of abuse, increase the number of perpetrators brought to justice, and ultimately to reduce the prevalence of violence against women and girls.[8]

Multiple changes in the law have been made towards achieving the aim of reducing violence against women and girls. These include the Marriage and Civil Partnership (Minimum Age) Act 2022. Introduced as a Private Member's Bill by Pauline Latham OBE MP, this change in law was approved by Parliament and came into force in February 2023. The law was designed to protect children aged 16–17, who were disproportionally female,[9] by making it illegal to subject to them forced marriages with parental consent. It means that 16- and 17-year-olds in England and Wales will no longer be allowed to marry, or enter a civil partnership, even when coercion has not been used.

---

2 UNGA Res 48/104 (20 Dec 1993).

3 Declaration on the Elimination of Violence against Women, UNGA Res 48/104 (20 Dec 1993).

4 "Domestic Abuse in England and Wales Overview: November 2024", 27 November 2024, www.ons.gov.uk/peoplepopulationandcommunity/crimeandjustice/bulletins/domesticabuseinenglandandwalesoverview/november2024#main-points accessed 3 December 2024.

5 "Domestic Abuse in England and Wales Overview: November 2024", 27 November 2024, www.ons.gov.uk/peoplepopulationandcommunity/crimeandjustice/bulletins/domesticabuseinenglandandwalesoverview/november2024#main-points accessed 3 December 2024.

6 "Domestic Abuse Victim Characteristics, England and Wales: Year Ending March 2024", 27 November 2024, www.ons.gov.uk/peoplepopulationandcommunity/crimeandjustice/articles/domesticabusevictimcharacteristicsenglandandwales/yearendingmarch2024#domestic-homicide, accessed 9 August 2024.

7 "The Lasting Impact of Violence against Women and Girls", 24 November 2021, www.ons.gov.uk/peoplepopulationandcommunity/crimeandjustice/articles/thelastingimpactofviolenceagainstwomenandgirls/2021-11-24, accessed 9 August 2024.

8 Home Office, "Tackling Violence against Women and Girls Strategy", 21 July 2021, www.gov.uk/government/publications/tackling-violence-against-women-and-girls-strategy, accessed 3 December 2024.

9 Statistics also show that girls are more likely to be impacted. For example, in England and Wales in 2018, 28 boys married under the age of 18 compared with 119 girls.

This includes non-legally binding "religious" ceremonies, which would still be viewed as marriages by the parties and their families. This means that it is now a criminal offence to exploit vulnerable children by arranging for them to marry, and those found guilty of arranging child marriages face sentences of up to 7 years in prison.

Another example of legislative change designed to further protect women and girls is the Online Safety Act 2023. The Government recognised that "the most harmful illegal online content disproportionately affects women and girls".[10] The Act places a duty on internet service providers to protect individuals from encountering priority illegal content online,[11] with extra protection provided for children.[12] Schedule 7 of the Online Safety Act 2023 sets out these priority offences. These include the offence of controlling and coercive behaviour in an intimate or family relationship under section 76 of the Serious Crime Act 2015.[13] Additionally, the offence of disclosing, or threatening to disclose, private sexual photographs and films with intent to cause distress under section 33 of the Criminal Justice and Courts Act 2015 is deemed a priority offence.[14] The Act also introduced a number of new criminal offences. These included sending photograph or film of genitals[15] and sharing or threatening to share intimate photograph or film.[16] These crimes, more commonly referred to respectively as cyberflashing and revenge porn, enable the law to prosecute and convict those charged with crimes that modern technology has made possible. The first successful prosecution for cyberflashing was seen in March 2024, shortly after the commencement of the Act in January of the same year. Nicholas Hawkes was convicted of two counts of cyberflashing under section 187 of the Online Safety Act 2023, after sending unsolicited photos of his erect penis to a 15-year-old girl and another woman in February 2024.[17] For these crimes he was sentenced to 1 year in prison.

Thus, it can be seen that government policy has a clear focus to reduce violence against women and girls. As such, the law is evolving to address the different ways that this can be affected.

In relation to domestic abuse specifically, one significant change in the law was the introduction of the Domestic Abuse Act 2021. This will be examined below.

13.3 Domestic Abuse

As discussed above, tackling violence against women and girls is a national, and international, policy objective. The UN made it clear that in the Declaration on the Elimination of Violence against Women they were referring to "any act of gender-based violence that results in, or is likely to result in, physical, sexual or psychological harm or suffering to women".[18] Given its ordinary meaning, however, the word "violence" suggests some kind of physical contact. Therefore, before the introduction of the Domestic Abuse Act 2021, the domestic courts were left to determine what kind of harm amounted to violence.

---

10 Department for Science, Innovation and Technology, "Online Safety Act: Explainer", 8 May 2024, www.gov.uk/government/publications/online-safety-act-explainer/online-safety-act-explainer#how-the-act-protects-women-and-girls, accessed 9 August 2024.

11 Online Safety Act 2023, section 10.

12 Online Safety Act 2023, section 12.

13 Online Safety Act 2023, schedule 7, paragraph 11. See more discussion of coercive and controlling behaviour below at Chapter 13.3.

14 Online Safety Act 2023, schedule 7, paragraph 30

15 Section 66A of the Sexual Offences Act 2003 as inserted by section 187 of the Online Safety Act 2023.

16 Section 66B of the Sexual Offences Act 2003 as inserted by section 188 of the Online Safety Act 2023.

17 "Prison Sentence in First Cyberflashing Case", 19 March 2024, www.cps.gov.uk/east-england/news/prison-sentence-first-cyberflashing-case, accessed 9 August 2024.

18 Article 1 of the Declaration on the Elimination of Violence against Women, UNGA Res 48/104 (20 Dec 1993).

This was the issue faced by the House of Lords in *R v Ireland*[19] when interpreting what was meant by "bodily harm" under the Offences against the Person Act 1861. The case involved the conjoined appeals of two defendants, Ireland and Burstow, who had both harassed women. Ireland was charged with actual bodily harm under section 47 of the Offences against the Person Act 1861[20] after making a series of silent phone calls to three women who then suffered psychological harm. Burstow was charged with grievous bodily harm under section 20 of the Offences against the Person Act 1861.[21] He had harassed a woman for eight months through silent phone calls, letters, and following her, after she ended a relationship with him. As a result, the woman suffered from a severe depressive illness. When the Offences against the Person Act 1861 was written psychiatry was in its infancy, and undoubtedly Parliament did not have such type of harm in mind.[22] Nonetheless, the court held that bodily harm "must be interpreted so as to include recognisable psychiatric illness".[23] Thus, there does not need to be physical injury to amount to a criminal offence. This interpretation seems to be in line with Parliament's intention as shortly after the Protection from Harassment Act 1997 came into force, which recognised the crime more commonly referred to as stalking.

While *R v Ireland* resolved the issue of what harm could amount to an offence against the person, this did not completely resolve the issue in the context of domestic abuse. In *Yemshaw v Hounslow LBC*[24] the Supreme Court were asked to decide whether "domestic violence" within section 177(1) of the Housing Act 1996 was limited to physical contact. The case involved the local housing authorities' duty to provide housing to people who are homeless. The law provided that a person could be considered homeless if:

> (1) It is not reasonable for a person to continue to occupy accommodation if it is probable that this will lead to domestic violence or other violence against him, or against –
> (a) a person who normally resides with him as a member of his family, or
> (b) any other person who might reasonably be expected to reside with him.[25]

The claimant left the matrimonial home with her two children following behaviour from her husband that would now most likely be recognised as coercive and controlling. She had nowhere else to live so sought help from the local authority, who decided that she was not homeless as her husband had never hit her nor threatened to do so. In the ground-breaking judgment from Lady Hale, it was stated that violence was not limited to physical violence or threats of such violence.[26] She stated that the definition of violence could change over time.[27] Thus, demonstrating how the law evolves to meet the moral standards acceptable in society as knowledge and understanding develops.

The type of abusive harm that Lady Hale refers to was later recognised by Parliament in section 76 of the Serious Crime Act 2015, with the introduction of the crime of coercive and

19 [1998] AC 147.
20 See Chapter 7.5.1 for the definition and further discussion of actual bodily harm.
21 See Chapter 7.5.1 for the definition and further discussion of grievous bodily harm.
22 *R v Ireland* [1998] AC 147, 158.
23 *R v Ireland* [1998] AC 147, 159.
24 [2011] UKSC 3
25 Section 177(1) of the Housing Act 1996 (before it was amended by the Domestic Abuse Act 2021 to include domestic abuse).
26 *Yemshaw v Hounslow LBC* [2011] UKSC 3, [28]–[32].
27 *Yemshaw v Hounslow LBC* [2011] UKSC 3, [27].

controlling behaviour in an intimate or family relationship.[28] This section aimed to better protect victims of domestic abuse. It provides that:

> 76(1) A person (A) commits an offence if –
> (a) A repeatedly or continuously engages in behaviour towards another person (B) that is controlling or coercive,
> (b) at the time of the behaviour, A and B are personally connected
> (c) the behaviour has a serious effect on B, and
> (d) A knows or ought to know that the behaviour will have a serious effect on B.

Since the introduction of this offence, the number of crimes recorded by the police has increased from 4,246 in the year from 2016 to 2017, to 45,310 in the year 2023 to 2024,[29] with 93 per cent to 94 per cent of victims being women and the perpetrators being almost exclusively male.[30]

The law was then further developed with the introduction of the Domestic Abuse Act 2021. The Act purposely uses the term abuse, rather than violence, in recognition that abuse can take many forms. This Act provides the first comprehensive definition of domestic abuse. Section 1 states:

> (1) This section defines "domestic abuse" for the purposes of this Act.
> (2) Behaviour of a person ("A") towards another person ("B") is "domestic abuse" if –
> (a) A and B are each aged 16 or over and are personally connected to each other, and
> (b) the behaviour is abusive.
> (3) Behaviour is "abusive" if it consists of any of the following –
> (a) physical or sexual abuse;
> (b) violent or threatening behaviour;
> (c) controlling or coercive behaviour;
> (d) economic abuse (see subsection (4)
> (e) psychological, emotional or other abuse;
> and it does not matter whether the behaviour consists of a single incident or a course of conduct.
> (4) "Economic abuse" means any behaviour that has a substantial adverse effect on B's ability to –
> (a) acquire, use or maintain money or other property, or
> (b) obtain goods or services.

This Act aimed to further improve the effectiveness of the justice system in providing protection for victims of domestic abuse and bringing perpetrators to justice. Some of the changes enacted included: Extending the controlling or coercive behaviour offence to cover post-separation abuse in recognition that domestic abuse often continues after separation; creating the offence of non-fatal strangulation or suffocation of another person;[31] and amending section 177(1) of the Housing Act 1996 to include domestic abuse, and to provide that all eligible homeless victims of domestic abuse automatically have "priority need" for homelessness assistance.

Despite the various developments in the law, domestic abuse remains an extensive issue. For example, worldwide a woman or girl is killed by someone in her own family on average once

---

28 See Vanessa Bettinson, "Aligning Partial Defences to Murder with the Offence of Coercive or Controlling Behaviour" [2019] J Crim L 71 for a comprehensive explanation of the meaning of coercive and controlling behaviour.

29 "Domestic Abuse Prevalence and Victim Characteristics", 27 November 2024, www.ons.gov.uk/peoplepopulationandcommunity/crimeandjustice/datasets/domesticabuseprevalenceandvictimcharacteristicsappendixtables, accessed 3 December 2024, table 20.

30 Home Office, "Review of Coercive or Controlling Behaviour Offence", 10 May 2021, www.gov.uk/government/publications/review-of-the-controlling-or-coercive-behaviour-offence/review-of-the-controlling-or-coercive-behaviour-offence#fnref:11, accessed 9 August 2024.

31 See Chapter 7.5.3 for more discussion of this offence.

every 11 minutes.[32] Nationally, research from the National Police Chief's Council shows that in the three-year period from 1 April 2020 to 31 March 2023 there were 723 deaths in individuals with a history of domestic abuse victimisation. This included 248 intimate partner homicides and 216 suspected victim suicides.[33] Leading to a Government acknowledgement that homicides were not the only type of death to result from domestic abuse.[34] Of the 100 domestic homicides in the year ending March 2023, 70% of the victims of domestic homicide were women, with these killings often being preceded by some form of domestic abuse.[35] Males were much less likely to be the victim of a domestic homicide, with only 8% of all male homicides being domestic-related for that year. In contrast, the number of domestic homicides against women accounts for almost half of all adult female homicide victims, with all but one being killed by a male suspect.[36] This demonstrates the gendered nature of domestic homicide.

13.4 Domestic Homicide

Nearly a quarter of all homicides are classified as domestic. Despite this, until 2024, schedule 21 of the Sentencing Act 2020 made no provision for the domestic context to be considered when setting the tariff for the mandatory life sentence for murder. Specifically, this meant that while coercive and controlling behaviour was recognised as a crime, the law did not reflect the seriousness of this non-physical abuse against victims before they were killed. Equally, it did not consider this abuse if the victim of coercive and controlling behaviour then killed the abuser. This anomaly in the law was addressed in the Wade report.[37] The recommendations included tougher sentences for murderers with a history of controlling or coercive behaviour against the victim and for "overkill", which is a phenomenon prevalent in domestic killing. This would amount to an aggravating factor. Conversely, the Wade report recommended that a history of coercive and controlling behaviour suffered by the victim should be a mitigating factor. These changes were bought into effect by the Sentencing Act 2020 being amended by the Sentencing Act 2020 (Amendment of Schedule 21) Regulations 2024.[38]

While this amendment to sentencing provides welcome recognition of the context that can lead to killing, it does not alter that the person is labelled as a murderer and faces a mandatory life sentence. As discussed in Chapter 13, this can cause specific issues for women who kill their abusers out of fear for their own lives, but are unable to plead self-defence or loss of control.[39] This is particularly a problem when the fear does not come from direct threats or use of violence, and from the fact that a woman is more likely than not to use a weapon to defend themselves. The result of this is

---

32 Swagata Sen, "Why Can't Women Escape Abusive Relationships?", 9 February 2020, www.rightsofequality.com/why-cant-women-escape-abusive-relationship, accessed 13 August 2024.

33 Vulnerability Knowledge and Practice Programme, "Domestic Homicides and Suspected Victim Suicides 2020–2023: Year 3 Report", March 2024, www.vkpp.org.uk/assets/Files/Domestic-Homicides-and-Suspected-Victim-Suicides-2021-2022/Domestic-Homicides-and-Suspected-Victim-Suicides-Year-3-Report_FINAL.pdf, accessed 9 August 2024.

34 Home Office and Laura Farris, "Fatal Domestic Abuse Reviews Renamed to Better Recognise Suicide Cases", 5 February 2024, www.gov.uk/government/news/fatal-domestic-abuse-reviews-renamed-to-better-recognise-suicide-cases, accessed 9 August 2024.

35 For further discussion, see Holly Johnson, Li Eriksson, Paul Mazerolle and Richard Wortley, "Intimate Femicide: The Role of Coercive Control" (2019) 14(1) Fem Criminology 3, 4.

36 Nick Stripe, "Homicide in England and Wales: Year Ending March 2023", 8 February 2024, www.ons.gov.uk/peoplepopulationandcommunity/crimeandjustice/articles/homicideinenglandandwales/yearendingmarch2023#the-relationship-between-victims-and-suspects, accessed 9 August 2024.

37 Clare Wade, "Domestic Homicide Sentencing Review", 17 March 2023, https://assets.publishing.service.gov.uk/media/6411ce52d3bf7f79df1aa9c4/domestic-homicide-sentencing-review.pdf, accessed 11 August 2024.

38 Schedule 21, section 9(ba) and 10(ca) of the Sentencing Act 2020 as amended by sections 3 and 4 of the Sentencing Act 2020 (Amendment of Schedule 21) Regulations 2024 (S.I. 2024/137).

39 See Chapter 13.3.1.

that the law criminalises women, who we might otherwise be burying,[40] for protecting themselves against their abuser. In a bid to mitigate this problem, diminished responsibility has been employed to provide a partial defence to women who kill their abusers.[41]

13.4.1 Diminished Responsibility

Diminished responsibility provides a defence to murder, reducing it to manslaughter. It is defined under section 2 of the Homicide Act 1957 as amended by section 52 of the Coroners and Justice Act 2009:

> Persons suffering from diminished responsibility (England and Wales)
>
> (1) A person ("D") who kills or is a party to the killing of another is not to be convicted of murder if D was suffering from an abnormality of mental functioning which –
> (a) arose from a recognised medical condition,
> (b) substantially impaired D's ability to do one or more of the things mentioned in subsection (1A), and
> (c) provides an explanation for D's acts and omissions in doing or being a party to the killing.
>
> (1A) Those things are –
> (a) to understand the nature of D's conduct;
> (b) to form a rational judgment;
> (c) to exercise self-control.
>
> (1B) For the purposes of subsection (1)(c), an abnormality of mental functioning provides an explanation for D's conduct if it causes, or is a significant contributory factor in causing, D to carry out that conduct.

This is an exemption-based defence constructed on the defendant's lack of capacity to make the right choice to adhere to the standard the law requires. This differs to an excusatory defence, which operates in limited, specified situations when the defendant has chosen to do the wrong thing.[42] In an exemption-based defence the defendant is not held fully to blame as this lack of capacity to make the right choice is due to an abnormality of mental functioning.[43] Therefore, the person avoids, or has reduced, criminal responsibility and punishment as they are incapable of meeting the objective standard that society requires of them.

The application of diminished responsibility can be seen by considering the scenarios at the start of the chapter. Azael could have a defence of diminished responsibility. The burden of proof would be on him to prove the defence on the balance of probabilities. The jury would need to decide whether he had an abnormality of mental functioning.[44] It would then need to be established that the abnormality came from a recognised medical condition. He has a diagnosed personality disorder that would likely qualify as a recognised medical condition.[45] Next it would need to be shown that this medical condition has impaired Azeal's ability to understand the nature of his conduct, form a rational judgment, or to exercise self-control. It could be considered that Azael's medical condition has impaired his ability to form a rational judgment.[46] This impairment must

---

40 Sophie Howes, "Women Who Kill: How the State Criminalises Women We Might Otherwise Be Burying" (Centre for Women's Justice, 17 February 2021).

41 Note, that while it is acknowledged that men can also be the victims of abuse, the term "woman" will be used in recognition of the statistical evidence that women are far more likely to be victims of abuse.

42 See Chapter 10.2 for more discussion on the nature of excusatory defences.

43 For more discussion, see Anthony Duff, *Answering for Crime: Responsibility and Liability in the Criminal Law* (Hart Publishing 2009), 287.

44 See, *R v Hussain* [2019] EWCA Crim 666.

45 For example, see, *R v Moyle* [2008] EWCA Crim 3059; *R v Martin* [2001] EWCA Crim 2245.

46 See, *R v Conroy* [2017] EWCA Crim 81.

be substantial. The Supreme Court in *R v Golds* clarified that the word substantial should be given its ordinary meaning, with the jury left to decide whether the impairment reaches the required level.[47] Finally, for Azael to have the defence he would need to show that it was the personality disorder that caused, or significantly contributed, to his conduct in killing Bodie. Thus, causation would need to be established. A successful plea would lead to Azael's conviction for murder being reduced to manslaughter, and the judge being given discretion in what sentence could be imposed.

While the defence of diminished responsibility is suitable to reduce blameworthiness in cases such as Azael's, the exemption-based theoretical underpinning means that this defence may not be suitable for women who kill their abusers. First, as stated above, the defendant must show that they are suffering from a recognised medical condition.[48] That a woman is a victim of abuse, without this leading to a diagnosable medical condition, will be insufficient.[49] Second, it assumes that the woman's mental functioning is at fault for the resultant killing, rather than the killing being a reasonable response to a fear of death or serious violence.[50] As Loveless expresses, "the legal debate shifts from the objective rationality of her actions to preserve her own life to those personal inadequacies which apparently explain her failure to flee from her abuser".[51] This feeds into the image of women who kill as being "bad, sad or mad",[52] raising issues of fair labelling and unwarranted stigmatisation, consequently leading to the syndromisation of women.[53] Nonetheless, as the law currently stands, diminished responsibility seems the only option of an available defence for abused women who kill their abuser. This is demonstrated in the case of *R v Challen*.[54]

R v Challen

Georgina Sarah Challen, known as Sally Challen, met her husband, Richard, when she was 15. They married 10 years later. During their 31-year marriage, Richard was unfaithful on several occasions, which caused Sally distress. She sought medical help and in 2009 was referred to a psychiatrist, but no recognised medical disorder was diagnosed. In 2009 the couple separated, but they then reconciled in 2010. This was on agreement that Sally entered a "post-nuptial agreement" that included denying her full financial entitlement in any subsequent divorce, and forbade her from interrupting Richard or speaking to strangers. Richard continued to have relations with other women. On the 14 August 2010, while having lunch, Sally took a hammer from her handbag that she had brought with her. In a frenzied attack, she killed Richard by repeatedly hitting him over the head with it.

47 *R v Golds* [2016] UKSC 61, [40].

48 Section 2(1)(a) of the Homicide Act 1957 as amended by section 52(1) of the Coroners and Justice Act 2009.

49 *R v Challen* [2019] EWCA Crim 916.

50 See Elizabeth Kenny, "Battered Women Who Kill: The Fight against Patriarchy" [2007] UCL Juris Rev 17; Aileen McColgan, "In Defence of Battered Women Who Kill" [1993] Oxford Journal of Legal Studies 508; and Celia Wells, "Battered Women Syndrome and Defences to Homicide" [1994], who argue that self-defence is a more appropriate than a partial defence of loss of control or diminished responsibility.

51 Janet Loveless, "R v GAC: Battered Woman 'Syndromization'" [2014] Crim LR 655, 665.

52 See Holly Pelvin, "The 'Normal' Woman Who Kills: Representations of Women's Intimate Partner Homicide" (2019) 14(3) Feminist Criminol 349, 349.

53 See, *R v Hobson* [1998] 1 Cr App R 31. For more discussion, see Isabel Grant, "The 'Syndromization' of Women's Experience" in D. Martinson et al., "A Forum on Lavallee v. R.: Women and Self-Defence" (1991) 25 UBC L Rev 23, 51, 53–54; Anne Coughlin, "Excusing Women" (1994) 82 Cal L Rev 1, 87; Marilyn McMahon, "Battered Women and Bad Science: The Limited Validity and Utility of the Battered Woman Syndrome" (1999) 6 Psychiatry, Psychology & Law 23.

54 [2019] EWCA Crim 916.

Sally was charged with murder. At her trial she was portrayed as a jealous and obsessive wife who had killed with premeditation. Sally raised the defence of diminished responsibility based on a depressive disorder. Despite not being raised by the defence, the judge also put the defence of provocation to the jury. Neither defence was accepted and Challen was convicted of murder. She was sentenced to the minimum tariff of 22 years in prison, which was reduced to 18 years on appeal.[55] Challen then appealed on the grounds of fresh medical evidence, and argued that Richard's coercive and controlling behaviour had led her to have an abnormality of the mind. Furthermore, that coercive control was relevant to the question of provocation. Challen's appeal was successful and a retrial ordered. This, however, never took place. The plea of manslaughter was finally accepted by the prosecution, and Sally was released after spending 9 years and 4 months in prison.

Thinking points:

- In *R v Challen*, there was evidence that Sally Challen had suffered years of coercive and controlling behaviour from her husband. Could this provide the basis of a defence of diminished responsibility?

In the earlier case of *R v Hobson*, battered women's syndrome was recognised as a medical condition for the basis of the defence of diminished responsibility.[56] The defendant had stabbed and killed her abusive and alcoholic partner during an argument. Evidence was provided at trial that in the 18 months leading up to the killing, she had reported the abuse to the police on 30 occasions. The defences of provocation and self-defence were left to the jury, but she was convicted of murder. Hobson appealed on the ground that in 1994 battered women's syndrome was added to the standard British classification of mental diseases and had become a recognised disorder. She provided medical evidence that at the time of the killing she was suffering from battered women's syndrome, a form of post-traumatic stress disorder, and her appeal was allowed.[57] Thus, a defence of diminished responsibility could be based on the medical condition of battered women's syndrome. The name of the condition, however, suggests that there needs to be physical violence. Therefore, as was the case in *Hobson*, that the woman needs to be battered.

In examining the scenarios at the start of the chapter, Celeste has suffered years of physical abuse at the hands of her abusive husband, Demetri. When she stabs and kills him she may not be able to successfully plead self-defence if it is considered that by using a weapon the force is disproportionate.[58] Therefore, as an alternative she could plead one, or both, of the partial defences of diminished responsibility and loss of control. For the defence of diminished responsibility, if she can show on the balance of probabilities that she had an abnormality of mental functioning caused by physical violence that resulted in battered women's syndrome, she may have a defence available to her.

In *R v Challen*, the abuse was psychological, stemming from years of intimidation, isolation, and control. When arrested for killing her husband Sally reported that, "everything had been on the [deceased's] terms" and despite her doing her best to please him he was always critical of her. Her cousin gave evidence that Richard had pulled the strings in their marriage, to which Sally

---

55 *R v Challen* [2011] EWCA Crim 916.

56 [1998] 1 Cr App R 31.

57 [1998] 1 Cr App R 31, 34.

58 See Chapter 12.3.1.

had "danced".[59] At the original trial there was a lack of understanding of coercive and controlling behaviour, and instead focus was placed on depression.

In the previous case of *R v Ahluwalia*, depression had been accepted as basis for the defence of diminished responsibility.[60] In that case the defendant had suffered years of physical abuse and humiliation from her husband, before setting his bedroom on fire and killing him. Her defence of provocation was rejected by the jury and she was convicted of murder. Despite evidence of her depressive disorder being available at trial, this was not presented. The Court of Appeal held that such evidence could lead to an arguable defence and allowed the appeal.[61]

Returning to the scenarios at the start of the chapter, Eliana has suffered years of abuse at the hands of her abusive husband, Fitz. Regardless of whether the abuse is physical or mental, the severe depressive illness she suffers at the time of the killing could provide a basis for the defence of diminished responsibility. The cause and type of abuse is irrelevant. The defence is based on Eliana's abnormality of mental functioning and whether this caused, or significantly contributed, to the killing.

In *R v Challen*, despite opposing evidence from the defence, medical evidence provided by Dr Paul Gilluley for the prosecution asserted that Sally Challen did not have a depressive disorder. Evidence that must have swayed the jury in them rejecting the defence of diminished responsibility and finding her guilty of murder. Thus, Challen could not establish physical violence leading to battered women's syndrome as in *R v Hobson*, and could not establish that the psychological abuse had led to a depressive disorder as in *R v Ahluwalia*. This left the question on appeal of whether the fresh evidence of coercive and controlling behaviour could amount to a basis for a defence of diminished responsibility.

The Court of Appeal concluded that coercive and controlling behaviour in itself was not a defence to murder. It could only be considered in context of the Parliamentary defined defences of diminished responsibility and provocation (now, loss of control). This raises the unanswerable question of whether coercive and controlling behaviour would have been included in the Coroners and Justice Act in 2009, if more had been known about its effects at that time. Nonetheless, while coercive and controlling behaviour was recognised as a crime in 2015,[62] it is not recognised as a defence.[63] Thus, suffering from coercive and controlling behaviour is not a medical condition that would fulfil the requirements of diminished responsibility.[64]

In the scenarios at the start of the chapter Gail has suffered years of coercive and controlling behaviour from her husband, Hector. Following the decision in *R v Challen*, despite her feeling trapped and unable to leave, she would have no defence of diminished responsibility available to her. It could not be said that her capacity to make the right choice had been reduced, and thus the exemption-based defence would not apply. Her alternative would be to plead loss of control, and argue that the coercive and controlling behaviour was a relevant circumstance beyond that of impacting her ability to exercise a normal degree of self-control.[65]

- As coercive and controlling behaviour is not a defence, what is its relevance in the context of diminished responsibility?

A person who kills their abuser, whether that abuse is physical or psychological, could be deemed morally less blameworthy than someone who kills without this context. While this is

59 [2019] EWCA Crim 916.
60 (1993) 96 Cr App R 133.
61 (1993) 96 Cr App R 133, 142–3.
62 Serious Crime Act 2015, section 76.
63 See, Tony Storey, "Coercive Control: An Offence but Not a Defence" [2019] J Crim L 513.
64 Under Coroners and Justice Act 2009, section 52(1)(a).
65 See Chapter 12.3.1. for more discussion of how the loss of control defence could apply.

not promulgating that individuals should take justice into their own hands, it is recognising that domestic abuse is a complex issue with serious consequences. The uninformed view asks why these women do not just leave instead of killing their abusers. Such a viewpoint fails to recognise the intensity of social entrapment and the evidence that a woman is actually just as much, if not more, at risk of harm when she does leave.[66] Midson makes the comparison between those experiencing coercive and controlling behaviour, to those who are kidnaped or in hostage situations. She argues that society would not hold kidnap or hostage victims as morally culpable of they killed to escape, so the same standard should apply to those experiencing coercive and controlling behaviour who kill their abusers.[67] Equally, Bettison criticises the result in *R v Challen* as it demonstrates "that victims who experience psychologically focused coercive control can be denied a reduction of moral responsibility when they commit crimes as a result of being subject to it".[68] Thus, even though a person who kills their abuser is morally less blameworthy than someone who has not been subjected to abuse, coercive and controlling behaviour is not a defence, and cannot result in a reduction of blameworthiness that is recognised within the law.

In *R v Challen*, it was argued that Sally Challen suffered from a borderline personality disorder and a severe mood disorder at the time of the killing. As such, her defence of diminished responsibility was still based on a recognised medical condition. The coercive and controlling behaviour was only relevant as it caused the more severe symptoms of these conditions to be masked during the time Richard and Sally Challen were living together. It meant that the medical conditions could only be properly diagnosed once she was free from his controlling presence.[69] As argued in Chapter 12,[70] part of the issue with abuse victims successfully pleading the partial defence of loss of control is the impact the abuse has on the way they present when interviewed by the police and in court. Perhaps, *R v Challen* goes some way to recognising and addressing this in relation to diminished responsibility.

In the final scenario given at the start of the chapter, Itzel has suffered years of coercive and controlling behaviour from her husband James. When she kills James there is no evidence of a recognised medical condition. Following *R v Challen* it could be argued that the coercive and controlling behaviour had prevented the, later diagnosed, medical condition from becoming apparent. If it could be established that the medial condition did exist at the time of the killing, despite the symptoms not being displayed, Itzel could have a defence of diminished responsibility. She would not be considered as blameworthy as the scenario involving Gail, as the medical condition could mean her capacity had been reduced. As such, she is not held fully responsible for the killing. The compromise is that her mental illness is viewed as the cause of the killing, and she is burdened with the stigma that results from this.

13.5 Conclusion

Domestic abuse is a predominantly gendered, national and international issue. In the UN and the UK there has been strong commitment to tackling domestic violence against women and girls. To achieve this policy aim, much domestic legislation has been introduced. This recognises the different ways abuse can be inflicted, and that harm caused can be psychological as well as physical. Nonetheless, domestic abuse, and domestic homicide, remains prevalent.

---

66 See, for example, "Why Don't Women Leave Abusive Relationships?", www.womensaid.org.uk/information-support/what-is-domestic-abuse/women-leave, accessed 14 August 2024.

67 Brenda Midson, "Coercive Control and Criminal Responsibility: Victims Who Kill their Abusers" (2016) 27(4) Crim L Forum 417, 433–434.

68 Vanessa Bettinson, "Aligning Partial Defences to Murder with the Offence of Coercive or Controlling Behaviour" [2019] J Crim L 71, 78.

69 [2019] EWCA Crim 916.

70 See Chapter 12.3.1.

As discussed in Chapter 12, the changes recommended by the Law Commission, and introduced by the Coroners and Justice Act 2009, were with a view to addressing the gender inequalities in the law relating to the partial defence of loss of control. As has been examined, despite these changes, victims of domestic abuse who kill their abusers may still find it difficult to successfully plead a loss of control defence in front of a jury.[71] The alternative is to plead diminished responsibility. Prior to the changes made by section 52 of the Coroners and Justice Act 2009, diminished responsibility had been successfully utilised when the abuse had meant that the killer had suffered from battered women's syndrome. Moreover, the defence could be utilised when the abuse had led to the killer suffering from depression. While this provided some relief to abused women who would otherwise be facing the label and sentence of a murderer, it unacceptably meant that the narrative had moved from the abuse suffered to the mental condition of the killer.

The case of *Challen* provided an opportunity to consider the significance of coercive and controlling behaviour, which resulted in the death of the abuser. This form of abuse, which does not rely on physical harm, had been recognised as a crime in 2015 by section 76 of the Serious Crime Act. The Court of Appeal, however, held that it could not provide a defence to killing. This is an understandable outcome when the defence of diminished responsibility is based on lack of capacity, which is determined by establishing that there is a recognised medical condition. Coercive and controlling behaviour is a crime focused on the wrong doing of the perpetrator, not a medical condition suffered by the victim of the abuse. Nonetheless, this does not change the assertion that a person who suffers social entrapment and kills is less morally blameworthy than someone who has not. Domestic abuse may be a relevant circumstance for establishing the defence of diminished responsibility, as shown in *R v Challen*, when it is concealing a recognised medical condition. Other than this, as the law currently stands, domestic abuse in itself will not reduce the blameworthiness of a murderer who kills their abuser to that of a manslayer. The only slight relief that is provided is from domestic abuse being considered as a mitigating factor when imposing the mandatory life sentence of those who kill their abuser.

13.6 Further Reading

Bettinson V, "Aligning Partial Defences to Murder with the Offence of Coercive or Controlling Behaviour" [2019] J Crim L 71

Clough A, "Coercive Control: Transforming Partial Defences to Murder in England and Wales" [2023] J Crim L 109

Midson B, "Coercive Control and Criminal Responsibility: Victims Who Kill their Abusers" [2016] Crim L Forum 417

Storey T, "Coercive Control: An Offence but Not a Defence" [2019] J Crim L 513

13.6.1 Websites

www.centreforwomensjustice.org.uk/home

www.justiceforwomen.org.uk

71 For example, see *R v Martin R v Martin* [2020] EWCA Crim 1798; *R v Magson* [2022] EWCA Crim 1064; *R v Cheng* [2024] EWCA Crim 1400.

Chapter 14

Imposing Liability on Corporations

Chapter Contents

DOI: 10.4324/9781003408383-15

14.1 Chapter Aims and Objectives

This chapter considers when corporations,[1] as legal entities, can be found criminally liable for their actions. In a criminal justice system that is based on establishing the fault of an individual, which can be deduced from establishing certain blameworthy states of mind, imposing liability on corporations presents a challenging problem. The courts have developed devices to enable corporations to face criminal liability within the confines of the *actus reus* and *mens rea* requirements, while Parliament has introduced a number of statutory provisions aimed solely at corporate liability. This has resulted in a piecemeal approach being adopted in determining when a corporation can be criminally liable.

By the end of this chapter, you should be able to:

- Identify and justify when corporate criminal liability can be imposed.
- Examine how legal principle was influenced by morals and policy in the decision of *Tesco Supermarkets Limited v Nattrass*.[2]
- Examine whether statutory corporate offences resolve the problem of when a corporation can justly be criminally liable.

> The issues that will be examined in this chapter can be illustrated through the following scenarios. Before starting the chapter, read the following scenarios and consider whether the corporations (indicated in italics) should be held responsible:
>
> - Anna works in a *grocery shop*. She alters the "best before" labels on produce and sells the produce to customers.
> - Bradley works in a *furniture shop*. He has an argument with a customer and hits them.
> - Claire works in a *hospital*. Despite her colleagues raising concerns with their line manager on multiple occasions about her treatment of patients, and the high morbidity rate of those in her care, nothing has been done. Following the recent death of one of her patients Claire has been convicted of gross negligence manslaughter.
> - Dakota works in the sales department of a *large manufacturer*. He is paid bonuses according to the amount of sales he achieves. Using company money, he pays a foreign official a bribe. This is so the manufacturing company that Dakota works for will win the contract to provide goods to that foreign country.
> - Ernie works for an *accountancy firm*. At the weekend, using the knowledge that he has learnt at work, he helps his girlfriend avoid paying taxes that she should be paying.
> - Freya works for a *bank*. She is accessing customer's account information and selling this on to cybercriminals to earn extra money for herself.

14.2 Imposing Liability on Corporations

Corporations pose a particular quandary for criminal law. As has been discussed throughout this book, it is clear that in certain situations criminal liability can be rightly attributed to an individual for their blameworthy actions. The devices of *actus reus* and *mens rea* are used to limit and justify who

---

1 The term corporation will be used throughout for ease and consistency, except for when the statute being discussed uses differing terminology.

2 [1972] AC 153.

will be held legally responsible. But, what if it is a corporation's acts or omissions that have led to wrongdoing occurring? Does a corporation have moral agency, which in turn means it can be attributed with moral blame for a criminal offence?

A corporation is a legal entity that is separate from its owners.[3] As such, following the enactment of Interpretation Act 1899,[4] all acts that have since referred to a person are interpreted to include a body of persons corporate or incorporate. Nonetheless, despite the suggestion of Lord Denning in *HL Bolton (Engineering) Co Ltd v TJ Graham & Sons Ltd* that "[a] company may in many ways be likened to a human body. It has a brain and a nerve centre which controls what it does",[5] it does not have a physical body to commit *actus reus* or a mind capable of forming *mens rea*. This means that certain crimes, for example rape, which requires that the defendant intentionally penetrates the vagina, anus or mouth of another person with his penis,[6] cannot physically be committed by a corporation.

There are certain situations whereby it is morally desirable, and attractive for policy reasons, to hold a corporation responsible. For example, when the harm to society, such as the pollution of rivers, has been caused by the way a corporation undertakes its activities. Or, when imposing criminal liability on a well-known corporation will provide greater, and more public, denunciation than prosecution of an individual. As such, criminal liability goes beyond the compensation for harm that can be afforded in a civil suit, and allows a public and moral judgment to be made on the actions of the corporation with the aim of future deterrence of the offending behaviour. Moreover, corporations may be best placed to stop certain kinds of harm being undertaken by their employees,[7] and thus corporations can fulfil a crime prevention role.[8]

Imposing liability on corporations does not present an insurmountable problem in crimes of strict liability. This is because if the criminal actions or omissions of an individual can be attributed to the corporation, then liability can be established without the need to prove *mens rea*. This form of derivative liability enables the law to punish corporations when the *actus reus* of their employees does not follow regulatory requirements and thus poses a danger, for example, to public health or the environment.

Crimes that do not fall into the category of strict liability are more problematic. This is because it is not enough to show that wrongdoing, by whatever means, has occurred. It must also be shown that the corporation have a guilty mind that accompanies these guilty actions or omissions. If it is agreed that corporations should hold criminal responsibility then a method needs to be devised to determine a corporation's guilty mind, and thus, their criminal liability. The method adopted by common law for crimes that require *actus reus* and *mens rea* is the identification principle. Similarly to the way strict liability offences operate, liability is again derived from individuals within the corporation. This fails to recognise a corporation as a separate complex entity with its own culture and characteristics.[9] To address this, and the issues that arise with the identification principle, Parliament are increasingly creating offences that are bespoke to corporations, such as corporate manslaughter and failure to prevent offences. These, however, still raise issues when determining if is just to impose criminal liability on corporations.

---

3 *Salomon v Salomon* [1897] AC 22.

4 Section 19, as now contained in Schedule 1 of the Interpretation Act 1978.

5 [1957] 1 QB 159, 172.

6 See section 1 of the Sexual Offences Act 2003.

7 For example, the Law Commission, *Reforming Bribery* (Law Com No 313, 2008) in discussing the introduction of a corporate offence of failure to prevent bribery (discussed further below at Chapter 14.6.2) states at para 6.14: "It is companies (and those acting on their behalf) who are undoubtedly in the best position to ensure that the enormous damage done by toleration of bribery – especially in relation to overseas trade – is reduced or even eliminated worldwide."

8 See Andrew Ashworth, "A New Generation of Omission Offences?" [2018] Crim LR 354, 360–363 for more discussion of the correct role of corporations in crime prevention.

9 See Neil Cavanagh, "Corporate Liability: An Assessment of the Models of Fault" [2011] J Crim L 414, 415 who argues for a non-derivative approach where "corporations are seen as free-standing entities, culpable for their own policies, procedures and system".

Even if criminal responsibility can be established, this still leaves the question of what punishment is suitable for a corporation. Furthermore, whether a penalty it is needed if an individual has already faced punishment for the wrongdoing. In a system designed to punish individuals the appropriate punishment for corporations becomes problematic. A corporation is a legal entity, but has no physical body, so cannot be sent to prison. Moreover, fining the corporation may result in punishing those, such as shareholders or service users, who had no knowledge or control over the criminal actions.[10] This does not effectively achieve the aims of sentencing.[11] One solution is the approach to punishment taken in the Corporate Manslaughter and Corporate Homicide Act 2007, which, as discussed below,[12] provides a wider range of penalties that if effectively utilised may achieve greater deterrence or reparation.

14.3 Strict Liability

Crimes of strict liability do not require the prosecution to prove *mens rea* for one or more aspects of the *actus reus*.[13] This means that a corporation can be found criminally liable without the difficulty of establishing whether a legal entity, which does not have a brain, has formed the requisite *mens rea* for the crime charged. Many of these crimes are regulatory in nature and have been created through acts of Parliament. Arguably the regulatory nature of these crimes means that they are not the proper subject of criminal law. This is because, "criminal law should be employed only when engagement in the prohibited conduct in question warrants official censure, because it involves a harm-related moral failing, not just a breach of a rule or simple departure from a standard."[14] The imposition of liability without *mens rea* can, however, be justified when it will make individuals and corporations more careful in carrying out functions that would otherwise create an issue of social concern. Moreover, it can make employers responsible for the acts of their employees.[15] In the House of Lords decision in *Tesco Supermarkets Limited v Nattrass*[16] Lord Diplock states:

> the most effective method of deterrence is to place upon the employer the responsibility of doing everything which lies within his power to prevent his employees from doing anything which will result in the commission of an offence. This, I apprehend, is the rational and moral justification for creating in the field of consumer protection, as also in the field of public health and safety, offences of "strict liability" for which an employer or principal, in the course of whose business the offences were committed, is criminally liable, notwithstanding that they are due to acts or omissions of his servants or agents which were done without his knowledge or consent or even were contrary to his orders.[17]

Examples, of such liability being imposed include: it is a strict liability offence to sell a lottery ticket to a person aged under 18 contrary to section 13 of the National Lottery Act 1993;[18] to sell

---

10 On the contrary, in *Balfour Beatty Rail Infrastructure Ltd* [2006] EWCA Crim 1586 when the Hatfield train crash lead to the railway company being convicted under section 3 of the Health and Safety at Work Act 1974 and sentenced to a £10 million fine, the Lord Chief Justice noted at [42] that raising concern among shareholders will act as a powerful incentive for management to comply with the health and safety duties. Thus, appropriate fines serve as a deterrent.

11 See Chapter 1.3.2 for more discussion of the policy aims of sentencing.

12 See Chapter 14.6.1 below.

13 See Chapter 9.3 for more discussion of strict liability in the context of sexual offences.

14 Law Commission, *Criminal Liability in Regulatory Contexts* (Law Com CP No 195, 2010) para 4.6.

15 See below at Chapter 14.4 for further discussion of vicarious liability.

16 See further discussion of *Tesco Supermarkets Limited v Nattrass* at Chapter 14.5 below.

17 *Tesco Supermarkets Limited v Nattrass* [1972] AC 153, 194.

18 *Harrow London Borough Council v Shah and Another* [2000] 1 WLR 83.

food not of the nature or substance or quality demanded under section 14 of the Food Safety Act 1990;[19] to provide a short measure of goods under section 28 of the Weights and Measures Act 1985; and to sell alcohol without a licence under section 137 of the Licensing Act 2003. Little difficulty arises in attributing the actions of the employee to the corporation through the principle of vicarious liability[20] in instances such as these. In such situations, the goods in question, which are then wrongly sold or supplied, are owned by the corporation. Therefore, while it might be an employee who has performed a particular transaction, the transfer of the legal title of the goods has gone from the corporation to the buyer. There are, however, limits to when this attribution principle can apply.[21] This could be due to the statutory language of the offence being charged as seen in *Attorney General's Reference* (No 2 of 2003).[22] The Court of Appeal held that a consultant obstetrician and gynaecologist who was the licensed person responsible for the supervision of activities of clinics[23] where the alleged offences had taken place, was not responsible for the offence of keeping, without storage, of an embryo intended for human application[24] committed by the sole embryologist at the clinics. Despite this being an offence of strict liability, nothing in the Act meant that his position as the licensed person automatically made him the "keeper" of the embryos. The court went on to say:

> If it had been intended that the person responsible should, as a matter of law, have been criminally liable for any contravention of section 3(1) by anyone else, or for administrative failures within the clinic in relation to the keeping and use of embryos, this could have been achieved, if Parliament had so intended, by clear language. Such language is not used.[25]

Thus, while the courts will impose liability on corporations for the actions of their employees, this is not a general rule. It will depend on the statutory construction.

Moreover, the moral justification of deterrence that Lord Diplock refers to above, in *Tesco Supermarkets Limited v Nattrass*, does not have blanket application to criminalise corporations when the corporation has tried to avoid the wrongful conduct taking place. As Lord Diplock goes on to state,

> this rational and moral justification does not extend to penalising an employer or principal who has done everything that he can reasonably be expected to do by supervision or inspection, by improvement of his business methods or by exhorting those whom he may be expected to control or influence to prevent the commission of the offence.[26]

Due to the oppressive nature of imposing strict criminal liability to corporations for the actions of their employees, many statutes include a defence of due diligence. Unlike some other common law jurisdictions,[27] England and Wales have no common law general defence of due diligence. Instead, a piecemeal approach means that corporations can avoid liability if the statute being

---

19 *Ruxton v Haston* [1997] 3 WLUK 527.

20 See Chapter 14.4 below for more discussion of Vicarious Liability.

21 For more discussion see David Ormerod, Karl Laird, and Matthew Gibson, *Smith, Hogan, and Ormerod's Criminal Law* (17th edition, Oxford University Press 2024) 291–293.

22 [2004] 1 WLR 2062.

23 Under section 17 Human Fertilisation and Embryology Act 1990.

24 Under section 3(1)(b) of the Human Fertilisation and Embryology Act 1990.

25 *Attorney General's Reference* (No 2 of 2003) [2004] 1 WLR 2062, [21].

26 *Tesco Supermarkets Limited v Nattrass* [1972] AC 153, 194.

27 For example, Canada has a developed a due diligence defence at common law that can apply to offences of strict liability. See *R v City of Sault Ste Marie* (1978) 85 DLR (3d) 161.

prosecuted under provides for such a defence. For example, section 34(1) of the Weights and Measures Act 1985 states:

> In any proceedings for an offence under this Part of this Act or any instrument made under this Part, it shall be a defence for the person charged to prove that he took all reasonable precautions and exercised all due diligence to avoid the commission of the offence.

Similarly, the Food Safety Act 1990, section 21(1) states:

> In any proceedings for an offence under any of the preceding provisions of this Part (in this section referred to as "the relevant provision"), it shall, subject to subsection (5) below, be a defence for the person charged to prove that he took all reasonable precautions and exercised all due diligence to avoid the commission of the offence by himself or by a person under his control.

These sections show that a corporation can avoid liability when they have not been negligent in trying to prevent the wrongdoing. Therefore, while it may be possible to attribute strict liability to a corporation for the actions of an employee, without the prosecution establishing *mens rea*, the corporation can then avoid liability by establishing that they had exercised due diligence and thus had not been negligent. The application of such a due diligence defence, contained in section 24(1) of the Trade Descriptions Act 1968, was the subject of the House of Lords consideration in *Tesco Supermarkets Limited v Nattrass*. This case is considered further below,[28] but one important aspect to note here is how corporate liability was attributed to Tesco Supermarkets Limited, and defended. As already discussed, in cases of strict liability, involving goods that belong to the corporation, there is little difficulty in imposing liability on a corporation by applying the principle of vicarious liability. To prove a defence, however, the corporation has the burden of establishing that they have assessed the risks and exercised due diligence, so that they are deemed not to be negligent. Therefore, while the wrongful actions require no *mens rea* to be established, the defence has the burden of establishing a lack of *mens rea* (negligence) in making out the defence. This meant that in *Tesco Supermarkets Limited v Nattrass*, the House of Lords held that while Tesco Supermarkets Limited could be vicariously strictly liable under section 11(2) of the Trade Descriptions Act 1968 for the actions of its employees, liability was avoided. Negligence by one of Tesco's managers, to exercise due diligence over store employees, was that of another legal individual who was separate to the corporation. As such, the corporation could establish its own lack of negligence for the purpose of allowing the due diligence defence in section 24(1).

14.4 Vicarious Liability

The principle of vicarious liability is well established in civil law. For example, in the tort of negligence an employer can be vicariously liable for the negligent actions of their employees,[29] for negligent actions of persons akin to employees,[30] and even criminal actions carried out by their employees if conducted in the course of their employment.[31] Within criminal law, where the key policy aims include punishment and deterrence,[32] such a wide approach is not accepted.

The only exception, as discussed above, is cases of strict liability.[33] For these offences, criminal liability, in addition to being imposed on an individual, can be vicariously imposed on a corporation

28 See below at Chapter 14.5.

29 *Century Insurance v Northern Ireland Road Transport* [1942] 1 All ER 491.

30 *Cox v MOJ* [2016] UKSC 10.

31 *Mohamud v W M Morrison Supermarkets* [2016] UKSC 11; *Armes v Nottinghamshire County Council* [2017] UKSC 60.

32 See Chapter 1.3.2.

33 *Tesco Supermarkets Limited v Nattrass* [1972] AC 153, 199.

regardless of the corporation's state of mind or blameworthiness.[34] Imposing liability on a corporation in this way can be justified as the corporation benefits from the employee's actions. Moreover, if the corporation goes unpunished this "undermines the operation of competitive business".[35]

Examining the scenario of Anna at the start of the chapter, as this would amount to a strict liability offence under section 14 of the Food Safety Act 1990, the grocery shop could vicariously liable for the actions of Anna. The grocery shop could avoid liability by proving a due diligence defence under section 21(1) of the Food Safety Act 1990. This would place the burden of proof on them to show that they had not been negligent in allowing the offence to happen.

Nonetheless, as already discussed,[36] not all strict liability offences will impose vicarious liability. Thus, the two concepts are not synonymous. Moreover, if the crime is one that requires *mens rea* it has long been held that vicarious liability is not appropriate.[37] As Lord Morris in *Tesco Supermarkets Limited v Nattrass* states: "In general criminal liability only results from personal fault. We do not punish people in criminal courts for the misdeeds of others. The principle of respondeat superior [let the master answer] is applicable in our civil courts but not generally in our criminal courts."[38] The importance of justice,[39] and the imposition of moral censure that is associated with criminal liability,[40] means that vicarious liability has no general application in the field of criminal law. Thus, a person can only be responsible for their own crimes.[41] Therefore, if an employee carried out a crime, it would be them who would face criminal liability and not the corporation. Thus, returning to the scenario of Bradley at the start of the chapter, it can be seen that the furniture shop will not be responsible for Bradley hitting a customer. This is because such a crime requires *actus reus* and *mens rea*, which will not be vicariously attributed to the furniture shop under the principles of criminal law.

This approach would mean that corporations would always avoid criminal liability where the crime charged required both *actus reus* and *mens rea*, as instead individuals would be prosecuted. This, however, does not achieve a desired deterrent effect on corporations. Therefore, instead of corporations being able to avoid liability, the courts have developed the identification principle to impute the *mens rea* of an individual to become the *mens rea* of the corporation.

14.5 The Identification Principle

As already stated above, when a crime requires both *actus reus* and *mens rea* to be proved it becomes difficult to establish criminal liability for a corporation. This is because the prosecution is not trying to establish if an individual is blameworthy, as is the norm for a criminal offence, but whether fault can be attributed to the corporation as a whole. As Wolf strongly asserts, "As long as the criminal law continues to include among its functions the expression of moral blame, the application of criminal law should be restricted to persons and other beings that have, not just cognitive

---

34 For example, see *R v British Steel* [1995] 1 WLR 1365; *Harrow London Borough Council v Shah and Another* [2000] 1 WLR 83.

35 See Celia Wells, "Corporate Failure to Prevent Economic Crime – a Proposal" [2017] Crim LR 426, 429 for a discussion in the context of bribery.

36 See the discussion at Chapter 14.3 above.

37 In *R v Huggins* (1730) 92 ER 518, Raymond CJ. "It is a point not to be disputed but that in criminal cases the principal is not answerable for the act of his deputy, as he is in civil cases; they must each answer for their own acts, and stand or fall by their own behaviour."

38 *Tesco Supermarkets Limited v Nattrass* [1972] AC 153, 179.

39 See Chapter 2.3.1.

40 See Chapter 1.3.1.

41 This extends to crimes committed by other individuals and corporations when, for example: the individual is aiding and abetting others under section 1 of the Accessories and Abettors Act 1861; conspiring with others to commit a crime, for example, under section 1 of the Criminal Law Act 1977; and encouraging and assisting a crime under sections 44–46 of the Serious Organised Crime Act 2007.

capacities, but souls."[42] Thus, if a corporation cannot be said to have its own moral agency, this would suggest that the corporation should avoid prosecution. As discussed above,[43] legal principle means that a corporation cannot be vicariously liable for the actions of others for crimes requiring *mens rea*. Instead, if the corporation is to be held criminally liable then this liability has to be directly imposed on them. As discussed in Chapter 5, different states of *mens rea* are used as a vehicle to determine how blameworthy someone is for a particular outcome. Therefore, using this formulation the *mens rea* of the corporation in itself has to be determined to establish its moral agency, criminal responsibility and the correct level of blameworthiness.

Historically, it was thought that a corporation could not be indicted for a crime for procedural reasons.[44] Over time the procedural position for indicting corporations altered as the law has changed.[45] In response, the courts developed the identification principle to enable moral agency to be derived from individuals and placed onto the corporation.[46] The principle holds that the acts and states of mind of corporation's directors and managers are imputed to become the *actus reus* and *mens rea* of the corporation, which can then be held liable for the wrongdoing. The identification principle was defined in the leading case of *Tesco Supermarkets Limited v Nattrass*.[47]

Tesco Supermarkets Limited v Nattrass

The defendant, a large limited company owning about 800 supermarket stores, was charged under section 11(2) of the Trade Descriptions Act 1968 for advertising a product at a promotional price that was not available for purchase at that price. Tesco had in place a system of training and supervision of its managers and employees to ensure that offences of this kind did not occur, but the manager of the store had not checked the work of his staff as he was required to do. This had led to the offence being committed. Tesco claimed that they had a defence under section 24(1)(a) of the Trade Descriptions Act 1968, as the wrongdoing had been done by "another person". In this case the manager of the store. Furthermore, that they had complied with section 24(1)(b) by taking all reasonable precautions and exercised due diligence to avoid the commission of the offence. In the original trial it was found that the store manager did not qualify as a "another person" separate from the company for the purpose of the Act. Tesco appealed to the Divisional Court and then further to the House of Lords. Lord Pearson in his judgment in the House of Lords stated that, "there are some officers of a company who may for some purposes be identified with it, as being or having its directing mind and will, its centre and ego, and its brains".[48] The appeal was allowed as the manager in this context could not be identified as being the company, and therefore was "another person" for the purpose of the defence.

---

42 S Wolf, "The Legal and Moral Responsibility of Organisations" in Ronald Pennock and John W Chapman, *Criminal Justice: Nomos 27* (New York University Press 1985), 286. For an opposing view see Neil Cavanagh, "Corporate Liability: An Assessment of the Models of Fault" [2011] J Crim L 414, 432 who states that corporations can have moral agency as "the requisite *mens rea* is found in the corporate culture rather than in the mind of an individual".

43 See Chapter 14.4.

44 *Anon* (1701) 12 Mod Rep 560 per Holt CJ, which noted that a personal appearance was required in court to enter a plea.

45 For example, Section 33(3) of the Criminal Justice Act 1925 provides that a corporation may enter a plea by a representative, or if the corporation fails to do so the court shall order a plea of not guilty to be entered and the trial shall proceed as though the corporation entered a not guilty plea.

46 For further discussion of the Identification Principle and its development, see Law Commission, *Criminal Liability in Regulatory Contexts* (Law Com CP No 195, 2010) Part 5.

47 [1972] AC 153.

48 [1972] AC 153, 190.

Thinking points:

- In the judgment of *Tesco Supermarkets Limited v Nattrass* Lord Reid stated: "Where a limited company is the employer difficult questions do arise in a wide variety of circumstances in deciding which of its officers or servants is to be identified with the company so that his guilt is the guilt of the company".[49] How do the courts determine who is the corporation's "directing mind and will, its centre and ego, and its brains"?

As discussed above,[50] Lord Diplock identifies there were policy reasons when passing the Trade Descriptions Act 1968 of wanting to protect consumers, but that allowing a due diligence defence provides rational and moral justification.[51] In other words, protecting consumers needs to be balanced against only finding those who are truly at fault to blame. One mechanism to achieve this balance is to restrict whose blameworthy state of mind can be considered to be that of the corporation. Or in this case, whether the manager's negligence was that of the corporation or "another person". This question of who can be identified as the corporation is not an easy one to answer. Even within the judgments given within the House of Lords in *Tesco Supermarkets Limited v Nattrass* slightly different approaches were used. Lord Reid seems to give a clear answer when he states: "Normally the board of directors, the managing director and perhaps other superior officers of a company carry out the functions of management and speak and act as the company".[52] This appears to give quite a closed and concise list of who can be identified as being the company. However, Lord Reid then goes on to add:

> But the board of directors may delegate some part of their functions of management giving to their delegate full discretion to act independently of instructions from them. I see no difficulty in holding that they have thereby put such a delegate in their place so that within the scope of the delegation he can act as the company. It may not always be easy to draw the line but there are cases in which the line must be drawn.[53]

There seems to be no further guidance of exactly where this line that Lord Reid is referring to should be drawn.

Alternatively, Lord Morris, in determining whether the manager in *Tesco Supermarkets Limited v Nattrass* could be identified as the company, states: "He was, so to speak, a cog in the machine which was devised: it was not left to him to devise it. Thus, the question becomes whether the employee who has conducted the wrongdoing is just a cog or the creator of the machine."[54] Lord Morris concluded that the manager was just a cog, but this leaves the matter to be determined as a question of fact for each different corporation in each case.

Viscount Dilhorne and Lord Diplock also take differing views. Viscount Dilhorne opines that it must be considered who is "in actual control of the operations of the company".[55] This suggests a pragmatic approach, which considers who can be identified as the corporation on what happens in practice. Whereas, Lord Diplock places emphasis on "identifying those natural persons who by the memorandum and articles of association or as a result of action taken by the directors, or by the

49 [1972] AC 153, 170.
50 See Chapter 14.3.
51 [1972] AC 153, 194–195.
52 [1972] AC 153, 170, 171.
53 [1972] AC 153, 170, 171.
54 [1972] AC 153, 170, 181.
55 [1972] AC 153, 170, 187.

company in general meeting pursuant to the articles, are entrusted with the exercise of the powers of the company".[56] These differing approaches demonstrate that there is not one single answer to which individuals can be identified as being the corporation.

In *Meridian Global Funds Management Asia Ltd v Securities Commission*, Lord Hoffman in the Privy Council tried to assert a more policy-based approach that considered the particular law that had been breached when determining who could be identified as the company.[57] This enabled a broader interpretation to be taken in determining which employees could be said to be the corporation. Nonetheless, this wider approach has since been rejected, with the narrower approach used in *Nattrass* being returned to.[58]

Adopting a narrower test for determining who will be deemed the directing will and mind of the corporation does not, however, necessarily diminish the policy aim of protecting consumers. Even if a relevant employee of the corporation cannot be identified as being the corporation, managers and employees can still face individual liability for their acts or omission (although not sought in *Tesco Supermarkets Limited v Nattrass*).[59] Nonetheless, individual punishment will not have the same deterrent effect on the corporation as corporate liability would, nor the potential for high-profile denunciation that would result from the prosecution of a well-known corporation.

Overall, the House of Lords' judgment in *Tesco Supermarkets Limited v Nattrass* favours ensuring that moral agency is not just blindly imputed onto a corporation. This is despite the policy aims that could be achieved from adopting a wider identification principle to hold more corporations responsible.

- Lord Pearson in *Tesco Supermarkets Limited v Nattrass* states that when identifying which people can be identified as the corporation, the constitution of the company concerned should be considered.[60] Why is the constitution of the company problematic in applying the identification principle?

One of the key issues with the identification principle is that the less complex or smaller the corporation is, the easier it is to identify an individual person as being the corporation. This means that smaller corporations are disproportionately penalised,[61] with larger complex corporations avoiding liability because a suitable person with the required *mens rea* that can be attributed to the corporation cannot be identified.[62] Thus, in a modern society where corporations are often global, employing hundreds, if not thousands of employees, the identification principle becomes redundant. This means that corporations that have a wide-ranging reach and impact, cannot be penalised when their acts or omissions cause damage. Therefore, resulting in the discriminatory application of the identification principle against small corporation and undermining the policy aim of legislation to protect individuals from harm.[63]

In summary, the common law identification principle is problematic. It tries to resolve the problem of attributing criminal liability to corporations when the crime requires *mens rea*. Legal principle provides that vicarious liability should not be generally adopted in criminal law, but the identification principle still requires criminal liability that is derivative from an identifiable individual. This makes imposing liability a difficult task, especially in large corporations. In the

---

56 [1972] AC 153, 170, 200.
57 [1995] UKPC 5.
58 *Attorney General's Reference (No 2 of 1999)* [2000] QB 796.
59 [1972] AC 153, 170, 183.
60 [1972] AC 153, 170, 191.
61 For example, see *R v OLL Ltd and Kite* [1996] 2 Cr App R 72.
62 For example, see *R v P & O European Ferries (Dover) Ltd* (1991) 93 Cr App R 295.
63 See Chapter 2.3.6 for discussion of the harm principle.

next section, it will be considered whether Parliament has managed to resolve the issue of how to effectively and fairly impose corporate liability, during their enactment of a range of statutory corporate offences.

14.6 Statutory Corporate Offences

So far, this chapter has considered how corporations can be criminally liable for crimes that also impose liability on individuals. The dual functionality of these offences has meant that the courts have found corporations vicariously liable for the actions of their employees in offences such as those requiring strict liability, and devised the identification principle to impute *mens rea* from an individual onto the corporation for crimes that require both *actus reus* and *mens rea*. This next section considers statutory offences that have been written by Parliament specifically with corporations in mind as the potential offenders: corporate manslaughter under the Corporate Manslaughter Act 2007; and failure to prevent offences under the Bribery Act 2010, the Criminal Finances Act 2017, and the Economic Crime and Corporate Transparency Act 2023. The introduction of these offences is policy driven to deal with specific issues that have arisen over time. Each has provided an opportunity to consider what basis corporate liability should be imposed on, and whether the law should move away from establishing individual wrongdoing that can then be imposed on a corporation through vicarious liability or through the identification principle.

14.6.1 Corporate Manslaughter

The offence of corporate manslaughter was enacted in the Corporate Manslaughter and Corporate Homicide Act 2007 after 13 years of deliberation.[64] This was in response to public disquiet at corporations avoiding liability for large-scale disasters.[65] The offence has limited application in that it only creates corporate liability for culpable killing, and no other offences. Moreover, the offence is aimed solely at corporations, and as such, individuals cannot be liable under its provisions.[66] The offence is supplementary to liability that can be imposed under the Health and Safety at Work Act 1974 and is aimed at providing a deterrence to reduce the number of avoidable workplace deaths.[67] Furthermore, it goes beyond health and safety legislation by attaching the label of manslaughter to corporations who are convicted, with the stigma and moral condemnation that accompanies this.[68] The offence of corporate manslaughter is constructed from the common law offence of gross negligence manslaughter, which prior to the Act was the main method of convicting corporations with the use of the identification principle.[69]

---

64 The Law Commission first considered reforming the law of corporate manslaughter in 1994: Law Commission, *Criminal Law: Involuntary Manslaughter* (Law Com CP 135, 1994), Part IV and Part V, G.

65 For example, the loss of 193 lives in the sinking of the P&O *Herald of Free Enterprise* in 1987, the loss of 31 lives in the Kings Cross Fire in 1987, the loss of 35 lives in the Clapham Rail Disaster in 1988, and the loss of 51 lives in the sinking of the *Marchioness*.

66 See James Gobert, "The Corporate Manslaughter and Corporate Homicide Act 2007 – Thirteen Years in the Making but Was it Worth the Wait?" (2008) 71(3) MLR 413 for further discussion and criticism of the decision to not include accessorial liability for senior managers under the Act.

67 See Victoria Roper, "The Corporate Manslaughter and Corporate Homicide Act 2007: A Re-evaluation 10 Years on from the First Case" [2022] Crim LR 290 for a discussion of how it has achieved this aim.

68 See Chapter 2.3.2 for further discussion of fair labelling.

69 As stated in *R v HM Coroner for East Kent Ex parte Spooner* (1987) 3 BCC 636, 642, "for a company to be criminally liable for manslaughter . . . requires that the mens rea and the actus reus of manslaughter should be established not against those who acted for or in the name of the company but against those who were to be identified as the embodiment of the company itself".

The Corporate Manslaughter and Corporate Homicide Act 2007, section 1(1) states that:

> An organisation to which this section applies is guilty of an offence if the way in which its activities are managed or organised –
>
> (a) causes a person's death, and
> (b) amounts to a gross breach of a relevant duty of care owed by the organisation to the deceased.

It has been observed that the "special policy considerations that flow from the unique harm of causing a death make it desirable for the corporate manslaughter provisions to apply to a wide range of organisations".[70] Thus, under section 1(2) organisations includes corporations[71] but is a much wider concept that also includes police forces,[72] and employers that are partnerships or a trade unions[73] As the organisations referred to under the Act can be both private and public organisations, this removes the Crown immunity that previously existed for certain public organisations. Notwithstanding this, most of the charges brought under this act have been against private corporations.

The intention of the Act was to enable liability to be imposed without the use of the identification principle, which was a potential bar to prosecution. As such, the culture and policies of the corporation may be considered.[74] Nonetheless, despite the offence of corporate manslaughter being aimed at direct liability for organisations, rather than derivative from individuals, it still does not completely leave the identification principle behind. The Law Commission's proposals, which referred to "management failure",[75] would have placed more focus directly on systematic failures. The Act, however, focuses on the failures of managers and considers the role of senior individuals within the organisation. Section 1(3) provides that: An organisation is guilty of an offence under this section only if the way in which its activities are managed or organised by its senior management is a substantial element in the breach referred to in subsection (1). This means that it still needs to be possible to identify who are the senior management and whether it is their actions that have led to a gross breach of the relevant duty. Section 1(4)(c) defines "senior management" as meaning the persons who play significant roles in:

> (i) the making of decisions about how the whole or a substantial part of its activities are to be managed or organised, or
> (ii) the actual managing or organising of the whole or a substantial part of those activities.

This has the benefit of referring to senior management as "persons". As such, this can refer to the actions of an aggregation of individuals, which was not permitted under the previous common law.[76] This better reflects the corporate reality of many organisations, where decisions are made by multiple people. Thus, the previous problem of liability depending on being able to identify just one person as the "directing mind and will" of the corporation is avoided.

---

70 David Ormerod, Karl Laird, and Matthew Gibson, *Smith, Hogan, and Ormerod's Criminal Law* (17th edition, Oxford University Press 2024) 263.
71 Corporate Manslaughter and Corporate Homicide Act 2007, section 1(2)(a).
72 Corporate Manslaughter and Corporate Homicide Act 2007, section 1(2)(c).
73 Corporate Manslaughter and Corporate Homicide Act 2007, section 1(2)(d).
74 Corporate Manslaughter and Corporate Homicide Act 2007, section 8(3)(a).
75 Law Commission, *Legislating the Criminal Code* (Law Com No 237, 1996), draft bill, section 4(1)(a).
76 See Chapter 1.3.2.

Nonetheless, the Corporate Manslaughter and Corporate Homicide Act 2007 has attracted much criticism, although some have argued unjustly so,[77] for its failure to effectively prosecute corporations.[78] The Act does not give clarity as to who is senior management. Furthermore, the words "significant role" and "substantial part" mean it is easier to identify relevant senior managers in smaller organisations. As Wells argues:

> By requiring the "substantial" involvement of "senior management" and then defining this body as "those persons who play significant roles" the Act gives . . . lie to the Government's claimed commitment to an organisational version of fault that is not dependent on the actions of specified individuals.[79]

Thus, like with the common law identification principle, the application of the Corporate Manslaughter and Corporate Homicide Act 2007 means discrimination against smaller corporations still exists. In an examination of the cases prosecuted in the first ten years of the Act, Field concludes: "The stringent senior management requirement in particular may well present insurmountable prosecutorial difficulties should a large corporation in which authority is diffused through a complex organisational structure find itself in the dock".[80] Therefore, despite the act's aim to move away from the identification principle, it is dependent on deriving liability from the actions of individuals. This means that the law does not enable prosecution for systematic failures that have led to death in large corporations. Moreover, because the organisation can only be liable for causing the death through the way in which its activities are managed or organised by its senior management, this poses a problem in establishing causation. The larger the organisation, the more distant a senior manager may be from the actions or inactions that actually caused the death. Conversely, establishing a causal link in small corporations may prove to be much easier.

The Corporate Manslaughter and Corporate Homicide Act 2007 provides a range of penalties for corporations who have been found liable under the Act. In addition to a fine that is specified under section 1(6), section 9 of the Act provides for remedial orders that require the organisation to remedy the failures that led to the death. Additionally, section 10 provides for publicity orders that require the corporation to publicise details of its conviction. Ormerod, Laird, and Gibson describe these innovative sentencing and disposal powers as one of the most welcome aspects of the Act.[81] Imposing punishments in these ways achieves the policy aims of deterrence, reparation and denunciation, which may not be achieved through fines alone.[82] Regardless, despite the good intentions of the Act, these sentencing powers have been criticised for being scantly used and ineffective for smaller corporations where there is little or no reputation to be lost.[83] Thus, while the policy aims of such provisions are sound, their adoption as a mode of punishment renders them of little use.

---

77 Victoria Roper, "The Corporate Manslaughter and Corporate Homicide Act 2007: A Re-evaluation 10 Years on from the First Case" [2022] Crim LR 290.

78 Dave Whyte, "The Fatal Flaws in the English Corporate Manslaughter Bill" (2005) 67 Employment Law Bulletin 4; James Gobert, "The Corporate Manslaughter and Corporate Homicide Act 2007 – Thirteen Years in the Making but Was it Worth the Wait?" (2008) 71(3) Modern L Rev 413; Gary Slapper, "Justice is Mocked if an Important Law is Unenforced" (2013) 77(2) J Crim L 91; Sarah Field, "Ten Years On: The Corporate Manslaughter and Corporate Homicide Act 2007: Plus ça Change?" (2018) 29(8) ICCLR 511; Steve Tombs, "The UK's Corporate Killing Law: Un/fit for Purpose?" (2018) 18(4) Criminol Crim Justice 488, 503.

79 Celia Wells, "Corporate Criminal Liability: A Ten Year Review" [2014] Crim LR 849, 857.

80 Sarah Field, "Ten Years on: the Corporate Manslaughter and Corporate Homicide Act 2007: Plus ca Change?" (2018) 29(8) ICCLR 511, 520.

81 David Ormerod, Karl Laird, and Matthew Gibson, *Smith, Hogan, and Ormerod's Criminal Law* (17th edition, Oxford University Press 2024) 276–277. See also, Paul Almond, *Corporate Manslaughter and Regulatory Reform* (Palgrave Macmillan 2013) 32.

82 See Chapter 1.3.2 for more discussion of the policy aims of criminal law.

83 Sarah Field, "Ten Years on: The Corporate Manslaughter and Corporate Homicide Act 2007: Plus ca Change?" [2018] ICCLR 511, 519.

Examining the actions of Claire from the scenario at the start of the chapter, it can be seen that the hospital is potentially liable for corporate manslaughter. It would need to be established that the death has been caused by the way the senior management manage or organise the work of the hospital, which has amounted to a gross breach. This may be a difficult threshold to meet as those who are senior enough to have a significant role in managing a substantial part of the hospital's activities, may have little awareness or direct control over the actions of Claire. Even if it can be established that there are systemic failures in the way the senior managers manage or organise the activities of the hospital, an objective threshold would need to be met to determine if this amounted to a gross breach. If all the criteria are met, the hospital can face liability as a public body under the Corporate Manslaughter and Corporate Homicide Act 2007. This would then leave the question of what would be an appropriate punishment. A fine could achieve future deterrence and make the hospital more careful in its staff monitoring and whistleblowing processes, but it is questionable whether it is morally palatable to fine a public not-for-profit corporation. Even if a fine was levied, the money would come from the public purse, just to go back into the public purse. Alternatively, or additionally, a publication order could be imposed. This may have wide reaching detrimental effects with public loss of confidence in the health service, and may be superfluous if the matter has already been investigated and reported by the media. Lastly, a remedial order could be imposed, which could be an effective way to ensure that such failings do not occur again. It is, however, likely that this could be dealt with as a regulatory matter through the relevant regulatory body without the need for criminal prosecution. Nonetheless, this may not achieve the moral condemnation and deterrence of a manslaughter conviction, which is the aim of the Act.

14.6.2 Failure to Prevent Bribery

Bribery poses a particularly difficult issue for the domestic criminal justice system, as not only are corporations the main offender of this type of offence, the offence tends to be carried out on a transnational level with transnational corporations filling the demand of corrupt officials. As such, "bribery is a widespread phenomenon in international business transactions, including trade and investment, which raises serious moral and political concerns, undermines good governance and economic development, and distorts international competitive conditions".[84] In 1997 the Convention on Combating Bribery of Foreign Public Officials in International Business Transactions was the first anti-corruption instrument focused on the "supply side" of the bribery transaction. The Convention established a legally binding standard to criminalise bribery of foreign public officials in international business transactions.[85] Article 12 of the Convention imposes a rigorous peer monitoring process on signatory states. As such, the UK was put under pressure by the Organisation for Economic Co-operation and Development's Working Group on Bribery[86] to change its bribery laws, and in particular remove the identification principle that prevented successful prosecution.[87] Despite the Law Commission concluding that the identification principle was not in contravention of the convention, it recommended an approach that moved away from identification and instead adopted a form of vicarious liability.[88] Therefore, unlike the approach taken by the

84 OECD, *Convention on Combating Bribery of Foreign Public Officials in International Business Transactions*, OECD/LEGAL/0293, 4.

85 OECD, *Convention on Combating Bribery of Foreign Public Officials in International Business Transactions*, OECD/LEGAL/0293, 3.

86 OECD, *Follow up Report on the Implementation of the Phase 2 Recommendations* [for UK] 2007, 21.

87 Law Commission, *Reforming Bribery* (Law Com CP No 185, 2007) para 9.13.

88 Law Commission, *Reforming Bribery* (Law Com No 313, 2008) Part 6.

Law Commission less than a decade earlier for corporate manslaughter,[89] the proposed liability for bribery was not aimed at being an extension of direct corporate liability.[90]

The Law Commission's proposals led to the enactment of the Bribery Act 2010. The Act has not completely abandoned the common law identification principle. Section 14 of the Act enables the bribery offences under sections 1, 2 and 6 to be committed by a corporation if they have been committed with the consent or connivance of a senior officer of the body corporate or a person purporting to act in such a capacity.[91] The requirement of identifying a senior officer and showing consent and connivance provides for a high burden to establish corporate liability. Alternatively, liability can be imposed against corporations under section 7 of the Act. This section imposes strict liability on commercial organisations if they fail to prevent bribery.[92] Section 7(1) states:

> A relevant commercial organisation ("C") is guilty of an offence under this section if a person ("A") associated with C bribes another person intending –
>
> (a) to obtain or retain business for C, or
> (b) to obtain or retain an advantage in the conduct of business for C.

Thus, a commercial organisation can be vicariously liable for the actions of an individual associated with the organisation.[93] Section 8(1) defines a person associated with the organisation as a person who performs services for, or on behalf of, the corporation. Ashworth criticises this model of liability by arguing that failure to prevent offences, such as this one, are extending the criminal law vertically, by adding a layer of criminal responsibility. In other words, it is not just the individual who can be liable, but also the corporation above that individual.[94] Moreover, this offence appears to approach the problem of identification by assuming a model of fault based on strict liability, which is normally reserved for regulatory offences. Thus, while the Act presented an opportunity to move away from the identification principle, and to introduce a new model of liability focussed on systematic failures or corporate culture that is not derivative from individuals,[95] it has instead adopted a mixture of vicarious strict liability and the identification principle to impose corporate liability.

The adoption of the strict liability approach under section 7 could be justified when considering the "serious moral and political concerns" that bribery offences raise. The result is, what has been described as, "the toughest anti-corruption law in the world".[96] A corporation can, however, avoid liability under section 7(2) of the Bribery Act 2010. This provides that it is a defence for the commercial organisation to prove that they had in place adequate procedures designed to prevent persons associated with the commercial organisation from undertaking such conduct. Therefore, providing a due diligence defence to remove the harshness of strict liability and find a balance when apportioning blame. This section can also be seen to have the opposite

---

89 Law Commission, *Legislating the Criminal Code* (Law Com No 237, 1996) Part VIII.

90 Law Commission, *Reforming Bribery* (Law Com No 313, 2008) para 6.35, explains this difference with reference to the required *mens rea* of the offences. As explained above, corporate manslaughter rests on an objective assessment of whether there has been a gross breach of a relevant duty, whereas Bribery has a subjective mental element.

91 Bribery Act 2010, section 14(2)(a) and (b).

92 This was contrary to the approach recommended by the Law Commission, *Reforming Bribery* (Law Com No 313, 2008) para 6.100, which stated that requiring strict liability "would run entirely counter to the normal approach to serious offences".

93 For example, in 2016 the Sweett Group plc were the first organisation convicted under section 7 of the Bribery Act 2010 and were fined £1.4m after pleading guilty.

94 Andrew Ashworth, "A New Generation of Omission Offences?" [2018] Crim LR 354.

95 For example, see Neil Cavanagh, "Corporate Criminal Liability: An Assessment of the Models of Fault" [2011] J Crim L 414, who argues for a non-derivative corporate model of fault.

96 Celia Wells, "Corporate Criminal Liability: A Ten Year Review" [2014] Crim LR 849, 868.

effect to corporate manslaughter when considering how it affects liability for small organisations. While the Corporate Manslaughter and Corporate Homicide Act 2007 favours imposing liability on smaller corporations for manslaughter, the associated guidance published with section 7(2) of the Bribery Act 2010[97] means that the onus of what amounts to adequate procedures will be far less for smaller organisations. Thus, making it easier for them to fulfil the requirements of the due diligence defence.

In the case of Dakota from the scenario at the start of the chapter, the manufacturer he works for could be liable under section under section 7 of the Bribery Act 2010 for its failure to prevent the bribery. The manufacturer has benefited from Dakota's actions by gaining business, and Dakota will be considered an associated person. It will be irrelevant that this is a large company so they may not be aware of the transactions being carried out by individuals, as they will be vicariously strictly liable for Dakota's actions. The only option the manufacturer has to avoid liability is to plead the due diligence defence. For this they will need to show that they had adequate safeguards in place that were adequate for the size and type of business.

14.6.3 Failure to Prevent Facilitation of Tax Evasion

Following the introduction of the offence of failure to prevent in section 7 of the Bribery Act 2010, sections 45 and 46 of the Criminal Finances Act 2017 introduced two new corporate liability failure to prevent offences. This Act again aimed to overcome the problems of the identification principle. As the government acknowledged, use of the common law identification principle "meant that bodies that refrained from implementing good corporate governance and strong reporting procedures were harder to prosecute, and in some cases lacked a strong incentive to invest in preventative procedures".[98] Similarly to section 7 of the Bribery Act 2010, sections 45 and 46 of the Criminal Finances Act 2017 impose corporate liability for their failures to prevent the substantive offence being committed by another. This extends liability for omissions into what Ashworth describes as: "A new generation of omission offences."[99] This creates the issue that criminal liability maybe harder to justify, as arguably an omission is not as blameworthy as an act.[100]

Section 45(1) of the Criminal Finances Act 2017 states:

> A relevant body (B) is guilty of an offence if a person commits a UK tax evasion facilitation offence when acting in the capacity of a person associated with B.

Section 46(1) also provides a similar provision for failure to prevent facilitation of foreign tax evasion offences. This Act provides slightly wider liability than the Bribery Act 2010. This is because an associated person is determined by the capacity in which they were acting, rather than the formal position they held. Moreover, the associated person does not need to be acting for the benefit of the corporation, which is a requirement of other failure to prevent offences under the Bribery Act 2010[101] and the Economic Crime and Corporate Transparency Act 2023.[102] This further undermines the justification for imposing corporate liability that holds that a corporation should be liable if they are receiving a benefit from the wrongdoing.

---

97 Ministry of Justice, "The Bribery Act 2010 – Guidance", 11 February 2012, https://assets.publishing.service.gov.uk/media/5d80cfc3ed915d51e9aff85a/bribery-act-2010-guidance.pdf, accessed 2 November 2024.

98 HMRC, "Tackling Tax Evasion: Government Guidance for the Corporate Offences of Failure to Prevent the Criminal Facilitation of Tax Evasion", 6 September 2017, https://assets.publishing.service.gov.uk/media/5a82aaa0e5274a2e8ab58b82/Tackling-tax-evasion-corporate-offences.pdf, accessed 3 November 2024, 3.

99 Andrew Ashworth, "A New Generation of Omission Offences?" [2018] Crim LR 354.

100 See Chapter 4 for further discussion.

101 See Chapter 14.6.2 above.

102 See Chapter 14.6.3 below.

The ambit of the Criminal Finances Act 2017 is additionally extended beyond that of the Bribery Act 2010, by introducing strict liability for a crime that is inchoate in nature. The associated person only has to facilitate tax evasion (although this does need to be in their capacity as an associated person), not actually carry out the tax evasion themselves. Therefore, the relevant body can be strictly liable for the tax evasion actions of another person that they are unaware of. Despite this potential for wide-ranging liability, a Home Office report in May 2024 reported that to date there had be no convictions for the offences under sections 45 and 46 of the Criminal Finances Act 2017. Thus, it is questionable how effective this model of liability is at imposing corporate liability.

Returning to Ernie in the scenario at the start of the chapter, it needs to be considered whether the accountancy firm can be found responsible for his actions under section 45 of the Criminal Finances Act 2017. Ernie has facilitated tax evasion. This does not need to be done for the benefit of the accountancy firm, but must be shown that it has been done while acting in the capacity of a person associated with the accountancy firm. Despite using the knowledge that he has learnt at work, it is unlikely that his actions will meet this threshold. Therefore, the accountancy firm will not be liable for his actions. Instead, an individual action would need to be taken against Dakota.

Similarly to the Bribery Act 2010, if a corporation is shown to be liable, a defence is provided to under section 45(2) of the Criminal Finances Act 2017.[103] This states:

> It is a defence for B to prove that, when the UK tax evasion facilitation offence was committed –
>
> (a) B had in place such prevention procedures as it was reasonable in all the circumstances to expect B to have in place, or
> (b) it was not reasonable in all the circumstances to expect B to have any prevention procedures in place.

Unlike section 7(2) of the Bribery Act 2010, this section requires "reasonable" procedures rather than "adequate" ones. It is unclear whether this makes any substantive difference. Moreover, section 45(2)(b) allows a corporation to avoid liability even if they have not got procedures in place. There is no equivalent section in the Bribery Act 2010. This gives a corporation more scope to avoid liability for the failure to prevent tax evasion offences than for the Failure to Prevent Bribery offence. Thus, while the scope of liability for failure to prevent tax evasion is more wide reaching than for the failure to prevent bribery, greater apportioning of liability is balanced with the availability of a broader defence.

14.6.4 Failure to Prevent Fraud

Fraud is now the most common offence in the UK, amounting to 41% of all crime in the year ending September 2022,[104] with an estimated £1.17 billion stolen in 2023.[105] The Fraud Act 2006 introduced a range of Fraud offences.[106] These offences require that a person is dishonest. As these offences depend on establishing this *mens rea* requirement, the identification principle is needed to establish a corporation's liability. To address the problems that arise from identifying

103 A similar defence is also provided for Foreign Tax Evasion under section 46(3) of the Criminal Finances Act 2017.

104 Home Office, Serious Fraud Office, HM Treasury, Department for Business and Trade, Ministry of Justice and Companies House, "Economic Crime and Corporate Transparency Act: Failure to Prevent Fraud Offence", 29 February 2024, www.gov.uk/government/publications/economic-crime-and-corporate-transparency-act-2023-factsheets/economic-crime-and-corporate-transparency-act-failure-to-prevent-fraud-offence, accessed 3 November 2024.

105 "Annual Fraud Report 2024", 3 June 2024, www.ukfinance.org.uk/system/files/2024-06/UK%20Finance%20Annual%20Fraud%20report%202024.pdf, accessed 3 November 2024, 6.

106 See Chapter 7.4.

an individual as the corporation, a new failure to prevent fraud offence aimed at corporations, has been introduced.[107]

Section 199(1) of the Economic Crime and Corporate Transparency Act 2023 provides:

> A relevant body which is a large organisation is guilty of an offence if, in a financial year of the body ("the year of the fraud offence"), a person who is associated with the body ("the associate") commits a fraud offence intending to benefit (whether directly or indirectly) –
>
> (a) the relevant body, or
> (b) any person to whom, or to whose subsidiary undertaking, the associate provides services on behalf of the relevant body.[108]

Corporate liability under this section differs to the other failure to prevent offences examined above. Section 199 of the Economic Crime and Corporate Transparency Act 2023 only applies to large organisations. Large organisations are defined under section 201 of the Act as when the corporation satisfies two or more of the following conditions in the financial year preceding the year in which the alleged fraud is said to have occurred: the company has (i) more than 250 employees; (ii) turnover of more than £36 million; and/or (iii) a balance sheet total of more than £18 million.[109] The effect of this is that large organisations can be strictly liable under the Economic Crime and Corporate Transparency Act 2023 for the actions of their associates under the principle of vicarious liability, but *mens rea* will still need to be established for small and medium corporations for fraud offences under the Fraud Act 2006 through the identification principle. This raises the question of why a higher threshold of establishing blameworthiness through *mens rea* is required to establish criminal liability for small and medium corporations. The justification given is to ensure burdens on businesses are proportionate.[110] This, however, ignores the fundamental principles of criminal law. Just because a corporation is more able to afford a fine does not alter its blameworthiness or how deserving it is of the moral condemnation that is associated with a criminal conviction.

The Economic Crime and Corporate Transparency Act 2023 requires that the fraud is undertaken by an associated person. There is no requirement that the associated person is convicted of fraud, just that they have committed one. Thus, while corporate liability derives from individual liability it is not dependent on proving it. Sections 199(7)–(9) of the Economic Crime and Corporate Transparency Act 2023 gives further guidance as to who is an associated person. As with the Criminal Finances Act 2017, importance is given to the services performed rather than the defined relationship held between the parties. Unlike the Bribery Act 2010, however, the associated person under the Economic Crime and Corporate Transparency Act 2023 must be acting for the benefit of the corporation. This does not necessarily mean a financial benefit, and has a broader scope than the Bribery Act 2010 that requires the obtainment or retainment of business or a business advantage.

Similarly to the other failure to prevent offences, section 199(4) of the Economic Crime and Corporate Transparency Act 2023 provides a due diligence defence that requires reasonable prevention procedures, or for the corporation to show that it was not reasonable to have prevention procedures in place. Section 199(3) provides further protection by stating that the relevant body is not guilty

---

107 At the time of writing the Failure to Prevent Fraud offence was not yet in force, but was expected to come into force during 2025.

108 Note, section 199(2) extends this offence to parent undertakings.

109 Section 202 provides a definition for parent undertakings.

110 Home Office, Serious Fraud Office, HM Treasury, Department for Business and Trade, Ministry of Justice and Companies House, "Economic Crime and Corporate Transparency Act: Failure to Prevent Fraud Offence", 29 February 2024, www.gov.uk/government/publications/economic-crime-and-corporate-transparency-act-2023-factsheets/economic-crime-and-corporate-transparency-act-failure-to-prevent-fraud-offence, accessed 3 November 2024.

of an offence if the body itself was, or was intended to be, a victim of the fraud offence. While the term "victim of a fraud offence" is not defined, this added protection provides some further balance between imposing strict liability to enable corporate liability to be established, and only convicting those who are blameworthy.

Finally, returning to Freya from the scenario at the start of the chapter, it needs to be determined whether the bank can be criminally liable under section 199 of the Economic Crime and Corporate Transparency Act 2023 for failing to prevent her fraud. Freya could be charged with fraud through an abuse of position under section 1 of the Fraud Act 2006. For this it would need to be shown, for example, that she dishonestly abused her position to make a gain for herself.[111] For the bank to be vicariously liable for Freya's actions it would first need to be established whether they met the criteria of a large organisation. If this failed, then to find corporate liability the identification principle would need to be used to show that Freya's dishonest actions, or anyone else's involved, amounted to the directing mind and will of the company. This could produce an insurmountable hurdle if she is not a senior employee. If the bank was classified as a large company, it may still avoid liability if it could establish that Freya was acting for the benefit of the bank. While this does not need to be a financial benefit, and the term "benefit" could have a broad application, it is unlikely that selling customer's details could be considered in the bank's benefit. Therefore, despite her potentially undertaking these actions at work, using the access that her position gives her, the bank will not be criminally responsible for her actions. Even if it was established that the bank was vicariously strictly liable, they could still present a due diligence defence. The burden of proof would be on the bank to show that it had taken reasonable prevention measure. Moreover, the bank will not face corporate liability if they can show that they were a victim of the fraud.

14.7 Conclusion

Corporations are a legal entity, on which imposing criminal liability can sometimes be beneficial and deserved. If a corporation's actions have led, for example, to unsafe food being sold to the public or rivers being polluted, then the corporation needs to face censure for this. Imposing criminal liability goes beyond the compensatory effect of civil law. It identifies and publicises that such behaviour is unwanted, and needs to be prevented. Despite, these persuasive reasons for the imposition of imposing criminal liability on corporations, throughout this chapter it has been shown that there are difficulties in determining when a corporation should be liable and what the basis for such liability should be.

Vicarious liability can be used to derive liability from an individual onto a corporation for strict liability offences. These offences tend to be regulatory in nature and not subject to the same moral condemnation as other criminal offences. As such, imposing criminal liability can be justified for the policy reasons of achieving deterrence and protecting the public, even though it may not have been established that the corporation itself has acting wrongfully. The introduction of failure to prevent offences removes the issue of the corporation being liable for the wrongful actions of an associated person, as it instead directs strict liability onto the corporation for its failure to prevent the wrongdoing. This further expands the criminal reach of liability for omissions. Moreover, despite the failure to prevent offences seeming to hold the same basis for liability, the slightly differing definitions lead to further complexity within the law.

Thus, in crimes of strict liability, liability is derived onto the corporation for the wrongful acts of associated persons. This is either by vicariously attributing the wrongful act of another to the corporation, or for the corporation's omission in preventing another from carrying out the wrongful

---

111 Fraud Act 2006, section 4.

act. No *mens rea* of the corporation is required to be established. Therefore, the policy aim of preventing the occurrence of certain types of crimes, recently financial crimes, seems to outweigh the fundamental principle of criminal law of *actus reus non facit reum nisi mens sit rea*.[112] Nonetheless, due diligence defences, which despite reversing the burden onto the corporation to establish that they have not been negligent, exist to protect the corporation from this derived liability and further ensure the raising of standards.

In crimes that require *mens rea*, when conviction does result in moral condemnation, imposition of liability cannot be justified without moral blameworthiness of the corporation being established. Common law has adopted the identification principle to address this, meaning that the blameworthiness of the individual could become the blameworthiness of the corporation. This is when it can be established that an individual is the will and directing mind of the corporation. This has resulted in difficulties in achieving successful prosecutions and discrimination against smaller corporations. The Corporate Manslaughter and Corporate Homicide Act 2007 tried to overcome this problem by introducing liability that is not derivative from an individual. This Act has, however, had limited effect on corporate liability in that it only applies to one type of corporate offence, and liability still requires a certain degree of identification.

Despite the increasing number of corporate offences being enacted, a comprehensive and universal approach of how liability should be imposed on corporations does not exist. Instead, a piecemeal approach has been taken to enact laws to address a variety of issues. A more systematic approach could have been adopted that looked at the corporate culture, and the blameworthiness of the corporation as a separate legal being to the individuals that make up the corporation. As no such approach currently different rules exist depending on the crime the corporation is being charged with.

14.8 Further Reading

Ashworth A, "A New Generation of Omissions Offences?" [2018] Crim LR 354

Cavanagh N, "Corporate Criminal Liability: An Assessment of the Models of Fault" (2011) 75 J Crim L 414

Field S, "Ten Years On: The Corporate Manslaughter and Corporate Homicide Act 2007: Plus ça Change?" (2018) 29 ICCLR 511

Jefferson M, "Corporate Criminal Liability: The Problems of Sanctions" (2001) 65 J Crim L 235

Laird K, "The Criminal Finances Act 2017 – an Introduction" [2017] Crim LR 915

Manchester C, "Knowledge, Due Diligence and Strict Liability in Regulatory Offences" [2006] Crim LR 213

Roper V, "The Corporate Manslaughter and Corporate Homicide Act 2007 – a Ten Year Review" (2018) J Crim L 48

Wells C, "Corporate Criminal Liability: A Ten Year Review" [2014] Crim LR 849

112 See Chapter 2.3.4 for further discussion of this legal principle.

Index

Kolibri 360 GmbH
Ferdinand-Jühlke-Straße 7
99095 Erfurt, Deutschland
produktsicherheit@kolibri360.de